THE FUTURE OF BUSINESS

Critical Insight into a Rapidly Changing World from 60 Future Thinkers

THE FUTURE OF BUSINESS

Critical Insight into a Rapidly Changing World from 60 Future Thinkers

Series Curator and Editor
Rohit Talwar

Co-Editors
Steve Wells
April Koury and Alberto Rizzoli

FutureScapes

THE FUTURE OF BUSINESS

First published in United Kingdom and United States of America by Fast Future Publishing 2015
FutureScapes is an imprint of Fast Future Publishing in 2015
www.fastfuturepublishing.com

For Information contact info@fastfuturepublishing.com

Paperback ISBN 978 0 9932958 0 5
Ebook 978 0 9932958 1 2

Cover and interior designed by Rachel Lawston, www.lawstondesign.com
Paperback interior was designed in collaboration with Alberto Rizzoli

*Rachel Lawston would like to give special thanks to
Alberto Rizzoli and April Koury for their support in the design process*

Ebook interior designed by Alberto Rizzoli

Printed by The Print Guild

Contents

CONTENTS

CONTENTS

CONTENTS

Index available on www.fob.fastfuturepublishing.com

References available on www.fob.fastfuturepublishing.com

Introduction

Business in the Age of Disruptive Convergence
By Rohit Talwar and Steve Wells

Welcome to the Future of Business

This book is aimed at the leaders of today and the pioneers of tomorrow. Our intention is to provide a broad perspective on the key forces, trends, developments, and ideas that could redefine our world over the next two decades. The intention is to highlight how these "future factors" are shaping the opportunities, challenges, implications, and resulting choices for those driving the future of business. The book draws on the ideas of over 60 futurists, future thinkers and experts in a range of domains from 22 countries on four continents.

Fundamental questions

In a world of constant and ever-more fundamental change, those charged with leadership, management and stewardship of large and small organizations alike are faced with a set of questions many of us never thought we would have to confront. These questions are becoming more prominent and real as we develop a better understanding of, and feeling for, the disruptive potential of what's coming over the horizon. So what are these questions that are making their way from fun discussions among futurists, innovators, and would-be world changers to the top of the business agenda? Well, here are ten that we see being discussed more frequently at the top table:

- **Strategy** How do we compete and make a profit in a world where automation and digitization are shortening business cycles, accelerating change, and driving the commoditization of many goods and services?
- **Workforce** How do we manage and motivate a workforce that could span in age from 16 to 90 years as people's life expectancy rises and, in order to survive, they are forced to keep working long past the historical age of retirement?
- **Human Enhancement** What's the impact on our business and the commercial opportunity arising from people using scientific advances to enhance the performance of their brains and bodies?
- **Resources** How will we produce our products if scarce natural resources run out or are rationed?
- **Mindset** Can we transfer exponential thinking from the technology world to other domains to address society's grand challenges in areas such as diversity, healthcare and education, and overcome the scarcity of key resources such as food, water and rare earth metals?
- **Artificial Intelligence** How close is the day when smart technologies such as artificial intelligence (AI) could replace 50 per cent or more of the workforce?
- **Automation** What could the fully automated company of tomorrow look like, and who will buy our goods and services if technology is eliminating jobs at every level of the workforce?
- **Unemployment** If technological unemployment results in 30 to 50 percent or more of the workforce being permanently unemployed, will we need a universal basic income and how will it be funded?
- **Money** How might the nature of money and financial systems evolve – what impact could these developments have on our business?
- **Purpose** What would be a sustainable driving purpose and societal role of business in a world being transformed by all these forces of change?

The Future of Business is designed to explore these questions and many more. Through their contributions, the authors help to illuminate the future factors shaping tomorrow's agenda, explore the resulting implications, and highlight the emerging choices for business leaders.

What's driving the change agenda?

Why are all these questions appearing in parallel – what's driving the need to tackle such a wide range of game changing issues at the same time? Throughout history, people have understood that tomorrow's business landscape will be shaped and influenced by the world around us. What is perhaps different today is the sheer speed at which our world is being transformed rapidly by a convergence of science-led innovations and the ideas they enable. We are entering a fascinating period in our history, where science and the technologies it spawns, are now at the heart of the agenda.

Our thinking about the future of society, government, and business is completely intertwined with the path of technological progress. Convergence between disciplines such nanotechnology, biotechnology, information and communications technology (ICT), and the cognitive sciences is opening up a world of possibilities – many of which are emerging within weeks and months of each other. These rapid and groundbreaking advances are creating the potential for humanity to evolve in almost unimaginable ways. These developments underpin and drive the need for new thinking and create new possibilities for the future of business.

These forces of change are also at play in the broader economy. They are combining with a general thrust towards increased globalization, rapidly evolving economies, shorter and faster business cycles, and the rise of cyber currencies. They are driving digital transformation – the rapid automation and digitization of work and the workplace. The rise of AI and robotics in particular are driving a debate about how far we should allow such technologies to permeate our lives, and the risks of technological unemployment, as even professional knowledge workers' roles are automated on a permanent basis. Developments such as blockchain technology are creating transparent electronic public activity ledgers that have the potential to revamp the nature of trade, contacts, and transactions in every sector. Indeed some argue that they could lay the foundation for a reworking of the entire economic system.

New possibilities, new strategies, new leadership mindsets

In the context of such rapid and wide-ranging changes, determining the future of business takes on far greater importance than simply defining the next three-year strategy and revenue targets. Fundamental questions are being raised about the purpose and nature of business, its relationship with society, and the meaning of profit in tomorrow's world. The answer to these will in turn drive us to re-evaluate the importance of brands, design and culture, and how to educate tomorrow's workers and citizens. Finally they have dramatic implications for national identity, values and governance. Collectively these forces and our responses to them will drive disruption, renewal, and transformation in every sector. They will shape the future of business.

In response to this "perfect storm" of change on the horizon, leaders in every current and emerging sector will be challenged to think hard about future strategies. New "conscious leadership" perspectives are required on how to deal with disruptive entrants and how to evolve products and services in the face of digital disruption. We are being forced to rethink manufacturing and distribution strategies, evolve business models and organization designs, and learn how to ensure effective stakeholder engagement in a fast changing world.

As leaders, we will be challenged to determine our responsibility around job creation – how can we ensure that people are earning the money to buy the goods and services we produce? These transformative changes and choices are in turn raising fundamental questions on the future nature and capabilities required of leadership and management. They will also shape our thinking on how to attract, develop, and retain the type of talent needed across the organization to ensure future relevance and growth. These are the issues which our authors explore in *The Future of Business*.

The aim and structure of the book

This book is designed to provide wide ranging visions of future possibilities and take us on a tour of the forces shaping the political, economic, and social environment. We explore the advances in science and technology that could have the greatest impact on society and drive business disruption. We examine the implications of these for how business will need to evolve and the new industries that could emerge over the next two decades. We highlight key tools, approaches, and ways of thinking about the future that can help organizations embed foresight at the heart of the management model. We conclude with a framework that highlights key choices we face in shaping the Future of Business.

We took an organic approach to the design of the book – allowing potential authors to propose topics, choosing those that would have the most relevance and resonance and then allowing a natural structure to emerge based on the content they provided. As a result, the book is structured into ten key sections, these are summarized below:

- **Visions of The Future** presents a series of broad perspectives on the global shifts on the horizon as a result of the ideas and developments discussed elsewhere in the book.
- **Tomorrow's Global Order** examines the emerging political and economic transformations that could reshape the environment for society and business.
- **Emerging Societal Landscape** explores the changing fabric of society – who we are becoming and how we will be educated, finance our futures, and choose where to live.
- **Social Technologies** highlights how tomorrow's technologies could permeate our everyday lives and blur the boundaries between humans and machines.
- **Disruptive Developments** explains the nature and potential impact of new technologies that will enable large-scale and transformative business innovation.
- **Surviving and Thriving** discusses how business can adapt to a rapidly changing reality and identifies some of the critical

success factors for business in a constantly evolving world.

- **Industry Futures** looks at how old industries might change and identifies a range of new ones that could emerge.
- **Embracing The Future** introduces a range of futures and foresight tools, methods and processes that businesses can use to explore, understand, and create the future.
- **Framing The Future** provides a set of views outlining why and how organizations should look at the future.
- **Conclusions** sets out a framework to help leaders respond to the ideas presented in the book to drive future strategy and navigate uncertainty and a rapidly changing reality.

A more detailed overview of the contributions within each section and their authors is presented below under *Chapter introductions*. Sections one to seven start with a brief overview of relevant critical driving forces.

The FutureScapes Series

The Future of Business is the first book in the FutureScapes series. Each book will explore a different aspect of the future. The aim is to make the content accessible to a broad audience and help individuals, organizations, and decision makers understand the factors shaping our world and the choices open to them. The concept was born at the beginning of February 2015 and our aim was to apply exponential thinking to the publishing sector. We had been told that to do a high quality multi-authored book of this nature would take 18 to 24 months. We wanted the ideas being presented to be fresh, so an 18-month delay between initiation and publishing simply wouldn't work. Instead we set ourselves the target of doing it four times faster. You are now reading the results of us achieving that ambitious goal. We hope you find it of interest and value.

Creating the book

We invited contributions from a range of people whose ideas we respected and also posted open invitations for proposals on a range of relevant online forums. Our aim was to get 20 good quality chapters but we ended up with 60! We allowed authors to decide whether they wrote 500, 1000, 2,000 or 3,000 words – we deliberately wanted to create variety and enable people share ideas in their own voice and in a short-form manner if they so desired. We received over 70 proposals. A number of people said they would have contributed but simply could not do it in the tight timescales we set for first and second drafts.

We selected 60 proposed contributions that we felt were suitable for the book and invited them to submit a draft chapter. These were all put through two edits. At that stage we rejected some on the basis of fit and quality and some dropped out because they didn't have time to bring their chapter up to the standard we required. The authors then produced second drafts based on our feedback and we then put them through two more stages of content editing and a two-step copy edit phase to create the text you are reading now. In total we have 60 chapters from 62 contributors.

Rethinking the publishing model

We decided early on that we did not want to just do one book. Our aim was to build a new type of publishing business which rebalanced the reward model to reflect the effort that goes into each book. In the traditional model the retailer and distributor typically take around 70% of the revenues – leaving little to share between those who actually created the book. That model also has huge in-built time delays. We decided that in order to achieve our ambitions, we had to take control of the entire process and rework the business model. Initially the book will therefore only be available from our website, and we are working with efficient partners to manage global distribution.

We have also adopted a profit sharing approach. The authors receive 25 percent of profits divided amongst them transparently according to the length of their chapters. A further 35 percent is divided among the core team – who have basically worked for free on the core activities of project management, author liaison, editorial, production, distribution, cover design web design, PR, marketing, social media, sales, and the myriad other tasks that went into creating the book.

A further ten percent of profits are being set aside to fund educational scholarships for people wanting to receive training in foresight and futures research. Our goal is to build capacity around the world that can help individuals and organizations anticipate and understand the changes on the horizon and then map their own preferred course. As the publisher underwriting the project and bearing all the risks we are taking 25 percent of profits and the final five percent has been set aside for contingencies. We expect this model to evolve as the business grows with a greater proportion of profits being shared with the authors as we take on a salaried staff.

A massive thank you to the team
We would like to thank the team who has worked with us to help turn a crazy vision into a finished product that we are all very proud of. Alberto Rizzoli, April Koury, D'shaun Guillory, Emma Pask, James Langton, Owen Richards and Rachel Lawston have at different times worked tirelessly (and largely without payment) over the life of the project to make it happen. Thank you.

References
A number of the authors have referenced a range of content in producing their chapters. In many cases these include web links which readers may want to follow up on. The reference numbers appear in the text and we have placed the relevant reference information on our website www.fob.fastfuturepublishing.com – where you can link directly to the underlying websites.

Chapter introductions
Below we summarize the content of the chapters in each section and provide a brief overview of each author. Their full profiles can be found on the website at www.fob.fastfuturepublishing.com.

SECTION 1 – Visions of the Future –
What are the global shifts on the horizon?

The Future of Business - Navigating the Next Horizon

Rohit Talwar is a global futurist, founder and CEO of Fast Future Research and Fast Future Publishing and the curator and lead editor of the Future of Business. His opening chapter presents a broad overview of the emerging ideas, fundamental tensions and technology developments shaping the future of business. Thirty key future industry sectors are identified, and possible future business behaviors and strategies are discussed along with the resulting choices for business leaders.

Forecasting Future Disruptions - Strategic Change Is Inevitable

William E. Halal is Professor Emeritus of Management, Technology, and Innovation at George Washington University, Washington, D.C. and founder of the Tech Cast forecasting system. He presents forecasts out to 2030 for critical technologies, social trends, and wild cards, and highlights their expected impacts and implications for society, nations, and business.

The Automated, Digitized, and Simulated Future

Gray Scott, a New York based futurist, techno-philosopher, speaker, writer, artist, and founder and CEO of SeriousWonder.com, outlines the relentless forces that are driving the deep and transformative penetration of digital technologies into every aspect of society.

Redefining the Relationship of Man and Machine

Gerd Leonhard is a Swiss-based Futurist, Keynote Speaker, Author, and CEO of The Futures Agency. He sets out the case for a Digital Ethics Treaty, ensuring that in the face of exponential waves of disruption, we focus on controlling these technologies and harnessing them to serve humanity and further human happiness.

Can 3D Printing Destroy Capitalism and Restore Government?

Jeffrey Joslin is a self-proclaimed "extraterrestrial from the Pleiades star cluster" and a writer on the advancement of technology. He argues that 3D printing could be the most disruptive innovation in history – reshaping industry value chains, enabling abundance, redistributing economic wealth, and rebalancing power and influence in political systems.

SECTION 2 – Tomorrow's Global Order – What are the emerging political and economic transformations that could reshape the environment for society and business?

The Prospect of Democracy 2.0

David Wood is a UK based futurist, technologist, writer, and chair of London Futurists. He sets out the case for embracing technology to help enable the transition from democracy 1.0 to a more open, participative, and informed democracy 2.0 model of governance in the digital era.

The Comeback of Value Creation as the True Measure of Results in Business

Pétur Albert Haraldsson is a business executive, entrepreneur and financial services change agent from Iceland. Petur presents a compelling vision of how the economic and financial system could evolve in the digital age to enable true market driven capitalism and a reframing of the future purpose and role of banks.

The Impact of Accelerating 3D Printing Technology on Economic Systems

Sally Morem is a freelance writer based in Northern Minnesota and Southwest Florida with an interest in emerging technologies, including space development and transhumanism. She highlights the highly disruptive potential impacts of the rise of 3D printing on business, consumers, the environment, and the wider economy.

The Future of the Global Monetary and Financial System – Time for a New Bretton Woods?

Professor Adrian Pop is a faculty member at the National University of Political Science and Public Administration in Bucharest Romania. Adrian highlights scenarios for how our international monetary and financial systems could evolve in the wake of the global financial crisis, continued economic uncertainty, and the scale of disruption taking place in financial markets, digital currencies, and global trade.

It's not Money until it's Postmoney

Dr. Boyan Ivantchev is an associate professor in behavioral finance and board member of a Bulgarian listed private equity fund. He examines the evolution of the role of money, its emergence as Postmoney and the potential future scenarios for the evolution of money in an increasingly digital world.

Investing in International Aid and Development

Norman Rebin is a Canadian based specialist in productivity and communications focused on global business. He outlines the drivers for and benefits of increasing future corporate involvement and investment in international aid and development.

SECTION 3 – Emerging Societal Landscape – Who are we becoming, how will we live?

Understanding Tomorrow's Consumer Landscape

Anne Lise Kjaer, a global futurist and trend observer based in Denmark, discusses how relationships between producer and consumer could change and the implications for how organizations will need to adapt to engage with ever-more demanding consumers.

Generation Z in the Workforce

Anne Boysen is a Norwegian futurist and researcher specializing in generational analysis. She examines the evolving nature, expectations, and workplace implications of those born after 1995 – often referred to as "Generation Z".

Education 2025 – Building a generation of problem solvers

Alberto Rizzoli is a young Italian futurist, educational innovation entrepreneur, and Singularity University student. Alberto explores how schools and learning could evolve as a result of the rapid adoption of new technologies and educational models.

The Future of Personal Income and Expenses

Michael Nuschke is a "Retirement Futurist" focusing on the impacts of emerging technologies on personal financial planning. He addresses the potentially dramatic future impacts on personal finances of rising life expectancy and accelerating technologies.

The Future Potential of Consciousness in Business

Rishi Haldanya is a U.S. student with a strong interest in personal development, consciousness, neuroscience and entrepreneurship. He highlights how working with human consciousness could enhance workplace performance and create opportunities across a growing number of sectors.

The Future Derives From Place Choices

Stephen Roulac is a San Francisco based Real estate expert, litigation consultant, strategy advisor, and author. He examines the range of factors that will influence our future decisions about where to live, work and locate our businesses and highlights implications of those choices for individuals, companies and society.

SECTION 4 – Social Technologies – How will tomorrow's technologies permeate our everyday lives?

The Future of the Internet

Rohit Talwar and Alexandra Whittington – a Houston based foresight researcher – describe key forces and factors shaping the next twenty years of the internet and discuss how its role in business and society could evolve

The Future of Digital Media – The Freexpensive Prerogative

Yates Buckley is a founding partner at UNIT9, an award winning UK digital production agency. He explores how we might use intelligent personal agents to integrate our technology ecosystem to best communicate with us, control access to our personal data, and serve our needs.

Mobile 2030: Scenarios for the Role of Mobile Technology in Society

Alexandra Whittington and Amir Bar – a technology and education professional – present four scenarios exploring how mobile technology could permeate every aspect of our social and professional lives by 2030.

The Impact of Wearable Lifestyle Technologies and Gamification on Business and Society

David Wortley is a Malaysian based author and expert on the strategic use of gamification and enabling technologies for the transformation of business and society. His chapter considers the future potential impact of wearable lifestyle sensor technologies, AI, mobile applications, and gaming concepts on personal and corporate health.

Body-Machine Convergence

Dr Ian Pearson, a globally acclaimed futurist and inventor, takes us on a journey to the frontiers of human enhancement, examining how scientific advances could turn the body into a technology platform and blur the boundaries between man and machine.

The Rise of Neurosocial Networks – The Prospects for Networking our Brains in the Next 20 Years

Martin Dinov is a PhD student and researcher at Imperial College London focused on modeling, understanding and improving attention, cognition and brain function. Andrew Vladimirov is an experienced Ukrainian neuroscientist specializing in stimulation technologies. The authors examine the potential developments in, and applications of, neurotechnologies that could allow people to network at a brain-to-brain level.

Life in 2035: Future Consciousness, Cyborgs and Wisdom

Victor Vahidi Motti, a noted and award-winning Iranian scholar and academic futurist, explores how rapid and radical advances in science and technology could disrupt and reformulate our understanding of human capability, wisdom and the nature of work.

The potential for technological singularity and its future impacts on society

Anish Mohammed, a UK-based technologist and security expert, explains the notion of the technological singularity, and examines the potential challenges it could create for humanity.

SECTION 5 – Disruptive Developments – How might new technologies enable business innovation?

The Decentralization of Everything - Exploring The Business of the Blockchain

In this chapter Alexandra Whittington and Rohit Talwar introduce the nuts and bolts of blockchain technology and explore its potential disruptive impacts for society, business and economies.

The Future of the Phone Call

Dean Bubley, a UK-based technology analyst and authority on the future of telecommunications, explore the potential evolution of the humble phone call and considers the implications of ever-more fragmented – but more functional and customized – forms of telecommunication.

Will AI Eat the World?

Calum Chace, a highly acclaimed author, international authority on artificial intelligence (AI) and experienced business executive, examines the likely benefits and risks of AI and so called "conscious machines" for business and society.

From Clouds to Networks Without Infrastructure
Dr. Peter Cochrane is a seasoned technology innovator and entrepreneur and former head of research and Chief Technology Officer for BT in the UK. Peter outlines the radical innovations required in networking infrastructures to support the projected growth in internet users, connected objects and internet traffic.

Future Developments and Opportunities for Deep Learning Artificial Neural Networks
Elias Rut, a freelance software engineer and student of computational intelligence at the Vienna University of Technology and Martin Dinov, a computational and experimental neuroscience PhD researcher at Imperial College. The authors introduce us to the power of deep learning Artificial Neural Networks as a tool that can have a transformative impact in fields as diverse as understanding the brain to financial decision making and economic risk analysis.

How Massive Simulation Models could Transform Decision Making in Business, Government and Society
Vinay Gupta's career has seen three distinct phases: software nerd, ecologist, and revolutionary. He is now the release manager for Ethereum – a new "trustless software platform for developing and running decentralized applications on the internet". He discusses the challenge of valuing complex assets such as ecosystem services and explores how large scale simulations could enabled us to value the impact of everything from climate change to a new business model.

The Future of Events and Networking
Tiana Sinclair is a UK based product manager, futurist and an advocate of emerging technologies and runs the Future Tech Track event for early technology adopters. Tiana highlights how a range of

advanced technology developments could be deployed to augment the live experience for attendees, event owners, sponsors, and planners.

Revolutionizing Interactive Entertainment and Marketing in Public Places through Ambient Interactivity

Michael Mascioni is a market research consultant, writer, and conference planner in digital media and clean energy. He provides an overview of how the use of ambient interactivity could play out to enhance user experiences and marketing effectiveness in public places.

SECTION 6 – Surviving and Thriving – How can business adapt to a rapidly changing reality? What are the critical success factors for business in a constantly evolving world?

Experience Rules: How Stakeholder Experiences will Drive Profit into the Future

Joyce Gioia is President and CEO of The Herman Group (U.S.) and a Strategic Business Futurist advising global clients on workforce and workplace trends. She highlights how maximizing the experience of each stakeholder group could be the most critical driver of future corporate profitability.

Acceleration of the Slow Movement

Dana Klisanin, an award-winning U.S. psychologist and expert on conscious living, explores how businesses in future may increasingly turn their back on the pursuit of speed and instead embrace the concepts of the Slow Movement.

Business Agility: The Future of Work

Laura Goodrich is a speaker, coach, advisor and Global Workforce Innovator focused on change and the future of work. She describes the fundamentals of business agility as a management methodology to ensure organizations have the capacity to respond rapidly and effectively to emerging and anticipated change.

The Future of Work, Talent and Recruitment

Matt Alder is a digital strategy expert who focuses on the future of work. He examines the critical forces of business change and how they are shaping tomorrow's organization designs and models of work and employment.

The Future of Talent Management: Recruiting, Workforce Planning, Leadership Development and Performance Management

Kevin Wheeler is a U.S. based author, consultant, teacher, and global speaker and Founder and President of The Future of Talent Institute. Kevin explains how the confluence of factors driving business change will force us to rethink every aspect of talent management in tomorrow's organization.

Making the Shift from Disruptive to Hyper Scalable

Omar Mohout, Professor of Entrepreneurship at Antwerp Management School discusses the limits of the disruptive innovation philosophy and argues that future success requires companies to adopt Hyper Scalable thinking to succeed in winner-takes-all markets.

SECTION 7 – Industry Futures – How might old industries change and what new ones could emerge?

The Future of Aviation

Andrew Charlton, a highly respected Geneva based aviation industry consultant and commentator, presents the case for reform of the aviation sector ecosystem to address the critical capacity constraints that could hold back global trade, employment, and economic growth.

Futures Journalism: a Manifesto

Anna Simpson, a Singapore-based author and curator of Forum for the Future's Futures Centre, examines the current crisis in the practice and institutions of journalism and news reporting, and argues the need for journalism to evolve by learning from the practices of futures and foresight research.

Shaping the Future of Journalism

Puruesh Chaudhary is a development and strategic communications professional and the Founder and President of AGAHI, an NGO focused on creating knowledge collaboration and information sharing platforms. She discusses how the practice of journalism needs to evolve in the face of continuous global change and rapid technological advancements.

Constructing the Future

Julian Snape is a UK-based adviser on the impacts of disruptive technologies for small to medium enterprises and one of the early co-founders of Transhumanism in the UK. He traces the rapid evolution of 3D printing and examines the transformative ways in which it could impact the construction sector.

The Future Business of Body Shops

B.J. Murphy, is a 24 year old American Technoprogressive Transhumanist, writer, editor, and social media manager for the futures magazine SeriousWonder.com. B.J. outlines a powerful vision for how advances in cybernetics, 3D printing, and the biohacking movement could drive the emergence of high street Body Shops performing a range of human enhancements.

The Rise of the Cosmeceutical Sector

David Saintloth, a U.S. entrepreneur, designer, and writer, highlights the market potential of a new cosmeceutical health and beauty sector that could emerge as a result of recent developments in gene editing technology.

The Great Energy Controversy of 2030

James H. Lee is a Delaware-based investment advisor and authority on emerging technologies and social trends. He examines the potential opportunities and risks associated with tapping in to fields of crystallized natural gas in the form of methane hydrates trapped in our oceans below the arctic permafrost.

Space-Based Solar Power and Wireless Power Transmission
Devin Daniels is a U.S. based physics student and technology innovator with a deep interest in space based ventures. Devin explores the transformational social and commercial potential and associated technological challenges of developing a space based solar power generation industry.

SECTION 8 – Embracing the Future – What are the futures and foresight tools, methods and processes that we can use to explore, understand and create the future?

Foresight Infused Strategy Development
Maree Conway is an experienced foresight and strategy consultant and the founder of Thinking Futures (Australia). She explores how to infuse foresight into existing corporate strategy processes to strengthen outcomes and execution.

Automated, Experiential, Open: How to Overcome "Futures Fatigue" with Emerging Foresight Practices
Cornelia Daheim, a leading German futurist and foresight consultant, highlights a growing trend towards the use of IT-based, participative and experiential approaches to invigorate and enhance the practice of corporate foresight.

Storifying Foresight: Scenario Planning as a Tool for Improved Change Management Processes
Dr. Claire Nelson is Ideation Leader of The Futures Forum USA and a White House Champion of Change. She explains the critical role of scenario planning and storytelling in helping organizations shape and share their desired visions of the future, and in delivering the resulting organizational changes.

Is the Future of Design Thinking in the Future of Business Foresight?
Jim Burke is a U.S. foresight coach focused on delivering innovation

and effective ways to think about and act on future. Jim highlights the growing use of Design Thinking as part of the foresight process, particularly for prototyping future scenarios.

SECTION 9 – Framing the Future – How should organizations look at the future?

What Works in Transforming Organizations and Institutions?
Professor Sohail Inayatullah is on the faculty at the Graduate Institute of Futures Studies, Tamkang University, Taiwan and Director of metafuture.org. He identifies critical insights and principles for how we can use foresight and a learning journey approach to framing new strategies and driving organizational transformation.

Futures Thinking - A Critical Organizational Skill
Hardin Tibbs, a highly experienced UK-based futurist, strategist, educator, and writer, highlights the importance of developing the critical future thinking skills that enable a organization to anticipate and adapt to change.

Critical Foresight Skills
Dr. Peter Bishop was Director of the Foresight program at the University of Houston and is now the Executive Director of Teach the Future which helps educators teach foresight. He highlights how organizations can acquire the key foresight skills required to create new adaptive strategies and drive change in uncertain times.

Business Management in a Time of Change: The Importance of Futures Studies
Professor Francisco Jose Martinez-Lopez from the University of Huelva, Spain, specializes in information technology and future studies, and Mercedes Garcia Ordaz is Associate Professor of the University of Huelva of the Department of Financial Economy, Accounting and Operations Management. They explore the critical importance of future studies and long term planning in an era of rapid change.

Is The Pace of Change Accelerating?
Stephen Aguilar-Millan is s consulting futurist from the UK and Director of Research at the European Futures Observatory. He examines the potential for the pace of change to stop accelerating and examines the possible consequences.

The Outside Context Problem, A Concerned Observer's Guide
Benjamin Mottram is a UK based future thinker and authority on crowd sourcing and gamification. He discusses how organizations can make sense of and address the unforeseen and complex problems that will be thrown up by a constantly changing operating environment over the next two decades.

Be There Now
Paul Brooks, a Hawaii-based researcher on social and economic emergence, stresses the importance of openness, dynamism and scalability in helping a business prepare for the future.

Section 10 – Conclusions – Navigating Uncertainty and a Rapidly Changing Reality

Lead Editor Rohit Talwar sets out a framework to help leaders respond to the ideas presented in the book to drive future strategy and navigate uncertainty and a rapidly changing reality.

SECTION 1

Visions of the Future - What are the global transformations on the horizon?

Exploring future possibility

In this opening section we explore some big picture views of how our world could play out in the next two decades and the potential implications for individuals, society, governments, and business. The authors examine how the key economic, social and technological forces, emerging ideas, and developments discussed in the rest of the book could come together to drive fundamental change. In particular they highlight critical current and future technology revolutions that could disrupt and reshape how we live, how we govern and the future purpose, role, nature, and conduct of business.

The five chapters in this section address the following topics:

The Future of Business - Navigating the Next Horizon (page 29) – In the opening chapter Rohit Talwar sets out a broad overview of how business could be reshaped over the next two decades by new ideas, disruptive technologies and emerging behaviors.

Forecasting Future Disruptions (page 50) - Strategic Change Is Inevitable – Professor Bill Halal presents forecasts of the technology revolution, social trends, wild cards and their expected impacts and argues the need to guide the path of creative disruption.

The Automated, Digitized, and Simulated Future (page 72) – Gray Scott explores how the relentless future pace of automation, digitization, and digital simulation could redefine our world.

Redefining the Relationship of Man and Machine (*page 82*) – Gerd Leonhard argues that in the face of such all-encompassing technological change, the purpose of business will evolve to focus on serving humanity and furthering human happiness.

Can 3D Printing Destroy Capitalism and Restore Government? (*page 94*) – Jeffrey Joslin examines the truly disruptive capability of 3D printing and its wide ranging potential to change everything from the purpose of business to the future of governance and democracy.

Global Drivers of Change

By April Koury, Iva Lazarova and Rohit Talwar

Below we examine a range of 14 drivers that are expected to be globally transformative and could set the high level context within which business and society generally will evolve. We focus in particular on four themes: Emerging Paradigms, Energy, Resources, and Climate and Environment.

Emerging Paradigms
- ***Age of Abundance*** – The Singularity movement argues that, counter to the peak proponents, advances in science and technology will lead to a world of post-scarcity or abundance between 2020 and 2050. Nanotechnology, genetic sciences, bio – and molecular manufacturing, robotics and AI will result in great efficiencies in resource usage and management, as well as offer up a whole new host of plentiful new materials. This will extend to lab grown meat, replacing the need for animal farming.
- ***Innovating to Zero*** – Innovating to zero is the idea of creating a "Zero Concept" world, where companies will deliver energy solutions, goods, and services with zero carbon emissions. Some extend the idea to include delivering goods and services with zero environmental impact. Technologies that will assist in the drive for zero emission include wind power, the travelling wave reactor (TWR), solar PV, and third generation biofuels

(biofuels derived from algae).

- *Circular Economies* – Traditional linear economies are based on a "take, make, dispose" model, whereas circular economies rely on the re-use of resources to extract maximum value and minimize waste before being safely returned to the biosphere. Governments as well as businesses are taking notice of the potential economic and ecological long-term benefits of investing in a circular economic model. In 2012 a report sponsored by the Ellen MacArthur Foundation found that a subset of the European Union manufacturing sector could realize net material cost savings of up to $630 billion per year by 2025 through switching to a circular economic model.[1]

- *Civic Ecology* – Civic ecology practices are community-based environmental stewardship actions that enhance the green infrastructure, ecosystem, and human well-being within urban areas. In essence, communities come together to care for nature typically in places marked by disaster, poverty, and environmental degradation. Activities include community gardening, tree planting, and park cleanup.[2] Civic ecology practices are growing in number as the need for global sustainability initiatives becomes increasing prominent.

- *Environmental Market-Based Instruments (MBIs)* – Environmental market-based instruments are policies that provide incentives to polluters to reduce their negative environmental impacts. Carbon taxes and "cap and trade" policies are the most widely adopted MBIs. Continued global growth is expected to increase the adoption of MBIs to encourage more sound behavior in carbon usage and provide the funds to finance ecological protection.

- *Community Sustainable Resource Management Schemes* – Local community initiatives are encouraging communities to reuse, recycle, repurpose, and share resources. In Mexico City, for example, at the Mercado del Trueque, families exchange recyclable materials for fresh produce. On its opening day the Mercado collected an estimated 11 tons of recyclables from

3,000 local families.[3]

Energy

- *Rising Energy Demand* – Global energy demand is expected to increase by one-third by 2035, with emerging economies accounting for more than 90 percent of that net energy demand growth, according to the International Energy Agency. Low-carbon energy sources like renewables and nuclear could meet about 40 percent of the growth in primary energy demand by 2035.[4]

- *Scale of Alternative Energy Adoption* – Oil prices are expected to rise in the longer term as the pressure on fossil fuel supplies drives up costs over time. This could result in a growth in the use of alternative energy by publicly owned energy utilities, existing private sector players, and new providers. Sources could include a combination of solar, geothermal, tidal, wind, biomass, nuclear, motion capture, and other forms of alternative energy. Self-managed alternative energy supplies are becoming increasingly popular at the corporate level. They provide firms with more options for fulfilling their energy needs, and allow them to decouple themselves from the price volatility of the public energy supply.

- *Growth of Fracking* – Hydraulic fracking involves drilling vertically into the earth to release gas and oil by using a high-pressure fluid to cause fractures and cracks in deep shale rock formations. Trillions of cubic feet of gas and oil may be extracted this way. Though the fracking market is expected grow from $13.33 billion in 2013 to $19.8 billion by 2020[5], environmental concerns and governmental regulations banning fracking may hobble this energy source.

Resources

- *Resource Scarcity* – Resource scarcity greatly impacts many aspects of business decision making, from location to securing raw materials and supplies. Every resource will become a battle ground as nations seek to secure access to food, water, raw materials, rare earth minerals and other energy resources. Sustainable resource management is gaining increased government attention due to the combined pressures of climate change, population growth, economic growth, and of course, resource scarcity.

- *Peak Everything* – According to peak everything proponents, humans are reaching the peak limits of our planetary resources including oil, water, carrying capacity, and all raw materials. For example, peak oil production is expected to hit between 2015 and 2020 (although advances in technology continually push that date into the future). The FAO warns that world food production needs to increase by at least 70 percent to meet the demands of a growing population by 2050.[6]

- *Food Security* – In the coming decades, population growth coupled with reduced access to fresh water and declining arable land will resulting in mounting pressure on food security globally.[7] The regions expected to have the largest population growth (Asia and Sub-Saharan Africa) by 2050 are currently seen as the least well equipped to meet these growing food demands and to deal with food security challenges, increasing the risk of conflict in the future. However, growing agricultural practices like permaculture, vertical farming, community gardening, edible landscaping, and urban fruit gleaning are redefining where and how we grow food, and will help alleviate future challenges to food security.

Climate and Environment

- *Climate Change* – Experts agree that the planet is experiencing a rapid change in global and regional climate patterns. This is predicted to lead to increased sea levels, changes in the amount and the pattern of precipitation, and the expansion of desserts in subtropical regions. In particular, extreme weather and heat, drought and heavy rain, maritime acidification, and the extinction of living organisms would lead to decreasing yields from agriculture and fisheries. Severe climate change effects could also lead to increasing numbers of refugees. Governments worldwide are facing the challenge of developing policies that mitigate these effects and also build resiliency into our systems. Many nations may simply be unable to cope with the costs of protecting against severe climatic incidents and remediation after they occur.

- *Developing Materiality of Biodiversity Impacts on Business* – Environmental impacts such as growing resource scarcity, biodiversity loss, and degradation of ecosystems provide new opportunities and risks to investors, shareholders and, insurers given corporate reliance on these assets.

The Future of Business – Navigating the Next Horizon

By Rohit Talwar

What are the forces, ideas, tensions, developments, opportunities, and choices shaping the future of business over the next twenty years?

Charting the Future of Business

The future of business over the next two decades will not be a linear extrapolation from the present day. There are many possible scenarios – each with multiple paths to get from where we are today to an uncertain tomorrow. Those scenarios arise from the complex interplay between a range of future factors:

- Socio-demographic changes, and the rapidly evolving values, needs, and expectations of individuals and societies.
- Political and economic shifts.
- Alternative possible trajectories for energy, resources, the environment, biodiversity, and sustainability.
- New business thinking and the impacts of an increasingly globalized business landscape.
- Rapid and convergent developments across a range of disciplines in science and technology with potentially disruptive impact.

This chapter examines the critical tensions and choices that are arise from the interplay of these forces and outlines the domains of science and technology that could catalyze the biggest changes in our world. I highlight emerging business sectors that could shape tomorrow's economy and examine the new business strategies and behaviors that these developments could enable. I conclude with an assessment of the critical decisions businesses need to make as they define their future purpose and strategy.

The central role of information and communications technology

The business landscape is being shaped by a number of major shifts that in turn are forcing us to rethink every aspect of our purpose, philosophy, culture, strategy, business model, capabilities, technology architecture, operational design, organizational architecture, HR approach, and financing options. At the heart of the story about tomorrow's business, is the impact of the ever quickening pace of advances in information and communications technology (ICT) in particular. We are experiencing exponential rates of development and declining costs for many of the underlying fields from computer power and storage capacity to communications speeds and data transmission bandwidths. These are enabling the spread of relatively low cost mobile devices across the globe, giving ever-larger numbers access to the internet, and driving the current dialogue around digital transformation and industry disruption.

When worlds collide

The pace of digital penetration into every aspect of our world is leading to an inevitable clash between two worlds. On the one hand we have the planet populated and largely still run by those **born physical**. They see the world as a very tangible entity with physical outputs – whether they build houses, produce cars, or provide financial services. In this world, despite digital advances, "analog" mindsets dominate aspirations and decision making, hence growth opportunities and business problems are tackled in a relatively linear manner – with technology as an enabler.

This physical world is on a headlong collision course with the inhabitants of "planet digital". The latter is inhabited by individuals and firms who are **born digital**. Instead of houses, cars, and savings products, all they see is data. They believe every challenge and problem can be addressed by finding the right software algorithm and deploying the appropriate mix of technologies. Crucially, they bring exponential thinking to business strategy. They want to break with linear approaches that typically limit them to 5 to 50 percent improvements on key measures of organizational performance. Instead, they are looking for ways to triple the number of houses built per week, reduce the time to produce a new model by 20 times or more, and quadruple the number of customers per employee.

Reworking the DNA of business

The challenge for those not raised with a digital mindset is to learn how to evolve and compete in the new environment. Can we get there by simply deploying more technology or do we need radical reframing of our way of seeing the landscape – do we need to develop a digital and exponential mindset? Some believe this evolution of their DNA can be achieved within the existing "rules of the game" – innovating within the standard industry practices, established ways of thinking and unspoken assumptions that shape the strategies of most players in the sector.

Others are trying to reinvent themselves by pursuing game changing approaches. In many sectors, the biggest disruption comes from new entrants who ignore the old rules and seek to change the game itself. For example, when Skype entered the telephony market it changed the game by taking the industry's core product – the humble phone call – and making it available for free. Skype has captured around 40 percent of international telephone traffic with a fraction of the total workforce of most telecommunications operators. Those adopting this path have to embrace a fundamentally different mindset and culture – rather than simply making the investment in more technology.

As you read through the chapters in this book, it becomes clear that businesses trying to carve a path to the future will have to respond to a number of significant tensions that are emerging across nations, society, and business. These opposing forces are driving the need for new thinking and new strategies, creating new opportunities and unveiling a whole new range and scale of risks.

Economic, political, and social tensions

As countries wrestle with the complex questions posed by a fast changing and highly interconnected world, the decisions they make have a fundamental bearing on the choices made by both national and international businesses.

- *Econo-Political Consolidation versus Fragmentation.* Some groupings such as the European Union, ASEAN and the Gulf States could see greater convergence on a range of economic and political policy issues. At the same time, a range of smaller and struggling developing nations may seek to merge. In both cases the drivers are the need for economies of scale and consolidated policy making in the face of an accelerating pace of change. These forces drive the need for nations to create critical economic strength, attract the investment required to serve their populations, and compete in the hyper-connected era. In parallel, we may see many regions seek to break away from countries in pursuit of economic and political independence.

- *Closed versus Open Flows.* Those who seek to control economic activity will be challenged by a relentless pursuit of the opportunities presented by globalization. Network technology in dismantling artificial barriers to the free global flow of information, knowledge, people, money, assets, services, and physical goods. A more dynamic, instantly responsive and rapidly evolving system will introduce new sources of opportunity, uncertainty, and volatility.

- *Ageing versus Youthful Societies.* In many nations, an ageing population with a declining birth rate will pressurize government finances and care systems. Developing nations with faster growing and younger populations will face the triple challenges of upgrading education models, creating employment and providing effective health and social systems.

- *Masculine versus Feminine.* Male-dominated power structures and systems in governance, business, society, and the family will continue to come under pressure. Females now outperform males at every level of the education system across the planet. Women's income levels are rising, as is the proportion of total national assets that they own. Together these developments will accelerate the drive for equal access to workplace opportunity, advancement, and rewards and be a transforming force in many economies. These in turn will challenge organizational thought processes, governing assumptions, dominant cultural metaphors, and workplace practices.

- *Power versus Profit.* Global energy demand is expected to outstrip supply for many decades to come. Warnings around the dangerous climatic and environmental impact of fossil fuels are ever-more frequent. Trillions of dollars of investment is required to ensure adequate and continuous power for a growing global population and the underlying infrastructure and business sectors that serve it. Massive growth is inevitable and necessary in the use of alternative energy sources from solar to wind, tidal, bio-waste and geothermal. The sheer level of financing required to develop and scale up this new global energy grid will require participation from governments, and the willingness of investors to accept lower returns than those traditionally achieved in the energy sector.

Commercial pressure points

Business will be reinvented as sector incumbents are challenged externally by brash new entrants and internally by a generation demanding change. These upstarts are embracing new ideas – fueled by technology advances, different generational attitudes, and shifting global perspectives on what emerging nations are capable of. This will be test each of the pillars upon which we have built modern business, global trade, and its governance systems.

- *Corporate Power versus Youthful Ambition.* Up to 50 percent of the Fortune 500 in 2025 probably doesn't exist in 2015. Many more traditional "linear thinking" companies may struggle to reinvent themselves with an "exponential mindset" for the digital age. They will be challenged by so called "hyper-growth companies" seeking "triple digit plus" rates of improvement and growth. These challengers could emerge in sectors like alternative energy, food production, genetics, driverless cars, 3D and 4D printing, and goods and services that we can't even conceive of today.

- *Old Money versus New Finance.* We'll still have financial services but not as we know them. The notion of public stock markets could be transformed by transparent blockchain-powered (see below) trading platforms and more efficient online crowd funding solutions. The widespread use of distributed digital currencies like Bitcoin, could effectively create a single global monetary system and eliminate currency markets and centralized regulation. By 2025 we should expect the industry to have been reshaped by open markets and crowd based solutions that bypass existing providers of everything from savings and insurance to equity investment and commercial financing.

- *Consolidation versus Distribution.* There is an increasing prospect of "winner takes almost all" in many technology-enabled markets and online services. As a result, unemployment could rise and the disparities between the rich and poor could grow – driving the rise of a global hyper-rich segment. Automation is decoupling economic growth from job creation and driving technological unemployment. Joblessness levels of 50 percent or more could become the norm without radical shifts in national economic strategies. This will drive down average income levels and increase demands for some form of guaranteed basic income for the whole population.

- *Safe Havens versus Wild Frontiers.* Business attention, investment, and talent will be attracted to rapidly growing emerging market mega-cities such as Mumbai, Delhi, Dhaka, Sao Paolo, Kinshasa, and Lagos. These cities are typically characterized by burgeoning populations and an increasing middle class. However, they often have fragile physical infrastructures and under-developed civil society frameworks. The opportunity will test the capacity of more rigid thinking Western corporations. To survive and thrive in these new arenas, they must learn how adapt and behave like water in the face of myriad obstacles. Will this shift in focus happen at the expense of slower-growing but better-understood mature economies that are struggling to adapt to a new world?

- *Manual versus Automated.* Advances in AI and robotics in particular could drive the replacement of humans by machines in every walk of life from retail assistants to airline pilots, accountants, and doctors. Businesses will increasingly have to make philosophical choices between continuing to employ people for the benefit of society and automating for profit maximization.

Science and technology choices

Rapid progress in existing domains coupled with the emergence of new fields of discovery will continue to excite and challenge governments, business, and society. Issues will arise over the extent to which we should seek to control and regulate research endeavors – and whether it is even feasible or realistic in the modern age. As, the boundaries between humans and machines continue to blur, and technology is increasingly embedded in our bodies, business will be forced to reassess how far it is prepared to go in pursuit of profit.

- *Human versus Machine Intelligence.* Battle lines could be drawn between those wanting to preserve the sovereignty of flesh over silicon, and the innovators keen to experiment with the possibilities created by Artificial Intelligence (AI), collective intelligence, and deep learning systems.
- *Enhanced versus Unenhanced Humans.* Our notions of what it means to be human will be challenged by advances that enable the chemical, genetic, electronic, and physical augmentation of

our brain and bodies. The use of smart drugs, genetic modification, direct brain stimulation, and exoskeletons could see the emergence of a new modified breed of Human 2.0 with far greater capabilities than their unenhanced counterparts.

- *Info versus Bio.* While most expert commentators expect information technology to be the centre of the economy for the next two decades, others believe the emergence of the biological era could have even greater impact. From gene therapies and gene editing to new materials and energy sources from synthetic biology – there is huge potential. The promise of DNA-based computing and could transform the information and communications technology (ICT) sector and see the human body become a computing platform.

- *Physical versus Virtual.* With everything from money and education to policing and governance moving to the digital realm, greater focus will be placed on virtual assets. The physical will become increasingly ICT enabled – with sensors, computing, and communications capability being embedded in everything from clothing to wallpaper. For example, the proportion of ICT functionality in the value of a new vehicle could rise from 30 to 50 percent today to 80 percent by 2035. The boundaries between physical and virtual will continue to blur through augmented and virtual reality.

New leadership capabilities

To navigate a coherent path through the choices being thrown up by these tensions, businesses will need to learn new decision making approaches. Central to the new leadership agenda will be the ability to master complexity, systems thinking, scenario planning, predictive modeling, collaboration, experimentation, and discovery-led innovation approaches. A clear challenge here is to develop the intellectual depth and resourcefulness required to address such a complex and fast-changing agenda. In response, an increasing number of leaders are turning to spiritual practices such as mindfulness meditation to help them tap into the capabilities of their subconscious mind and tune into their intuition. A range of research studies have demonstrated the positive impact of such regular practices on health, wellbeing, mental outlook, and performance.

The revolution will be intelligent, automated, synthesized, and broadcast

A range of transformative science and technology developments promise to revolutionize old industries and give birth to new sectors. Summarized below are fifteen areas of development with significant disruptive potential over the next two decades.

Information and Communications Technology

- *Exponential Technologies.* The power, capacity and functionality of a range of technologies will continue to increase. For example, some experts believe that by 2025 we could see computers capable of operating at the speed of the human brain – roughly 10,000 trillion cycles per second.
- *New Computing Architectures.* A range of initiatives are underway to replace silicon as the base material of our computing devices. Developments in areas such as Optical, Quantum and DNA-based devices could deliver massive leaps in performance using radically different concepts and models of computing.
- *The Hyperconnected Internet of Humanity.* The internet could reach five to seven billion people by 2035. The content of the web will be available to all – mainly via their mobile devices. Anywhere from 50 to 250 billion devices could be connected to the web, along with a trillion or more sensors embedded in those devices and other objects such as furniture and product packaging. Cisco estimated this hyperconnected *Internet of Humanity* could generate $19 trillion[8] of value through better use of assets, increased employee productivity, elimination of supply chain process inefficiencies, improved customer experiences, and technology innovation.
- *Blockchain Technology.* The blockchain is a highly secure protocol that enables the direct digital transfers of information

without an intermediary. It can be used for money (Bitcoin), personal data, stocks, transaction records, and contracts. The distributed and secure model that underpins blockchain based systems could transform financial services, eliminating the clearing house role. It is already facilitating the creation of smart self-activating contracts and driving the idea of **Decentralized Autonomous Organizations** (DAOs). These largely automated entities would combine blockchain approaches and AI to conduct the business of the organization according to a precise set of business rules. Some say blockchain and what it enables are the basis for a transformation of the economy and could have an impact bigger than the internet.

- *Immersivity and Mixed Reality Living.* Our physical environment will have ever-greater capability to identify and interact with us – tailoring the experience to each individual based on the information we are willing to share. Multi-sensory stimulation will take augmented and virtual reality to the next level. Online retail could be transformed when we can add touch, taste and smell sensations.
- *Artificial Intelligence / Conscious Technology.* We are entering a phase where advances in AI could yield systems that come close to matching human capability. The next evolutions could see the development of so called strong AI, Artificial General Intelligence (AGI) and SuperIntelligence. These tools could exceed human reasoning capabilities and outstrip us in every intellectual endeavor – potentially behaving in ways beyond our current comprehension.

There is widespread disagreement within the AI-community over whether and when such advances could occur. If they do happen, these developments could be just 10-20 years away. Over the next decade we will definitely see the emergence of more highly intelligent and adaptive personal ecosystems. Our intelligent agents will learn from our behaviors, act on our behalf in the digital realm, anticipate our needs, provide us with timely information, and guide our choices.

Advancement of Humanity

- *Healthcare Transformation.* Wearable and embedded sensors and devices could transform everything from condition monitoring to drug delivery and treatment. Big data and AI will enhance diagnosis and care planning. Telemedicine and robotic surgery could enable improved life expectancy in remote areas. Low cost 3D printing, stem cell treatments, and new tissue growing capabilities will make reliable organ replacement safer, faster, and cheaper.

- *Human Augmentation.* Humans will increasingly "upgrade" their brains using a combination of nootropic cognitive enhancing smart drugs, and electronic brain stimulation. Our physical performance could be augmented through gene editing and gene replacement, physical modifications, 3D printed electro-mechanical replacements, and exoskeleton body strengthening attachments. We could see genetic treatments to eliminate conditions such as rage and obesity. In their chapters, B J Murphy and David Saintloth suggest we could see the emergence of high street **Body Shops** and treatment centers offering a range of such augmentations.

- *Brain Uploading.* A number of major research initiatives are working on mapping how the human brain stores information, which could be achieved by 2025. Technology companies will compete to "back up" our brains online.

- *Transformation of the Food Chain.* Global food demand is increasing at more than double the growth rate of food supply. Radical solutions are required to feed a planet with rising incomes and consumption aspirations. A range of innovations are being explored to meet those demands over the next two decades. These include genetically engineered crops, saltwater agriculture, open-sourced food research, vertical farming, precision agriculture, 3D printed food, and organic crop management. On the next horizon are robot farmers, bioprinting of meat and other foodstuffs – combining tissue engineering and 3D printing, localized food production, plant-based meat alternatives, personalized nutrition, AI-designed foods and recipes, and low-cost foodstuffs developed for nutrition rather than taste.

Domestic Infrastructure and Manufacturing Systems

- *Robotics / Drones.* From driverless cars to construction and elder care – robots and their drone cousins are entering our world in large volumes and the price is falling dramatically. The speed, dexterity, balance, reasoning capability, and emotional intelligence of robots could increase to the point where robotic companions could be commonplace by 2030.
- *3D / 4D Printing.* The speed, functionality, choice of materials, and range of applications for 3D printing will continue to increase. Everything from blood vessels, to food and buildings are already being 3D printed. Neighborhood maker centers could become increasingly prominent – allowing individuals to download product design "recipes" from the internet or create their own designs and then fabricate them using these shared community facilities. The evolution to 4D printing will enable the manufacture of objects that can self-assemble and change their shape and properties – for example producing limbs that could reinforce themselves as we age.
- *Nanotechnology and Atomically Precise Manufacturing (APM).* Nanotechnology is the manipulation of matter at the atomic, molecular, or nanoscale – working with particles roughly 1 to 100 nanometers in size. Advances in physics, chemistry and biology have enabled us to engineer materials and nano-systems. Already in use in many sectors such as chip manufacturing, the next big stage of development could impact many industries. The goal is to build products with atomic precision – literally assembling them atom by atom to give the precise properties we desire and eliminate waste in the manufacturing process. This could deliver low-cost, high-performance components and systems. APM would enable the production of stronger, lighter, safer, lower emission, and more efficient physical structures,

engines, medical devices, drugs, energy sources, and foodstuffs.

- **Synthetic Biology.** There are a range of developments that could result from applying engineering disciplines to biology. This could enable development of low-cost drugs, new materials, foodstuffs, chemicals, and energy sources. It could provide tools to clean up toxic spills and remediate environmental pollution. The potential to engineer entirely new lifeforms is also being explored. The so-called NBIC convergence between nanotechnology, biology, information technology and the cognitive sciences could in future yield smart, adaptive and self-healing materials and entire biological systems.

- **Energy Innovation.** Energy demand is rising driven in part by a mobile device-enabled web-connected population – driving concerns over the environmental impact of fossil fuels. The argument is building for increased investment in alternative sources of energy supply. The debate over nuclear safety will rumble on but a significant expansion of global nuclear generating capability seems inevitable.

A range of cleaner alternatives such as solar, tidal, geothermal, wind, and bio-waste will take a larger share of total energy supply. However, governmental inertia, corporate hesitancy, lack of investment, and continued debate over the right energy mix could hold back alternative energy development. Later in this book, Devin Daniels and James Lee highlight the potential of space-based solar power and tapping into fields of methane hydrates (crystallized natural gas) trapped below the arctic permafrost in our oceans.

Viewed collectively, these developments could drive significant shifts in every aspect of our world in 2035. The impacts range from what it will mean to be human and how health and wellness services are delivered through to future energy supply, the cars we drive, the homes we live in, and the ways in which goods are produced.

Industries of the future

The transformative tensions and developments outlined above will in turn spawn a range of new industries – many of which are discussed elsewhere in this book. The likes of Mckinsey,[9] Volans,[10] and others have done extensive research on emerging sectors that could drive the next wave of $100 billion to $1 trillion plus global industries. Tables 1-3 below identify thirty existing and emerging sectors that we believe could account for 50 to 60 percent or more of the entire global economy over the next two decades. These will become an increasingly focus for innovators, entrepreneurs, investors and those who might provide products and services to these sectors.

TABLE 1 – Critical Sectors – Technology, Citizen and Domestic

Information and Communications Technology	Citizen and Domestic
Mobile Internet – Devices, Infrastructure, Commerce and Services	Healthcare Innovation
Next Generation Intelligent, Personalized Internet	Elder Care
Cloud Based Applications, Infrastructure and Services	Human Augmentation / Body Shops
Internet of Things / Internet of Everything / Internet of Humanity	Clean Domestic Water and Sanitation
Big Data, Data Mining and the Automation of Knowledge	Smart Homes – Intelligent Devices, Air Conditioning, Waste to Power
Artificial Intelligence and Deep Learning	Green Vehicles / Electric Cars / Autonomous and Near-Autonomous Vehicles
Blockchain-Based Systems and Distributed Autonomous Organizations	Education Systems Transformation

TABLE 2 – Critical Sectors – Production and Societal Infrastructure and Services

Production Technologies and Systems	Societal Infrastructure and Services
Advanced Robotics / Drones	New Food and Agriculture Solutions
3D and 4D Printing and Advanced Materials	Sharing / Circular Economy Solutions – Repurpose Recycle, Reuse, Repair
Genomics and Synthetic Biology	Smart City Infrastructures and Services
Biomimcry Applied to Design of Products and Engineered Systems	Intelligent Transport Systems
Rapid / Green / Sustainable Construction	E-Government

TABLE 3 – Critical Sectors – Industry Transformation, Energy and Environment

Industry Transformation	Energy and Environment
Global Infrastructure – Roads, Transport, Energy, Water	Alternative and Renewable Energy / Energy Storage
Automation of Professional Services – E.g. Accounting, Legal, Consultancy, and Architecture	Advanced Oil and Gas Exploration and Recovery – Including Fracking, Methane Hydrates
Financial Services Technologies	Geo-Engineering, Climate / Environmental Protection, Disaster Recovery, and Remediation

New business strategies and behaviors

So how might businesses respond in the face of these forces of disruptive change and the potential opportunities and risk they could create? Here are ten types of response that might emerge and which – in some instances – we can already see evidence of. Some of these behaviors will become strategies in their own right; other firms might form their strategies by combining a range of these behaviors.

- *Exponential Thinkers.* A growing number of firms are already looking to apply exponential thinking to the design of their organizations – driving 100 per cent or more improvement. Table 4 below highlights examples of the kinds of performance improvement that can be achieved over more traditional competitors by applying such thinking in both the digital and physical domains.

TABLE 4 – Performance Improvements from Exponential Thinking[11]

Business/Sector	Exponential Improvement
AirBnB Hotels	90x more listings per employee
GitHub Software	109x more listings per employee
Local Motors Automorive	1000x cheaper to develop a new car model 5-22x faster to manufacture an individual car
Quirky Consumer Goods	10x faster product development (29 vs 300 days)
Google Ventures Investments	2.5x more investments in early stage start-ups 10x faster through design process
Valve Gaming	30x more market cap per employee
Tesla Automotive	30x more market cap per employee
Tangerine (formerly ING Direct Canada) Banking	7x more customers per employee 4x more deposits per customer

Such strategies can also have a dramatic financial impact (table 5). We expect the potential benefits to drive a growing interest in how to apply exponential thinking both to existing organizations and to new and early stage businesses that want to pursue a hyper-growth trajectory.

TABLE 5 – Exponential Improvements in Market Capitalization[12]

Company	Age (years)	2011 Valuation	2014 Valuation	Increase
Haier	30	$19 billion	$60 billion	3x
Valve	18	$1.5 billion	$4.5 billion	3x
Google	17	$150 billion	$400 billion	2.5x
Uber	7	$2 billion	$40 billion	20x
AirBnB	6	$2 billion	$10 billion	5x
Github	6	$500 million (est.)	$7 billion	14x
Waze	6	$25 million	$1 billion (2013)	50x
Qirky	5	$50 million	$2 billion	40x
Snapchat	3	0	$10 billion	10,000x +

- **Intimacy Freaks.** A growing number of businesses will begin to understand the power of the information they hold about their customers. Using big data, predictive analytics, and AI they will be able to forecast customer intentions and behaviour with unerring accuracy. This will drive the desire to increase the frequency of contact, and extend the relationship with customers. The providers of the most popular devices and services such as Apple, Samsung, Google and Facebook already own the customer interface to large numbers of customers. They will fight to deepen these relationships, increase the dependency upon them, and erect barriers to prevent others from stealing away customers.

- **Barbarians.** As data becomes central to the understanding of any market, challengers will be ever-more willing to enter a sector, ignore the existing rules of combat and adopt approaches that effectively change the game and savage and paralyze the incumbents. This is happening already in the home delivery market where digital brands with deep customer intimacy are able to offer a range of products and services from other retailers. By positioning their own brand as the purchasing portal, they are effectively diminishing the power of the underlying brands. To whom do born digital customers have greater loyalty – Amazon, Google and Facebook or Target, Wal-Mart and Home Depot from who the intermediary might be buying the items?
- **Aliens.** In the face of digital transformation and market disruption, established industry players may choose to adopt strategies that break ranks, ignore established rules of engagement and change the game. Such strategies will be pursued with the aim of pre-empting external challengers and seeking a first mover advantage over existing competitors. China's Broad Group[13] has pursued such a strategy using rapid construction approaches to overturn traditional industry timelines by pre-fabricating the sections in the factory prior to onsite assembly. For example, they have erected a 30-storey hotel in just fifteen days.
- **Magicians.** Rapid automation is driving the potential commoditization of many products and services. In response, businesses will be challenged to differentiate themselves by creating moments of magic in the customer experience that deliver a genuine wow factor. What aspects of your offering and customer experience exceed expectations and have customers telling stories about you?
- **Adoption Agencies / Buy a Future.** Some organizations may begin to recognize that they are ill-equipped to succeed in the emerging landscape. Their survival strategy may be to effectively "adopt" the players who they think can create that future for them – investing in firms who can drive the necessary internal and market-facing metamorphosis. These might be smaller

and more nimble rivals in the sector, bold new competitors, or consulting firms who truly understand what it takes to win in uncertain times. Others may deliberately target their corporate venturing arms to buy into firms that could change the game and destroy the core business. Indeed this is already becoming more commonplace in the venturing sector.

- **Business Light.** The challenges of refocusing and aligning large organizations can be slow and painful. In response, some may feel the best way forward is to strip the organization back to its bare bones. Such **business light** entities might comprise a small core staff that frames strategy, creates key ecosystem partnerships, and manages finances and stakeholder relationships. Literally everything else from product design and manufacturing through to marketing, sales and distribution would be delivered by a network of outsourced partners and service providers.

- **Trekkies.** Bold ambition is becoming fashionable. Competitions like the X-Prize, **moonshot initiatives** such as Google's "We Solve for 'X'", and institutions like Singularity University are all focused on deploying radical science and technology ideas to address global problems and challenges. Investors, entrepreneurs and innovators are increasingly focused on the pursuit of the seemingly impossible with venture ranging from low cost sustainable housing and universal education, through to hypersonic travel, colonizing space, and asteroid mining. This desire "to boldly go" where others dare not tread will drive a constant stream of ever-more ambitious initiatives. These will go well beyond normal corporate agendas and blur the boundaries between the roles of the public and private sector.

- **Automation Junkies.** The promise of the entirely automated enterprise will be a magnet for many entrepreneurs attracted by the notion of establishing a Distributed Autonomous Organization (DAO) that can eliminate the uncertain human element and exist almost entirely in software and silicon. This in turn could give rise to the notion of **companies as technologies** and corporate conglomerates and investment funds as platforms for the aggregation of multiple DAOs.

- **The Non-Owned Enterprise.** In the same way as no one can lay claim to ownership of the outputs of the open source initiatives in software development, plant research or car design, we may see similar **non-owned** open source models of organizations emerge. These could be DAOs where some form of rewards are given to those who write the rules and house the distributed infrastructure for the business, but where no one actually owns it. We could see a growing movement towards firms which seek to compensate those who provide services or infrastructure but have no shareholders. They may recycle any profits to fund operations and future developments. They might also make voluntary contributions to national guaranteed income funds to help those who have little or no chance of employment.

Conclusion – choosing a future

A range of high-impact forces are reshaping the business landscape. The central role of ICT is accelerating the collision between the physical and digital worlds and driving choices around how we rework our organizational DNA. Changes in the economic, political, social, commercial, scientific, and technological domains are transforming every aspect of society. The change process is surfacing fundamental tensions and shaping key choices facing business over the next two decades. A range of critical science and technology developments is creating the potential for disruption of old sectors and the emergence of new ones – these could form the heart of the global economy over the 2025-2035 timeframe.

In response to these forces, a range of new behaviors and strategies are starting to emerge for the conduct of business in the decades ahead. Our response to the underlying tensions, technology developments, behavioral options and strategy choices will shape the course of organizations. I believe five key sets of decisions will drive those responses:

- **Being** – *What kind of organization do want to be in the future?*

(Purpose, ambition, societal impact, stakeholders, values, ethics, behavior, governance, products, services, and markets)

- **Behavior** – *What strategies, operating structures, and organization designs do we need to achieve our purpose?*
- **Financial Orientation** – *What business models will we use to fulfill our ambitions? (Profit orientation, ownership, asset and infrastructure financing, innovation funding, revenue models)*
- **Talent** – *What human resources models could best deliver our people ambitions? (Balance between humans and machines, levels of employment, critical roles, leadership, development, enhancement opportunities, rewards, community engagement)*
- **Delivery** – *What mindset, capabilities, and technologies do we need to ensure we can survive and thrive in a rapidly changing world?*

Forecasting Future Disruptions – Strategic Change Is Inevitable

By Professor Bill Halal

What are the key forecasts to 2030 for emerging technologies, social trends, and wild cards – what are the possible impacts?

Identifying the next wave of change

This chapter draws upon a state-of-the-art foresight system to present forecasts of the technology revolution, social trends, wild cards, and their expected impacts. Based on a macro-forecast of this wave of change, the most likely scenario for the critical period of 2020-30 is outlined. To better understand how to survive this transformation, guidelines for strategic planning are presented and illustrated with examples of corporate success. The forces of strategic change are so vast and relentless today that new directions are inevitable. Our choice is to guide creative destruction or submit to the alternative – chaos.

Good planning is rarely practiced

Sound strategic planning is rarely practiced in most organizations today, and at a critical time when the world is changing dramatically, it has never been more necessary.

Some corporations and governments do a fine job scanning the horizon for disruptive trends in technology, markets, and society, and devising strategies to adapt, or even use the disruptive forces to their advantage. For example, Netflix leads in video services because the founder beat Blockbuster to the holy grail of streaming movies and developed a virtual organization that delivered great customer service. Apple took the dominant position in the IT industry from Microsoft by capturing the lead in high-quality products for the mobile era. Toyota saw the coming of green cars and moved ahead of this market tsunami that is now sweeping the planet, displacing GM as the world's biggest car maker. Germany developed solar and wind energy sources to avoid a reliance on fossil fuels and nuclear, and now gets the bulk of its energy from renewable sources.

These exemplars are the exception, unfortunately. Most people are preoccupied with their current work and have difficulty finding time for strategic thinking. When they do, there is often uncertainty about how to approach such a daunting challenge. It does not help that opinion varies enormously on the merits of various strategy methods, the benefits of strategic visions and goals, the value of fore-casting, and how to involve the organization. Many simply focus on how to achieve relatively near-term goals, ignoring the rush of change surrounding them and the difficult issues that prevent progress. Even when done well, strategic thinking requires us to confront difficult realities, and increasingly, to find a way through crisis.

Today, the challenges ahead are so unprecedented and so danger-ous that they cannot be ignored. Hence tough strategic choices are increasingly being forced upon us by default. The most striking example is the issue of climate change. The onset of serious climate change is obvious to all but the most fervent deniers, yet there is no working agreement among major nations on a plan to reduce emis-sions. The planet passed through what scientists consider the tripping point of 400 ppm (parts per million) of Carbon Dioxide CO^2 in the atmosphere in 2014, and concentrations are still increasing.

Yes, there are hopeful trends, but there are also grave doubts about the outcome. To put it bluntly, we may be too late. The planet is so enormous that decades are needed to change its atmosphere significantly, even if policies enacted now were sufficient to head off what appears to be a looming climate disaster.

Movement in new strategic directions is inevitable, and the basic question is, can we guide the forces of change or will they force us into directions we may not like? I submit the answer to this existential dilemma is good foresight-led strategic planning that confronts the issues and turns them to advantage.

This article aims to help readers consider the challenges posed by the technology revolution, globalization, and social changes, and to explore how to get your organization on the right side of history. I have drawn on key findings from our work at the TechCast Project[14], including forecasts of emerging technologies, social trends, and wild cards. These cover the entire strategic landscape for planners and decision makers.

Forecasting the strategic environment

To better understand where the world is heading, the TechCast Project aims to provide authoritative forecasts across the technological and social spectrum. The research method uses collective intelligence to pool the knowledge of 130 high-tech CEOs, scientists, engineers, academics, consultants, futurists, and other experts worldwide to forecast breakthroughs in a comprehensive range of fields. No forecast can be really accurate, of course, but validation studies confirm that this approach provides estimates accurate enough to put decision-makers in the right ballpark. The results show that technological and social advances, their adoption patterns, and impacts follow well-defined cycles that can be forecast rather accurately. [15]

The following analysis highlights how these advances are likely to unfold over the following few decades. The tables presented below for Emerging Technologies, Social Trends, and Wild Cards summarize all three types of forecast results. These are useful for suggesting patterns in the data and identifying forecasts of particular interest for various business sectors. Please note that these highlights are drawn from the website, and so details and references can be found at http://www.techcastglobal.com.

The technology revolution

In tables 1 to 3[16] the first column displays a range of critical technologies and the percentage of the relevant market they could capture or impact by 2030. The following columns present the three key dimensions of our technology forecast data:

- The most likely year each technology will reach its next adoption level.
- The potential global market size in US$ at saturation, and
- The confidence level of the experts for each forecast.

The adoption level forecasts cluster around the 2015-2030 period, outlining what now appears to be the crest of this historic wave of innovation. Some think of it as the emergence of the technological singularity. Futurist Ray Kurzweil defines the Singularity as "a future period during which the pace of technological change will be so rapid, its impact so deep, that human life will be irreversibly transformed".[17]

TABLE 1 – Emerging Technologies Forecasts – Digital Economy
and Information Technology

Technology (% of the market they could capture or impact by 2030)	Most Likely Year	Market Size ($Billions)	Expert Confidence (%)
Digital Economy			
E-Government – 30%	2019	275	68
E-Commerce – 15%	2017	1815	69
Entertainment – 50%	2017	706	68
Global Brain – 50%	2019	1000	72
Virtual Education – 30%	2020	410	70
Intelligent Web – 30%	2018	447	70
Information Technology			
Biometrics – 30%	2020	100	66
Intelligent Interface – 30%	2021	579	68
Next Gen Computing – >0%	2026	1095	65
Virtual Reality – 30%	2022	333	67
Thought Power – 30%	2030	463	61
AI – 30%	2024	770	63
Cloud/Grid – 30%	2017	667	70
Internet of Things – 30%	2021	1319	69

TABLE 2 – Emerging Technologies Forecasts – Manufacturing, Robotics, Energy, Environment, Medicine and Biogenetics

Technology (% of the market they could capture or impact by 2030)	Most Likely Year	Market Size ($Billions)	Expert Confidence (%)
Manufacturing & Robotics			
Nanotechnology – 30%	2024	642	66
Smart Robots – 30%	2027	655	65
Modular Buildings – 30%	2025	2165	62
Power Storage – 30%	2023	736	65
3-D Printing – >0%	2017	393	64
Energy & Environment			
Alternative Energy – 30%	2027	2248	61
Aquaculture – 70%	2025	205	60
GMO Crops – 30%	2024	635	60
Smart Grids – 30%	2025	944	64
Water Purification – 90%	2023	709	63
Green Economy – 30%	2021	2757	62
Organic Farming – 30%	2031	641	64
Precision Farming – 30%	2023	790	66
Climate Control – >0%	2017	570	67
Medicine & Biogenetics			
Child Traits – 30%	2035	246	50
Gene Therapy – 30%	2031	614	58
Replacement Parts – >0%	2026	744	60
Life Extension – 100 years	2037	1410	62
Personal Medicine – 30%	2026	846	63
E-Medicine – 30%	2021	642	67
Cancer Cure – >0%	2029	825	58
Synthetic Biology – >0%	2022	617	62
Neurotechnology – 30%	2034	462	57

TABLE 3 – Emerging Technologies Forecasts –
Space and Transportation

Technology (% of the market they could capture or impact by 2030)	Most Likely Year	Market Size ($Billions)	Expert Confidence (%)
Space			
Moon Base – >0%	2034	289	59
Space Tourism – >0%	2018	105	71
Humans On Mars – >0%	2034	438	53
Star Travel – >0%	2055	2624	58
Commercial Space – >0%	2023	583	58
Solar Satellites – >0%	2031	461	59
Transportation			
Hybrid Cars – 30%	2021	887	67
Fuel Cell Cars – >0%	2018	433	64
Intelligent Cars – 30%	2022	1124	67
High-Speed Rail – 30%	2029	344	61
Electric Cars – 30%	2027	1172	63
Small Vehicles – 30%	2022	431	65

The following sections summarize the most significant breakthroughs in each of seven fields. Please note that the Information Technology and E-Commerce fields are most advanced with critical technologies arriving earlier and driving the subsequent progress of the other fields. The dominant theme is breakthroughs everywhere.

Computer Power should continue to double every two years as a "second generation" of optical, biological, and quantum computers takes over. Artificial intelligence (AI) is automating routine tasks and is expected to have an increasingly significant and widespread impact – for example transforming the internet. The Web is now the same age as television (TV) was when it dominated the 20th century. Working, shopping, learning, and most other social functions are likely to move online to a virtual world that is ever-present and intelligent. You might buy something by talking with a virtual robot that greets you by name, knows all the merchandise, answers questions, and has infinite patience – the perfect salesperson.[18]

E-Commerce today operates at ten percent adoption levels, but online shopping, publishing, education, entertainment, and other services are likely to reach the critical 30 percent adoption level soon as new geographic markets take off. The huge populations of China, India, Brazil, and other developing countries are moving in droves to the Internet. Five to seven billion people could soon create online markets of several trillion dollars.[19]

Green practices are likely to take off in the near future (for example, 2015-2020) and governments are likely to increase their efforts to tackle global warming about that time. Alternative energy sources – such as solar, wind, and biofuels – are growing 30-40 percent per year. This is another manifestation of Moore's Law, which observes that computer power has been doubling every 18-24 months for decades. The global market for green technologies is expected to reach about $10 trillion in two to three decades, turning the current environmental mess into an opportunity for future economic growth.

Manufacturing systems are becoming intelligent and can produce sophisticated goods cheaply, quickly, and is enabling easier customization to individual requirements. Fuelled by cheap labor and new markets, industrialization should raise living standards dramatically in most poor nations over the next few decades. This will be a boon to business, but making it sustainable is an enormous challenge. Progress creates potential challenges around mounting demands for energy, ecological damage, and clashes between diverse cultures.

Medicine advances in healthcare are increasingly able to confer mastery over life. Artificial organs can already replace almost all bodily functions, and stem cell research can repair and grow organs. Over time, electronic medical records, online doctor's visits, computerized diagnostics, and other forms of telemedicine should curtail rising costs and improve quality of care. Just as the Industrial Age mastered most aspects of the physical world, these advances are making it possible to master the biological world.

Transportation is moving faster and farther. Our forecasts show that a new wave of green vehicles such as hybrid and electric cars should become main-stream by about 2020, and we are likely to see intelligent cars that drive themselves. It may seem that information systems could replace travel, but information forms a virtual world that parallels the physical world rather than replacing it. People will always want to visit each other, handle the merchandise, and hammer out tough decisions together.

Space is going private. Commercial rockets now service the International Space Station, and other competitors are planning visits to the Moon and the creation of space hotels. Just a few years ago the idea of commercializing space seemed bold. However, it now looks like will soon open the "final frontier" to private ventures. As access to space becomes widely available, it's easy to imagine how crossing this watershed from government control to private enterprise could unleash a rush of space pioneering.

Social Trends

Our forecasts of Social Trends are summarized in tables 4 and 5.[20]

The results are presented in a similar way to the technology forecasts, estimating when a social trend is likely to reach critical adoption levels and expert confidence in the forecast. But market saturation makes little sense for social trends, so instead we estimate the impact.

A common theme of **higher-order values** seems to be emerging across these diverse social trends – social responsibility, transparency, growing economies, environment, diversity, women, education, and global ethics.

TABLE 4 – Social Trend Forecasts –
Business, Economics, Government, Politics and War

Social Trend	Most Likely Year to Reach Adoption	Social Impact (-10 to +10)	Expert Confidence (%)
Business & Economics			
Market Concentration – 51%	2026	3.1	49
Old Nations Grow – 3%	2018	3.7	61
New Nations Dominate – 50%	2023	3.3	63
Consumerism Triumphant – 67%	2022	3.3	59
Travel Soars – $10 trillion	2020	2.9	59
Jobs Failure – 10%	2021	-3.5	61
Services Dominate – 50%	2021	2.7	66
Government & Politics			
Privacy Dying	2019	-0.7	70
Environmental Demands	2022	5.5	64
Transparency	2022	4.9	58
Extremism Growing	2018	-2.5	62
War			
Water Wars – 1+	2026	-1.8	53

TABLE 5 – Social Trend Forecasts –
Demographics, Lifestyles, Values, Spirituality, Nature and Science

Social Trend	Most Likely Year to Reach Adoption	Social Impact (-10 to +10)	Expert Confidence (%)
Demographics & Lifestyles			
Global Graying – 25%	2032	0.5	64
Mass Migration – 20%	2026	2.9	55
Generation Change – 50%	2021	3.2	67
Urbanization – 60%	2021	0.3	64
Fertility Falls – 1%	2028	2.4	58
Diversity Accepted – 51%	2026	5.1	56
Working Women – 70%	2026	4.3	65
Values & Spirituality			
Legal Pot – 33%	2021	1.8	61
Global Ethics – 30%	2032	4.5	56
Education Expands – 50%	2026	5.7	64
Social Responsibility – 50%	2021	4.0	63
Nature & Science			
Fragile Systems – 33%	2019	-2.0	58

In Economics, our experts see a trend toward bigger global corporations with increasing market dominance, and undeveloped nations modernizing quickly. Services and travel are likely to grow, and unemployment is expected to remain a problem. The gap between rich and poor could reach worrisome levels, with some attempts at reform.

Government is expected to struggle with mounting demands for environmental safety, while privacy and transparency will become even more important. Extreme political views are not likely to dissipate and may grow more severe, especially in the Muslim world where a major clash is underway between Sunnis and Shias.

Water is destined to become the next critical resource after oil. Fully two-thirds of the world's population could be living in regions with chronic, widespread shortages of water. Conflict is likely as demand for fresh water outstrips supplies, causing political instability, reducing economic growth, and endangering food supplies.

Demographics suggest the population will likely become older and increasingly diverse, with fewer children and more women working. The proportion of people living in cities could increase to 60 percent by the early twenties. We are also likely to witness an historic shift in leadership from the old guard to a younger generation with different views and values.

Values and Lifestyles are undergoing dramatic change. Look for increasing demands for social responsibility, global ethics, diversity, and education. The legalization of mild drugs like marijuana and the acceptance of many variations in gender and lifestyles are growing in modern nations, which will be startling to many.

Technology is creating ever more complex systems that are fragile and failure prone. These vulnerabilities grow with increasing size and myriad connections. Modern electronics now covers the globe in an infinitely complex mega-system that can produce power blackouts, Internet crashes, unexpected drug interactions, and other surprises. A small failure in one part of the global system can cascade into catastrophe.

Wild Cards

Wild cards are high-impact, low-probability events, like an asteroid strike. Often called **black swans**, they can introduce threats and sometimes windfall opportunities. Tables 6 and 7[21] sum up our forecasts. Because wild cards are different in nature than technology or social trends, the variables we focus on differ also. The TechCast experts estimate the probability of a wild card occurring, its potential social impact and their view of its likely Impact.

TABLE 6 – Wild Card Forecasts
– Business, Economic, Government, Politics and War

	Probability of Occurrence (%)	Potential Social Impact (-10 to +10)	Expected Impact (%)
Business & Economics			
Democratic Enterprise	28	3.9	1.2
Bank Nationalization	22	-0.1	0.2
Global Depression	30	-3.9	-1.1
Government & Politics			
Peace in Palestine	13	4.0	0.5
Climate Shift	50	-4.1	-1.8
UN Collapses	11	-2.7	-0.3
China Falls	25	-2.3	-0.4
War			
Israel Conquered	2	-2.8	-0.1
Nuclear War	9	-7.0	-0.7
Energy Weapons	59	-0.2	-0.1

TABLE 7 – Wild Card Forecasts
– Demographics, Lifestyles, Values, Spirituality, Nature and Science

	Probability of Occurrence (%)	Potential Social Impact (-10 to +10)	Expected Impact (%)
Demographics & Lifestyles			
Alien Contact	13	3.3	0.4
Superbugs	38	-3.9	-1.3
Global Pandemic	24	-4.5	-1.2
Values & Spirituality			
Paranormal Proved	12	1.4	0.4
Human Cloning	40	0.7	0.6
Nature & Science			
Solar Storm	34	-4.4	-1.4
Weather Control	30	3.8	1.4
Singularity Arrives	43	4.6	2.5
Asteroid Hit	3	-6.2	-0.1

Likely Wild Cards are the most common aspect of our results. The large number of likely Wild Cards is striking: Climate Shift – 52 percent; Energy Weapons – 49 percent; Human Cloning – 39 percent; Global Pandemic – 39 percent; Superbugs – 35 percent; and Solar Storm – 34 percent. The impacts of these high probability wild cards average about five on our scale of one (utopia) to ten (catastrophe), so decision-makers should pay heed.

Unlikely Wild Cards make up the other end of the spectrum: Israel Conquered – two percent; Asteroid Hit – three percent; UN Collapses – 11 percent; and Nuclear War – nine percent.

Global Economics and Politics could be changed by a number of critical events: China Falls – 18 percent; Bank Nationalization – 24 percent; Democratic Enterprise – 26 percent; and the Singularity arrives – 34 percent.

Intriguing Possibilities with some chance of occurring include Alien Contact – 17 percent; Paranormal Proven – 15 percent; and Peace in Palestine – 17 percent.

Marco-Forecasting the critical decades

Our collective forecasts are aggregated below to **macro-forecast** the strategic environment over the next decade or two. This analysis suggests that the Great Recession has run its course and a new wave of economic growth began to take off around 2015.

Macro-Forecast of 2020-30

- **Sustainability Arrives:** Green business, alternative energy, climate control, GMO, smart grids.
- **Green Transportation:** Hybrid/electric/smart cars, hi-speed trains, small aircraft, hypersonic flight.
- **Mastery Over Life:** Artificial organs, DNA testing, grown organs, cancer cure, life extension, neurotech.
- **Infinite Knowledge and Intelligence:** Second generation IT (bio, optical, quantum), AI, robotics, virtual reality, automation of routine thought.
- **Higher-Order Values:** Social responsibility, growing economies, environment, diversity, women, education, global ethics.
- **Threats Across the Spectrum:** Economic depression, banking crisis, automation of jobs, global warming, Singularity arrives.
- **Global Consciousness:** Movement beyond knowledge to address global challenges, restructuring of institutions.

2015 as a point of take off – The period starting around 2015 is significant because the cluster of green technologies, information systems, e-commerce, and advanced auto designs suggests a resurgence of economic growth is taking off about that time. This also coincides with the pattern of 35 year cycles that roughly govern U.S. stock markets. Look at a 100 year graph of the Dow Jones Industrial Average on a log scale and you will find three 35-year cycles. The Roaring Twenties was the peak of a 35-year cycle that ended with the Great Crash of 1929. The Eisenhower boom of the sixties started about 1945 and was followed by the Reagan boom that began with his election in 1980. The 2008 economic crisis marked the end of the Reagan 35 year cycle, and it is likely to be followed by a new worldwide boom starting about 2015 based on the technologies noted above.

The rise of new sectors and solutions – As the Technology Revolution picks up speed about 2020, we expect to see personal medicine, intelligent cars, alternative energy, and the other advanced technologies shown. This period is also likely to enjoy near-infinite computing power using second generation architectures (optical, bio, nano, and quantum). Smart robots are likely to enter homes and offices, and good AI is likely to automate routine tasks in the same way GPS navigation solved the problem of travelling from point A to point B.

The emergence of green growth – One of our most striking conclusions is that a green revolution is imminent – driving a new wave of sustainable economic growth. Today's surge of green business should reach mainstream use soon, and governments are likely to take serious steps to curb global warming and climate change. Alternative energy sources – largely wind, biofuels, solar, and nuclear – are growing globally at 30-50 percent per year and are likely to provide 30 percent of all energy use by about 2020. This growth rate is comparable to Moore's Law that forecast skyrocketing IT systems, so we should expect a similar rapid build-up of sustainable technology.

Led by the EU, Japan, China, and other nations, this green sector is expected to reach trade volumes of $10-20 trillion by 2020 – exceeding automotive, health care, and defense. In short, the present mess in energy and environment policy actually offers a great opportunity to convert a potential crisis into sustainable, unifying growth. This green boom could even serve to defuse the race toward weapons of mass destruction, terrorism, and conflict generally, as diverse cultures are more closely integrated into the fabric of a global community.

Automation of knowledge tasks – As the Technology Revolution picks up speed by about 2020, we predict a wide-spread use of genetic therapy, synthetic life, nanotechnology, personal medicine, and cancer cures. As already highlighted, this period is also likely to enjoy near-infinite computing power. Smart robots are likely to enter homes and offices, and AI should also become sufficiently sophisticated to automate routine knowledge. As endless intelligent devices take over routine tasks, we are increasingly shifting attention beyond knowledge to focus on values, beliefs, ideology, vision, and other higher levels of thought. This pivotal shift is occurring not out of noble motives alone but simply out of the sheer necessity of dealing with the global megacrisis.

Connecting the planet – Information Technology may be the most powerful force shaping the world today, igniting endless innovations in online publishing and virtual education. It is enabling different forms of e-commerce that will soon reach the critical point where new industries take off. The huge populations of China, India, Brazil, and other developing countries are moving in droves to PCs, the Internet, smart phones, and mobile devices. Forecasts suggest that between five and seven billion people will soon inhabit a digital world that is far larger and more intelligent, creating online markets of several trillion dollars, and producing massive social impacts, for better or worse.

Harnessing AI and unleashing human consciousness – The central role of AI will shift the relationship between humans and machines in profound ways. Contrary to assertions that AI will surpass people and make us obsolete, AI can liberate us from mental drudgery and release the unique human capability for higher consciousness, at a time when the world is heading toward unprecedented challenges. This is not a coincidence but rather the playing out of developmental forces that are driving the life cycle of the planet from our old stage of development to the next.

Harnessing strategic foresight to prepare us for transformation

With such bold prospects ahead, it is essential to prepare for a world in transformation. Whatever their purpose and methods, leaders need to develop a well-thought through system to forecast and adapt to future waves of technological, economic, and social change. There may be uncertainty about specific trends and breakthroughs, but there is little doubt that we will see plenty of strategic change over the planning horizon.

Forming a good strategy is inherently an uncertain process and all leaders do it somewhat differently, of course. Organizations are affected by different technologies, so leading companies identify and monitor the progress of those that are strategic for their organization. Disruptive technologies that could change an industry are especially important and require creative thought to develop viable responses and build new business ventures. A strategy must not only be sound, its implementation must also be timed quite precisely. Taking a big risk a few years too early can invite bleeding-edge failures, while a few years too late and the field could be dominated by competitors.

We have studied exemplars of creative strategy and use these insights to outline guides for creating strategic change. The following examples from Netflix, Apple, and Toyota illustrate the need to track key forces in the external environment, look for creative opportunities, collaborate with key stakeholders, and learn from failure. [22]

Netflix steams to success

Netflix illustrates the central role of a technology-inspired vision in transforming a field. A decade ago, the founder Reed Hastings could see that it would soon be feasible to stream movies, and understood this shift in technology would change the rules of the game. Netflix also knew that having employees run shops, charging for rentals, and imposing late fees were outmoded relics of the past, while online service delivered by a virtual organization offered unbeatable value.

A critical threshold occurred in 2005 when thirty percent of Americans gained broadband. YouTube was launched and its instant success signaled quite dramatically that the streaming video take-off point had arrived. Today, video comprises roughly ninety percent of all Internet traffic, and is expected to reach 3.5 billion viewers around the globe in 2015 – a huge new market hungry for movies, TV, and other digital entertainment.[23]

By monitoring the rise of these crucial enabling technologies, Netflix could time its move to deliver movies online and transform the industry into a larger more functional whole. Reed Hastings effectively formed a collaborative ecosystem of talented staff, media companies, Internet firms, and accepting viewers to make streaming video a reality.

Apple leads the mobile revolution

Another great example is Apple's brilliant use of mobile technology to create a long line of stunning and revolutionary products. In 1999, the company was skirting bankruptcy while Microsoft dominated business with a market value of $620 billion. However, Steve Jobs convinced the record companies that the future lay in online music sold for $0.99 per song, demonstrating the power of collaboration. The striking success of the IPod and iTunes laid the foundation for subsequent mobile devices – the iPhone, iPad and Apple Watch.

Jobs' genius lay in a unique talent for combining functionality and beauty to create breakthrough products. He didn't do market research because he was planning transformative products that few yet understood. He thought success requires "listening to the technology" in order to discover the potential products waiting to be invented.[24] Jobs said: "If I had asked someone who only used a calculator what a Mac should be like, they couldn't have told me. There's no way to do consumer research so I had to create it and then show it to them. It's not the customer's job to know what they want." [25]

Jobs also demonstrated the learning value of failure. Apple's long list of failures prepared him to create great products when he returned from exile. Long after John Sculley became CEO and Jobs was sent into the computing wilderness, Sculley acknowledged: "I'm convinced that if Steve hadn't come back when he did ... Apple would have been history". [26] In fact, Jobs' approach to developing strong new products is based on failure. Here's how he selected the best concepts: "Killing bad ideas is not hard – what is really hard is killing good ideas." [27]

The iPod, iTunes, iPad, and iPhone went on to transform entertainment and communications. In 2014, Apple became the biggest company in history, with market capitalization of $683 billion while Microsoft's value dropped to $338 billion.[28] Apple is likely to become the first trillion dollar company in history.

Toyota pioneers a green car

Toyota offers a model of strategic planning that helped it succeed in using a disruptive technology to gain leadership of the global automotive industry. Two to three decades ago, Japanese carmakers struggled to compete with the Big Three U.S. carmakers – General Motors (GM), Ford and Chrysler. The Big Three ruled the industry with profitable cars and trucks averaging 12 miles per gallon (MPG). GM alone held almost half the U.S. market at one time.

By anticipating the rise of environmental threats, the end of cheap oil, and the development of hybrid technology, Toyota led the way to an era of energy-efficient, green car design. It surpassed GM as the world's biggest car maker in 2010. How did they pull this upset off?

Toyota began planning their game-changing Prius hybrid because forecasts indicated declining oil supplies and growing public concern over the environment. They tracked the development of high-performance Lithium-ion batteries, hybrid technology, the coming of **peak oil** and environmental concerns. The obstacles were considerable because batteries were not adequate, hybrid technology would take many years to develop, and costs would remain high.

They thought the obstacles could be overcome, and the demand for green autos looked promising. They invested $1 billion in R&D and a design that looked most promising – the Prius Hybrid – because it embodied powerful advantages in environmental sustainability, low energy use, and advances in car batteries.

While GM, Ford, and other car companies procrastinated, Toyota executives had the foresight to envision a new generation of energy efficient, non-polluting hybrid cars. The Prius is the top selling auto in Japan, Consumer Reports suggests: "Toyota is the most recognizable car brand in the U.S.",[29] and Toyota expects the Prius to lead the American market by 2020.

Today's decisions set tomorrow's headlines

As we look to the future, nobody doubts the enormity of the problems that are certain to emerge on route. Despite vows that the 2008 financial crises marked an end to profligate behavior, it's hard to imagine how this transformation can be achieved in a world that still celebrates power politics, money, consumerism, and self-interest. We are experiencing significant shifts in products, industries, markets, organizational forms, consumption patterns, and the rules of competition. As a result, executives in all fields face constant challenges to redefine their mission and purpose, cultivate new customers with cutting edge products and services, and withstand external threats. We are being forced to readjust careers, downshift to sustainable lifestyles, and rethink our priorities. The uncertain nature of this transition also makes it hard to know which nations and corporations will lead and which will fail, while war, economic failures, and political stalling are not about to disappear.

The long ascent of civilization has always managed to overcome what appeared to be insurmountable obstacles: the Ice Age; the Fall of Rome; the Dark Ages; World Wars I and II; and the Nuclear Age. Our next challenge is how we address the likely emergence of a high-tech global order. This process is larger and more powerful than mere individuals, and it is likely to alter rock-hard convictions in ways that may shock us. With increasingly pressing problems, the outmoded practices of the industrial age could be sloughed off like an animal shedding its hide with the seasons. How we approach the urgent need to plan for this onslaught of strategic change over the next decade may determine if the headlines of tomorrow are dismal with disaster or buoyant with success.

Our forecasts of emerging technologies, social trends, and wild cards raise some critical questions for business:

- *What are the most critical issues your organization is likely to face because of this emerging wave of change?*
- *What strategic alternatives can you consider to resolve the emerging issues, ideally to your advantage?*
- *How can you involve the key stakeholders to produce the most productive strategy and lead the organization to success?*

The Automated, Digitized, and Simulated Future

By Gray Scott

How can we prepare for the deep technological transformations shaping the next two decades?

The goal of this chapter is to help facilitate a deeper understanding of ubiquitous digitization and the role this will play in our future. The article is broken down into three primary concepts: **Automation of Everything (AOE); Digitization of Everything (DOE);** and **The Simulated Reality Singularity (TSRS).**

The path to 2035 – a vision of deep technological disruption

Over the next two decades, I firmly believe we will witness the unfolding of a future that will be automated, decentralized, digitized, and eventually simulated. By 2035, our homes, cars, and most of our jobs could be automated. Automation will decentralize and disrupt almost every industry. The world economy will face a new future – filled with 3D printers, personal artificially intelligent (AI) assistants, and digital real-time healthcare applications that we can access on our personal smart devices.

Robots, algorithms, and simulations will dominate the world in the near future. We are becoming a digitized species. I believe we are heading towards a virtual simulated reality of big data that knows everything about us. It will be a transparent realm without secrets and void of privacy. We will use brain implants, electroencephalography (EEG) devices, and virtual reality (VR) glasses to access this world with ease.

It appears that we are heading toward what I call **The Simulated Reality Singularity** (TSRS). I have created a formula that may be useful to help understand and simplify the road ahead:

Automation of Everything (AOE) + Digitization of Everything (DOE) = The Simulated Reality Singularity (TSRS)

The TSRS is a state of pure digital reality that is indistinguishable from the reality that we see around us now. Every sensorial experience will be replicated in the TSRS. Our digital avatars will become digitally immortal inside the TSRS. We will also use time dilation, the ability to speed up or slow down time, inside these advanced simulations. This will enable millions of years to pass in a matter of hours. We will be able to reverse the simulation, fast forward or pause it. Eventually, our digitally simulated avatars inside the simulation will become artificially intelligent. Will they ask who their creator is? Will they send probes out into the edges of the simulation?

Every innovation we are creating appears to be leading in the direction of the TSRS. From the most current visual effects (VFX) films, research into growing brains on computer chips (yes this is happening now), to the latest Oculus Rift VR headset, we appear determined to digitize our reality and ourselves. The question is why? We will get to that, but first let me lay out the steps to this future.

Automation of Everything (AOE)

The first stage and the one we are about to enter is the Automation of Everything (AOE). To evolve as a species, we must automate away the distractions, the mundane, and the repetitive processes of our lives. In the future, no one should stand in a factory doing repetitive labor. Just as we crawled out of the oceans at one time, we are now evolving again. A new membrane is developing around us that will facilitate our digital evolution. Think of the AOE as a digital cocoon. Once it is fully developed, we will be free to move on to the next stage of our digital evolution.

To live in an abundant future, we need raw materials. How can we automate this process? Imagine a future filled with self-replicating autonomous artificially intelligent robots. Imagine that these robots are sent off planet to harvest raw materials from near earth asteroids. These asteroid mining robots could manufacture products directly on the asteroid and then ship the goods back to earth, the Moon or even Mars.

Automated asteroid mining may sound like science fiction. However, as of 2015, astronomers have discovered 11,000 near-Earth orbit asteroids and there are, according to a company called Planetary Resources, over 1,000 more being discovered each year. Planetary Resources is working to turn this asteroid mining scenario into science fact. According to their website, "A single 500-meter platinum-rich asteroid contains more platinum group metals than have ever been mined in human history."[30]

With the help of AI industrial robots, we could potentially build an entire space station directly on these near-earth asteroids. I understand that this idea may sound hard to believe. It is easy to dismiss this as fantasy. Only three hundred years ago the idea of men walking on the Moon was also thought of as fantasy, even heresy.

Imagine what this would do to our world. We could stop most if not all mining here on earth. No need to send humans into space to do this dangerous mining work. We can create AI robots that do the heavy lifting for us. We could also control these mining robots from the safety of our offices and homes here on earth. Space is rich with raw materials as well as water. If we can automate, harvest, and manufacture our products we can move away from a monetary economy to a resource based economy. Think of it this way. Right now, we have a Star Wars economy. An economy based on scarcity, pay walls, and resource hoarding. Innovations in technologies like automation and 3D printing however, could create an economy more like Star Trek – where money no longer exists – enabling us to explore our creativity and our dreams.

Worldwide shipments of multipurpose industrial robots are forecast to exceed 207,000 units in 2015. Each of these robots can do the job of several human workers and can work 24 hours a day without breaks or holidays. By 2035 we may see robots in most of our hotels, restaurants, and homes. This is not a far future trend. The robot revolution has arrived. One example is the Henn-Na Hotel set to open in July 2015.[31] Ten humanlike robots are being developed by Osaka University and manufactured by the humanoid robotics company Kokomo to work alongside ten human workers in the 72-bedroom hotel. These humanoid robots will mimic breathing and blinking and will be fluent in Japanese, Korean, Chinese and English. Hospitality automation is not just a gimmick. Eliminating human workers will lower costs for the developers and the customers. The rooms will start at $60 (7,000 yen) per night.

Climate change threatens to cause major droughts and famine in the near future, but we already have a solution. Agricultural farm bots will grow and harvest food from urban underground vertical **Pink Farms** lit by light emitting diodes (LEDs). These Farms use red and blue LED lights to grow food indoors without it ever seeing sunlight or pesticides. Pink Farms are not a far future idea. They exist today. In fact, in Japan a botanist named Shigeharu Shimamura has converted an old Sony semiconductor factory into a LED Pink Farm that produces up to 10,000 heads of lettuce every day.[32]

If we automate these Pink Farms and place them around the world in urban areas, we could finally become a decentralized and automated agricultural society. With abundant solar and wind energy to run the automated Pink Farms, food in the future could theoretically become free. With no workers to pay and free energy to run the automated farm bots, we could provide the nutritional requirements of every person on this planet. It sounds like a utopian dream but the technologies are here and the steps to achieve this vision are undeniable.

Autonomous self-driving cars will become the standard form of transportation in urban areas. Automated planes, trains, and drones will deliver products directly to our doors, and home service robots will be waiting to accept our deliveries. So where are all of the robots that will help us automate our lives? They are here now. Japanese telecommunications giant SoftBank plans to begin selling a robot named

Pepper in the U.S. in 2015 for around $1,700.[33] Pepper understands human emotions and can respond accordingly. Pepper may not fold your laundry or wash your car in its first incarnation. Just like other technologies however, newer models of the Pepper robot may evolve into a multidimensional service robot.

Care-o-bot 4 is another interesting robot that we may see in our homes and hotels in the near future.[34] It will help you cook and may even babysit your children. These robots will also take care of all the maintenance in our future smart homes. It will be common in the future to have 3D printed homes that harvest solar and wind power. They will utilize advanced stationary batteries to store excess energy that the homeowner can then trade for other goods and services.

Can corporations as we know them survive a decentralized automated future if everyone can harvest energy, food, and raw materials? Maybe, if these corporations change their core ideologies. They need to acknowledge that the future is not about acquiring wealth for CEOs and shareholders. It is about providing pathways to abundance for humanity. Today's biggest companies may be dismantled by tomorrow's automation if they continue to use outdated operational models and ways of thinking. If jobs are replaced by automation, who will buy their products and services? No one. Companies that continue to sell products with pre-automation prices in the post-automation era will disappear. The companies that reduce and produce will survive.

Companies that ignore these tectonic movements will suffer the wrath of exponential change in the future. The robots are coming, and they are only going to get more intelligent and industrious.

So now that we have automated everything and all of our basic needs are met, what will we do next? We digitize our world, of course. And so begins the Digitization of Everything (DOE).

Digitization of Everything (DOE)

Automation and digitization go hand in hand. Like a digital fetus in fetu that cannot be separated. Automation will set off a chain reaction that will lead to the Digitization of Everything (DOE). It has already begun. We digitize pictures of our food, our holidays, and the faces of friends and families. Every 3D scan, every photo or video we take, and every word we type on our digital devices adds to the DOE. Every second, humanity is generating unimaginable amounts of hidden code. Like a virtual tsunami, this code flows into the cloud and into the web, carving out a new digital landscape. The DOE is all around us, and we are constantly feeding it, while it is gathering our deepest thoughts and feelings. In fact, if the psychotherapist Carl Jung were alive today to see this, I think he would have viewed this as the awakening of the global digital unconscious mind. The DOE is creating a global digital brain. It may not be conscious or aware yet but if this continues we may eventually create a global artificial intelligence.

If Blockbuster had used foresight to see the DOE, they might have prevented NetFlix from ever being created. They should have seen this coming but instead they ignored this truth until it was too late. Now Netflix and services like Apple TV and iTunes are all part of the DOE. We are digitizing old films, books, and photos. Dorothy will forever walk the yellow brick road in a land called Oz thanks to the DOE. Her performance has been guaranteed digital immortality. She and her cowardly lion will be bound to our species no matter what planet or moon we inhabit in the far future.

The web is the primary version of our future simulation. In fact, the web 3.0 will not be random HTML pages called up by keyword searches on Google. It will be a simulated 3D virtual reality filled with avatar replicas of our minds and bodies that greet our customers and friends when we are offline. These avatars will be automated and propagated with big data from our lives. Advanced AI algorithms will harvest information from our real world. In the future it won't be big brother watching us; it will be the AI simulation. Even without logging on to the digital simulation it will gather big data from the real world. Using face and emotion recognition, it will use public cameras to watch you and learn from your experiences just by reading your facial expressions and body language.

Computers, as we know them today, will fade into the background of our lives. In the past, we used our hands to operated looms that made our fabrics. These looms were once a common household item. Today however, automation has removed looms from most modern homes and communities. Automated machines weave and manufacture fabrics faster today than any human could have created by hand in the past. The same thing will happen to modern computers. They will still exist, just not as we know them today. They will become ubiquitous. Everything will be a computer. You home, your car, your desk chair will all be a smart computing object filling the digital simulation with information.

The Simulated Reality Singularity (TSRS)

The simulation hypothesis proposed by Oxford University philosopher and futurist Nick Bostrom suggests that the reality that we find ourselves in may be a sophisticated simulation created by an advanced post-human society. We may be digital beings in a digital system that is being simulated by a more advanced future intelligence. Even if our current reality is not a simulation, I do think a great simulation is near. Everything about us will be quantified, calculated, predicted, and digitized in the future. Big Data will feed a never ending ubiquitous membrane of all seeing, all knowing data flowing freely into the digital simulation.

We are entering a brave new simulated future. The concept of real will become irrelevant. The groundwork for this simulated future has already begun. The age of mechanization, automation and digitization is creating exponential change on our planet. Although it is just the beginning, it will continue until we reach an inevitable state of pure digital simulation. A future in which our brains can no longer distinguish between the real and the digital. An advanced simulation so immersive that some people will choose to reside primarily in the simulated domain. I expect that these **simulation junkies** will spend most of their time in this digital reality. The simulation will be the preferred drug in the future. We will drift in and out of these worlds with ease. We may even become indifferent to what reality we are in.

Horizontal and ubiquitous adaptation of new technologies may not be possible in the near future. Poverty, Luddism, and technophobia (fear of technology) will keep some people from experiencing the benefits of digitization and automation. Early adopters may prosper from new technologies but they may also suffer the consequences of the mistakes and sidesteps that new technologies sometimes bring. The wealthy in Ancient Rome who could afford new lead pots and utensils suffered lead poisoning because of their ability to adopt new technologies before the general population. We may see some interesting side effects from a future filled with virtual realities and egomaniacs who can control warships with their minds using EEG technologies.

We are now a species that can control our environment using EEG devices and wireless technologies. EEG headsets use small electrodes that sit on the forehead or scalp. These electrodes read the brainwaves of the user and this information can then be sent wirelessly to any EEG enabled device or item of electronic hardware, including drones and robotic arms. Imagine using the power of your thoughts alone to move a construction crane or to fly an airplane. Think of it as digitally assisted telekinesis.

This technology will enable us to manifest our thoughts and desires into reality. It will also make it easier to scan and digitize everything around us. We will digitize and upload our imagination and dreams into the simulation. If this sounds impossible we should consider that we are already flying jet plane simulations with our minds. Recently a paraplegic woman named Jan Sheuermann used her mind alone to pilot an F-35 Joint Strike Fighter flight simulator. The project was a collaboration between the University of Pittsburgh Medical Center and the Defense Advanced Research Projects Agency (DARPA). They used microelectrodes and neurosignaling to achieve what would have been called magic 50 years ago.[35]

In a simulated digital reality, you can be anyone or anything. In the digital simulation, we will have total morphological freedom. Just like the virtual world *Second Life*, we will be free to become everything from robots to dragons in the digital simulation. Advanced simulations are already here today. Simulations help scientists understand our current reality. From the big bang to how viruses work, we are already an advanced simulating species. As advancements in VFXs continue, like understanding micro facial movements and how to simulate hair that looks and moves like the real thing, we are getting closer to a truly convincing digital reality.

In fact, in many ways we have already crossed into the VFX singularity. Many of the moving images on TV and in theaters are created using advanced VFX. How much of what you see on TV do you think was shot in-camera and how much do you think was created in some VFX studio? Twenty, sixty, seventy-five percent? Today's VFX have become so advanced that the brain can no longer tell the difference between simulated footage and what is real. The best VFX studios create images that blend seamlessly into our brain's historical image references. The face is the most complex to simulate with accuracy. Until recently you could tell instantly if an actor's face was real or VFX. However, today that is not the case. Imagine how advanced the VFX will be by 2035. Using real human actors in films may become an antiquated notion.

Emerging technologies like 3D scanners that scan faces and the interiors of our homes will make it easier to digitize our world. We will scan every inch of our world and replicate this inside the digital simulation.

So how will humanity react to a brave new simulated reality? Simulated care assistance retreats (SCARs) may become a new industry. We may see **simulation junkies** checking themselves into these SCAR's as a new form of **digitalcation**. Why travel to the Maldives if you can simulate the vacation at a local luxury SCAR? It may become mandatory to spend time in these simulated realities in the future. Just as Facebook and LinkedIn have become a necessary tool for business today, simulated reality in the future may become the new normal. Want to close a major new deal? You might need to check into a SCAR center while you virtually golf with your new clients.

Bostrom's simulation theory may sound unbelievable until we use foresight to see the precursory innovations that keep the arrow of time pointing in one direction – towards a digital future. Our current emerging technologies appear to have a singular unconscious intention. It appears we intend to become simulations and simulators of the future. The future horizon is becoming clear. We are heading toward an automated, digitized and simulated future.

So what are some of the key questions this vision of the future raises for business?

- *What opportunities and challenges would the transition to an automated, digitized and simulated future create for your business?*
- *How deep and extensive is the digital vision for your organization – is it moving fast enough?*
- *How might notions of business, commerce and profit evolve in a world of true abundance?*

Redefining the Relationship of Man and Machine

By Gerd Leonhard

What are the challenges and opportunities facing society in the next 10 years as a result of an accelerating pace of technological development?

From technology disruption to furthering human happiness
This chapter aims to provide important context framing for the mission-critical business decisions that we will all need to make in the next few years in strategy, business model development, marketing, and HR. Remaining relevant, unique, purposeful, and indispensable in the future is obviously a key objective for every business every-where, yet technology will no doubt continue to generate exponential waves of disruptions at an ever-faster pace. Soon – once technology has made almost everything efficient and abundant – I believe that we will need to focus on the truly human values of business, i.e. to transcend technology. Successful business will no longer be about running a well-oiled machine; rather it will be about uniquely furthering human happiness.

Exponential and combinatorial: we're at the pivot point
We are witnessing dramatic digitization, automation, virtualization, and robotization all around us, in all sectors of society, government,

and business – and this is only the beginning. I believe these trends will continue to grow exponentially over the next decade as we head towards a world of five to six billion Internet users by 2020, and possibly as many as 100 billion connected devices in the **Internet of Things,** such as sensors, wearables, and trackers.

Beyond any doubt, machines of all kinds – both software and hardware – will play an increasingly larger role in our future, and progressively more intelligent machines will impact how we live our lives at every turn. Netscape's founder turned venture capitalist Marc Andreessen already highlighted this phenomena in a 2011 Wall Street Journal opinion piece entitled *Why Software is Eating the World*[36] – a prescient headline that is certain to play out in force in our imminent future.

We are already nearing the pivot point where very few ideas seem to remain in the realm of science fiction for very long. This can be witnessed in areas such as automated, real-time translation (SayHi, Google Translate, Skype Translate) and self-driving and semi-autonomous cars (Google, Tesla, Volvo). The fiction-reality boundary is also being crossed by developments such as intelligent personal agents (Cortana, Siri, Google Now), augmented and virtual reality (Microsoft Hololens, Oculus Rift) and many other recent breakthroughs. Our world is being reshaped by developments that used to only exist in the scripts of Hollywood blockbusters such as *Blade Runner, Her, Minority Report, Transcendence* and *The Matrix.* (On that note, let's be sure not to give these blockbuster movies too much credit as far as realistic foresight is concerned).

Technology: it's no longer about IF or HOW but about WHY

The urgent need for clear man-machine ethics is amplified by the view that we should probably no longer be concerned whether technology can actually do something, but whether it **should** do something. The how is being replaced by the why (followed by who, when and where).

For example, why would we want to be able to alter our DNA so that we can shape what our babies look like? And who should be able to afford or have access to such treatments? What would be the limits? In machine intelligence, should we go beyond mere **deductive** reasoning and allow smart software, robots, and artificial intelligence (AI) to advance to adductive reasoning (i.e. to make unique decisions based on new or incomplete facts and rules)? If autonomous machines are to be a part of our future (as is already a certainty in the military), will we need to provide them with some kind of moral agency, i.e. a human-like capacity to decide what is right or wrong even if the facts are incomplete?

"Hellven" challenges

Tremendous scientific progress in sectors such as energy, transportation, water, environment, and food can be expected in the next 10-20 years. I believe most of these achievements will have an overall positive effect on humanity, and hopefully on human happiness (which I would suggest should be the ultimate goal) as well. This would clearly be the **heavenly** side of the coin.

At the same time, on the **hell** side we are now approaching a series of complex intersections at very high speeds. Soon, every single junction we navigate could either lead to more human-centric gains or result in serious aberrations and grave dangers. It has often been said that, "technology is not good or evil – it just is". It is now becoming clear that the good / bad part will probably be for us to decide, every day, globally and locally, collectively and individually. Clearly, if we assume that machines will be an inevitably large part of that future, we will need to decide both what we want them to be, and perhaps more importantly, what we want to be as humans – and we need to do it soon.

Artificial Intelligence (AI) is the most significant "hellven" challenge

Most technologies, software and hardware alike, are not only becoming much faster and cheaper but also increasingly intelligent. The spectrum of rapid recent advances runs the gamut from the kind of **simple algorithmic** intelligence it takes to win against a chess master, to the advent of thinking machines and IBM's neuromorphic chips (i.e. chips that attempt to mirror our own neural networks) and their ambitious **cognitive computing** initiative. Buzzwords such as AI and deep learning are already making the headlines every single day, and this is just the tip of the iceberg. Looking at the investments by the leading venture capitalists and funds, AI has already become a top priority in Silicon Valley and in China, often a certain sign of what's to come.

At the same time, almost every single major information and communications technology (ICT) company already has several initiatives in this man-machine convergence arena. Google and Facebook are busy acquiring small and large companies in a wide range of AI and robotics-related fields. They clearly realize that the future is not just about **big data**, mobile, and **connected everything**. They see the next horizon as embedding capability to make every process, every object, and every machine truly **functionally intelligent**, albeit not (yet) humanly intelligent as far as social or emotional traits are concerned. But maybe this is just a question of when rather than if?

Just imagine what AI could do to our everyday activities such as searching the web (as we call it today), and you can get a glimpse of what's at stake here. In the very near future, who will bother with typing a precise two-word search phrase into a box when **the system** already knows everything about you, your schedule, your location, your likes, your connections, your transactions, and much more? Based on the situational context, your **external brain** i.e. the **AI in the cloud** will already know what you need, before you even think of it, and will propose the most desirable actions as easily as today's Google maps propose walking directions. Hellven, once again, depends on your standpoint.

IBM, the creator of Watson Analytics, a leading commercially available AI product, appears to be betting the farm on this future. IBM is investing billions of dollars into neurosynaptic chips and cognitive computing – designed to emulate the human neural systems with the intention of creating a **holistic computing experience**, i.e. computing that feels as natural as breathing. Computing is no longer outside of us – a thought both scary and exhilarating. Apart from

IBM, Google is working on its own **Global Brain** project and the École Polytechnique Fédérale de Lausanne (EPFL) in Switzerland is pushing the EU's hotly contested **Human Brain project**. China's Baidu has also signaled its ambitions to discover the holy grails of AI by hiring top-level researchers in that field including Stanford's Andrew Ng, and by opening up a Silicon Valley AI center. The list goes on. Clearly, man-machine convergence is on top of the global agenda and investors smell enormous profits.

But: machines don't have ethics

The AI gold-rush has only just started, and this is probably a very good time to be more concerned about whether Silicon Valley's leading venture capital firms have enough foresight to consider more than their financial returns. After all, it is they who are funding commercial applications of man-machine technologies that might have potentially catastrophic side effects on humanity. In my view, the issue of how man and machine will inter-relate in the future should not be viewed from a profit-only perspective. Machines don't have ethics and neither does money. The coming combination of these forces that operate beyond and above human values strikes me as even more dangerous.

Some futurist colleagues predict that we will soon reach a point where the capacity of **thinking machines** will exceed that of the human brain; a point that Ray Kurzweil, scientist and author of *How to Create a Mind*, calls The Singularity, with 2029 as the likely ETA. At this point, if not earlier, even larger and deeply wicked problems will emerge. For example, if we maintain that technology does not (and will not) have ethics, it would probably be downright stupid for anyone to expect that any current or future software program, machine, or robot would be able to act based on human morals, values, or ethics. Thus, the **morals of machines** will emerge as a major factor in the future of humanity, and the issues around what I call **Digital Ethics** (see below) will quickly become more essential as technology spirals into the future.

Every algorithm will need a "humarithm"

I coined the **humarithm** neologism in 2012 – as a wordplay that riffs off algorithms – because I believe that the chains of logic, formulas and **if this then that** rules urgently need to be paralleled with corresponding systems of ethics, values and assumptions, and new if we believe this we must do that rules. I believe that every time we offload a task to an algorithm (a machine) we will also need to think about what kind of humarithm we need to offset the side-effects, i.e. how to best deal with the unintended consequences which are certain to arise.

For example, we may eventually come to the conclusion that commercial airliners can indeed be better piloted by software and robots than by human beings; most research already indicates that this is indeed the case. But if so, we must certainly think about how the passengers will feel about traveling inside a large metal tube that is steered entirely by a robot. This may well be a typical case of where efficiency should not trump humanity.

Who's serving who? The trap of machine-thinking

In my view, the issue is less likely to be the cookie-cutter, dystopian Hollywood plot that we have watched dozens of times, i.e. the elimination of humanity by AIs. The much bigger concern is that we as humans, might soon be forced to effectively behave more like – or even become – machines in order to remain productive or useful in a machine-age economy. Just imagine a world where you simply cannot compete or even keep up without some kind of wearable augmented reality (AR) or virtual reality (VR) device, or without an implant, or other mental or physical augmentations. Given that many of us are already utterly dependent on our mobile devices, and often feel alone or incomplete without them, these scenarios may become reality a lot faster than we think. Which university professor would not want to have the world's knowledge available instantly in the lecture theater using a Wikipedia-app controlled via a contact lens or an unobtrusive brain-computer-interface (BCI)? Which doctor would not want IBM's Watson Analytics VR-display to provide him with real-time medical information and thereby protect him from malpractice lawsuits?

Once these technologies are cheap, easy to use, and ubiquitous their utter convenience will be extremely tempting.

The real question for now is probably not if and when the machines will attempt to control, replace, or even eliminate us. The more fundamental and timely concern is whether and how we can remain truly human in a world that is quickly becoming a kind of global-brain-machine. A machine comprised of super-intelligent software, hardware, and processes, with human traits being increasingly removed from the equation because they are simply slowing things down too much. Imagine a world without serendipity, boredom, mistakes, mystery, and surprise. A world in which everything has become efficient, optimized, hyper-connected, intelligent, and real-time? In that world, what will happen to us humans, the limited wetware, the eight to nine billion people who may inhabit the planet in the next 20 years?

If this strikes you as a wicked problem, consider that this gigantic man-machine operating system (OS) might in fact be what some of the leading global technology companies are already striving for. LinkedIn is busy building a global **economic graph**; a kind of proprietary OS for work, jobs, and HR that uses Big Data and AI to predict hiring trends and training needs (among many other things). Facebook already has its own global OS for social and commercial relationships, and Google has its Global Brain project (amid its numerous investments in AI, robotics and deep learning companies). Clearly, the future is already here.

The future of work and jobs: moving towards the right-brain

We now have to face the distinct possibility that as machines rapidly become more capable of doing what we used to do, particularly with our left brains, we will probably need to become more human and increasingly less like machines. Ironically, this is completely the opposite of what traditional MBAs looked like, avoiding emotions, limiting imagination, and sticking to schedules and plans. If you believe that non-algorithmic i.e. emotional or subconscious factors such as trust, purpose, ethics, and values will remain at the core of human societies in the foreseeable future, this will clearly put a much stronger emphasis on the right brain. Education, training and learning will be changed forever as a consequence and we are already seeing the tip of that iceberg emerging.

What if – in the near future – many routine business activities or operations are actually handled by algorithms and intelligent agents acting on our behalf? In sectors such as procurement, logistics, or telecommunications network management it might well be possible to have intelligent, self-learning software, and reasoning robots take care of 50-100 percent of the frequent and repetitive tasks, within a decade from today. This would obviously lead to huge increases in efficiency and potentially massive costs savings, bringing much lower prices for consumers but also a crushing commoditization for those companies (and people) that currently provide these services. Clearly, human operators cannot and should not compete here – the only way for us is to move up the food-chain, i.e. above the API (application program interface).

Who will have stewardship and control?

Some urgent questions arise as we enter the age of man-machine convergence: who will actually have stewardship of these issues? Who is in charge of what is ignored, allowed, or sanctioned? Should it be trusted to the likes of Defense Advanced Research Projects Agency (DARPA) or the United Nations? If this is not just about technology and business but also about ethics, values, and culture, who would have authority over these matters? What will happen to our collective, cultural and social concerns, i.e. those beyond the commercial agenda? How will our social contracts change because of this, and will these achievements make us happier?

The challenges of unintended consequences

In my view, unintended consequences of exponential technological progress are by far the biggest challenge that we will need to tackle in this coming age of smart machines – and hopefully not *Our Final Invention* as James Barrat presents in his brilliant 2013 book[37].

Exponential technological advancements are certain to have a myriad of unintended yet even inter-related and combinatorial consequences. In many cases I believe, these must be considered more seriously before we proceed.

Some will prove to be rather harmless and more easily remedied such as using smartphones while driving becoming an increasing cause of accidents. Others may have potentially catastrophic outcomes – such as AIs that could learn how to fix and augment themselves, leading to a so-called **AI explosion** and **superintelligence** that could spell the end of humanity as we know it (again, as Hollywood likes to depict so deftly).

Drones also make for a very good example here. There is certainly some logic in augmenting or even replacing postal and delivery services with drones in urban areas or even in places that lack infrastructure such as in Africa. If we were actually to pursue this however, we are certain to face a slew of unintended consequences which may well void most benefits we may otherwise derive from it. Consider issues such as these drones providing the perfect means for real-time surveillance, or the likelihood of citizens acquiring weapons or other means of disabling those drones that have become a nuisance to them.

Such wicked problems may well become the default in the very near future. How do we harness the positive outcomes of these new technologies without creating monsters on the flip side?

Opportunities and challenges driven by abundance

Through exponential technological progress we will soon reach new levels of man-machine relationships. This clearly has the potential to solve many challenges that are subject to bold scientific endeavors – such as energy, food, water, and the environment. Connecting everyone and everything (the Internet of Everything) will generate very powerful network effects that – among many other things – will allow us to further perfect crowd-sourcing, crowd-funding, and crowd/peer-creation. While this in itself is hardly a panacea either, it does enable business models that were impossible before, generating increased abundance at an even faster pace and quickly challenging our economic logic to the core – as we are already seeing in the debates about Uber and AirBnB. What would be the purpose of increasing consumption if almost everything is abundant? When the price of most goods goes towards zero because they can be reproduced instantly, why do I need to work for a living, and what would my money still buy me?

On the flip side, the challenges of actually reaching abundance driven by a highly evolved **man-machine OS** will be numerous. For example, we will very likely see potentially dramatic job losses – technological unemployment – on a global scale and especially in the BRICs/CIVETS. This could result in social unrest, increased crime, and terrorism born out of sheer hopelessness. There is also the quite real threat of creating a truly perfect real-time surveillance network where nothing, not even your thoughts, would remain private. Finally, there is the dramatic and global rise of **machine thinking** (see above). This is accompanied by an increasingly popular mindset that treats human idiosyncrasies like story-telling, mystery, boredom, contemplation, and imagination as mostly wasteful and inefficient, and wishes to make an algorithm out of everything. The combined effect of these challenges could certainly be considered a kind of hell that would rival George Orwell's worst fears.

Digital ethics are becoming crucial as man and machine converge

To be ready for this coming age of intelligent machines and increasing man-machine convergence I believe we urgently need to start debating and crafting a global **Digital Ethics Treaty**. This would delineate what is and what is not acceptable under different circumstances and conditions, and specify who would be in charge of monitoring digressions and aberrations. No small feat clearly, but maybe the process and the result could be similar to the guidelines that came out of the 1975 Asilomar Conference on Recombinant DNA – a framework that seems to have guided the development of biotechnology deftly and effectively for the last 35 years.

I believe a **Digital Ethics Treaty** will soon prove as important as the nuclear non-proliferation treaties (NPT) that are already in place, and that have indeed proven to be enforceable (if not entirely without friction). So here are some admittedly still fairly raw rules I would like to propose for inclusion in such a treaty:

- We should not allow humans to actually become technology (in the sense of fundamental augmentation of the human body or mind).
- We should not allow humans to be effectively governed by intelligent technologies.
- We should not allow the fundamental altering of human nature and the **manufacturing** of new creatures with the help of technology (such as large scale genetic manipulation).
- We should not allow robots and intelligent machines to upgrade, fix or alter themselves.
- We should not allow the open or inadvertent discrimination of humans that chose not to use technology to increase their efficiency or competitiveness.
- W should not require or allow robots to make ethical decisions, i.e. to become sentient or develop some kind of moral agency.

"The best way to predict the future is to create it", (to quote Peter Drucker, Abraham Lincoln and Alan Kay).

The bottom line is that if you are running a business or an organization today, you will probably encounter these man-machine-convergence challenges very soon, or maybe it will be more of a **gradually then suddenly** event for you.

Either way, the future of how we relate to and intertwine with machines is being defined at this very moment, and it raises some fundamental questions:

- *How are you shaping the debate about the future direction of your business – are you building towards the human future or the machine future?*
- *Heaven or hell – how should society seek to shape evolution and*

ethical governance of technological innovation and the boundaries between man and machine?

- *What sort or organizational structures, strategies and business models will we need to survive and thrive in a world of abundance, declining prices and high technological unemployment?*

Can 3D Printing Destroy Capitalism and Restore Government?

By Jeffrey Joslin

How can business leaders adapt to the radically different economy and government models that could arise from 3D printing and similar innovations?

In this chapter I explore the potential of 3D printing to disrupt literally every business sector and drive major economic shifts as goods become cheaper. I then examine the implications for the distribution of wealth and power across society and the potential transformations that could occur in governance.

How fundamentally disruptive could 3D printing be?
We often fail to acknowledge the implications of a single invention until they become truly obvious. In the case of 3D printing, it is transitioning into the mainstream, and smart business leaders are approaching the technology with caution, as they should. Perhaps no innovation since the advent of the internet has had similar potential to change how our society functions at the most fundamental level. 3D printing could overturn centuries of flawed democracy and revolutionize the way we do business. Will we heed history's warning and be ready to meet this

new world head on? *The answer isn't a simple one.*

What can we learn from historical examples of breakthrough innovations?

Many believe a single invention could never change our economy, government, or social orders so drastically, but they perhaps forget the historical context of similar – yet much simpler – inventions. The printing press changed the world during the transition from the Middle Ages to the Renaissance. It created new social strata while destroying others. Arguably, this made possible the biblical notion that all human beings were created equal instead of only the richest or those lucky enough to be born into a certain family. It paved the way for democracy as we know it.

During the Middle Ages, books were expensive, literacy was low, and the autocracy certainly fought to keep it that way. Although many rudimentary forms of the printing press were available centuries earlier, Johannes Gutenberg is credited for the advent of the mechanical movable-type printing press that was widespread in Europe by the mid-fifteenth century.

This invention was a requisite factor in the eventual mass production of books, which consequently became much cheaper and more widely available. This created a cascade effect. First, the literacy of the lower classes slowly increased as they sought to further their education. Second, news began to travel faster and with greater accuracy due to a new mass media in the form of newspapers or "the press". Third, all forms of governmental and religious authority was threatened by the emerging middle class. Eventually, capitalism and a weak form of democracy were born as a result.

Without the printing press, none of these developments would have been possible. While the printing press gave birth to capitalism, the 3D printer could be the invention that kills it.

Unlocking the transformational potential of 3D printing

Instead of printing a single layer of ink onto a seemingly two-dimensional piece of paper, imagine a new invention which can manufacture almost everything using a simple set of blueprints easily downloaded from the internet. That is 3D printing. The device essentially lays down layer upon layer of a material, fusing them together until the completed design is manufactured. We can print homes, pharmaceutical drugs, chemicals, foods, and even human organs. Soon, products will be bought, sold, and manufactured from the comfort of our own homes instead of stores or factories.

Such a shift could fundamentally change how businesses deliver goods and services and, eventually, upend our economy while strengthening democratic forms of government. People will no longer need to leave their homes to make purchases which currently require a trip to the store. If you have the option of printing a toy from the comfort of your own home, will toy stores stay in business? Possibly not. In the decades ahead, many businesses will no longer require physical premises. They will sell downloadable blueprints instead of physical products or risk going out of business. Those that maintain a physical presence are likely to evolve into experience centers. Imagine stores becoming a networking and learning hub where customers can exhibit their creations, share knowledge from each other, and receive expert guidance from professionals in the relevant domain.

Because we can 3D print pharmaceuticals, doctors could write prescriptions and provide emailed blueprints so you can produce a needed drug from home. This is a far-future example since pharmaceutical components will have to be closely regulated, but the point is clear: many services will need to adapt to changing business models due to the radical shift in manufacturing. Inevitably, almost every business will own many 3D printers. Anything that can be 3D printed most probably will be. In some specialist cases such as the pharmaceutical example, we could see the growth of neighborhood fabrication centers where communities share the specialist 3D printing tools and feed stocks.

Currently, China's economy thrives because it dominates manufacturing. What might happen to it when 3D printing is the dominant form of production; when we can print products from our living rooms? 3D printers can already print food. What happens to the concept of a grocery store when we no longer need to leave the house to obtain nourishment? Scientists are printing human tissues and organs. What could happen to human life spans when we need no longer die due to organ failure, and how might that affect social structures around the world?

Put all the puzzle pieces together, and certain conclusions can be drawn. For example, 3D printing could place countries on a more even playing field in manufacturing, changing global commerce. But more important implications are on the horizon.

3D printing and the evolution of democracy

How would you define communism? In many countries, we are taught to hate even the idea of communism, but few of us can define it accurately. Communism is the simple idea of goods and services becoming so abundant that the price falls to a negligible point. Most instances of communism up to this point in history have been administered by authoritarian governments which have distorted the basic ideology to fit their control ambitions. That isn't real communism.

How would you define democracy? We generally define it as a government for the people, by the people. All voices are equal. Of course, most of us have never experienced this kind of democracy. Here in the U.S., those with the most money seek to control the key political gestures of those in power. Those with no money have less of an impact. That isn't real democracy.

We're nearing the point in time at which a person with a 3D printer can print the parts required to construct another printer. Whereas the printing press provided us with cheaper books and libraries (and the internet has provided a medium through which we can download them for free), 3D printing will provide us with cheaper forms of everything. This is a major point of departure from everything we know and understand about how economies work.

The transition will be long-winded and depend on other technologies such as renewable energy. Some have estimated that solar power will have reached the point at which it can provide for the entire world's energy needs by 2030. Although 3D printing drains a lot of energy and is therefore still expensive to use, the day is coming when energy will no longer be an impediment to the widespread use of the technology.

When that day comes, 3D printing, along with other technologies such as drones and automation, will cause a similar cascade of events to those which occurred after the advent of the printing press. Goods will become abundant and cheap, forcing capitalist enterprises worldwide to rethink their strategies and business plans. Money will lose value and class structures could begin to collapse as people we be able to afford more with less. In such circumstances the super rich seem likely to lose their power.

When this happens, governments will capitulate to the needs of the many instead of the needs of those with the most money and influence. Some cynics say that if voting made a difference, they wouldn't give us the opportunity to do it. They have a point because money often wins elections. When we all have access to the same goods and the widening gap between rich and poor finally crumbles, our democracy should become stronger.

Who wins in the new economy?

Even today, many social commentators and analysts accept that our society is transitioning into one based on information, the only real commodity left to us, and the hardest to put a price tag on. This could lead to an economy naturally evolving towards economic communism, which would in turn lead to a more robust form of democracy than we enjoy today. Couple these possibilities with the growing anger and resentment of the poor and the middle classes towards the super-rich, and it's easy to see a revolution in the making.

Sure, 3D printing has the capacity to destroy capitalism as we know it while redefining democracy to the point that the old systems will become unrecognizable, but will business leaders fight these transitions? Or will they adapt to meet the new paradigms which will inevitably form? If the response of the autocracy during the transition from the Middle Ages to the Renaissance is any indication, there will be strong resistance from business and political leaders. But the end result seems inevitable.

And that might be okay. Communism and democracy seem to work together like peanut butter and jelly; you can have one without the other, but they just don't seem to work as well as they do together. We'll find out soon, one way or another.

Here are three questions to consider:

- *Will world economies naturally transition to economic communism because of new technologies, or will capitalism linger? Either way, how quickly will businesses adapt to and accept 3D printing devices, should they become main-stream?*
- *Will those holding the vast majority of the world's wealth be able to retain their assets and influence, or will 3D printing lead to economic and governmental changes which weaken the power of the superrich and massive global corporations?*
- *Could once-successful business models within developed nations be dislocated to developing nations where they might still be economically viable?*

Section 2

Tomorrow's Global Order – What are the emerging political and economic transformations that could reshape the environment for society and business?

New systems and structures for a new era

This section provides a wide ranging discussion of ways in which political and economic governance systems need to be reformed to serve the needs of society and provide a sound footing for the future conduct of business. At the heart of the each discussion is the twin recognition that technology is creating new possibilities and society's expectation of these systems is evolving rapidly. There is a clear acknowledgement of a growing demand for transparency, equity, participation, and access for the whole of society.

The six chapters cover the following themes:

The Prospect of Democracy 2.0 (page 111) – David Wood outlines the need to embrace technology to facilitate the transition to a more open, participative and informed model of governance and democracy in the digital era.

The Comeback of Value Creation as the True Measure of Results in Business (page 123) – Petur Albert Haraldsson argues for a reframing of the future purpose and role of banks and presents a compelling vision of how economic and financial systems should evolve to enable true market driven capitalism.

The Impact of Accelerating 3D Printing Technology on Economic Systems (page 129) – Sally Morem highlights the highly disruptive potential impact of 3D printing on business, consumers, the environment, and the wider economy.

The Future of the Global Monetary and Financial System - Time for a New Bretton Woods? (page 134) – Professor Adrian Pop sets out scenarios for how the international monetary and financial systems could evolve in response to the immense forces for change.

It's not Money until it's Postmoney (page 139) – Dr. Boyan Ivantchev examines the evolution of the role of money, its emergence as Postmoney and the potential future scenarios for the evolution of money in an increasingly digital world.

Investing in International Aid and Development (page 147) – Norman Rebin outlines the drivers for and benefits of increasing future corporate involvement and investment in international aid and development.

Global Drivers of Change

By April Koury, Iva Lazarova and Rohit Talwar

We have identified thirty key drivers of change that are likely to set the context for future political and economic transformation. These are categorized under three headings: Policy and Governance, Economics, and Economic Systems.

Policy and Governance

- *Rate of Democratic Transition* – As one regime after another toppled in the wake of the Arab Spring, expectation rose that more nations would move to a democratic form of government either through conflict or peaceful means. Now, however, the resulting difficulties of adopting a democratic model have highlighted the capacity building challenges and the hurdles inherent in transforming governmental and social structures in such a short timeframe.
- *Reframing of Global Governance Institutions* – The global shifts of wealth, power, and influence toward the emerging economic giants is driving demand for the restructuring of global institutions like the United Nation, the World Bank, and the International Monetary Fund. Power will continue to flow to the populous and increasingly economically strong nations – led in particular by China, India and Brazil. New alliances and groupings will form such as the Shanghai Co-operation Organization and ASEAN (Association of Southeast Asian

Nations) and they will seek to increase trade and political ties, bypassing the West in many cases.

- *Democracy 2.0* – The rise in digital technology has given many citizens easier access to governments – who in turn have greater access to the thoughts, opinions, needs, and wants of all citizens in a flexible, adaptable, and real time manner. Individual citizens can increasingly be consulted on any matter and are able to bring their issues to government attention.

- *Country Mergers* – Many governments will struggle to finance everything they are expected to by their citizens, from policing and social welfare, to education, climate change protection, and economic development. The map of the globe will change, driven by economic and environmental forces. Many smaller and poorer countries may find it impossible to cope on their own with the accelerating pace of change and the cost of keeping up to speed with a globally connected planet. By 2025, we could see 20-25 country mergers, with "at risk" nations seeking to come together to create the critical economic strength and attract the investment required to serve their populations and compete in the hyperconnected era.

- *Country Fissions* – New countries could also emerge. Since 1945, the number of countries worldwide has grown from 60 to 196 today. New states developed with decolonization in the 1960s and 1970s, and even more gained sovereignty with the break-up of the USSR. Now, Catalonia, Brittany, Scotland, the Western Sahara, sections of Myanmar, Iraq, Syria, Libya, and even Saudi Arabia are among the many regions today that could break apart and form new nations in the next two decades.[38] Alongside country mergers, we may also face a future of an increasing number of smaller, independent nations.

- *Neo-Cold War* – Tension could increase between Russia and Europe / the U.S., particularly if Russia's economic situation declines further and it continues to seek to annex former parts of the Soviet Union. A new cold war between China and the U.S. / Europe could arise if China is seen to become too strong economically and to be pursuing a global political stance that goes against the western nations' wishes. Additionally, the proliferation of nuclear, biological, and chemical weapons could introduce new state players into this situation.

- **Rise of Brutal Fundamentalism** – A growing number of fundamentalist groups may emerge from a variety of religions and worldviews as their leaders seek to pursue religious, political, social, and economic ambitions through the bullet rather than the pulpit or ballot box. Governments and global institutions will struggle to respond effectively because of the lack of desire to engage in ground conflict and the increasingly outdated notion of outright victory in such conflicts.

- **Networking and Automation of the World's Legal System** – While world law may not exist in the foreseeable future, the world's legal systems are expected to become increasingly networked. This could lead to ever closer alignment of legal frameworks and the increasing automation of the law as it becomes embedded in our environment – for example vehicles that automatically fine us if we exceed the speed limit.

- **Political Experimentation** – Worldwide, there is a growing view that current governance models simply are not appropriate for a world in transition in the digital age. Democracy, single party states, dictatorships, and monarchic rule are being scrutinized as governments experiment to see which new models can best serve national goals. In increasing instances where the government has been viewed as utterly ineffective, citizens have joined together to solve problems that were traditionally handled by the government.

- **Empowered Populations** – New models of government coupled with technology advances are empowering populations to share knowledge, be aware of their environment, and make informed and responsible decisions. One challenge to leveraging all of this data and information is the ever growing shortage of data scientists. However, these empowered communities are still able to challenge the roles of the decision makers currently running politics, health, education, and welfare systems.

- *Civic Hacktivism* – Civic hacktivism is the combination of civic activism and the digital world. Civic hacktivists use their coding and computer programming knowhow to replace slow, outdated government bureaucracy with fast, usually internet based solutions. By networking citizens, governments, and technologists together, local problems can be discussed, ideas brainstormed, and apps developed which solve the initial problems. By streamlining government bureaucracy, citizens are better able to understand and participate in their local governments, and governments are made more transparent and accountable to their constituents.

- *Rise in E-Government* – Globally, countries are pushing for more e-government projects in order to cut costs and improve internal communication, as well as to gain a better understanding of – and provide services to – their citizens. These initiatives are already changing the way businesses and citizens interact with, and access, government services.

- *Privatization of Public Services* – Worldwide, governments are increasingly turning to the private sector to deliver public goods and services. Often commercial providers are more efficient, cheaper, and have a quicker response time than government-run public services. However, when an increasing number of public services are delivered by the private sector, questions around governance, transparency and risk emerge.

Economics

- *Economic Growth* – Despite economic uncertainty and systemic fragility, economic growth (global GDP) is expected to continue growing into the next decades. According to projections, the global economy is expected to grow at an average rate of over three percent per year from 2011 to 2050, doubling in size by 2030, and again by 2050

- *Public Debt* – Public debt is the total amount owed by a central government to its creditors. The global financial crisis and the

Eurozone sovereign debt crisis have both left developed economies with high levels of indebtedness. Total debt for OECD has
risen from 79.9 percent of total OECD GDP in 2008 to 111.2
percent in 2014 according to OECD figures.[39]

- **Economic Power Shifts** – Emerging economies are experiencing growth, allowing them to exert more influence over the
global economy. This shift in power may lead to the rise of a
new international system. Leading the way for the last decade
were the growing economic juggernauts of Brazil, Russia,
India, China and – to a lesser extent – South Africa. Potentially
following in their wake are the so-called "Next 11" countries –
Bangladesh, Egypt, Indonesia, Iran, Mexico, Nigeria, Pakistan,
the Philippines, South Korea, Turkey, and Vietnam. These are
identified as having the potential to become some of the world's
largest economies in this century.

- **Global Flows** – As the world becomes more interconnected,
the flow of goods, services, people, and finance across borders
continues to grow. These global flows represent over 36 percent
of global GDP and are creating new degrees of interconnect-
edness between countries.[40] The degree of connectedness of a
nation is seen as an indication of its current and potential prosperity. It is estimated that countries with a larger number of
connections in the network of global flows increase their GDP
growth by up to 40 percent more than less connected countries.

- **Feminomics** – In both developed and emerging markets,
by 2020 roughly one billion women who had been living at
a subsistence level will enter the global economy for the first
time – as middle class consumers, producers, entrepreneurs,
and employees. They will have roughly as much economic
influence as the populations of India or China. Governments
will need to address any gender-based discrimination that may
arise. Businesses will need to reassess not only what goods and
services to provide these new consumers, but also how to meet
the needs of these new employees.

- **New Trading Zones** – Worldwide, governments are entering into new trade agreements, which in turn will stimulate the development of new trading hubs, creating new growth markets and increasing trade volumes by 2020.

- **Global Inequality** – Over the past 20 years, global inequality has increased dramatically, a trend expected to continue into the future. In 2014, Oxfam reported that 85 of the world's wealthiest individuals had a combined wealth equal to that of the bottom 50 percent of the world's population, or about 3.5 billion people. It is projected that by 2016, the wealthiest one percent will own more than half of all global wealth.[41] Research indicates that greater income inequality within countries correlates with higher unemployment and crime rates, and lower than average health and social mobility.

- **Continued Globalization** – As the world shrinks through transport improvements and ever faster communications technology, so the flows of goods, services, people, and capital moving between nations and across continents continues to increase. While globalization tends to lead to market liberalization and expand trade in most countries, concerns arise over the additional levels of complexity it adds to business decision making and the potential for cultural dilution.

- **Technological Long-Term Unemployment** – By 2025, it is estimated that up to 50 percent of current jobs at every level will be replaced by software, robots, or smart machines. As more jobs are automated, fewer are being created by the emerging sectors; those that are created require higher skills and fewer people. This could result in long-term unemployment, placing massive pressure on governments, businesses, and society to rethink business policies. It will also force a re-evaluation of approaches to education, lifelong learning, job creation, and job placement assistance. Long-term unemployment would strain government social security budgets, lead to a rise in poverty, and drive the expansion of the shadow economy as people seek to work outside of the tax system.

Economic Systems

- *Systemic Fragility* – The global financial crisis of 2008 illustrated just how fragile and interconnected today's global operating environment is. Every aspect of finance, government, and commerce was affected by this systemic fragility. This growing sense of risk is driven by continued economic volatility, continuing rich-poor divides, the complexities of financial markets, declining government spending, the disruptive impact of crowd financing, and cybercurrencies, increasing polarities between political groups, and the demand for truly sustainable infrastructure investment and resource allocation.

- *Systemic Antifragility* – Risk analyst Nassim Taleb introduced the concept of antifragility[42] to systems thinking, with the idea that a system improves as it is exposed to stress. While a rigid system may seem more stable, in the long run it is unable to cope with unexpected shocks. Conversely, an antifragile system contains built in redundancies that help it thrive and adapt to changing forces and pressures. Governments and businesses are exploring antifragility concepts to develop better policies and regulations concerning financial systems in particular.

- *Networked Economy* – The networked economy is the emerging economic environment that is driven by the massive, multilayered, exponentially-growing, real-time connections between people, devices, and businesses. It is the convergence of social networks, business networks, and the network of devices connected to the Internet of Things. SAP estimates that the networked economy will be valued at $90 trillion over the next 10 to 15 years.[43] To adapt to the new economy, businesses will need to become mobile, social, and "always connected" to both internal and external business and social networks. Because the networked economy hinges on information, companies will need to address issues concerning the ownership, privacy, and security of that information.

- *Global Derivatives Market* – The global derivatives market is an integral part of the international finance system and global economy. Worldwide, businesses use derivatives to hedge risks and reduce uncertainty about future prices. Defaults on sub-prime mortgages, a type of financial derivative instrument, partially triggered the last global financial crisis. Most financial derivatives are not traded on any exchange and so total exposure is difficult to determine. Estimates vary greatly – and some suggest the face value of all derivatives outstanding is over three quadrillion (3,000 trillion) dollars, or more than 40 times the entire world's annual GDP.[44]

- *Full Reserve Banking* – Full reserve banking only allows banks to lend out the assets they actually hold. This is the alternative to the dominant fractional reserve banking system, which many believe has created unmanageable instabilities in the global economy that will drive future economic collapses. Full reserve banking requires that banks keep the full amount of depositors' funds at all times, and that they may only lend out the actual assets they possess. Some economists argue that full reserve banking is more robust and less liable to create the types of credit bubbles, systemic risk, or "too big to fail" scenarios that occur under fractional reserve banking.

- *Technological Hegemony* – Countries with ownership of core technologies typically enjoy higher levels of added value as a result. Hence a country's science and technology development level could decide its status in the international arena.

- *Socio-Economic Unrest* – With debt issues unresolved and a hyper-volatile global economy, the potential for further downturns is very real. The costs of recovery could see further redundancies and austerity measures similar to those experienced in Greece. Populations may not be willing to put up with this while others continue to make disproportionate gains in wealth, further widening the gap between rich and poor.

- *Governing the Shadow Economy* – The shadow economy exists alongside a country's official economy, and consists of illicit economic activities like undeclared work and black market transactions that avoid government regulation, oversight, and taxation. Current estimates place the annual market value of the global shadow economy at $1,829 billion.[45] Many countries who once tried to control the shadow economy are now moving toward a model of acceptance, acknowledging that in some instances it can deliver many of the services governments are failing to provide, such as policing, education, and healthcare.

The Prospect of Democracy 2.0

By David Wood

How concerned should business people be about the future of politics?

In this chapter, I will describe an important potential transition from **democracy 1.0** to what can be called **democracy 2.0**. This transition will allow many more people than at present to make positive contributions to the operation of politics. I see this transition as a key enabler for the favorable future of business. However, as I will explain, the transition is by no means inevitable. Instead of democracy 2.0 we might end up with **democracy 0.0**.

The key role of politics

Here's why anyone interested in the future of business should be paying attention to the future of politics. Politics exerts powerful influence over the complex mix of factors that guide and constrain how business evolves. These factors include markets, incentives, subsidies, regulations, standards, public funding, public expectations, and technology. All these factors are impacted by political decisions. In turn, these factors mold the business environment – sometimes for better, sometimes for worse.

Present-day political systems however, are proving themselves inadequate to keep up with an increasing pace of change. Politicians are often solving yesterday's problems rather than addressing tomorrow's challenges. As such, the influence which politics exerts is frequently malign rather than beneficial. That's something which should concern all of us. That is a reason we should be looking for ways to help politics improve.

I expect this conclusion to be unpopular. It may be regarded as a forlorn hope. Politics is messy, people say. Politicians have a reputation for being brutally self-serving. "Stay well away from politics," is a common piece of advice. Yet, to echo a quote attributed to Edmund Burke, "All that is necessary for the triumph of evil is that good men should look on and do nothing." If we view politics as inherently messy and self-serving, that's the way it's likely going to stay. Happily, it's going to become easier for people of good will to do more than simply offering armchair criticism. Rather than just looking on, we will be able to get involved in reshaping the political landscape. As I will explain, we will have technology to thank for this change.

Anticipating democracy 2.0

My choice of the term democracy 2.0 echoes the **web 2.0** revolution which took place in the world of software from around 2004 to 2010. As someone heavily involved in mobile software over that period, I witnessed that revolution at close quarters, from my vantage point on the executive leadership team at smartphone OS pioneer Symbian.

Web 2.0 is characterized by features such as blogging, social media, and collaboratively edited encyclopedias. Prior to web 2.0, the World Wide Web generally had the flavor of a library – it was somewhere that people visited in order to find and consume content. It could also be described as an encyclopedia. Content was added to the web by central hubs. But in web 2.0, the web took on the flavor of a conversation. People were no longer just consumers of media, but creators of it. The network of web interactions jumped forward in capability, with much greater intelligence at the edge of the web than before. The tangible sign of this increased intelligence is the huge swathe of user-originated content generated in applications such as Wikipedia, Facebook, Twitter, Instagram, and YouTube.

It can be the same with politics. New applications, coupled with revised political processes, can transform politics from being **centrally controlled** to being **collaboratively directed**. Rather than political leadership lagging behind the technology curve, politics could stay abreast – or even ahead – of the true challenges and opportunities of the time. We could all be benefiting from the greater wisdom at the edges of political structures – wisdom in the skills of people that, presently, have little to do with politics.

Democracy is, after all, meant to be (in the words of Abraham Lincoln) "…government of the people, by the people, for the people." Let us emphasize the phrase **by the people**. Indeed, voters in regions all over the world have, from time to time, the power to dismiss their elected authorities. They can also raise petitions, write pamphlets (nowadays blogs), and newspaper leader articles. But the political establishment has a disproportionate influence. Voters are frustrated that they frequently have what they perceive as a limited choice of genuinely alternative options. Reflecting this disillusionment, membership of political parties has plummeted in many parts of the world.

This trend can be reversed. The factor that enables this reverse is similar to the factor that allowed web 2.0 to emerge from the midst of web 1.0. Critically, web 2.0 relied on more sophisticated software than had been used previously. This included clever features such as scripting, as well as the means to chain together different services in what became known as **mashups**. Via mashups, enhancements by different software writers could be combined together in innovative ways. For example, maps and calendars started appearing in lots of different applications. Moreover, it became easier for enthusiastic end-users to create their own applications, complete with graphically appealing user interfaces, without needing to attend lengthy training courses. This was all enabled by powerful new development tools and so-called **integrated development environments**.

The factor that can enable democracy 2.0 to emerge in the midst of voter frustrations with democracy 1.0 is, similarly, new technology. Accelerating technology is already radically transforming many areas of life – including education, entertainment, health, transport, the environment, and warfare. Technology has, in the same way, the potential to radically transform politics. It can do this by enabling improved collective decision-making, by instant fact-checking of claims made by politicians, by evaluating options in a way free from human bias, and by identifying which are the most significant points in a large sea of noisy democratic discussion.

It will be like when Google gently asks us, "Did you mean to type. . . ?", and when Google draws our attention to improved navigation routes through cities we thought we already knew well. Technology will, similarly, be suggesting innovative new policy, perhaps better than anything dreamt up by human analysts. New technology can also offer improved alternatives to archaic first-past-the-post voting systems, in which electors are unable to express their actual preferences.

That's the potential. But will it happen?

Different futures

There are a couple of complications. First, like all new developments, the technologies of decision-making can be misused. They could enable a horrific state of oppression and alienation, rather than the positive vision of democracy 2.0 that I have started to sketch. The proud descriptive adjective **Big** in **Big Data** has an uncomfortable potential re-use in **Big Brother**. Second, more broadly, technology could veer off in any number of disastrous directions.

Some emerging technologies – in particular artificial general intelligence and nanotechnology – are so powerful as to produce changes more dramatic than anything since the agricultural revolution. The outcomes could be extraordinarily positive for humanity, but they could also threaten our very existence.

Existing technologies already pose potential catastrophic risks to the well-being of humanity – the risk persists of accidental nuclear warfare and runaway climate change might be triggered by unchecked emissions of greenhouse gases that push global temperatures beyond sudden tipping points.

There are further complications from relatively easy access by alienated, destructive individuals to weapons of mass destruction such as dirty bombs and synthetic pathogens. Technology has always had the nature of being a two-edged sword, but it's now sharper and more potent than ever before. The same YouTube that provides free access to wonderful Khan Academy educational videos also distributes contemptible footage of atrocities, inducing widespread outrage and hatred. The same synthetic biology that can repair and improve damaged human organs can also produce deadly pathogens with virulence beyond the worst existing diseases. The same computer guidance systems that navigate us to holiday destinations can also navigate lethal cruise missiles to explode in the midst of large human populations.

What is it that will determine whether the powerful force of 21st century technology is a blessing rather than a curse? What will influence whether technology enhances our ability to heal, educate, and flourish, rather than our capability to wreak havoc? This brings me back to the central theme of this chapter: politics.

Politicians out of touch

Speaking personally, my biggest concern about politics is about the reverse of the influence that I described earlier. The influence runs in both directions. At the same time as technology could be transforming politics (giving rise to democracy 2.0 to supersede the weaknesses of democracy 1.0), politics could be transforming technology. However, politicians are – by and large – failing to exert what I view as the necessary support for the positive potential of technology.

Far too often, national political discussion essentially neglects the technological dimension. Technology is relegated to having a minor role in the debate, rather than being recognized, as it should be, as potentially the single most important change agent. Current policymakers do, from time to time, speculate about the development of technologies. However, they rarely tackle the issue of **convergent disruptive technologies** – advances whose development paths unexpectedly influence each other. This means politicians tend to react to each new disruption with surprise, after it appears, rather than anticipating it with informed policy and strategy.

It's tempting (but a mistake) to compare the flight path of change in any one technology area with the trajectory of a golf ball. Once struck, a golf ball flies through the air under the influence of well-understood laws of gravity and aerodynamics. Bounces may be hard to predict with precision, but the influences on where the ball will eventually come to rest are relatively few in number. Contrast that situation with predicting the outcome of a snooker ball, on a table containing many balls, all set in motion by an initial cue strike. Balls repeatedly bang into each other, changing their direction multiple times. Initial uncertainties multiply rapidly. It is this latter situation which bears greater resemblance to the evolution of technology. In the crucible of technological progress, numerous different technological and market trends keep impacting and transforming each other. These trends are also influenced heavily by social and psychological trends, which are, likewise, hard to predict. These trends are said to **converge**, although the word **collide** is equally valid.

Society has already seen remarkable changes in the last 10-20 years as a result of rapid progress in fields such as electronics, computers, digitization, and automation. In each case, the description "revolution" is appropriate. Even these revolutions pale in significance to the changes that will, potentially, arise in the next 10-20 years from extraordinary developments in healthcare, brain sciences, atomically precise manufacturing, 3D printing, distributed production of renewable energy, artificial intelligence (AI), and improved knowledge management. Indeed, the next two decades look set to witness four profound convergences:

- *Between artificial intelligence and human intelligence* – with next generation systems increasingly embodying so-called **deep learning**, **hybrid intelligence**, and even **artificial emotional intelligence**
- *Between machine and human* – with smart technology

evolving from **mobile** to wearable and then to embeddable, and with the emergence of exoskeletons and other cyborg technology
- *Between software and biology* – with programming moving from silicon (semiconductor) to carbon (DNA and beyond), with the expansion of synthetic biology, and with the application of genetic engineering
- *Between virtual and physical* – with the prevalence of augmented reality vision systems, augmented reality education via new massive open online courses (MOOCs), cryptocurrencies that remove the need for centralized audit authorities, and lots more.

Each of these four grand convergences will be far-reaching in its own right, but the combination of all four happening in parallel injects additional large elements of uncertainty.

In principle, technological developments have the potential to generate abundance – plenty of material possessions, healthy longevity, uplifting mental life, and profound experiences to dissolve the worries of electors around the world. As a result, voters would no longer need to hustle and campaign for adequate provision of welfare services, such as pensions, education, and healthcare.

However, there are many uncertainties that influence technology – both how it is developed and how it is deployed. Technology does not determine its own outcome. Instead, the allocation of resources to technological development is strongly impacted, as mentioned earlier, by the operation of markets, incentives, subsidies, regulations, and public expectations. In turn, all of these factors are impacted by politics – either by commission or omission. Due to politicians' comparative lack of active interest in technology, the impact is frequently one of omission.

As an important representative example, green technologies are progressing too slowly. Too many financial subsidies are diverted into defending carbon-based energy resources that, in contrast to green technologies, have highly polluting side effects. A desired transition to cleaner lifestyles, long discussed, remains fitful and erratic. In contrast to the future vision of humanity living in positive harmony with the environment, present-day societies are pushing the planet close to devastating tipping points. Vested interests, driven by short-term financial concerns, are obstructing a rational allocation of research and development resources. That's why politicians ought to be exerting much greater green leadership by:

- Championing a wide-ranging investigation into which green technologies are the most promising
- Where needed, orchestrating patient, long-term investment, and adjusting regulatory frameworks, and
- Opposing any distortions that short-term interests exert on the R&D landscape.

To help politicians reach such decisions and to follow through on the necessary policy implementations arising, democracy 2.0 can play a big role.

Improving rationality

For positive open discussion to take place in a society, informing politicians of both the real issues and the potential solutions, a number of underpinnings need to be in place. These include digital rights, trusted safe identities, robust infrastructure, and the ability to communicate freely without fear of recrimination or persecution. Hence, I believe we have a common interest in the following policies:

- Accelerating the development and deployment of tools ensuring personal privacy and improved cyber-security
- Ensuring the protection of critical Internet services even for the cases of wars and other emergencies (these services will include web archival, Wikipedia, source code repositories, trusted root encryption keys, etc). For comparison, this protection is just as vital as storing the seeds of critical food plants in the Norwegian Doomsday Vault.

- Extending governmental open data initiatives
- Championing the development and adoption of online digital tools to improve knowledge-sharing, fact-checking, and collective decision-making
- Increasing the usefulness and effectiveness of online petitions, and
- Restricting the undue influence which finance can have over the electoral and legislative process.

In line with the dictum that government policy should be based on evidence rather than ideology, we should advocate that:

- Insights from the emerging field of cognitive biases are adapted into decision-making processes
- New committees and organizations be designed so that they are less likely to suffer groupthink, and
- AI systems should increasingly be used to support smart decision making.

Finally, to guard against a different form of oppression of free debate, I believe there is a strong case that all laws restricting free speech based on the concept of personal offence should be revoked (note that this is a concept distinct from the crime of harassment). While potentially contentious, my personal view is that, before anyone is accepted into a country, whether as a visitor or as an immigrant, they must confirm that they fully accept the principle of free speech, and renounce any use of legal or extralegal means to silence those who offend their religion or worldview.

With these safeguards all in place, the impact of politics on the development and deployment of technology should become beneficial rather than adverse. It will contribute to the creation of a positive feedback network of influences.

Improving education
In readiness for a radically different future, one other set of political

changes needs to be enacted: carrying out critical reforms in education. A greater proportion of the time spent in education and training (whether formal or informal) should be future-focused, exploring:

- Which future scenarios are technically feasible, and which are fantasies
- Which future scenarios are desirable once their **future shock** has been accepted
- What actions can be taken to accelerate the desirable outcomes and avoid the undesirable ones
- How to achieve an interdisciplinary understanding of future scenarios
- How resilience can be promoted, rather than society just having a focus on efficiency, and
- How creativity can be promoted, rather than society just having a focus on consumption.

The intelligent management of risk

Once again, there's a technology angle to this transition. Education can take greater advantage of MOOCs, augmented by smart AI teaching software. We can anticipate a time, not too far into the future, when, apart from laboratory work, the entire content of tertiary education could be delivered online. Progress towards this outcome of enhanced education for everyone can be accelerated through a mandate that each university and educational establishment should make an increasing proportion of their material accessible freely online every year. The outcome of these changes should be that:

- Citizens will be more informed about fast-changing technological and business issues
- Citizens will be aware of cognitive biases and other flaws in reasoning, and will collectively become better able to resist these fallacies, and
- There will be a big increase in the number of people working productively on positive solutions to the challenges being faced

by business, politics, the environment, and society.

An alternative future: democracy fails

Many people tend to think that the future will resemble the present. They recognize that new technologies will be adopted, in various fields, but they imagine that the overall operation of politics and business will be largely unchanged. That's not a view I share. I see two scenarios ahead, which can be named as **Democracy 2.0** and **Democracy 0.0**. The former scenario is the one I've mainly described in this chapter. But in the latter scenario, democratic influence and involvement will decline:

- The benefits of new technology will be widely perceived to be taken disproportionately by the people who already do well in society – the so-called one percent – rather than being shared
- Popular dissatisfaction with the existing political parties and the associated establishment will increase
- Powerful surveillance tools will quickly crack down on anyone showing dissent
- In parallel, other technologies will be used to placate and distract people – via beguiling video games, immersive soap operas, and befuddling recreational drugs
- Major decisions about national priorities and government investment will increasingly take place behind closed doors, manipulated by vested interests
- With ineffective government, powerful monopoly interests will gain the upper hand, and
- Without public oversight, it is likely that adverse uses of new technologies will increase, in warfare, suppression, crime, and terrorism.

Here are some questions for society and business to consider:

- *Is a middle way, keep calm and muddle through, credible as an alternative to the two stark alternatives presented above? Can* the momentum be taken out of the powerful change engine of disruptive technology, in order that the pace of change can be slowed down?

- Which of the threats of Democracy 0.0 are the most pressing? Which demand the most urgent response and discussion?
- Are there significant business opportunities associated with developing the tools that will advance Democracy 2.0? Will these tools be owned by the existing giants of the information age?

The Comeback of Value Creation as the True Measure of Results in Business

By Pétur Albert Haraldsson

Will banks be relevant in ten years; are they relevant today?

In this chapter I explore how the role of banks has become distorted in western economies. I present a vision of how the economic and financial system might evolve in the digital age to enable true market driven capitalism and examine how the role of banks could revert back to that of a low-cost transaction provider facilitating trade in the real economy.

The evolution of banks and banking

For the last two decades, the banking industry has driven inflation by pushing excessive spending by consumers and encouraging the use of leverage in business and real estate. Fortunes have been made and lost with hype-driven speculation and the introduction of financial products designed to provide instant financial gain without the need to create real value.

The resulting market volatility has been at the cost of investors and pensioners who need to think long-term. Institutions previously trusted to mediate risk and ensure stable returns over time have been lured with the instant gratification of commissions and management fees based on short-term returns. The resulting disconnection of interest between investors and financial institutions may be the root of the serious economic and financial problems western economies are experiencing. It is therefore high time to re-instate capitalism where real value creation is the basis of wealth and the main measure of results.

The banking industry's strong influence in western economies has made it the face of capitalism. This is manifested in the common misconception that the aim of capitalism is to earn interest on idle money by manipulating markets, inflating prices, and encouraging excessive consumption. But a real capitalistic economy uses private resources to build on existing value and produce new value with the aim of making a profit on the difference between the input and the output. In a capitalistic economy, the banks' role should be to facilitate this process with the tools exclusively available to them as government sponsored intermediaries. However, banks have repeatedly stepped out of this role by meddling in markets and giving the wrong signals to their managers by profusely rewarding gambling at their customers' expense.

The big opportunity here is to harness the brainpower of the brilliant individuals that the banks have recruited for the benefit of the capitalistic economy. Everyone will clearly profit when the world's smartest graduates use their gifts to build truly sustainable companies rather than inventing clever ways to "blow into bubbles" and avoid tax on the proceeds. Having been taught to ignore real value creation and focus on short-term financial gains, they could now bring back prosperity based on tangible results and good values.

As Albert Einstein pointed out, "We can't solve problems by using the same kind of thinking we used when we created them." Banks do not seem to have learned their lesson as they have generally reacted to a change by entangling their clients in debt rather than investing in their ability to provide relevant support in an evolving capitalistic economy.

The transition from an inflation-driven economy to sustainable-market driven economy

The transition to a market-driven economy from an inflation-driven economy will require the transfer of power from preconditioned bankers to open-minded business people. Business people understand that money has no value in itself, and that the foundation of an economy is value created with the production of goods and services the market needs and wants. A truly market-driven economy will therefore reward intellect and entrepreneurship handsomely while remunerating providers of brokerage and value exchange platforms in proportion to the limited real value of their input.

Three concurrent shifts will lead to the full transition to sustainable capitalism; social enlightenment, system replacement, and sustainable progress. The shifts will be driven by smart educators, resourceful business people, and individuals weary of the continuous battle with a faceless enemy: inflation. Whilst these shifts may only be considered **weak signals** of emerging change today, I believe supporting trends already taking place in society are accumulating fast and their combined impact is about to burst. As these shifts are the result of a need to correct a faulty system, the barriers to entry for new players and innovative solutions should be easy to overcome. Therefore a true paradigm shift may take place in the next decade or so.

Social enlightenment

At the core of the enlightenment will be a new breed of thought leaders teaching that conforming to a system that is unacceptable to a vast majority of stakeholders makes no sense. The foundation of the coming economic reform will be the realization of societies that democracy is a natural state of things, not something that can be bought, sold, or compromised with meaningless mantras. Just like a flock of birds turns and twists in unison and makes progress without apparent leadership, people will start following the enlightened path provided by readily available real knowledge and the natural instincts of crowds.

We will experience the revenge of the nerds – beyond seeing video game geeks and technology buffs become the richest people on the planet. We will learn that Bertrand Russell was probably not consoling grumpy nerds when he said: "The whole problem with the world is that fools and fanatics are always so certain of themselves and wiser people so full of doubts." We will realize that he was simply describing the unexplainable and yet entirely reversible slant of fortunes in favor of the intellectually challenged.

The enlightenment will climax in the realization that capitalism is a good thing and that the way it works is not complicated at all. Complications are simply the creations of those that make a living by skimming profits from the results.

System replacement

It seems unlikely that banks will re-establish a position of trust in society after having failed repeatedly to perform the simple task of facilitating transactions in the economy with a government backed mechanism. Governments will therefore be forced by citizens to revoke the banks' longstanding monopoly on supplying money to the economy. To avoid further damage and future crashes, the supply of money will be regulated by a transparent system based on an algorithm that optimizes the supply of money to sustain the economy.

New mediums like barter platforms and global cyber-currencies will continue to emerge and further neutralize the influence of banks in business. Revised textbooks will emphasize that money is of no value in itself and is only one of many tools for exchanging real value. Rating agencies funded by the very banks they are rating will be a thing of the past. Rating of services and comparisons of products and fees will be in the hands of independent comparison websites using real time information from service providers.

Eventually, currency markets will be replaced with a Universal Sustainability Index that will be the basis of all transactions involving goods and services. The baseline of the index will be the status of the sustainable supply of all of the earth's finite resources. It will ensure that companies and countries producing goods and services that damage the environment and deplete resources will earn less than their sustainable counterparts. With time, strong demand for cheaper sustainable goods and services will benefit all aspects of life.

Resumed progress

A successful transition to market-driven capitalism will result in a streamlined value chain focused on results. Inherent friction between distinct and differently motivated groups of individuals in business, finance, and professional services will be eliminated. Instead of wasting time and energy reconciling differences between wildly different schools of thought, a shared focus on sustainable results will give birth to a new kind of entity: **The Business Facilitator**. These multidisciplinary entities will design strategies and solutions for entrepreneurs that optimize the tangible results of their businesses and ideas.

Profitability of companies will improve as banking, the most expensive and least valuable layer of the economy, resumes its intended role of facilitating transactions. Business owners will realize that steady growth based on earned demand for their product is better than leveraged growth that demands speedy unsustainable expansion and costly forced demand. By de-leveraging and re-investing in the business they will have breathing space to make decisions based on market forces and value creation rather than short-term financial gain demanded by creditors.

As business owners will become focused on sustainable growth and the development of intellectual capital to support it, employees will become increasingly involved in the operation. With involvement comes loyalty and trust that opens new avenues that are equally bene-ficial to employers and employees alike. Companies will, for example, start offering their employees the opportunity to take their salaries as needed and in the form they prefer, for example currency, benefits, shares or goods and services. The company will pay the employee interest on the balance.

As B2B processing units on the outskirts of cities clustered around data centers, banks will become efficient and their services cheaper. They will be able to lower their overheads and only charge a fraction of the fees they charged in the past. Banks will play a vital role in processing transactions for a multitude of new solution providers focused on helping business and individuals create value.

Ex-banking executives will become productive contributors to the real economy where they will experience firsthand that banks exist because of economic activity and not vice versa. As account executives in Business Facilitators they will be able to leverage their banking experience to develop ways to maximize business profits with bespoke multi-source funding solutions. As highly driven individuals, they will continue to thrive on lucrative rewards, with bonuses that are based on the effect of their solutions on the client's bottom line.

When the market realizes that intellectual capital is a much more valuable ingredient than money in business, demand for third-party capital will decline. The cost of capital will therefore go down – reflecting its limited role in the value creation process rather than what its provider demands on the basis of an outdated system. Companies will increasingly expand by collaborating with other companies and individuals that can add real value in the form of relevant know-how, capital goods, or labor. The exchange medium for the value input will be shares in a company or project that the contributor has the option to exchange through crowd funding platforms. In this way, strategic **real value** investors will gradually replace debt as a way to sustain company growth and eliminate the waste that results from expanding with idle capital.

Here are three questions for businesses to consider on banking:

- *What is the total real cost of financial intermediation in your company?*
- *What roles do companies need banks to perform in the modern global economy?*
- *What would be the possible impacts of governments removing the banks' monopoly position in the economy?*

The Impact of Accelerating 3D Printing Technology on Economic Systems

By Sally Morem

Could accelerating technological development usher in the world's first economic system based on true abundance with no scarcities at all?

As acceleration occurs in the development of technologies such as 3D printing, goods and services are getting easier and easier to produce and the costs are dropping. Technological deflation is taking place. As a result, the production of genuinely new wealth is increasing at an exponential rate. In this chapter I explore the potential impacts of the rise of 3D printing on business, consumers, the environment, and the wider economy.

Acceleration of automation

Acceleration is largely centered on the automation of production systems. Automation has long ceased to be merely a matter of replacing human workers with machines. The capacity and productivity of the machines has already far surpassed that of humans in a number of industrial sectors. For example, our marvelously dexterous fingers and thumbs have been rendered immense ungainly at the scale of miniaturization already required for modern industrial processes such as the manufacture of computer chips. Our most skilled machinists simply cannot work to those kinds of tolerances. It has been years since any human has made a computer chip.

Picture the traditional factory a hundred years ago: a huge, noisy place, involving large numbers of workers. By modern standards they were extremely expensive to run, and yet extremely effective in producing millions of replicas of the original product design. However, just as the electronic computer became smaller, more precise, more readily replicated, and with greater computational speed, so has the factory. As I write this chapter, the factory is being replaced by the 3D printer.

The unstoppable rise of 3D printing

Today, 3D printers already produce houses, tools, toys, shoes, machine parts, cars, bricks, reconstructed fossils, even bones, and body tissues. Ever-faster machines are coming to market and the latest printers can print electronic devices with the use of special toner that allows it to embed circuitry within the device. Thin layers of toner are laid down on a base guided by Computer-Aided Design (CAD) software until the object has been completed. A printer can print the object exactly to specification again and again and again.

If your business deals with engineering prototypes, you will probably soon be using 3D printers if you are not already. Work that took days or weeks of rig building and machining to produce a single prototype now takes hours. Your prototype will be available and ready for testing the same day on-site. Your boss will not worry so much about costs and delays when you propose a project. When you ask for permission, your boss will more readily say, "Go ahead." A wider range of prototypes can also be produced at lower cost and in a far shorter timescale. This allows engineers and designers to perfect a product without worrying about the time or costs involved in multiple prototype iterations.

If your company supplies parts to other companies or consumers, fabrication steps may be reduced to just a few or perhaps just one. The need to stockpile spare parts for those steps will reduce. Bottlenecks will disappear. Costs will fall. Your boss will be happy. If your shop sells custom-made tools, you can reduce the size of your inventory drastically to a few show pieces and keep thousands of tools in CAD form on your computer, ready to be printed on demand. You can customize these to your customer's needs with a few keystrokes.

The broader benefits of 3D printing

3D printing decentralizes the production process – moving fabrication closer to the customer – bringing major potential benefits for production, shipping, infrastructure maintenance, and energy demand. Decentralization of design work and ready replication of CAD programs mean we need far less transport of finished goods to stores and warehouses. This means far less need for transport vehicles of all kinds. This also means far less wear and tear on bridges and roadways. All of which can help to reduce energy demand.

Consider the implications for the environment: any system producing printer toner out of any raw material can be thought of as a digestive system. The system eats the feedstock, reducing it to elemental components, and them reconfiguring them to be building blocks for the printing of desired products. There are endless ways in which this will have beneficial impacts on environmental rules, controls, effluent discharges, garbage disposal, pollution handling, and waste management.

In agriculture our ability to control the properties of foodstuffs and reduce production waste will continue to grow as replication of anything becomes easier and easier. Very simple foods have already been printed. It is only a matter of time until the development of precision food printers – replicating all foods to exacting standards. The impact on farming will be drastic. Farmers may wind up growing toner of all kinds for themselves and their neighbors instead of crops. Animals will no longer be needed for food. Neither will plants.

We are reaching the point, where it will soon be possible to use advanced printers to print copies of themselves and all the CAD programs they run. Those printers will become dirt cheap—perhaps literally. The 3D printer will then become the replicator. At that point we may all have them in our homes or share them in community fabrication centers. When almost everything we do, make, and know can be digitized and programmed with extreme precision, when everything becomes information, when everything is automated, this could be the day when all scarcities cease to exist.

3D printing and the "Abundance Society"

What happens when the producer and the customer become one and the same—the owner and user of the means of production? What happens when our technology gets so advanced, decentralized, and inexpensive that each one of us will be able to command the potential creative and fabricating power of today's multinational corporations and nation-states? This is what happens: the "Abundance Society".

But it won't stop there. The Abundance Society will speed up innovation even more by permitting millions of people to create more and more advanced technology in their own time. Inventors will participate in a fully open-sourced system on the Internet, posting **recipes** for their latest ideas. Since they won't have to worry about working for a living, their time will be freed up to innovate without worrying about bosses or even customers. Inventors and **invention software** (yes, invention itself may well be automated) will cut development time to hours or even minutes. And designs will fly through the Net at light speed, further triggering the thoughts of inventive genius around the world.

Perhaps we will achieve a truly historic irony: making socialists' wildest dreams come true, not through politics, but with capitalism—through the motive force of accelerating technology.

Key questions:

- *How can businesses manage the wrenching changes accelerating technology will impose on their design, production, and distribution functions?*
- *How might government, labor unions and society respond to the potentially massive resulting rise in unemployment?*

- *How will customers deal with radical shifts that enable them to become producers in their own right?*

The Future of the Global Monetary and Financial System – Time for a New Bretton Woods?

By Adrian Pop

What are the possible futures for the global monetary and financial system and their likely influence on the business environment?

The backbone of global business

The effective functioning of global business relies on a set of monetary, exchange rate management and financial regulatory systems that stem from landmark decisions made towards the end of the Second World War – often referred to as the **Bretton Woods Agreement**.[46] The key mechanisms of the International Bank of Reconstruction and Development (IBRD) and the International Monetary Fund (IMF) originated from the United Nations Monetary and Financial Conference held at Bretton Woods, New Hampshire, USA July 1-22, 1944, with the participation of 44 countries. The Bretton Woods Conference represented the initial attack on the problems of post-war economic reconstruction and drafted the Articles for Agreement for the IBRD and IMF.

The global financial and economic crisis, the economic power shift from the U.S. and Europe towards the rising powers in Asia, and the setting up by the BRICS countries in 2014 of a new development bank have all reinforced the trend towards reconfiguration of the global financial and economic order. Viewed by some as a new Bretton Woods, this major overhaul of the global financial and economic architecture currently evolves on four different, although interdependent tracks which are explained below along with their possible implications for business.

The international monetary system

The first track would be to re-base the international monetary system on a dollar-renminbi-euro triad or, at least, in case of a deepening of the euro crisis, on the dollar and renminbi (RMB), which is tantamount to a reversion to regionalism.[47] According to a Bruegel analysis, somewhere around 2019-22, it is deemed that China would be able to raise the status of the RMB over and above that of the yen or even possibly the British pound or Swiss franc. Moreover, by 2027-33 the RMB could become a very serious challenger to the euro and by 2037-42 it could overtake both the Euro and the dollar as the predominant global currency.[48]

Recognizing the role of emerging economies in global governance

The second track of establishing a new Bretton Woods would be to rightly match the emerging and developing countries' weight in the global economy, with their power and influence in setting the rules and institutional arrangements of the world economy. Emerging powers deem that major governance reforms are needed. In particular, they are requesting changes in quotas, voting rights, executive board representation, and transparency in the management selection process for global economic institutions. Although the IMF, the World Bank, and the World Trade Organization (WTO) have taken important steps to increase representation to reflect the shift in economic power towards developing countries, many rising powers remain unsatisfied. Institutions such as the Bank for International

Settlements (BIS) and International Accounting Standards Board (IASB) are behind the curve in giving adequate representation to China, India, Brazil, and other rising powers. Additionally, further reforms are needed at the level of the IMF, World Bank, and G20.[49]

Reinforcement of the special drawing rights

The third track is focused on the reinforcement of the Special Drawing Rights (SDRs) by enlarging the **basket of currencies** on which it is based to all major economies.[50] Any reform of the international monetary and financial system geared to making the SDRs a global reserve medium however, would have to address the issues of SDRs allocation[51] and creating the critical mass for the SDRs to become a world reserve currency. A solution would be to create a **substitution account** at the IMF denominated in SDRs to create the possibility for central banks to convert their dollars into SDRs. A more practical approach would be to include in the current SDR basket of currencies both the BRICS country currencies, but also those currencies that reflect the evolution of the prices of aluminium, iron, gold or crude oil. This means including the currencies of countries such as Australia, Canada, Chile, and Norway, thus linking the SDRs with the cycles of these key commodities.

Restoration of the gold standard

The fourth track of establishing a new Bretton Woods would be a restoration of the gold standard.[52] The New York Federal Reserve acts as the custodian of the gold owned by 122 account holders which include the U.S. government, more than 60 foreign governments, other central banks, and a few international organizations including the IMF. According to the New York Fed's own estimations, approximately 98 percent of the gold bars stored in its Lower Manhattan vaults belong to central banks of foreign countries. Much of the gold bullion arrived during and after the Second World War as many countries wanted to have a place of safe-keeping for their gold reserves. The volume of the gold stored continued to expand and climaxed in 1973, immediately after the U.S. suspended convertibility of dollars into gold for foreign governments.

The UK was a role model for the gradual adoption by other countries of the gold standard in the 19th century. Hence, a resumption of the gold standard could come about through the impetus given by a powerful actor on the international stage rather than through international agreement.[53] The impressive accumulation of gold reserves by Russia and China throughout the current crisis – as well as the diversification of the IMF's revenues through the creation of a fund supplied with gains from the sale of gold – both surely work in that direction.[54]

Scenarios for the evolution of the international monetary system
Three scenarios could be outlined for the possible evolution of the international monetary system:

- The **Repair and Improve Scenario** assumes the continuation of the on-going policy efforts to improve the functioning of the current system organised around the U.S. dollar through incremental reforms.
- The **Multi-polar/Bipolar Scenario** envisages that the U.S. dollar remains the main international currency but other currencies also play a key role in the international monetary system as reserve currencies, anchor currencies, and on international markets for goods and assets. Among the latter one would include the euro and the RMB (or only the RMB), as well as a possible single currency of East Asia or a BRICS currency.
- The **Renewed Multilateralism Scenario** posits renewed, possibly crisis-led, steps towards building a multilateral international monetary order. Since neither the RMB nor the Euro would emerge as major international currencies, the need for diversifying official and private reserves is met by the emergence of SDRs as a widely used quasi-currency.

Although all three scenarios would offer improvements compared to the current system, the Multi-polar/Bipolar Scenario would best correspond to structural changes in the world economy and mitigate some of the imperfections of the current system.[55] The Multi-polar scenario is seen as the most likely in the medium term. This is confirmed by early estimates of the U.S. National Intelligence Council at the beginning of the global financial crisis,[56] and by more recent assessments which speak about the likelihood of an uneven multiple international currency system.[57]

So what could this mean for global business?

An understanding of the future functioning of the global monetary and financial systems is critical for businesses that trade internationally. Everything from the pricing of global transaction, to exchange rate strategy, and currency hedging will be affected. The global balance of power and decision making influence within the governing bodies of international institutions may also impact on corporate choices in terms of where to locate headquarters functions and regional operating centers.

Hence this analysis raises some critical questions for the development of future business strategy:

- *What are the implications of each scenario for business hedging against foreign exchange / currency risks in the future?*
- *What strategies are required as the weight of international trade pivots towards rising economic powers?*
- *What role could commodity pricing receptiveness play in strategy development?*

It's Not Money Until It's Postmoney

By Boyan Ivantchev, Ph.D.

What is the possible future of money in a rapidly changing global economy?

Business relies on a common understanding of money as a means of exchange, a store of value, and a mechanism for rewarding employees and investors alike. In a rapidly changing global economy, notions of money may evolve and force us to rethink its purpose in quite fundamental ways. In this article I will look at the history of money, its role as a simple tool for payments, exchange, and a measure of value. I will then go on to examine the evolution of the concept of **Postmoney**[58] and highlight possible scenarios for the future of money.

The standard economic paradigm and the complexity of money

The standard economic paradigm defines money as a medium of exchange, unit of account and store of value.[59] [60] Equally its function is defined as having, "...universal acceptability for payment, exchange and measure of value."[61]

It is somewhat bizarre how the comprehensive role of money today is expressed only through its simple technical characteristics as a tool. The origin of money is a complex process that began with primitive and ancient forms of exchange around 3,000 years B.C. progressing to coinage around approximately 600 B.C. The history of money suggests that its meaning, role, and importance are also evolving – not only in its physical form, value, and methods of payment, as per standard economics – but also in the "inner nature" and **soul** of what we consider to be money.

The origin of money was define by Glyn in the following way:

"Money originated very largely from non-economic causes: from tribute as well as from trade, from blood-money and bride-money as well as from barter, from ceremonial and religious rites as well as from commerce, from ostentatious ornamentation as well as from acting as the common drudge between economic men."[62] This definition shows that money has origin, value, and functions related to anthropology, history, culture studies, morality and ethics, customs and laws, occultism and religion, wars, and social and economic development. It is also closely tied to the psyche and the psychology of individuals and nations. Why then does the standard economic paradigm continue to perceive money only as a means?

The dematerialization of money

Money has had many complex uses over time: as compensation for people killed; to purchase slaves and sexual services; as a dowry and compensation for the lost labor force in the family of the bride; for the sale of a son or daughter as farmhand laborers and soldiers; for magic spells and sacrificial offerings; to finance bribes and the remission of sins; and to purchase social status and public rank. Today it is also used for drug distribution, to finance of weapons of mass destruction, terrorism, and attempts to upgrade the human body and achieve immortality. These actions can hardly be valued in terms of money and its functions as a means only. Historically money appeared in order to support the exchange of goods and the development of trade, but gradually it started living its own life away from trading, and its functions ceased to be perceived solely as facilitating trade. It has become dematerialized.

Contemporary forms of dematerialized money and digital banking allow for the transfer of money between continents in seconds, money laundering, and reinvestment of the dematerialized money. Only a century ago that was impossible. How should we interpret the appearance of virtual money? Bitcoins have a market capitalization of approximately $4 billion as of March 2015.[63] The virtual economy of Second Life is valued at around $6-700 million. The global market of virtual items and identities (characters) and currencies was approximately $2.1 billion in 2007,[64] and five years later in 2012 it was $14.8 billion. It was projected to increase at an annual growth rate of 12.5 percent to 2016.[65]

Step by step, the dematerialization of money has led to disengagement – the decoupling of the digital form from the original carrier – and the beginning of new and independent existence. We can express the assertion that trading with virtual goods, services, and identities is a consequence of the existence of dematerialized electronic money and the globalization of various electronic payment systems. Already, the presence of virtualized money leads to the emergence of virtual worlds, products, identities and services that serve the existence of dematerialized money rather than as previously – money to serve physical trade in material goods.

The emergence of Postmoney

The virtualization of money and its value enables the existence of virtual worlds, economies, and currencies. If we accept the statement that: "Time in the virtual worlds means nothing,"[66] then it shall be measured only through a price expressed in money, arbitrating between saved and spent earth time to achieve a level, goods, images, and services in virtual worlds. Therefore, we can make the following hypothesis: the immateriality of time leads to the immateriality of everything else, i.e. of virtual goods and services, identities, etc. and so they have no commensurate point of reference in the physical world. As a result money is longer just a means, but has become an aim in itself.

This transition from physical to virtual and from means into an aim creates the notion of Postmoney. Serge Moscovici explains: ". . . but what is this mystery? It was money that led the way and has succeeded best in it, for money's entire significance does not lie in itself but rather in its transformation into other values. Now this evolution is contrary to reason and almost smacks of a modern miracle. In fact, how is it possible that a means has been elevated to the dignity of becoming an ultimate goal? In this resides the magic of money and its authority over all the rest."[67]

Virtualized money today is partially separated from the role of central bank money, as acknowledged by one of the Members of the Executive Board of the ECB,[68] because money creation – to a great extent – is already performed by the commercial banks. Indicative of the size of the Postmoney modern financial system is the volume of financial futures and options. The nominal value of these Over the Counter Market (OTC) derivatives amounted to $598 trillion in 2008 – the beginning of global financial crisis.[69] This was three times more than total value of global financial assets (securities, public and private debt and bank deposits) which amounted to only $178 trillion.[70] Here in a pure form is demonstrated the degree of leverage and speculation on the financial markets and the virtualization of global financial assets, which are no longer served by physical money. Instead, the assets themselves are serving Postmoney rather than any physical trade. They have become both the purpose and underlying assets for the enormous leverage taking place with derivative instruments.

Physical money has given way to commercial bank issued money and electronic money. As of March 2015 in the United States the value of coins and banknotes in circulation was $ 2987.70[71] billion (known as M1) while the M2 monetary aggregate[72] was $11845.60 billion.[73] The fact is that since 2006, the U.S. Federal Reserve is no longer publishing M3 money supply figures.[74] The last published figure in the U.S. for M3 was February 2006 and amounted to $10.3 trillion, more than two times greater than the M3 for 1996.[75]

The increasing lack of physical money leads us to forget what is written on American dollars – "In God We Trust", and if we believe in God, we must remember as well what is written in the bible: *"For the love of money is a root of all sorts of evil, and some by longing for it have wandered away from the faith and pierced themselves with many griefs (1 Timothy 6:10)."*

The future

Today money has become mystified and its aim per se is Postmoney. It has become a measure of human greed and low passions, immorality and all of the values associated with it, manifesting its delinquency by determining life and death with prices. These processes – mediated, induced, and self-generated by money – recall the thought of the ancient philosophers that: "Money is socially destructive, and may seem to belong to nature rather than culture. . . Money may seem unlimited internally (homogeneous) and externally – there is no limit to the sequence of exchanges by which it is accumulated."[76] To my great astonishment, in modern literature this subject is taboo and very few authors go deeper in the study of money from this perspective.

From where we stand today there are many possible futures for money and its role in society:

- Exchange coupons valid only in a single city
- Proposals to return to the gold standard
- The re-materialization of money through the common currency within the European Union (EU)
- Theories of a single world currency
- Transformation of the notions of money through the increasing use of virtual currencies such as Bitcoins and Linden Dollars

Let us examine some of these ideas in greater detail. The return to naive forms of money valid for a specific city or village – such as the Bristol Pound introduced in the English city of Bristol and valid for 350 public companies – represents a form of centrifugal force gathering momentum in recent years worldwide. Some futurists suggest that in the future Europe will be split into many very small states – as it was hundreds of years ago. Then such local currencies would have an increasing role in economic life. I believe these forecasts are rather unlikely and are feasible only in the case of destruction of the global financial and banking system, for example, the collapse of the SWIFT global payment system – comprising over 10,800 financial institution members from over 200 countries.

Some theorists are arguing that the growing range of alternative payment methods available and on the horizon – such as mobile payments, Apple Pay, and future possible Facebook platforms – will lead to fragmentation and eventually disrupt and destroy the established banking system and payment mechanisms. However, theories of International Economics and International Politics tell us that international integration in the modern world is so advanced that the processes of disintegration would be much more expensive than the efforts to strengthen this international integration. So I believe these exotic forms of currency development and alternative payment methods are unlikely to buck the trend towards integration. Through trial and error we will find a way of encompassing them within a larger "system of systems" of payment methods.

The arguments for a return to the gold standard (for example basing the standard economic unit of account on a fixed quantity of gold), the re-materialization of money, and the recovery of its value have become stronger over recent years. Contributory factors to these arguments include bloated national budget deficits, rising debt of the United States, seemingly unsustainable monetary policies focused on liquidity infusion through quantitative easing, continued reductions in the amount gold backing the available supply of coins and banknotes, and the continued growth of the monetary aggregate M2. While a return to the gold standard is not impossible, it would necessitate close coordination of the leading market economies and joint actions in this respect. Whilst difficult to implement, the benefits of ensuring integration would far outweigh the risks of nations pursuing their own path and the global disintegration that could result.

Despite the numerous criticisms of the EU and the Euro, it has emerged as the second most important currency in the world. Following the global financial crisis and national economic crises across the Union, the reputation of the currency has suffered. However this does not mean that there are many regions around the world, which – once the global financial crisis is over – will not renew their efforts to create regional monetary unions and introduce regional currencies. So, the mid-term future could see two or three new possible common currency zones emerge – e.g. in Asia, the Middle East, and Latin America. We could also see the emergence of a strong alternative to the International Monetary Fund (IMF) and the World Bank coming from the New Development Bank – the multilateral development bank created by the BRICS nations (Brazil, Russia, India, China and South Africa).

The historical success of the Euro Zone is fueling the arguments of supporters of a common global currency. The possible exit of Greece (Grexit) and other nations from the EU has so not as yet destroyed the idea of single currency. Indeed, there are many significant potential benefits of a common global currency, including:

- Uniform monetary policy
- A reduction in currency fluctuations and the risk of market manipulation
- Elimination of currency wars
- Significantly reduced costs for international trade and globalization
- A greater degree of economical and political predictability, and
- A smoothness and symmetry in the monetary measures in use across nations.

The idea of electronic cash emerged from a research paper by Dr. David Chaum at the end of the 1980's. Since then, we have seen very significant steps taken towards cashless societies – led by Nordic countries and the broader focus on e-money[77] and digital cash. The first steps in that direction have been made in the EU with the adoption of its E-money Directive (2009/110/EC).[78]

In the longer term, one can envisage an evolution from the current day experiences of the Euro, digital cash, e-money, and crypto currencies. I imagine that the money of the leading economies could be replaced by a global currency of government issued electronic points which would be used exclusively for the purchase of medical treatments and food. A variety of other systems would then be used to purchase goods and services across society using electronic points as the underlying currency. These in turn may disappear over time as goods and services effectively become free as a result of exponential technological developments that lead to a near-cashless society. The global adoption of electronic points should also terminate the possibility of money laundering and tax evasion, destroy billions of dirty physically stored banknotes, and help decrease crime and terrorism dramatically.

The philosophical leader of such a future step might be the European Union. However, in practice, only the USA today is in a position to drive such an initiative. Why is that? Because the biggest portion of world currency trades takes place in US dollars. This is actually on the increase. The Bank for International Settlements (BIS) reports that the US dollar's share of global currency trade rose from 42.5 percent in 2010 to 43.5 percent in 2013. The next biggest currency is the Euro which saw its share fall from 19.5 percent to 16.7 percent over the period.

This would also be a step towards returning money to its functions of means and termination of its deviant nature as Postmoney. Until the occurrence of this transformation we have to remember that: "It's not Money until it's Postmoney."

Questions:

- *What future business models might we need to adopt if everything except medical treatments and food were effectively available for free?*
- *How might the banking sector be transformed after the disappearance of cash?*
- *If money issues typically associated with Money Sickness Syndrome[79] will disappear in the future, what are the implications for financial services and the asset and wealth management sectors?*

Investing in International Aid and Development

By Norman Rebin

Investing in international aid and development will increase signifi-cantly for business but how will it be different from today?

This chapter explores the drivers for and benefits of increasing future corporate involvement and investment in international aid and development.

The need

The number of hungry in the world exceeds the populations of Canada, the U.S. and the European Union combined. According to the Food and Agriculture Organization, the annual shortfall needed to end it is $30 billion.[80] In addition to hunger, over 100 million children lack health care, schooling, and basic shelter. The nightly news points out the rise in those figures as more refugees flee the latest attacks from militants.

Drivers for increased involvement

In the face of the anticipated growth in the range of global grand challenges facing society, there is a clear and growing set of arguments for businesses in particular to play a more active role in international aid and development – through investment and direct involvement. Let's examine two of the key arguments – public relations and innovation.

Public Relations – Let's look at current television commercials. Slogans such as: "We help the world feed itself" are increasingly commonplace. Yet, these are not messages of charitable organizations: these are corporate ads. In contrast to the image that every business is cut throat, research has shown that the stakeholders react much better to a business that has a softer side. Involvement in international aid and especially development (the idea that people will eventually be self-sufficient), can personify an enterprise as both **caring** and **competitive**.

Innovation – For most of us, innovation is less a function of imagination than of sustainability. Steven Jobs knew that, so he and Apple introduced a regular flow of new products; a well known story. Yet some of the world's most intriguing business innovations, mostly unknown to the vast majority of us, affect large numbers of people on a daily basis. They have all been triggered by business foresight and an interest in foreign aid and development.

In their blog, *Innovative Solutions to Poverty and Hunger* the Borgen Project outlines some of these significant new products.[81] Among them are the Roughrider wheel chair which does not need a smooth surface to travel on; a packaged food that can immediately turn a malnourished child into a healthy one; and micro irrigation solutions for totally arid conditions. While these new products serve an immediate need, they also serve as the basis for expanded product development.

Transformative influences

Driven by the stark realities of need, the scale of international aid and development is expected to grow exponentially. However, the increasing involvement of businesses will change the delivery to more results-oriented projects. An example of this is the rise in private sector funding through the United States **Feed the Future** initiative which saw an increase of $40 million or 25 percent from 2012 to 2013.[82] Recent increases appear to follow the same pattern.

Partnering

There is a major trend in international aid and development towards partnering and specifically public-private partnering. Although the partnership is often developed domestically, the public partner is frequently an international agency which has the experience to bring a project to fruition.

Partnering will drive a second major expected trend – the segregation of aid and development initiatives into mega-projects, and mini – or even micro-projects. While the allure of partnering in a large project has the significant benefits of limited hands-on responsibility for the corporate partner, there can be dilution of the impact because of bureaucracy and the need for local government co-operation. In addition, there is usually considerably more satisfaction for both organizations and their staff in direct involvement with recipients. Although smaller, the projects can still be business-like and sustainable. Businesses will determine which approach best serves their purposes.

Involvement of China and India and the technology community

As part of its long-term economic, political, and social strategy China's business leaders have forged valuable trade connections to developing countries through aid. China's economic strategy includes initiatives to enhance education, health, and economic stability in key partner nations. A prime example is "South-South Cooperation" where China and other countries share information and strategy to enhance impoverished nation trade and aid. Through this process, China has developed strong and enduring markets and will continue to push other countries to follow their lead[83].

India has taken a different approach. It has been creating ultra low cost computers and other technology solutions for domestic consumption and then offered them to other developing regions. India is not only evolving a computer literate workforce, but has produced an export and aid product line. In addition to India's example, there is a strong movement by aid and development specialists and major technology companies to introduce the internet to the entire planet, more or less as a do-it-yourself tool.

All of the factors highlighted above will serve to drive an increase in foreign aid and development, and lead to growth in trade with now impoverished countries.

Questions to ponder:

- *How effective are the aid and development strategies your organization has pursued to date?*
- *When you start to do business in a developing country, which do you do first: invest in the business or invest in development?*
- *Apart from the feel good elements, what specific benefits do you think your organization could gain from an increased future investment in aid and development?*

Section 3

The Emerging Societal Landscape – Who are we becoming, how will we live?

The emerging societal landscape will present challenges and opportunities to our perspective on being human and how we'll live our lives. The chapters explore the emerging consumer landscape, the impact of Generation Z in society and the workplace and how technology could change education. We also explore how the management of our personal finances may need to evolve, the growing importance of understanding consciousness and mindfulness, and how we will make our choices around where to live and work.

These topics are explored in the following six chapters:

Understanding Tomorrow's Consumer Landscape (page 163) – Anne Lise Kjaer discusses how relationships between producer and consumer could change and the implications for future market strategies.

Generation Z in the Workforce (page 169) – Anne Boysen examines the evolving nature, expectations and workplace implications of those born after 1995 – often referred to as Generation Z.

Education 2025 – Building a generation of problem solvers (page 177) – Alberto Rizzoli explores how schools and learning could evolve through rapid adoption of new technologies and educational models.

The Future of Personal Income and Expenses (page 182) – Michael Nuschke addresses the wide ranging impacts of rising life expectancy and accelerating technologies on personal finances.

The Future Potential of Consciousness in Business *(page 187)* – Rishi Haldanya highlights how unlocking human consciousness could enhance workplace performance and create new business opportunities.

The Future Derives From Place Choices *(page 190)* – Stephen Roulac is a San Francisco based Real estate expert, litigation consultant, strategy advisor and author. He examines the range of factors that will influence our future decisions about where to live, work and locate our businesses and highlights implications of those choices for individuals, companies and society.

Global Drivers of Change

By April Koury, Iva Lazarova and Rohit Talwar

Thirty-three critical drivers of transformation are identified across seven key categories: Population and Demographics, Health and Wellbeing, Social Structures, Social Welfare, Lifestyles, Education and Skills, and Culture and Values.

Population and Demographics

- *Population Growth* – Global population is expected to continue increasing until 2050, when median estimates place it at 9.3 billion.[84] While birth rates in developed countries are often at or below replacement levels, developing countries in Africa, Asia, and the Middle East continue to maintain high birth rates. Continued population growth will be advantageous in providing a younger workforce and a larger consumer market whilst creating increasing competition for resources.
- *Urbanization* – Globally, the urban population has grown from 34 percent of total population in 1960, to 54 percent by 2014.[85] By 2050, that number is expected to rise to about 70 percent of total population.[86] This upsurge poses many challenges concerning how to provide such large populations with economic opportunities within cities, and how to manage city infrastructure, public services, sanitation, food, clean water, education, and healthcare for millions of urban citizens.
- *Megacities* – A megacity is a metropolitan area with a total

population of at least ten million people. As urbanization continues to increase, so too will the number of megacities. In 1985 only nine megacities existed, and by 2004 that number had grown to 19. As of 2015, 35 megacities exist, including Tokyo (the largest), Delhi, Mexico City, Sao Paulo, and New York. The world is projected to have 41 megacities by 2030.[87]

- *Generational Diversity* – Because of increasing life spans and new notions of retirement, Builders (born) 1925-45; Baby Boomers (1946-1964), Generation X (1965-1979), Generation Y (Millennials) (1981-1994) and Generation Z (1995 to the present day), will increasingly have to work together in the future. These generations each have differing values, communication styles, working methods, and lifestyle preferences that may clash. With the entrance of the Millennials into the workforce, companies are already dealing with conflicts between the print generations (Baby Boomers and Gen X) and the born-digital Millennial generation.

- *Super Aged Society* – Advances in science, technology, and medicine are increasing average life expectancy in many nations – often at a quite dramatic rate. By 2025, lifespans of 120 years or more may not be uncommon in the developed world. In most developed economies, the over-80's represent the fastest growing age group. Business, government, and society will need to evolve to address the issues of an aging population. How will we address the implications for housing demand, resource usage, health services, social care, and pensions? Aging societies could see marriages lasting over 80 years and increasing divorce rates among the elderly with potentially devastating financial impacts. Rising lifespans could also see people working well into their 90's. Entirely new service sectors will need to develop to meet the financial, physical, emotional, and spiritual needs of the elderly population.

- *New Notions of Retirement* – Retirement as we know it may cease to exist in the future; rather, people may take long breaks early in their careers and then step in and out of work for regular periods in their final 20 to 30 years of working life.

- *Eldercare* – The demographic trends of living longer and having fewer children later in life, especially in developed economies, suggests that elder care may become a huge burden on society and especially on the average worker. When an only child becomes a working adult, they may end up supporting not only their aging parents, but also their aging maternal and paternal grandparents. This, in turn could put a drag on geographic mobility and economic opportunity for working adults.

Health and Wellbeing

- *New Diseases* – For the last 40 years, new diseases have emerged every year, 20 kinds of which have grown to become drug resistant. Along with the increase of new diseases, issues such as poverty, urbanization, travel, migration, trade, invasion of mankind into the habitat of animals, and the increase of livestock farming have occurred, which raises concerns regarding the rapid spread of new diseases.
- *Health Divide* – In both developed and emerging economies, the gap between those with good and poor health continues to increase. This inequality will threaten the prospects for social development, growth, and stability.
- *E-Health* – E-health uses digital technology for the provision of better healthcare. Mobile, wearable, and ultimately embedded technologies will increasingly empower people to focus on their well-being, to monitor their health, and to take actions to improve it. The constant monitoring e-health provides will enable pre-emptive intervention and early warnings for problems like impending heart attacks and seizures.
- *Customized Health Care* – Advances in genetics, personal health monitoring technology, and hyper connectivity are leading to customized health care, where medical decisions, practices, and products are tailored to an individual. Already companies like 23andMe are able to map an individual's DNA,

and personal health tracking devices monitor and record biometrics daily. The next step will be tailoring treatments based on genetics and biological data gathered from networked health trackers. Additionally, diagnosis and treatment will take place through care-anywhere networks, and virtual doctor's visits and patient monitoring services could be available from any location.

Social Structures

- **Religion** – A number of existing trends and emerging ideas are helping to shape the future of religion. In Western Europe and East Asia the traditional religions are in decline; meanwhile Pentecostal groups are flourishing in Latin America, and Islam and Christianity continue to grow in Africa.[88] Recent projections from Pew Research Center estimate that by 2050, the number of Muslims will nearly equal the number of Christians worldwide, that India, while retaining a Hindu majority, will contain the largest Muslim population of any country, and the four out of every ten Christians will reside in sub-Saharan Africa.[89]

  However, decline in belief is happening globally, and very few countries are as religious today as they were 50 years ago (Iran and the U.S. are stark outliers to this trend). According to a Gallup survey, of more than 50,000 people in 57 countries, those claiming to be religious fell from 77 percent to 68 percent, and self-identified atheists rose from 10 percent to 13 percent between 2005 and 2011.[90] The countries that report the highest rates of atheism tend to have high economic, political, and existential stability. As stability increases globally, perhaps religious belief will decrease; or, as resource scarcity, systemic frailty, and economic uncertainty increases, perhaps faith will increase. As ideas continue to spread at the speed of the internet and people increasingly migrate from one culture to another, wider acceptance and tolerance of religious belief (or lack thereof) will become absolutely essential.

- **Female Shift** – Traditional gender roles continue to shift as women gain freedom and equality worldwide. Girls now outperform boys at every level in the education system in OECD countries. In the U.S., more people are employed by women-owned businesses than by Fortune 500 companies. Women will increasingly influence the economy, society, and government and profound shifts will happen in their personal and private lives. These developments will require changes at different levels, such as legal rights, work-life balance, family roles and structures, and organizational leadership.

- *Individualization* – Worldwide, individuals could increasingly be empowered to shape their own lives and influence governments through advances in technology, education, and health. Already, citizens are increasingly unwilling to accept the authority and decisions of the traditional ruling elite. The desire for transparency and exposure of abuses of power will drive citizens to demand a greater say. The public in many nations will become increasingly influential through mass uprisings, campaigning, and agitation via social media, mass petitions, and voting in more frequent e-elections and referendums. This move from the collective to the individual is forcing governments and businesses to reassess and change how they meet the needs of their customers / constituents.

Social Welfare

- *Universal / Guaranteed Basic Income* – The adoption of robots, automation, and artificial intelligence (AI) could eliminate millions of jobs in the coming decades.[91] Emerging sectors are expected to require fewer highly educated workers – increasing the risk of technological unemployment. Hence, many now argue that a guaranteed basic income will become a necessity in order to prevent social and economic collapse. Universal or guaranteed basic income is a system of social security in which all citizens are provided with an unconditional basic sum of money to live on. The system has been trialed successfully in Namibia and Manitoba, Canada.

- *Local Exchange Trading System (LETS)* – As the potential for technological unemployment rises, interest increases around the mechanisms that will enable people to access goods and services without resorting to money. Local exchanges trading systems are one such mechanism. LETS use a system of community credits which are given for providing a service, and which can be spent on whatever is offered by others within the system. Common forms of services exchanged include childcare, transportation, food, home repairs, and the renting of tools and equipment. LETS circumvent the formal economy by allowing people to trade work directly with one another. There is growing debate as to whether LETS forms part of the shadow economy, and if governments should seek to tax LETS activities.

Lifestyles

- *Cohousing* – Disenchanted with the isolation of modern, single households, an increasing number of people are opting for cohousing. Cohousing is a type of intentional, collaborative housing where residents are active in the design and operation of their community. Individuals and families live in private housing, but the neighborhood's physical design encourages community activities and involvement. In a decade it is estimated that the number of cohousing communities within the U.S. will double, driven by Baby Boomers seeking to downsize as they retire.[92]
- *Multiple Identities* – Now that individuals can exist both in the physical and digital world, many have taken on multiple identities. Virtual world avatars demonstrate people's desire to establish online personas, which are sometime completely different than their actual, physical identities.
- *Gender Identity* – Societal acceptance of gender identities outside of the traditional male/female genders will continue to grow. Already, social media giant Facebook provides over 50 gender identity options for its users.[93] Businesses and

governments alike will need to enact policies and practices that accommodate and protect this widening field of personal identities.

- **Greater Cultural Diversity in the Workplace** – The UN forecasts that Europe will need 1.6 million immigrants per year until 2050 to maintain its 2011 population levels. Since the majority of these are likely to come from emerging economies, European societies will need to accommodate greater cultural diversity.

- **Growing Middle Class in Emerging Economies** – The global middle class is projected to increase from roughly two billion in 2012 to an estimated 3.2 billion by 2020 and 4.9 billion by 2030. The majority of that growth is expected to come from Asia, which could represent 66 percent of the global middle class and 59 percent of middle class consumption by 2030.[94]

- **Multiple Careers** – As people live longer and fewer companies offer life-long job security, people are likely to have multiple careers. A university graduate today may hold anywhere from five to twenty careers over the span of her lifetime, which could stretch to 2090 and beyond. Currently, the average worker stays at each of her jobs for about 4.4 years; 91 percent of Millennials surveyed in 2012 expect to stay in a job for less than 3 years.[95]

- **Social Innovation** – There is growing interest in the concept of social innovation – pursuit of new solutions to social problems that are more efficient, effective, sustainable, or fair than the current solution. The value created by social innovation adds to society as a whole. There is a growing interest in taking approaches pioneered in delivering business change and using them to drive social innovation. The goal is to develop and implement new ideas for products, services, and models that meet social needs more effectively and create new social relationships and collaborations.[96] Emerging applications range from social housing, to emissions trading and education.

- **Geo-Socialization** – Based on geographic services and capabilities like geo-location, geo-socialization matches people's profiles, interests, and other personal data with location-based services, allowing people to connect with surrounding people, events, and businesses. It opens up new avenues of opportunity for enterprises to reach out and connect with consumers, and for people to connect and interact with each other.

Education and Skills

- *New Skillsets* – The Institute of the Future identified ten critical skillsets people need to thrive in the 21st century work environment. The forecasted skillsets deal with the drivers that will disrupt and reshape the workforce landscape of the future. The skillsets include sense-making, novel and adaptive thinking, social intelligence, trans-disciplinarity, new media literacy, computational thinking, and cognitive load management, cross cultural competency, a design mindset, and virtual collaboration.

- *Imbalances between High and Low Skill Labor* – A growing mismatch exists between what employers need and the skills of the labor pool. In the U.S. in 2011, an MGI survey found that despite the nine percent unemployment rate, 30 percent of U.S. companies had positions open for more than six months because they could not find workers skilled enough to fill them. Eighty percent of companies in Japan reported similar gaps. By 2020, it is estimated that the U.S. may have 1.5 million too few workers with college or graduate degrees and about six million too many who haven't completed high school.[97] Clearly these estimates run completely counter to the view that widespread automation could drive unemployment to record levels.

- *Reverse Brain-Drain* – Historically the educated workforce left developing countries for more opportunities in developed ones. Now, as economic and social conditions improve worldwide, the educated and skilled are predicted to return to their homelands by 2020. India, China, and Brazil are expected to see the largest returns.

- *Proliferation of Digital and Online Tools for Learning* – The development and evolution of new digital and internet-based tools like virtual classrooms has had a significant impact on education and the position of learning in daily life. The combination of social media applications and mobile devices has decoupled learning from the traditional classroom setting, allowing it to become personalized, interactive, and social. Classrooms are increasingly accessible to all.

- **Open Digital Learning** – Free massive open online courses (MOOCS) are now offered by thousands of educational bodies, including established institutions like MIT and Harvard. The growing availability of MOOCs, free online education tools, and people-to-people learning platforms could have a transformative impact in developed and developing countries alike. In the developing world it will enable students to access courses and gain a university education when their financial situation would never have allowed them to attend in person. In the developed world, as middle aged employees lose their jobs, free education offers the potential for lifelong learning support to enable people to retrain for new careers on a regular basis at little or no cost.

Culture and Values

- **Growth of Selfishness** – In a volatile world with the risks of further economic downturns, technological unemployment and greater competition for jobs, there is a risk that some sections in society could become increasingly self-centered and selfish. Individuals may seem themselves as being in competition for everything from jobs and housing to resources and a life partner.
- **Erosion of Trust** – As services become more automated and it becomes increasingly difficult to "talk to a human", trust may be eroded. Individuals will find it harder and harder to trust governments and businesses that constantly monitor people and use their personal data without their knowledge.
- **Rise of Big Brother and Decline of Privacy** – Societal concerns

may grow over the number of ways in which our every activity is monitored. Now even our TV can be monitoring our every move. A backlash could occur if people try to go off-grid. New privacy thinking, principles and treaties will be required to enable individuals to protect themselves in a world where every device can be listening in. Some believe we may require a digital ethics treaty to protect individual rights.

- ***Extinction of Languages and Culture*** – Some analysts argue that – due to the widespread use of smartphones and globalization – languages with less than 100 million users could gradually become extinct. Already, 2,000 out of 6,000 languages around the world are facing extinction, and 90 percent of languages spoken by African tribes have already become extinct. English, Mandarin (China), and Hindi (India) could become de facto universal languages.

Understanding Tomorrow's Consumer Landscape

By Anne Lise Kjaer

How can we engage with tomorrow's consumers?

It is not only consumption patterns that have changed over time, but also the very notion of what it means to be a consumer. This article considers the changing relationship between producer and consumer and the ways in which organizations will need to adapt to engage with audiences who will demand much more from you than simply goods and services.

The rise of conspicuous consumption

Debates about our consumer society are nothing new. The sociologist Thorstein Veblen coined the term **conspicuous consumption** in *The Theory of the Leisure Class* in 1899[98], and over recent years there has been a critical reappraisal of our role as consumers. In the documentary series *The Century of the Self*, filmmaker Adam Curtis[99] explored the evolution of consumerist society along ferociously cynical lines. He highlighted how the father of public relations, Edward Bernays, instigated everything from product placement to psychological persuasion techniques to trigger purchase decisions by consumers. While Bernays masterminded a consumerist society in America, economist John Maynard Keynes was contemplating alternatives in

England. In *Economic Possibilities for our Grandchildren* in 1930, he predicted that by 2030, living standards in "progressive countries" would be eight times higher and a 15-hour-working week would be the norm because we would: "...have enough to lead the good life."[100]

Towards a Good Life Society and "enoughism"

Just before the dawn of the new millennium, Naomi Klein's book *No Logo*[101] fuelled an anti-consumerism movement by shining a light on conspicuous consumption and mass manipulation by brands. While consumption is a fundamental part of life, it has become increasingly embroiled with our concerns about the impact and ethics of current patterns of production and lifestyle behavior. Having fulfilled our fundamental needs in western societies, a less materialistic and acquisitive perspective is taking shape, aided by disruptive new models where **access** over **ownership** is being explored. The evolution of consumption diagram (figure 1), inspired by Abraham Maslow's Hierarchy of Needs pyramid, charts this progression.

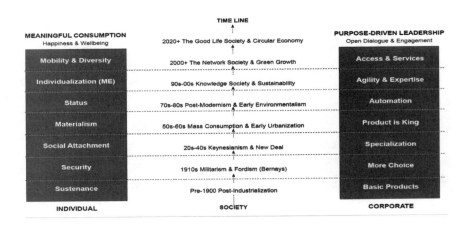

FIGURE 1 – The evolution of consumption details the change in consumer behavior and the impact on society and business. SOURCE: *Kjaer Global.*

Two issues prevail in the global consumption dialogue: first is the growing recognition that existing patterns of consuming are unsustainable; and second is that – rather than acquiring more stuff – we need to embrace **enoughism**. Hence the question arises: is a future with more considered and meaningful consumption a realistic proposition?

The 4P model and brand storytelling

At present, Keynes' vision of the future seems unlikely and, despite increased prosperity, we are not more content or less busy than we were 50 years ago.[102] Clearly, before projecting future consumption patterns we must consider the question: who sets the measure of what is enough? This requires us to redefine our notions about prosperity. Consider the 4P business model as the framework for delivering a sustainable bottom line.[103] By factoring in people, planet, and purpose alongside profit in any business strategy, organizations can be guided by a clearer and more customer-centric vision. Research suggests that broadcasting a firm's unique history and giving people what they actually need and want remains the biggest guarantee of an authentic brand experience. A Stanford study found that storytelling is up to 22 times more memorable than facts alone.[104] In order to build these stories, we need inspiring future scenarios to imagine tomorrow's people and their values and needs (figure 2).

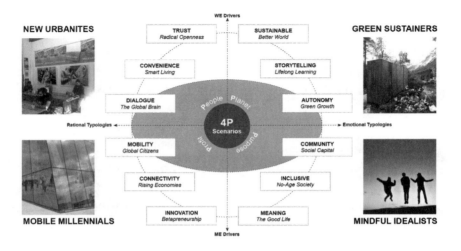

FIGURE 2 – Consumer Mindset Map projecting 2030+: Snapshot of tomorrow's people showing four core scenarios.
SOURCE: *Kjaer Global*

Factoring in People and Planet

A core futures discussion focuses on how to move from a waste-based model to a **repair and regenerate** model. Here research suggests that sustainability narratives need an urgent makeover. A survey by the World Economic Forum found that only 28 percent of people in the U.S. know what terms like **environmentally friendly** and **green** actually mean and only 44 percent trust these claims from big brands.[105]

Cutting through choice overload is a major challenge, as we see a preference for simple and meaningful products and services that improve our wellbeing and sustain our planet. New models that address current unsustainable consumption include the circular economy (CE) – already bringing together organizations and innovators globally to create products and services that enshrine the principles of **reuse and remake** at the initial design and development stage.[106]

Balancing Profit with Purpose

Major societal and sustainability challenges must be considered when thinking about future consumption patterns; these include hyper-urbanization, mass-mobility, global warming, ageing populations, health challenges, and – most pressing of all – wealth inequalities. To engage with these issues, organizations must consider a much wider circle of stakeholders. By adopting a **glocal** approach, global brands can reconnect with their stakeholders in a local context while contributing to the ecosystems within which they operate. Many visionary entrepreneurs, including co-founder of Whole Foods Market John Mackey[107] and Patagonia founder Yvon Chouinard, argue that there is plenty of data to prove that conscious businesses outperform traditionally run companies in the long run, while also creating value on multiple levels. Business models delivering products and services to match real needs, while considering the 4Ps, will be nurtured through **betapreneurship**, using agility and real-time responsiveness to ensure a more mindful approach to doing business.

A Betterness Consumption Paradigm

Increasingly people will be asking, "How does this product make me feel?" , "How is it made and how will it impact the environment?" Business must start exploring the impact of the products and services they offer beyond face value, and this means more equal partnerships with their stakeholders to be a force for good. Aiming for **betterness** participation and experiences will be key in the future. A recent study by psychologists Leaf Van Boven and Thomas Gilovich verifies this, indicating two key principles of consumption: first, doing things makes people happier than having things; second, anticipation of an experience is more exciting than anticipation of a material purchase – regardless of the price of the acquisition.[108]

Making purpose a guiding principle in our leadership models fosters a brand proposition where sustainability and inclusiveness become the foundation of any future proof strategy. It is clear that "good life aspirations" are central to tomorrow's lifestyle choices (figure 3) and successful brands will be those that understand and balance the 4Ps, incorporating long-term social, emotional, and economic value into product and service development.

20TH CENTURY	21ST CENTURY

HYPER CONSUMPTION	MEANINGFUL CONSUMPTION
Ego	Community
Meconomincs	Weconomincs
Ownership & Credit	Access & Sharing
Social Status	Reputation
Unsustainable	Sustainable
Capital P = Profit	Capital P = Purpose

FIGURE 3 – Tomorrow's lifestyle choices:
We are moving from **Meconomics** to **Weconomics**.
SOURCE: *Kjaer Global.*

For organizations, there are three clear issues that need to be addressed now in order to engage successfully with tomorrow's consumers:

- *How well do we know the current and likely future motivations of existing and potential audiences?*
- *As an organization, how well does our actual performance and behavior align with our purpose and brand promise?*
- *How are we embedding sustainability and authenticity as central goals in all our product or service strategies – how engaged are internal stakeholders in the ongoing process of improvement?*

Generation Z in the Workforce

By Anne Boysen

Generation Z represent over 25 percent of the population in 2015 and will soon start entering the workforce, how can business and society prepare for them?

This article looks at various macro trends that are shaping the demographic makeup of Generation Z. I examine the attitudes, preferences, and expectations that this group of highly diverse youngsters will have in common and the possible implications for their employers.

What constitutes Generation Z?

There is always some debate about when each generational cohort starts and ends. For the purposes of this article, I use the following definitions:

- Builders 1925-45
- Baby Boomers 1946-64
- Generation X 1965-79
- Generation Y 1980-94

Then it becomes more complex. From surveys and reports to think pieces and their acerbic comment sections, it's clear that we are far from a universal agreement on when generation Z was first conceived.

Were they born in the mid-nineties or mid-noughties? What should they be called?

It doesn't help that we are dealing with two different classification systems that are often used interchangeably. In the mid-nineties, the popular publication AdAge suggested that the transition between generation Y and Z happened around 1995, a cut-off point which was subsequently considered arbitrary and not cohesive with any underlying theory of social change. The authors behind the Millennial moniker, historians William Strauss and Neil Howe on the other hand foresaw a "crisis era" developing around the mid-2000s, which would kick off a new generational zeitgeist.[109] Following the dot-com bust, terrorist attacks and financial collapse of 2008, it became clear that a cascade of crisis-related events had indeed catapulted us into a new era that would most likely bring on a new generational zeitgeist almost a decade after Ad Age had suggested.

Unable to agree on precise timescales, many dismiss generational theories altogether. While this article does not aspire to settle the debate, the reader should be aware of the controversy – so as not to be confused by the current cacophony of generational labels and eras. This article chooses to use a cut-off point of 1995 between generation Y and Z – not because it is the most accurate – but because it is the most frequently used. Moreover, data is more readily available for this category. While data from the west is more easily obtainable, special efforts have been made to include globally representative data.

The family environment

Generation Z has come of age during a time when over-zealous and interventionist parental styles have been characterized in our modern vernacular through terms like **helicopter parenting**, **curling parenting**, and **tiger moms**. A news cycle that feeds on fear has convinced many parents that an array of horrific threat lurks around the corner. This has significantly reduced the amount of free outdoor play for Millennial and Generation Z children. The truth is that the world is safer today than it has ever been.[110] This long-neglected truth is finally starting to seep into the mainstream, along with the idea that excessive parental protectiveness probably comes with its own costs. As a result, the younger crop of parents tends to intentionally raise their children differently from how they themselves were reared.

Rather than relying on experts and grandmothers, young parents turn to social networks and friends. This leads to more nuanced advice enabled by modern information technology. We might witness more parents who shoot for simply being "good enough". The ultra-devout parent who waits impatiently outside the dean's office to profess their snowflake's special brand is headed for the comics. So too is the sports-obsessed parent who rants uncontrollably from the sidelines at their kids' soccer games. This shift in parenting attitudes could reinforce the move away from the blue-sky aspirations that were so emblematic of the Millennials' childhoods towards more pragmatic goal setting.

A web of global peers and strangers

Generation Z will live their most productive years during a global population peak. At the same time, the economic gap between OECD and non-OECD countries is expected to narrow. However, while economic growth decreases the income gap between countries, it is gradually increasing the income discrepancies within them. This economic globalization leads to new cultural ties between geographically remote regions, while geographically closer sub-regions grow apart culturally, hence the growing urban-rural divide in many countries. A middle class teenager in London might feel that she has much in common with a teenager in Sao Paulo while feeling estranged from another teen just a few boroughs away. We can expect these new geographical alignments to have consequences for how young people chose to study, work, collaborate, and compete.

Most forecasts and scenarios suggest global economic power will shift toward Asia, which is affecting the distribution of work in the global knowledge economy. By 2020, globally around 40 percent of Generation Z with higher education will be from China or India. This is due to those countries having a larger share of the youth population and also to competitive factors.[111] Emerging economies are experiencing more rapid growth than the west, so we should expect to see a shift from manufacturing jobs to more high tech, high skilled employment opportunities in those countries. Moreover, women – in these countries in particular – are outnumbering men in the educational arena and are choosing fields of study that will be in high demand in the coming decades, such as those in science, technology, engineering, and mathematics (STEM).

Peak education in the West

Surprisingly, while tertiary education should continue to rise in most BRIC countries, higher education might level off and even decline with Generation Z in some western countries. There are several reasons for this.

Teens and tweens are developing their societal awareness at a time when many white collar jobs seem not to pay off. During the last recession they saw their parents and older siblings be laid off in droves or demoted to positions that they are over-educated for. The sluggish world economy has put a damper on recruitment and prevented advancement opportunities for younger generations, as Baby Boomers hold on to their senior positions and postpones retirement. Consequently, younger generations are likely to perceive education as a less than safe investment.

Furthermore, potential employers are increasingly outspoken about a growing skills gap which they believe is caused by outdated educational systems which fail to fill workplace needs. In response, traditional education models and approaches are being overturned. For example, while U.S. college tuition charges rose by almost 80 percent more than cost increases in any other sector between August 2003 and August 2013[112] – access to knowledge in the internet age is nearly ubiquitous and cost-free. Consequently, formal education's traditional stamp of knowledge authority is fading. Into this vacuum emerge Silicon Valley tycoons like Peter Thiel – who encourages students to drop out of college to start entrepreneurial careers.[113] While this strategy is undoubtedly risky for most startup-hopefuls, the intervention has engendered social debates which embolden our youngest generation to consider career alternatives outside the well beaten path of academia.

In 2030 we are likely to see an increasingly diversely educated workforce – encompassing entrepreneurs who developed their own brands of expertise by means of various **hacker approaches,** along with apprenticeships, online courses, and peer-to-peer arrangements. In this emerging skills universe, traditional university degrees could become a thing of the past, or a rare symbol of exclusivity for the upper class – similar to designer brands and luxury cars. This is partly due to a trend where today's affluent parents often display their social rank through the Ivy League status of their heirs.

Entrepreneurial world-savers

Millennials are often believed to be our most entrepreneurial generation. Survey data reveal that they might, in fact, be the most risk averse and least entrepreneurial when compared to Boomers and Generation X. On the other hand, 61 percent of Generation Z say they would rather be an entrepreneur than an employee after college.[114] While it remains to be seen if this attitude will persist as they encounter the challenges associated with adult life, the aforementioned educational trends suggest that we could expect to see a deluge of start-ups and freelancers in the next decade.

If history is any guide, then some start-up ventures will succeed but most will fail. While the social stigma around business failure is declining, the monetary aspects could be harder to handle than ever before. At the time of writing, new tech start-ups are experiencing a surge of venture capital investments, but rumors that many of these tech enterprises might be overvalued could burst the capital bubble, possibly affecting the volume of seed money available to future start-ups. With technology that permits competitors to scale globally, the idea of market share gives way to market dominance. The result is an unsustainable global entrepreneurial dynamic with few winners and many losers.

Real or perceived risk could abate Generation Z's interest in going solo and convince them to exercise their entrepreneurial spirits as

intrapeneurs in large companies instead. Younger generations also tend to be favorable to governmental subsidies and industrial clusters that can help absorb some of these risks and provide economic and social support for solo entrepreneurs. Generation Z's financial pragmatism and relatively risk-averse flavor suggest that they will be more open to use political means to level the playing field or provide better social security. This could be one reason why American Generation Z teenagers are more likely to support universal healthcare than any other generation before them.[115] [116] We should also not be surprised if Generation Z voters in many countries put pressure on legislators to introduce basic guaranteed incomes.

A strengthened healthcare system means more than just getting treatment when you're sick. It also provides jobs. As Boomers age, degrees and certificates in gerontology will be in high demand even as we start outsourcing more functions to medical technology. One issue is privacy concerns, in which health data is particularly vulnerable. Furthermore, the human aspects of health care are difficult to robotize – but not impossible. For example, Paro – the robotic companion seal – has taken off in Japan, comforting the elderly in lieu of health care personnel. Skeptics are concerned an important human component will disappear from healthcare should computerized solutions take over. Professor Sherry Turkle at MIT researches human-robot relationships, and claims that despite our growing tolerance for substituting human emotional relations with robots, these relationships are deceptive.[117]

Technology in the workplace

While older generations may recoil at the idea of emotional robotization, it is possible that younger generations will find this more natural. Also called "Digital Natives", Generation Z has grown up in the constant presence of interactive screens and digital personal assistants. Surprisingly they confess a preference for face-to-face interaction,[118] but it is quite likely that they will at least tolerate substituting physical presence with digital interfaces better than past generations. A casual attitude towards blurring the lines between physical and digital will also influence their workplace behaviors and expectations. More cloud based work means that Generation Z will expect to work anyhow, anywhere, anytime. Just as brick and mortar schools disintegrate with shifting attitudes toward education, so too could workplaces.

As retiring Boomers start vacating jobs to younger generations, Generation Z may experience greater demand and start dictating their desired working conditions more than employers experienced with dutiful Generation Xers and opportunity-pinched Millennials. Generation Z might expect to report to work on their own preferences, working on a project basis rather than by the hour. Employers who provide engaging work tasks will gain from these arrangements, especially since they can spur serendipitous encounters in creative communities and co-working arrangements, which are hard to replicate in office environments.

When work is no longer a physical place, **bring-your-own-device** and **find your own nook** could become the new normal under the imperative of lean business management. Alas, job seekers' ability to absorb what used to be considered corporate expenses could exacerbate the new class divides we are already starting to see in a digital reputation economy – adding to a growing skills gap. The most attractive workers will be those who can take on these expenses or who possess qualities that let them negotiate better work agreements.

Conclusion

Will Generation Z become paralyzed by the misgivings of a troubled future they cannot create, but only mend? Or will their spirited entrepreneurialism circumvent business and society and kindle new types of sustainable and equitable prosperity? Efforts to collect comprehensive data on Generation Z are just beginning, so we are only starting to see the possible contours of our youngest generation's collective personality. Inferring singular traits about populations the size of whole generations is no small feat. The attributes sketched out in this chapter are at best suggestive. Even in the wake of big data, longitudinal observations are costly to collect and the internal variations within generations are significant. We can at best brush with broad strokes. But can we afford not to try to understand our successors because our methods are imperfect?

The evolution of Generation Z raises some critical questions for business:

- *How does your organization currently go about understanding and addressing the needs of different generations in the workforce?*
- *What are the implications of the needs and expectations of Generation Z for recruitment, training and development, leadership, remuneration and rewards?*
- *What are the challenges of serving the growing Generation Z customer base?*

Education 2025 – Building a Generation of Problem Solvers

By Alberto Rizzoli

How might schools and learning evolve with technology?

A new education agenda

The future promises widespread automation, dawning and dying industries, and an overall faster rate of change. So what skills will young people need to help them navigate an uncertain future and a life expectancy of 100 years or more?

In this chapter I explore the future of education in public and state schools (ages five to 18). A future where experience becomes the new definition of knowledge and teaching methods will need to be transformed, and where third-party education companies could propel the global delivery of education. The exponential growth of online learning and the transformation of school environments will work together to develop what is potentially going to be the most impactful generation of young persons in human history. Whether you are an entrepreneur, educator or technologist, you can take part in building this future today.

Meet the teachers

Let's walk into a classroom of ten year old students in the year 2025. I believe two main characters will lead the teaching efforts: a teacher who oversees the educational and social development of children and an artificial intelligence (AI).

The AI will reside in the children's digital devices, acting as the classroom's dictionary, calculator, bespoke tutor, and personal librarian. Great teachers, sometimes called **"rockstar teachers"**, are those who inspire students to achieve greatness, understand their own potential, and ultimately weigh in as an invaluable factor to their success.[119] Ten years from now I think we will see demand for inspirational teachers soar, while assessment and evaluation will mostly be outsourceable to an intelligent assistant or automated applications. This new relationship format will bring far-reaching changes to a student's development, by reclassifying teachers as friendly coaches and sources of advice, and liberating them from being perceived as subjective, draconian evaluators.[120] [121]

The machine assistant will act as a Socratic advisor, aware of each student's progress. Present both within computers, and in some cases robotic staff, it will be responsible for evaluating the now mostly-digital school work. It will understand an individual's points of strength, weaknesses, and progress through the use of machine learning. Assessment will be made on an international scale, as happens today in all-digital schools, granting an overview of – and comparison to – worldwide education standards. This last point may initially receive opposition from schools, but should eventually succeed once its benefits become evident in online education.

Learning methods during knowledge abundance

In the past decade Finland has consistently received the highest PISA (Program for International Student Assessment) score, an international measure of scholastic performance, among western countries[122] – distinguishing itself thanks to motivated, supportive teachers and highly autonomous schools.[123] [124] [125] One characteristic of Finnish education stands out with the potential to become a widespread standard – a focus on discovery-based learning. For example, in year five mathematics class after being given a series of problems, the students are asked to **discover the Pythagorean Theorem**. It seems increasingly likely that discovery-based education will be the norm in a future where facts and answers are readily available through digital assistants. Likewise, young students will explore their way through basic chemistry, algebra, economics, retracing the steps of Isaac Newton and Archimedes, and gaining reasoning skills and academic confidence. In order to attain this, AI assistants will apply the Socratic Method in teaching, inviting learners to explore subjects to reach answers rather than providing them directly.

Revolutionizing tools

The worldwide education app market was estimated to have grown from $640 million in 2009 to $1.46 billion in 2014, with growth expected to continue accelerating.[126] This market – estimated to be worth $1.8 billion today in 2015[127] is propelled by developing nations – where education apps receive 17% more downloads per mobile device than in Europe or the U.S.[128] The learning management system market, which lays the foundations for the spread of e-learning in schools, exceeded growth forecasts from $1.9 billion in 2013, a value estimated only one year prior by Bersin and Associates,[129] to $2.25 billion.[130] This explosive growth happened thanks to widespread adoption of cloud infrastructure, allowing much faster implementation of digital tools and significant savings.[131] This presents an opportunity for entrepreneurs to enter the education market without the assistance of publishers and distributors, while creating a multi-million dollar impact.

By 2025, we can expect an agile startup environment in the creation of educational tools, overcoming the slow-paced publishing industry. Not every tool will be digital, neither will we always substitute painting with touch screen gestures. The rapidly growing range of tools will however, be data-driven and able to learn from student input to create **customized coached experiences**. Some apps are already capable of this today.

Two factors will help these tools transform education: big data and gamification. By 2025, augmented reality in online learning could be so immersive that in many cases it will substitute real experiences due to superior quality and lower costs. Big data will drive personal development and allow the education app ecosystem to improve based on evidence. Also, in a future of abundance where education is not necessary for survival, it is crucial that young people understand the effect that it will have on their lives later on. Forecasting analysis will be applied to learning efforts to show what students can achieve if they succeed. Software could show a 16 year old what he could be in his 30's if he obtains an A grade in mathematics and digitally project his image as a healthy person in a sports car or on a luxurious holiday. Allowing the student to then view the same predicted individual if he failed the course will likely improve his results.

Will online education take over?

By 2020, many high quality fee-paying schools could be offering virtual reality attendance, either for those who live too far away to attend or for low-income learners. Meanwhile, simulation software is being built today for practical activities like laboratory work, making physical schools less necessary. Nevertheless, staying home won't be enough to provide future young students with the appropriate mindset to succeed. Healthy social, sexual and intimate relationships for example, cannot be experienced and developed purely through an online learning environment.

Relationship building, teamwork, negotiation and conflict resolution are just some of the experiences that should not be acquired solely online. Students will need to be around other people for a comprehensive social and academic education. However, this does not mean that today's school systems are the solution. A worldwide phenomenon of independent study groups, especially prevalent in developing countries, could take advantage of online instruments to create the education equivalent of a startup environment, motivated by worldwide rankings and opportunities for funding.

The trend of decentralization will therefore also affect schools.

Whether it is crowd funded independent start-up academies, or schools gaining greater autonomy through technology. A market-place of educational gamified experiences, tools, and simulations will accelerate the spread of high quality learning. Tomorrow's student will be a creative problem solver, raised to pursue great challenges, and confident that solutions are within their reach.

What are the critical questions that businesses, educators and individuals should consider?

- *As an entrepreneur or business, how can you tap into the rapidly growing app market that could disrupt traditional textbook education through gaming, virtual reality, and interactive digital tools?*
- *As an educator, how do you plan to inspire and retain the respect and attention of your students in an increasingly digital classroom environment, and are you ready to assume greater autonomy over national curricula?*
- *As an individual, how can you ensure that your children, grandchildren, or young relatives are competitively educated in a future where high-quality learning is heavily democratized?*

The Future of Personal Income and Expenses

By Michael Nuschke

How might increasing life spans and technological advances impact the individual wallet?

In any economic system, the finances of the individual or consumer are a key driver. This chapter takes a brief look at the possible dramatic impacts of rising life expectancy and accelerating technologies on personal finances, both income and expenses.

Longevity, disruptive technology and personal finances

Two major themes will have significant impacts on the future of personal income and expenses; an increase in longevity (healthy life extension) and widespread technological disruption. Having awareness of how these two key factors will impact an individual's finances will be crucial for individuals and the businesses that serve and employ them. Let's consider the key impacts for both of these major drivers of changes.

Eight key impacts for personal finances from increased longevity

A wide and ever-increasing range of emerging and expected therapies, drugs, and devices will slow and eventually reverse aging. Biology, as a physical system, can and is being re-engineered or reprogrammed (i.e. DNA can be seen as our human reprogrammable software) towards longer and healthier outcomes. With continued advances in biotechnology, medical devices, genetic therapies, nanotechnology, and other related developments, widely available anti-aging interventions are likely within ten to twenty years.[132] I expect these to impact personal finances in eight critical ways:

- *Cutbacks in pension income:* Rising life expectancy for retirees along with challenging investment markets will pose major threats to pension sustainability.

- *Retirement savings shortfalls:* Funding an extended retirement will make many rethink the timing or even the whole idea of retirement.

- *Extra medical expenses:* As new medical treatments are developed that promise mental and physical restoration and early detection, the associated increased level of personal healthcare expenditure will tap the savings of individuals. The speed of innovation in new medical treatments will produce a lag in those being covered by medical plans. Thus a higher percentage of medical expenses will need to be funded out of our pockets.

- *The mushrooming of medical tourism:* Medical and technological innovations reach across borders. Many new treatments to restore and enhance health will first become available outside one's home country. This could become a major new expense category for a significant percentage of the population.

- *Spending our kids' inheritance - squashing expectations of "inheritances as a retirement plan":* Life extension therapies could extend the lives of Baby Boomers (born 1946-64) and even those aged 70 or more today (the so-called "Builder Generation") – giving them more years to spend more of their estate. Increasingly, the expectation and reality of receiving an inheritance will fade away.

- *Greater awareness and rejection of environmental toxins:* Longer life spans mean greater potential damage to health from the gradual buildup of toxins. More and more, the ingesting of pollutants, pesticides, and other contaminants in our water and food chains will be rejected in favor of organic food sources. Switching to organic and pure sources of nutrition could easily add 10 to 30 percent to food costs.

- *Spending more for longer:* Longer and healthier lives will fuel increased spending on adult education, travel, and entertainment.

- *Multigenerational families plus income stagnation:* Income stagnation for Generation-X (1965-79), Generation-Y (1980-94) and the Millennials (1995-today) will result in increasing demands on boomer parents. Already in the U.S. over 30 percent of Baby Boomers provide financial support to their children.

Eight impacts on personal finances from technological disruption

Developments in exponentially growing technologies will induce disruption in many areas of the economy. Many of these developments will have out-of-pocket impacts on individual consumers. Here I highlight eight of the most critical impact points:

- *Continued ultra-low interest rates:* Technology driven price deflation for goods and services will dampen economic growth potential and act to keep prices and inflation low. In turn, investment returns on interest rate sensitive investments will continue to be challenged.

- *Dividend income disruption:* Many dividend paying stocks will be challenged to maintain their payouts as their business is undercut by technologically superior competitors. For example, electrical utility stocks (and bonds) being disrupted by solar and alternative energy providers.[133]

- *Technological unemployment:* Large job losses from human roles being replaced by advances in robotics and coming years. While many new jobs and industries may arise, there is considerable evidence that job losses will far exceed job creation.[134]

- *Universal guaranteed income (UGI):* One well supported

response to dealing with future technological unemployment is to provide everyone with a guaranteed base income. How this could be funded is under debate, but if the consumer cost-of-living drops as some expect (see below) UGI may be affordable.

- **Investment in continual learning:** Technological acceleration will produce a demand for retraining in more advanced areas. Career and life coaching will mushroom. Educational costs will become a growing part of the worker's budget.

- **New must-have gadgets:** We are already used to how quickly consumers want an updated model of smart phones, but this escalation is just the beginning. Innovations in hard-to-resist technological gadgets will expand this personal expense category. Virtual reality, augmented reality, digital assistants, and wearable medical technology will increasingly strain the pocket books of those riding the technology wave.

- **Technologies will drive consumer costs lower:** By 2020, 3D printing capabilities will include nearly all manufactured items, including printing your own electronics, pharmaceuticals, household items, and clothing. As manufactured goods ride the IT exponential impacts of **cheaper-faster-better-smaller**, this could become a very significant development in terms of personal finances.

- **Cost of Housing:** Ten thousand dollar houses? 3D printing is already being used in the construction of houses and industrial buildings. Again, as cheaper-faster-better-smaller impacts this area (currently the largest consumer expense category), other new expenditures may become affordable.

Consumers to take on more personal responsibility for financial security

As we can see from this brief review, the two-fold forces of increased longevity and technological disruption will reshape the landscape of the consumer's income and expenses. While the makeup of the individual's expenditures has always been in gradual flux, the speed of technological disruption and medical advances will bring an unprecedented acceleration in these changes. The ability of govern-ments and institutions to respond in a timely fashion will likely lag the speed of change – thereby forcing individuals to take more responsibility in order to survive and hopefully thrive in the extraor-dinary future ahead.

What other questions are posed by this review?

- *How might the timing of these consumer cash flow changes impact our discretionary income?*
- *What are the scenarios for how technological unemployment and the trend for retirees to want keep working play out?*
- *Which major industries will be disrupted first by new technology driven start-ups?*

The Future Potential of Consciousness in Business

By Rishi Haldanya

How might growing interest in the field of consciousness influence the future of business?

This article explains why entrepreneurs and business leaders should follow advances in consciousness, for themselves and their teams, and highlights how working with human consciousness could create opportunities across a growing number of sectors.

Unlocking the power of consciousness

There is a growing understanding that tapping into human consciousness is all about unlocking the exponentially more powerful subconscious mind. In some respect this parallels the growing interests in technologies and businesses that have the capacity to grow exponentially. Consciousness has traditionally been left to philosophers pondering the nature of things. However, such a phenomena at the core of who we are was bound to exert a greater influence over time. There is a growing body of research that demonstrates the value of tapping into consciousness through practices such as mindfulness meditation. Just as it permeates our being it permeates our lives. Consciousness will increasingly be seen as cutting edge science that can unlock human potential and hence be of critical important to business. Let's examine some of the potential implications and applications of bringing consciousness practices into business and the workplace.

Workplace implications – the value of "being in the zone"

Personal development is critical to the effective leader or entrepreneur. Consciousness practices such as meditation have been demonstrated to lead to better sleep and improvements in creativity, focus, motivation, memory, and learning. Enabling employees to harness their conscious power and thus increase their focus could help counter the estimated two hours lost each working day recovering from distractions.[135] Practices such as Yoga Nidra, Meditation, and Mindfulness which help people do this, could dramatically transform the working day and are increasingly being used by businesses.[136]

There is also growing interest in the idea of getting into a state of consciousness know as **Flow**. This essentially means focusing our energy and attention to enable complete absorption in tasks. Again this has been demonstrated to yield significant benefits in terms of creativity, clarity, and productivity. Flow is the ideal state any ambitious entrepreneur or leader wants for themselves and their teams in order for them to be truly productive.[137]

Sector opportunities

Tapping into human consciousness could have a range of applications. At one level the holy grail of artificial intelligence (AI) is to develop systems that can replicate and potentially enhance human consciousness. The application of AI could help create the ultimate internet search engine which shows us whatever is mostly closely aligned with our conscious minds.

The gaming industry is projected to be worth $100 billion by 2017.[138] One of the goals of developers is to be able to understand and then alter human consciousness through virtual reality. Furthermore, gamification is a major trend in education technology, a sector which is aiming to disrupt learning itself and recently attracting a milestone $2 billion investment.[139] A deeper understanding of consciousness would allow the development of ever-more powerful and effective learning solutions that worked on both the conscious and sub-conscious level.

Another major opportunity is presented by the world's largest industry – Healthcare. For example, there is clear value in knowing the level of consciousness of patients in a coma, on an operating table, or in recovery from major trauma. There is also a growing focus on the economic benefits of enhancing our mental, physical, emotional, even spiritual wellbeing, individually and as a society. Hence many doctors are now recommending consciousness practices as alternatives to drug treatment. Billions are also spent on the **war on drugs**[140] – addressing a market of people who want to alter our conscious experience through chemical means. A more natural approach to achieving such heightened consciousness could have beneficial social and economic effects for the individual, police forces, drug treatment services, and society as a whole.

It is clear that harnessing consciousness has wide ranging implications and benefits already. With our growing understanding of the field, the opportunities for positive impact look set to increase. Its influence cannot be ignored and philosophies that propound the quest for enlightenment, clearly state the importance of being aware of happenings in this world. Surely this is a trait every entrepreneur should strive for.

What are the questions for business that these insights to consciousness inform?

- *What is our attitude to bringing consciousness practices into the organization?*
- *How could we overcome potential cynicism at the introduction of such practices?*
- *What commercial opportunities could be created by the growing interest in tapping and altering human consciousness?*

The Future Derives From Place Choices

By Stephen Roulac

What are the critical factors that will drive future place choice and what impact could they have on individuals and organizations?

The power of place

It used to be that most people had very little choice about their physical place, their social place, their economic place, or their work place. More and more, people can now choose where they live and aspirations for social, economic, and professional standing of their own making.

Place choice changes everything, introducing dynamism and discontinuity in every aspect of society, culture, and institutions; transforming the lives of individuals and enterprises; and changing places, both subtlety and profoundly. The intersection of seven critical technologies, preferences and values, rules, and regulations shape, define, and realign the character of our places and therefore the quality of our lives. This chapter explores the consequences — examining the rewards, risks, opportunities, and threats resulting from of how technology defines the possible, culture shapes the desired, and rules prescribe the possible.

Place as a growing locus of attention

Our choices profoundly change people, society, culture, commerce, and places themselves. With choice has come more interaction and larger scale social, political, and commercial focus and organization around the concept of place.

Places are one of the three critical essentials of life, along with work and relationships. They are changing as dramatically now as ever before. Their future has profound ripple effects, as it makes for different work and different relationships. The capacity to make more choices about places leads to the capacity to make more choices about work and relationships. So, to understand the future of work and relationships, you must understand the future of places.

From the 17th century to the 21st, place choice has been the most significant differentiation of individuals' opportunities, social structure, and economic opportunities. This decision is driven by technology advances, hence understanding and acceptance of these developments and their implications is fundamental to comprehending future choices.

Comprehending places in the future will be ever more critical because they are becoming more complex, more dynamic, more functional, and multi-cultural. They are also becoming more accountable with the advent of video observation technology, coupled with roving monitors. For example, the casual observer who happens to capture with a cell phone a crucial incident that leads to criminal indictment for conduct that in earlier times might go undetected.

Most of us are innocent of how the prospects for and consequences of innovation may change, transform—even render irrelevant—our places. Presuming that they somehow are exempt from the forces of creative destruction and disruptive innovation can be precarious. Their future will derive from the appeal to those who choose where to live, work, shop, build businesses, create jobs, and invest capital. In the future, even more so than in the past, those that are the most appealing and conducive to people's desired lifestyles shall thrive, while the least appealing may not survive.

For example, Detroit was one of the largest, and most powerful and prominent—even dominant—metros. But no more. It became the victim of creative destruction, losing its leadership position. Detroit and its car-dependent economy have deteriorated from leadership to laggard. In contrast, San Francisco has thrived, especially its car economy culture—with Tesla being one of the most successful IPOs in recent times—and Uber commanding a record valuation. This focus on individuals and cars is key. As community and connection become ever-more important, the number of tools to enable access, way finding, and enhanced user experiences increases. With car growth outpacing parking spaces, applications such as ParkNav—applying predictive analytics to find parking spots—help to improve utilization and experience.

In the future, a significant the expansion of car services could reduce car ownership – with a reduction of the 70 percent of urban areas currently devoted to streets and parking. This would realign spatial patterns, property values, and regional economic status. These technology advances transform places, realigning the property process in the context of the supply chain and value chain, thereby altering roles, stature, and prosperity.

Future place choices – Seven primary technologies

Throughout history – and for the foreseeable future – seven primary technologies define "the possible" for our places, society's connection to them and the resulting creation and use of properties. Collectively and individually, these TICMELM (Transportation, Information, Communications, Making, Energy (power), Learning, Money) technologies enable and facilitate the resulting choices and experiences. Concurrently, in their more advanced forms, these TICMELM technologies are also substitutes for the need for property and offer alternative forms of place experience. Let's examine some of the ways these seven primary technologies define place and property choices and experiences:

- *Transportation* – The means by which people, materials, and products are moved within and between locations has a major impact upon their accessibility, appeal, and value.

- *Information* – The means by which information is captured, stored, disseminated, and accessed influences place experiences, property functions of and our ability to work in and between multiple locations.
- *Communications* – Extending the reach of messages and the span of connections has profound implications on the role, appeal, and therefore value of different property locations.
- *Making* – The technologies and inventive applications that shape and construct materials, products, properties, and machines, determine our experiences of properties and places. Advances in making technologies (for example 3D printing)—specifically facilitate design ingenuity—can substitute automation and machine enabled function and performance for human labor in assembling enormous structures.
- *Energy* – The means to provide light, heat, cooling, and move people and goods between locations can transform the experience of places and the property function.
- *Learning* – The mechanisms by which we capture, transfer, and record knowledge are fundamental to societal and economic progress. The ability to transfer knowledge rapidly and freely is having a transformative impact on where we choose to live and work.
- *Money* – Portable currencies and the free flow of money across borders has had a transformational impact on people's mobility. More flexible, creative, and innovative financial products and payments systems also enhance a location's prosperity and the resulting value of local properties.

The TICMELM technology changes clearly have profound implications, defining possibility and establishing the menu of options; our values then determine what is chosen. Values—as expressed in beliefs and attitudes, the sources and manifestations of psychology—determine which of the innovations made possible by technology are favored, adopted, and embraced. TICMELM innovations that are implemented and widely embraced can define, transform and shape the experiences in places.

Technology advances that transform TICMELM can also create and destroy industries and enterprises. Consider in the 19th century a number of American companies thrived distributing ice worldwide, with some 10 million tons of ice being harvested and sold by frozen water companies as of 1880. In Maine, 36 companies operated more than 50 ice houses, with capacity exceeding a million tons. The introduction of refrigeration destroyed their businesses.

Choosing our futures – moving to new places

People will choose to move from their origin to a new destination for two primary reasons: to escape intolerable home conditions; and for the attraction of the new. These two motivating forces are relative and absolute. Very bad absolute conditions may motivate the decision to leave. If existing conditions are generally tolerable, then the extraordinary attraction of a new option might motivate exodus.

Until the 18th century, the vast majority of people had very limited choice. From the 18th century onwards, the role of place choice has increased dramatically. As a result:

- Individuals can make their own life rather than having others decide what it might be.
- In the 17th century and before, local places enjoyed a monopoly position as that was all that people knew, could experience, or consider. With the advent of choice, people could consider alternatives – giving access to more things, and more possibilities.
- The more options that people have to leave, the more this competition motivates places to be accommodating, appealing, and supportive than those in a relative monopoly position.
- Choice enables people to select more attractive locations over less favorable ones.
- The demise of relative monopoly has driven change – with places being influenced both by those who leave and new arrivals.

- Choice introduces competition between places – even if it takes a long time for them to realize it.
- Some recognize the opportunity of choice, while others that do not often see an outflow of people, jobs, companies, and capital.

Prior to place choice, the very concepts of self-determination and democratic governance, which are so fundamental to the vast majority of societies throughout the world in the 21st century, was alien. Because locations were isolated and self-contained, people had few options. Places' destiny, particularly their economies, were largely independent. Benefits that might be derived elsewhere were not even available for consideration. Likewise, the risks or detriments of being exposed to external activities – save for the daunting consequences of military invasion – were similarly limited. Notably, in circumstances with limited competition and choice, individual aspirations were confined to a very narrow range of possible decisions as there was very limited differentiation.

The immigrants arriving in Massachusetts from 1629-1640 became the country's Yankee population—doubling in number every generation for two centuries, increasing to 100,000 by 1700 and to at least one million by 1800, six million by 1900, and nearly 16 million by 1988; all descended from 21,000 original English immigrants. A century ago more than half of the country's population was of British or Irish ancestry, yet today that figure is less than a third. This shift from nearly 100 percent three centuries ago is a striking example on the consequences of the escalating range of choices for people from countries other than Britain.

Can future place choices conquer consequences?
As we plan our futures, for individuals and local governments alike it is important to understand that choice profoundly changes our places and experiences of them in so many ways – evidenced by the way that essential characteristics of society can be very different after choice, compared to before.

These factors include:

Elements	Before Place Choice	After Place Choice
Culture	One/simple	Multi/complex
People	One race	Multi race
Values	Largely common/ homogenous	Divergent/conflicting
Social network	Small, straight forward	Large, complex
Social interactions	Simple, within class	Complex interactions, across classes
Social economic structure	Continuing and stability	Hyper-discontinuity and volatility
Commerce	Agriculture and small crafts	Information and innovative

In this context, Guttenberg's invention of the moveable type printing press has had profound implications. Instead of the storyteller and the audience needing to be together at the same time, the story could be told once and then read by geographically dispersed people at different times.

Future responses to change

Over the last half century, the average U.S. house size increased by over 50 percent, while the number of persons per dwelling decreased, leading to ever larger space per person ratios. With growing populations and construction limits, these patterns should shift, with declining average house sizes and less space per person. People will increasingly need to use their spaces in a smarter and more efficient manner. One of the innovative companies responding to such forces is Roost, a sharing economy new venture considered the Airbnb of storage for personal and commercial purposes.

The continuous rise in the creation, sharing, and consumption of knowledge has led to more insights about, aspirations for, and multi-faceted interactions about and between people and places. The increasing transfer of information and messages has parallel consequences to the growth in transportation of materials, products, and people, facilitating exchange, satisfying wants, rewarding entrepreneurial initiative, and creating wealth.

The analogy between media and transportation goes to the core concept of how transportation and communication technologies both connect and substitute for place. Canals, roads, and highways facilitate the transfer of tangibles, whereas electronic media facilitates the transfer of intangibles. The digitalization of content, replacing the three dimensional with the digitized image, has profound implications for individuals, society, businesses, governments, places, and the relationships between them.

An example comes from The Port Authority of New York and New Jersey[141] which sought to pursue a venture intended to respond to the decline of New York's role as a goods making, processing, and distribution center (connecting and deriving from its shipping dominance). The Port Authority elected to construct the World Trade Center. The structure was envisioned to facilitate the commerce of trade, rather than the physical trade process of moving goods and materials.

One distinctive TICMELM innovative application is the urban utilization of a gondola transit system. The closed cars run on wires suspended between support structures most commonly employed for the movement of people vertically, up a steep incline or slope. These are most often used in skiing locations and to provide access to otherwise difficult to access remote places.

Rio de Janeiro recently implemented a gondola line to facilitate movement and accessibility in the favelas, serving an area that previously had very limited transit access. The system has six stopping points in the Complexo do Alemao, shrinking a 90 minute journey—along very narrow alleys, switchbacks and up and down stairs—to sixteen minutes. The 152 gondola transit system is symbolic because it physically removes the separation between the informal and formal city, making them one.

Our future is the future of our places

With place choice being an ever more important and influential force in society, most people and locations are ill equipped to make informed decisions. To help this process, place type profiles can help individuals' and local governments determine personal place preferences. A critical factor here is the choice of property. Basic human needs for shelter plus economic activity create the need and demand for property. The relationships between places, property, and the economy are symbiotic and interdependent e.g. when the economy in a place is strong, that place and its properties are typically strong. A weakness in any of these three factors can in turn weaken the other two. An understanding of the forces and factors discussed here should help local and national governments in shaping future place strategy and enable individuals to make appropriate place choices.

Three key questions:

- *What factors are most central to your organization's future place choices?*
- *Given the rise of remote working and the globally dispersed nature of talent, how important is the availability of good local housing stock in making your place decisions?*
- *What opportunities could arise for your organization from growing workforce mobility and widespread availability of information and advice on individuals' decisions about place choice?*

Section 4

Social Technologies – How will tomorrow's technologies permeate our everyday lives?

The blurring of boundaries

There is little doubt that accelerating and ever-more impactful advances in science and technology will play an increasingly significant part in our everyday lives. This section highlights how these rapid advances are changing the way we might live and work and the way in which we manage our relationship with technology. A number of chapters also explore the blurring of the boundaries between humans and machines and examine the logical extension of this to the point of emergence of the so-called "technological singularity".

These issues are discussed across eight chapters.

The Future of the Internet (*page 205*) – Rohit Talwar and Alexandra Whittington – describe key forces and factors shaping the next twenty years of the internet and discuss how its role in business and society could evolve.

The Future of Digital Media - The Freexpensive Prerogative (*page 224*) – Yates Buckley explores how we might use intelligent personal agents to integrate our technology ecosystem and manage our personal data.

Mobile 2030: Scenarios for the Role of Mobile Technology in Society (*page 233*) – Alexandra Whittington and Amir Bar present four scenarios exploring how mobile technology could permeate every aspects of our social and professional lives by 2030

The Impact of Wearable Lifestyle Technologies and Gamification on Business and Society *(page 246)* – David Wortley considers the potential impact on personal and corporate health of wearable lifestyle sensor technologies, AI, mobile applications and gaming concepts.

Body-Machine Convergence *(page 255)* – Dr. Ian Pearson journeys to the frontiers of human enhancement, examining how scientific advances could turn the body into a technology platform and blur the boundaries between man and machine

The Rise of Neurosocial Networks – The Prospects for Networking our Brains in the Next 20 Years *(page 265)* – Martin Dinov and Andrew Vladimirov examine the potential developments in and applications of neurotechnologies that could allow people to network at a brain-to-brain level.

Life in 2035: Future Consciousness, Cyborgs and Wisdom *(page 273)* – Victor Vahidi Motti explores how rapid advances in science and technology could disrupt and reformulate our understanding of human capability, wisdom and the nature of work.

The potential for technological singularity and its future impacts on society *(page 281)* – Anish Mohammed explains the technological singularity and the challenges it could create for humanity.

Global Drivers of Change

By April Koury, Iva Lazarova and Rohit Talwar

Eleven key drivers of change illustrate the breadth of the anticipated technological impact.

- ***Evolving Personal Tech Ecosystems*** – The personal technology we use daily has evolved from desktop to luggable, from luggable to portable, from portable to wearable, and we are beginning to see an evolution into embedded / implantable technology. Wearable technology is becoming prevalent in smart watches, intelligent clothing, and personal health trackers like FitBit, while embedded technology now stretches beyond medical necessities like pacemakers and cochlear implants, to subdural microchips that operate lights, doors, and other computers remotely.[142]

- ***The Internet – Increasing Ease of Access and Worldwide Penetration*** – The internet is already a critical part of the operational infrastructure for individuals, businesses, and governments within the developed world. As technology becomes faster, cheaper, and more globally accessible, even individuals in the most remote regions on earth will gain access to the internet. It continues to transform access to services like education, and encourages entrepreneurship by giving people with limited resources the ability to reach the entire world and have unimaginable amounts of information at their fingertips. By

2025, experts forecast that more than 91 percent of people in developed countries and nearly 69 percent of those in emerging economies will be using the internet. The expectation is that we will rise from about three billion users today to up to 7.6 billion over the next decade.

- *The Internet of Things (IoT) / Internet of Everything (IoE) / Internet of Humanity* – The IoT is a further development of the internet, where items are connected to the network and can send and receive data. These everyday objects can communicate with each other and transmit information to people and systems. Everything from street lights to refrigerators to cars is now being connected. In 2015, Gartner estimates that 4.9 billion "things" will be connect to the internet, and by 2020, that number is expected to increase anywhere from 25 billion to 100 billion things.[143]

- *Intelligent Web* – The intelligent web is the evolution of the internet as we know it. Increasingly complex algorithms and artificial intelligence will become smart enough to search web data and draw meaningful inferences. The system will understand spoken questions, gather the relevant information, and form a meaningful answer to inquiries. The intelligent web will transform the way we access information and interact with each other on the web.

- *Virtual Worlds* – Virtual worlds are computer-based, 3D simulated environments where online communities of users can interact with each other. Massively multiplayer online games like World of Warcraft create a fantasy virtual world, whereas the virtual world of Second Life represents the real world. Beyond gaming, virtual worlds are increasingly used for online conferences and meeting spaces for businesses and education.

- *Digital Currencies* – Digital currencies like Bitcoin are an internet-based medium of exchange similar to paper currency, but they are "borderless" and allow for instant transfer between accounts anywhere in the world. The currencies are usually decentralized, controlled by users, outside of any governmental regulatory bodies, and transactions are anonymous.

- **Smart Cities** – Smart cities utilized digital technologies to connect with their citizens, improve overall wellbeing and reduce costs and unnecessary waste. Everyday city objects such as electric grids, roads, sewer systems, buildings and cars will be connected to the internet of everything, enabling object-to-object and people-to-object interactions. The belief is that these connections will open up vast new possibilities for sustainable, healthy communities, safer streets, and economic growth and development. At the same time, there will be push-back from privacy advocates who are concerned about the massive data collection associated with smart cities. Smart city initiatives are being pioneered in Boston, Copenhagen, Dublin, Masdar Abu Dhabi, Rio, and Singapore.

- **Augmented Reality (AR)** – Augmented reality is the process of overlaying objects in the physical world with digitally gen-erated content like maps, video, and sound. Generally, this is accomplished through smartphones or tablets, but advances in wearable devices like Google Glass and Hololens, and research into AR-enabled contact lenses will result in a much more physically integrated AR experience.

- **Virtual Reality (VR)** – Virtual reality uses computer modeling and simulation to generate real and imagined 3D worlds, 3D objects, and even sensations with which people can interact. Oculus VR, makers of the most recognizable VR headsets on the market, believe VR will reshape many fields in the future, including medicine, architecture, education, and business.[144]

- **Human Enhancement** – Human enhancement is defined as any attempt via augmentation to overcome the limitations of our bodies through chemical, genetic, or technological means. Enhancements range from improving mental performance, to boosting physical speed, strength, and stamina. It is predicted that by 2025 humans will have "hacked" every aspects of their bodies, creating a new breed of human 2.0 and 3.0. All of these enhancements will be monitored and managed constantly by a variety of wearable technologies and devices implanted into the body, which will track every vital sign and link directly to personal hand held devices and to monitoring services provided by healthcare providers.

- *Brain-Computer Interfaces (BCI)* – Using EEG signals detected by electrodes attached to the scalp, a BCI system records the brain's electrical activity, and as the user thinks of a certain concept or command, patterns in the EEG are deciphered by machine-learning software. The resulting information enables applications which communicate these commands wirelessly to computers and other objects. A new venture by Braingate hopes to commercialize a wireless device that can be attached to a person's skull and transmit the thought commands of paralyzed patients to various devices in the room.[145]

The Future of the Internet

By Rohit Talwar and Alexandra Whittington

How might the technologies, functionality and governance of the internet evolve – what could this mean for individuals, society, business and government?

Envisaging tomorrow's Internet

Advances in information and communications technology (ICT) are opening up many possible paths to the future of cyberspace as we know it. The resulting visions for tomorrow's Internet vary quite dramatically – on one of the spectrum are the notions of a smart public servant that anticipates and serves our every need while protecting our information fiercely. Somewhere in the middle (depending on your perspective) is the notion of the Web as a synthesized reality which blurs seamlessly with our physical one. At the other extreme lie dystopian visions where our every action is monitored by governments and commercial interests and where we have to trade our privacy in return for access to goods and services. This Chapter discusses the forces and factors shaping the future possible evolution of the Internet and highlights how its role in business and society could evolve over the next twenty years.

Introduction – the internet as a central backbone for the planet

Since the birth of the World Wide Web (WWW) in 1991, the idea of the public internet has become established as central part of life for many in the developed world in particular. There is often confusion between the Internet as the underlying communications infrastructure and the World Wide Web – the globally distributed network of public websites that we access via the Internet.

So what else can we access via the Internet? Estimates suggest that 60 to 90 percent of all traffic on the internet goes to the so called **Dark Web** – also known as the **Deep Web, Deepnet, Invisible Web, Hidden Web, and Dark Internet**. These are publicly accessible sites that have hidden their IP addresses either for privacy, security or illicit reasons. They hide their IP address using encryption tools such as TOR and I2P and the users have to know where to find these sites and use the same encryption tools to gain access. Some argue that the evolution of the Dark Web may drive developments in the public Internet.

Today there are an estimated 3.13 billion public Internet users worldwide and this is projected to rise to 4.7 billion by 2025.[146] [147] We estimate this could reach anywhere from five to seven billion by 2035. Andrew Ellis, professor of optical communications at Aston University, told the Sunday Times that Internet usage in the UK "... is growing so fast, currently at an exponential rate, that, in theory, it could be using all the UK power generation by 2035."[148]

As the Internet becomes increasingly mobile, and the capabilities and speed of the underlying technologies improve, the scale and reach of the internet and World Wide Web of websites that reside on it are expected to grow over that same period. Most experts believe it will be the first truly global infrastructure service – reaching far more people than centralized electricity distribution or public water supplies.

How might the growing scale, functionality, sophistication and intelligence of the internet impact the way we live, how society operates, and the nature of business, government, and the economy? What could a truly multi-sensory internet be like – how would the addition of touch, taste, smell, and direct brain stimulation change our experience of the Web? Can we maintain **net neutrality** with all data being treated equally; will the net remain an open access public good or fall under commercial or governmental control? How will we power tomorrow's Internet and avoid the risk of it draining public energy supplies? What are the implications for privacy, work, jobs, incomes, and social interactions? An exploration of the future of the internet must encompass all of these issues if we are to develop true insight on this phenomenon that is set to become the central nervous system of the planet over the next two decades.

In addressing these issues, we also need to ask ourselves some fundamental questions about the purpose, intent, role, ownership, and control of this increasingly powerful tool that many of us take for granted. What is the Internet, what is it for, what does it do, and should anyone own it? To help address these questions we will draw on three simple but powerful metaphors that describe the critical forces at play here:

- **When Worlds Collide** – the growing sense of urgency and shock arising from the clash between older physical entities and their newer "born digital" challengers.
- **Masters of the Universe** – the notion of emerging entities with boundless ambition, wielding almost mythical power, and displaying heroic leadership in their quest to take on any and every challenge.
- **DNA Evolution** – the rapid technological changes and resulting social shifts that could change the code of life itself.

These forces are driven by a relentless pace of development of the underlying technologies that serve up the Internet and through which we access it. This evolution is also changing our understanding of where the internet "lives". We have already watched computing and Internet access graduate from our desktops to portable and mobile devices. We are now in the phase of wearable access and evolving to one where our devices could increasingly be embedded in our brains and bodies.

On a 10 to 20 year timeframe the notion of devices being grown or grafted into to our bodies is not beyond the realms of possibility given the advances being made in the underlying scientific disciplines. On the short horizon is mass connectivity of everyday objects via the

Internet of Things (IoT) – with projections of anywhere between 50 and 250 billion net-connected objects over the next 20 years. The future of the Internet over the next two decades and beyond is most likely to see a whole new hyperconnected world of networked people, objects, and systems capable of transforming, reframing, and undermining the established norms of business and society.

When Worlds Collide - The internet is becoming the battleground between those born physical and their born digital challengers. There is a fundamental clash of mindset and assumptions here. The former see and conceive the world as physical objects or concepts – people, homes, bank accounts. In contrast, the born digital community views everything as data, with every requirement, problem, or challenge resolvable by finding the right algorithms, with the solutions deliverable via the Web. As a result, they believe that the solution to every problem from education to food shortages and environmental issues can be tackled by applying a digital mindset and deploying the right exponential technologies. The internet is the critical ingredient that enables the scaling up and global co-ordination, management and distribution of solutions.

Masters of the Universe - The companies that provide essential and increasingly universal internet services are reaching across industry and product lines to come up with game-changing solutions. With such profound capacities going forward, the analogy "Masters of the Universe" seems suitable to express a sense that the data and insight being gathered via the Web allows firms like Google, Facebook, and the rest to believe they can do anything.

Critically, they own the user interface and the platforms through which users interact on a daily basis. This enables the providers of popular social media platforms, search engines, and mobile devices to capture far more data about our lifestyles on a daily basis than any retailer, bank, or other service provider can possibly hope to. They own the interface and brand experience for their customers and have a level of customer loyalty that is powering their ambitions. As a result life extension, self-driving automobiles, banking, and healthcare are just some of the sectors that the "Masters of the Universe" view as within reach and prime for dominance and / or disruption.

This group see themselves as both the saviors and the ultimate inheritors of the planet in a winner-takes-all race to conquer a digitally-enabled and cyber-dependent world. As the technology elites continue to throw their hats into the ring, it becomes clear there are few endeavors they will not attempt. CNN columnist Andrew Keen suggests this new class of leadership resembles, "....a pre-industrial cultural economy of patronage determined by the whims of a narrow cultural and economic elite rather than by the democracy of the marketplace."[149]

Mutations in the DNA – As the internet evolves, it seems likely that businesses will favor early identification of opportunities to use it to ensure access to new markets, customers, and relationships. As the internet's functionality expands and the IoT blurs the boundaries between physical and virtual, so we will see continuous growth in the proportion of daily life that is Web-enabled, Web-dependent or Web-embedded. In this environment, accurate market insight and the choice of strategic actions will depend on having a solid grasp of the oncoming waves of technological advances.

An ever-expanding array of technology tools will increasingly define, expand, and enhance the parameters of daily life and the ways in which it could unfold. This shift to the Web is driving the mutation of DNA – how the internet will enable disruptors to change the game within sector after sector rather than playing within the rules. Some of the major mutations in the social and business DNA are gaining ground already and could have explosive impact in the coming decades – a number of such possibilities are explored later in the chapter.

Future internet visions and scenarios

A number of potentially competing views are emerging for how the internet could play out over the next 20 years. The Pew Research Digital Life 2025 project, surveyed over 2,500 experts on the future of the internet.[150] A key outcome was the notion of the internet as a utility that will soon "flow like electricity," being a simple fact of life for which there is little concern or recognition as a separate thing from the machines it runs.[151]

The study outlined 15 predictions that provide a sense of the challenges, risks, trade-offs, and choices that will confront society, governments, and business leaders when considering a technology that runs the risk of fading into the background. The predictions provide a useful framework for understanding the potential breadth and depth of impact:[152]

Functionality and Usage

- Information sharing over the Internet will be so effortlessly interwoven into daily life that it will become invisible, flowing like electricity, often through machine intermediaries.
- The Internet of Things, artificial intelligence (AI) and big data will make people more aware of their world and their own behavior.
- Augmented reality and wearable devices will be implemented to monitor and give quick feedback on daily life, especially in regard to personal health.
- The Internet will become "the Internets" as access, systems and principles are renegotiated.

Societal Impact

- The spread of the Internet will enhance global connectivity, fostering more positive relationships among societies.
- Political awareness and action will be facilitated and more peaceful change, and more public uprisings like the Arab Spring will emerge.
- The spread of the "Ubernet" will diminish the meaning of borders, and new "nations" of those with shared interests may emerge online and exist beyond the capacity of current nation-states to control.
- An Internet-enabled revolution in education will spread more opportunities with less money spent on buildings and teachers.

Emerging Risks

- Dangerous divides between haves and have-nots may expand, resulting in resentment and possible violence.

- Abuses and abusers will 'evolve and scale.' Human nature isn't changing; there's laziness, bullying, stalking, stupidity, pornography, dirty tricks, crime, and the offenders will have new capacity to make life miserable for others.
- Pressured by these changes, governments and corporations will try to assert power – and at times succeed – as they invoke security and cultural norms.

Societal Adaptation

- People will continue – sometimes grudgingly – to make tradeoffs favoring convenience and perceived immediate gains over privacy; and privacy will be something only the upscale will enjoy.
- Humans and their current organizations may not respond quickly enough to challenges presented by complex networks.
- Most people are not yet noticing the profound changes today's communications networks are already bringing about; these networks will be even more disruptive in the future.
- Foresight and accurate predictions can make a difference; "The best way to predict the future is to invent it."

The IoT is emerging as a common feature in most future visions and scenarios. The result of the proliferation of sensors and the embedding of intelligence and connectivity in a range of objects from domestic appliances and clothing to street signs, anywhere from 50 to 250 billion objects could potentially by connected to the internet over the next two decades. The World Economic Forum warns that the IoT: "Will have profound social, political and economic consequences, and increasingly form part of our everyday lives, from the cars we drive and medicines we take, to the jobs we do and the governance systems we live in."[153]

This extreme level of "Hyperconnectivity" would make globalization seem quaint on a comparative scale of impact. The same principles that minimized the Earth's cultural and economic barriers will now do so in a way that engages inanimate objects in the Global

Village. The social and economic impact could be far-reaching across intertwined networks of people, places, processes, transform markets, supply chains, living patterns, and the nature of work.

Microsoft's June 2014 report *Cyberspace 2025: Today's Decisions, Tomorrow's Terrain*[154] seeks to aggregate these diverse drivers and identifies three scenarios for the possible evolution of the internet and the resulting implications – **Plateau, Peak** and **Canyon:**

Plateau – This scenario is characterized by asymmetry. Political, economic, and societal forces both bolster and hinder technological progress and cybersecurity. Some governments have inconsistent policies and standards with varied levels of stakeholder participation and international cooperation, while other governments form clusters of open trade and foreign direct investment (FDI). Some countries are able to leverage technology to advance economic and socioeconomic development, while other countries are left behind technologically, unable to fulfill the potential of ICT. This fragmented and uneven approach to governance and the economy leads to a less than optimal global cybersecurity landscape.

Peak – This scenario is characterized by clear, effective government policies and standards across economies, and strong collaboration between governments to support open trade and promote FDI. This is a scenario of innovation, in which ICT fulfills its potential to strengthen governance models, economies, and societies. The actions of governments, businesses, and societal organizations foster the widespread and rapid adoption of technology. Political, economic, and social support leads to accelerated economic and technology growth and improved global cybersecurity.

Canyon – This scenario is characterized by obstructionist government policies and standards, protectionist stances, and isolation. These significantly restrict trade and FDI and undermine relationships across industrial sectors within countries as well as between countries. In this scenario, economic and technology growth is slower, with limited adoption of ICT and deep failures in cybersecurity.

These and other internet scenarios highlight the multitude of choices and possible paths that could enhance or impair its societal and commercial value. When we go beyond the near-term horizon a number of even more dramatic possibilities start to emerge such as being able to email physical objects, the integration of holographic technology into social interactions, books that feature "sensory fiction", direct connection of our brains to the internet, and the networking of our thoughts and dreams.[155] We are in a phase where the speed of advance is such that developments we think are a hundred years away could be delivered in 20.[156]

The scenarios and future possibilities raise fundamental questions about how customer preferences and product cycles might adjust in response, what our strategies should be, how we evolve business models, and how frequently we will need to update them. What is the most effective way of designing our organizations to respond where 20 years of technology—less than one generation—could drive a century's worth of social change? The ramifications will be immense for consumer profiling, marketing, advertising, and customer relationships.

The quest to make the internet a central life support system

The major players have all embarked on strategies to deepen the penetration of the internet into our everyday lives and into the fabric of commerce and government – thus strengthening our dependency upon it. Eric Schmidt, Executive Chairman of Google, argues the ubiquitous Internet's future will be "part of your presence all the time".[157] Given Google's strategy of branching out into everything from life-extension biology to self-driving cars, AI, robotics, and augmented reality, it is clear to see why it would want the Internet to be part of us all the time.

Interestingly, as the present incarnation of the Web is so woven into ordinary life, Vint Cerf, the "father of the internet" warns of dire consequences once today's open technology yields to more proprietary versions of the internet. He fears a "dark age" if we don't ensure that our collective online store of digital information (pictures, messages, experiences) is transferrable to future iterations of the Internet.[158] If this digital history is lost, the risk is that future generations may view our time on earth (1950-2050, perhaps?) as an empty void.[159] That the Internet will continue to expand and transform is a central tenet and assumption in the Masters of the Universe narrative.

A major focus for these would-be cyber-overlords is making internet access universal. Though it is one of their key talking points, obstacles persist. These firms are undertaking or planning a range of initiatives to extend internet access across the planet through satellites, mobile devices and so called "walled garden" applications which would restrict the access to what the provider chose to offer. While the firms claim they are serving the needs of humanity, other observers suggest this is simply an attempt to lock an ever growing audience into a proprietary version of the Web over which the provider has total control and surveillance.

A Facebook study found that, in the developed world, 76 percent of the population is online, compared to just 29.8 percent in developing countries.[160]

Developed markets are reaching saturation and 2014 saw a declining rate of growth in the number of global internet users for the fourth consecutive year.[161]

Hence, reaching this unconnected 70 per cent is central to future strategy as it would provide access to a further three to five billion potential customers over the next two decades. Is the universality of the internet a fact of life or a narrative imposed on behalf of those who stand to gain from its expansion?

Bitcoin, blockchain, Ethereum and the battle to reclaim the Internet

The Internet, though "free," is still effectively controlled by the companies who control the data. Meanwhile, it is clear that a backlash against the controlling power of the internet elite is taking shape.

Several of the most exciting emerging and anticipated technology breakthroughs will challenge the currently centralized nature of the internet. The cybercurrency Bitcoin brought this in to sharp focus with its decentralized payment mechanism that enabled users to buy and sell goods services via the Bitcoin network, without the need for a central banking system. The most interesting and disruptive aspect of Bitcoin is the underlying use of blockchain technology. This provides a secure mechanism for encoding transactions and a continuously updated distributed public ledger that records them.

A more recent venture called Ethereum builds upon the blockchain concept with a goal of decentralizing the communications, contracts, and transactions that occur in both the physical world and cyberspace.[162]

It provides tools that enable users to program self-activating self-managing **smart contracts**. Some suggest that this could lead to a more secure, transparent, and democratic internet that could outstrip the current one in scale and usage.

Another wave of potential disruption could come from what Cloudflare CEO Matthew Prince calls **The Second Crypto War**: "Companies like Apple, Google, Facebook, and others have acted as a centralized repository of user data that law enforcement could turn to during an investigation. As the second Crypto War heats up, these companies are engineering new ways to lock their users' data away even from legal process."[163]

Next generation technologies driving DNA mutations Connectivity – A technology that could have a major impact on connectivity is The Outernet – the idea of taking connectivity to space via satellite and transmitting data in a fashion analogous to radio transmission rather than wifi.[164]

This is seen as a temporary fix for universal internet access until more permanent infrastructure can be implemented in developing countries and remote areas.[165]

On a completely different scale, light fidelity, or Li-Fi, offers new avenues for highly localized bi-directional data transmission at theoretical speeds of up to 224 Gbps – which compares to theoretical speeds of eight to 1,300 Mbps for wifi transmission today.[166]

As light is blocked by solid objects, like walls, Li-Fi would be limited by physical barriers, providing a more individualized, localized and hence potentially more secure internet experience.[167]

Products and Services – Advances in machine learning, speech and gesture recognition, and other forms of AI will enable micropersonalization – a personality-centric future technology, where "interfaces will be obsessed with meeting your individual needs."[168]

Futurists John Smart and Ray Kurzweil – Google's Director of Engineering – suggest another highly intimate development could be possible by 2020, whereby our AI "digital twins" or "Cybernetic Friends" might be able to mimic their owners, including sharing the same worldview and expressions, even "hold conversations and have faces".[169][170]

AI is becoming an increasingly important internet technology and will be central to concepts such as the semantic Web (see below), intelligent interfaces, and customer service avatars. It will lead to intelligent agents that do our bidding on the Web, and ever-smarter text, image, and video-based search. Proponents of the technological singularity such as Ray Kurzweil argue that by 2029 we could see AI having advanced to the point where it exceeds human intelligence – a turning point beyond which it then becomes hard to predict what might happen. On route to this point of departure, the expectation is that AI will increasingly enable us to draw on a collective intelligence in the cloud, where all human knowledge will gather.[171]

For a number of the most promising developments to take root, it will be essential to raise society's trust and comfort levels – with both products and providers – around using and transacting with technology. The shift is happening as more and more services become digital-access only and a born digital generation grows up assuming ever-greater penetration of technology. For example, a Pew internet study found the majority (65 percent) of technology experts think that mobile payments will be the norm within five years.[172] The next iteration could see a range of biometric payment options from fingerprint recognition to "paying with a smile" via a facial scan.[173]

Smart Objects – Over the next few years society will become increasingly accustomed to and potentially more accepting of an environment populated by "smart" things, mostly connected through the IoT. We will also see the gradual transformation of inanimate objects (20 billion or more, excluding PCs, tablets, or smartphones) with the ability to know and express information, as well as gather data from their environment—including data about us.[174] In February 2015 Samsung generated considerable debate when it launched a TV with built-in voice recognition, where our conversations could be recorded and shared with third parties. Cisco's projections suggest the Internet of Everything (IoE) has the potential to reach $19 trillion of value by 2022.[175] As the social fabric is redefined by IoT and IoE, the implications – like DNA mutations—will be adaptive and evolutionary. Objects will play a much more active role in daily life.

Work – The DNA or work itself could evolve as a result of the push to connect essentially everything via online workflow software that manages every stage of activity – encompassing "companies, systems, technology, apps, and people."[176] Experts predict workflow software will help to ". . . solve the big data problem, the cloud security problem, and many of the roadblocks facing software technology today".[177] We are laying the foundations for the fully automated enterprise – companies that are effectively a giant distributed rules-based engine with little or no human intervention once the business rules have been defined.

Platforms such as Ethereum are catering for the emergence of these **Decentralized Autonomous Organizations (DAOs)** and **Decentralized Autonomous Corporations (DACs).** This gives rise to the notion of **Corporations as Technology** and the **Fully Automated Business Entity.** In this environment, stakeholder requirements will change. Customer expectations will be different. So will the expectations and needs of those who are still employed or contracted in to perform specific tasks that the DAC cannot as yet automate. What will work become when software enables most of it to be done automatically, almost intuitively? The companies that arrive early at solutions to these major puzzles could thrive and / or face a major potential public backlash at the notion of an entirely digital corporation.

Knowledge Management – On the horizon is the notion of the Semantic Web – increasing the intelligence and intuition of the Web, by annotating its content with self-descriptive information to enable more precise searching based on the context as well as the terms of the user enquiry. Inventor of the World Wide Web Tim Berners-Lee created the concept, foreseeing "... a number of ways in which developers and authors, singly or in collaborations, can use self-descriptions and other techniques so that context-understanding programs can selectively find what users want."[178]

A number of developments are underway in this domain and a range of platforms are beginning to incorporate basic semantic technologies, for example:[179] [180]

- Google's Knowledge Graph – providing information on "entities" such as people and places and the relationship between them.
- Hummingbird – drawing on your geographical location, search history, social activity, and other cues to personalize the search.
- Schema.org – a collaborative, community activity with a mission to create, maintain, and promote schemas (cognitive frameworks to help present and interpret data) and a common vocabulary for the capture and use of structured data on the Internet, on Web pages, in email messages, and beyond.[181]

An interesting aspect of the Semantic Web is that it will require new partnerships involving creative, humanistic, and emotionally intelligent participants to harness its full potential. Some of the most powerful applications are expected to come in domains such as travel and leisure, incorporating richer descriptions and multi-sensory information to enhance the presentation of content to would-be travelers. The sector is expected to embrace semantic search powered by AI and it could become standard in travel customer service by 2020.[182]

Care Giving – The expectation that, technologically speaking, society evolves with each step forward is threatened by the sense that many products and services come at too high a social price. One of the truths casting a harsh light on the future of the internet is that as we become more highly connected, we also become more highly observed. Becoming overly managed by our devices is one concern: the notion of "Big Mother" telling us how many calories to eat, reminding us of important social engagements, and introducing us to possible love interests.[183]

Our smart homes will be capable of conducting surveillance to the point of knowing how strong a batch of coffee should be brewed (based on how late you stayed out last night) or a bracelet that vibrates when the baby wakes in his crib.[184] Now more than ever, we can see how technology can transform social roles and relationships, especially when it mimics the work of caring for others. When roles that were traditionally, inextricably based on human interaction are taken up by machines, there will be a blurring of gender, family and social roles like never before. Again, the DNA comparison seems appropriate—technological change is reshaping who we are.

Home and Family – The home is the prime staging area for many significant developments related to the future of the internet. Semantic, ethnographic and media research studies are becoming critical to developing the next generation of products and services for the home. Some examples include:

- Like-a-Hug: a jacket that inflates every time someone "likes" us on Facebook.[185]
- Facebook's Coffee Table: a smart object that uses real-time speech analysis to pick up keywords from your conversation to pull up corresponding Facebook images.[186]

- Google's Latitude Doorbell: chimes a different tune for each family members when they are nearing home.[187]

A key concern is that most of these smart objects are being developed independently so there is no industry standard for how they work, much less a clear pattern for how they will work together. [188] Samsung has announced plans to invest $100 million in developing IoT solutions, with the goal of setting future systems standards. [189] However, the notion of dominating the IoT rests on several assumptions, the main one being that it's what the public wants at all.

Risks – An all-knowing all-seeing internet informed by networks of smart things opens up a range of possible risks such as the hacking of wireless pacemakers.[190] On a broader scale, concern is rising over the potential expansion of ransomware opportunities and the associated costs of dealing with "malware that seizes data until targets pay up within a certain time frame". [191] The appeal of rewriting societal DNA will extend beyond innovators and their investors, to the criminal element that can see new potential for illicit gain. So far, ransomware is reported to have hit at least one million victims – costing them $1.8 million. Even law enforcement has been impacted—it cost one American police department $500 to regain data seized from official computers.[192]

Clearly these technologies also offer the opportunity to both expand the malicious side of the Dark Web, and – potentially – to control it. Previously the domain of the illicit, the Masters of the Universe are being usurped by government in arriving on the scene. A Pentagon-developed search engine called Memex is claimed to be able access 95% of the information that a Google search can't, reaching "the deep, dark recesses of the World Wide Web".[193]

Recently, the Global Commission on Internet Governance (GCIG) said it anticipates fragmentation in criminals using the Dark Web, making it even more challenging to investigate.[194] Some of the strategies planned by GCIC include monitoring of customer data, semantic analysis to track future illegal activities and "marketplace profiling" to gather information about sellers, users, and goods.[195] Though these measures are meant to catch criminals, it is important to consider how legitimate businesses might get wrapped into the extra surveillance needed to combat crime. Particularly as the IoT is implemented, it will be important to figure out how to keep our "things" (and our most personal information) out of the hands of bad guys, and possibly the good guys too.

Protection of the Common Good – Alongside its murkier inhabitants, the Dark Web also serves as the "unofficial" internet, placing a destabilizing pressure on Masters of the Universe – acting as source of ideas, innovation and developments that lie outside their control. Furthermore, Defense Advanced Research Projects Agency's (DARPA) attempts to track hidden cybercrime rings could yield wider positive outcomes: "Aside from going after human traffickers, terrorists, and other criminals, DARPA says Memex can become particularly useful to government, military, and commercial organizations in finding and organizing 'mission critical' information on the Internet. Emergency responders, for example, can quickly find information on the worst hit areas in the event of a natural disaster."[196]

There are several new perspectives that support the notion of the internet as a **common good**. Tim Berners-Lee argues: "Affordable access to the Internet should be recognized as a human right."[197] It could also be a tool to fight injustice, providing a guarantee of online equality and rights.[198] If used fairly, in ways that enhance social justice, it might become the key technology that emancipates society from living at the mercy of imperfect political and economic systems. This is the line of thought being pursued vigorously by those involved in Ethereum and other similar decentralized developments. They argue that the transparency and security of the blockchain could provide new levels of openness and protection for citizens and lay bare the details of decisions and transactions that might otherwise be hidden from them.

Conclusion – who's net is it anyway?

As the analysis above suggests, in a constantly evolving environment with an accelerating pace of technological development and ever-greater potential gains, there are inevitably far more questions than answer right now about the future of the internet. At the heart of the matter is the issue of ownership.

A fundamental question for business and policy leaders alike is whether the internet can be both a "right" and a for-profit product or service? Despite the central nature of the question, it is in some respects being overtaken by events, with billions of "things" expected to arrive online within the next five to ten years. Will the Masters of the Universe have sidelined the issue by making the Web so central to our lives that we are willing to trade privacy and access to our personal data in return for rides on their branded internet wonderwolrd? From where we stand today, the "almost certain probable future" is that, a decade from now, our things will be talking to each other and busier than us moving data around in cyberspace. A lot of that data will be about us.

In this **Nextnet,** populated by connected things and our intelligent agents, what role will there be for the discussion about rights, morals, net neutrality, and ownership? Will the proponents of net neutrality succeed in their mission to have all data treated equally, or could we see a privatized, segmented net of nets emerge where corporations and governments set the rules and we get what we are willing to pay for? Will Ethereum and its like have populated cyberspace with a network of DAOs that operate largely unattended and whose transparency and openness challenges the authority of current and would-be Master of its Universe? On the other hand, would removing a human element from the Internet make it a much less appealing place and create the space for a completely new development to take place to fill the need for social interactions?

Might Dark Web 2.0 emerge as the place to escape the "things" and spend time in a human online ecosystem? A place to fly under the radar of companion objects and AI-enabled agents (and the companies that want to know what data they hold) might become a necessary and sought after refuge.

What's clear is that the scale and functionality of the Web and the underlying Internet are likely to expand dramatically. Innovators will deliver internet solutions that tempt us, rework the DNA of every aspect of society, and challenge our assumptions about the boundaries between public and private, free and paid, open and controlled. The born digital Masters of the Universe will continue to drive for winner-takes-all dominance in sector after sector – physical and digital alike. In response, the born physical business community will be challenged to rework its DNA and find ways of fighting back and transforming into entities capable of competing and winning when these worlds collide.

Closing Questions:

- *What new possibilities will the future evolution of the internet create for your business?*
- *How is the likely development of the internet being factored into your overall business strategy?*
- *How might the emergence of novel internet features change the way we market, sell, charge for and deliver goods and services?*

The Future of Digital Media – The Freexpensive Prerogative

By Yates Buckley

How can we integrate the technology that surrounds us to best communicate to us, and serve our needs?

This chapter explores the intrinsic question of how we can address issues of user privacy in an era where ever-more of our lives are being captured in digital form. Technology can only optimize how it serves us through the information that is stored about us. The long-term solution is that we endow a virtual intelligent agent that we can oversee to negotiate on our behalf and return to us control over what is deemed personal information.

Screens everywhere

Screens everywhere – we're used to them – a bit taxed by their constant demand for attention but we are also adapting to ignore them. When you sit in a public space, try counting the number of screens you see whether personal or public broadcast devices. Right now at an airport I see more than 15 digital devices: seven mobile users, two tablet, one laptop and mobile businessman, two TVs with news, two billboard style advercontent screens, and two ad billboards (big TV's on their side). This is the new normal and what is strange is that each one of these devices is capable of almost all the features of the other. They offer a kind of ubiquity of media and function. What differentiates them is how the owner of the device has decided to use them in the environment and what business model they participate in: selling ads, creating shared space in a bar, enabling personal communication, entertainment, or work.

Emerging and future technology developments will expand the device pool: glasses, watches, car interfaces, buttons, shoes, contact lenses – bringing with them the demand for a more integrated media use. You cannot use the watch the same way you do a phone but there is no technical reason you could not. The specialization of how we use these things is a user preference. So how do we cross the divide between all the devices that will serve us in the future and create an integrated voice? How will we bring this concert of technology under our personal control? The answer is a transformation of the person. You will no longer be only physical, but will be wearing your personal **metadata** – give us a means of controlling this and we can then control all of the other technology to ensure it serves us.

Digital media and the free versus expensive trade off

First, a bit of background: **digital media** is a broad category. It includes almost every kind of content including traditional mediums like film, radio, and TV when they are presented on a digital platform. This is because when things become digital they can be combined with other digital content and be adapted to different platforms: what can work on a mobile phone can be adapted to a virtual reality (VR) video game for example. The term digital media also includes the many different digital wrappers that can apply to traditional content such as a YouTube video, with its ratings, comments, and related videos.

The fluidity of this medium was best captured in a quote by Stewart Brand: "Information wants to be free, but it also wants to be expensive."[199] He noted a constant struggle between trying to create more and more valuable information and the increasing ease with which technology would allow information to spread. The image I have in mind is this: imagine your neighbor's life depended on you for some piece of information. It would be immoral for you not to share it with them.

But what if you had spent your life trying to get this information? And what if the whole world needs this information? What if instead of saving the neighbor's life it would simply allow them to live a little better? At some stage you will end up wanting to find a way to control access to this valuable information so you can make a living off it. In parallel, other people will be trying to crack your control so they can benefit from your information. This is the key force in the evolution of digital media: the friction between free and expensive.

Digital media – as with any other media – is also about the economy that sustains it. The free/expensive friction has defined how digital media has evolved since its birth in the '80s. Video games used to have physical cartridges to stop people from making copies, then we had cardboard decoders and special license keys, videos were supplied in physical CD/DVD/BlueRay formats and music came on CDs and specialized players. All of these variations in the media support platforms have really been about trying to keep the liquid-like digital-media in a bottle so it could be sold. At the same time, the fact that you can copy information indefinitely has led to a constant clash between two ends of the spectrum: either unusually high profits for locked copies or pirate versions for free – and we've yet to find a balance.

Digital media and the network

The evolution of the commercial Internet has been about resolving the same free/expensive conflict in a diffuse way. Each new wave of services that transform the internet has grown at the boundary between providing information access to users, while obtaining value from it at the same time. A search through the web, or an app store, or in your social network are the most obvious examples: you can find what you are looking for but you may also not be allowed to access it because you are in the wrong country. Crucially, for this kind of mechanism to work, there is one key requirement: that the user really is who they say they are, otherwise all bets are off.

The network has placed us, with our digital identity, at the negotiating table. Do we lie about our age to see some content? Can we lie to our friends on a social network? Can we lie about our phone number when we need a special two-step password authentication? Our personal data acts as a balancing tool in the expensive/free tension. What sort of theme do you like? What about your friends? What was the last film you saw? Did you actually pay to read this book?

The metadata opportunity

I picture a future where I and my metadata are walking around the world with strings connecting me to all my contacts. I walk around with this network. When I enter a shop they know me already, they know what I like, I save time, get smiles, and a discount. However, another fellow human that decides to be anonymous gets none of that, and might even trigger a silent alarm on a CCTV that tracks him trudging out of the shop with the wrong pair of socks.

Our personal metadata is very much like our clothes. If I wear a pin-stripe suit some people seem to treat me with more respect and if I wear sportswear at a wedding they will steer clear. The difference is that with personal metadata only some of it is really personal in the sense that you can control it. Most data about you is out there in the digital ether and there is not so much you can do to get it back or change it. What this tells us is that the current model of personal metadata being out there, without you having some oversight on it, is societally awkward. We should expect a different kind of mediated control over our digital identity in the future.

Our networks will have power and will command attention. The difference between being an influencer and being a consumer of digital media will blur. We are entering a space where we will bring media with us wherever we go and it will be our personal broadcast tool. We will be seeding information to reinforce our networks, and taking our networks to the streets to win people over to our lifestyle basket.

Digital media: a closer future

One way to read the trend of digital media is to think about how close a device is to the user. A close device is one that knows more about you, not just physically closer. A tablet that is highly customized to your settings is closer for example than an exercise wrist-band that only knows about your arm moving. The future of digital media is going to be about all our devices getting closer. Indeed, a new generation of devices will emerge which are so close it will be hard to understand the dividing line between the person and their extension.

There is commercial value for advertisers in media that is aware of who is watching it. This means being able to report effectiveness of a product on the basis of specific target groups. Billboards are being prototyped to use computer vision to identify a target audience and to project specifically to that user only. Augmented reality (AR) tools like HoloLens and Magic Leap will extend your information to the room that surrounds you, so your digital media is so close that only you can see it and you interact with it using objects in your real room. Personal computer interfaces involving direct implants into people's brains will be more and more common; this is the limit where the extension is so close you can't easily divide the person from the medium.

Close media also means that everything we see and use in digital media will be filtered through the metadata of our network. For example, if all our friends love a film, we will most certainly end up seeing that very ad on a billboard, online, or as a bonus in a game. We may find this disturbing and bothersome but there are not many ways to resolve the tension between expensive and free information. Whatever we get for free will have a converse mechanism to deliver value to the information provider. In the extreme, if it's hard to quit Facebook now, imagine if it was part of who you actually are, an implanted extension.

The AI-PA and deep future of digital media

The solution to the problem of free/expensive around personal data, will likely be resolved around commercialization of artificial intelligence (AI) powered agents that negotiate different interfaces on your behalf. Ray Kurzweil describes something similar: a personal assistant (PA) that can help with many everyday tasks.[200] This AI-PA will be something you will need to both trust so you will have abundant control over it, and understand the general principles that guide and teach it.

The user experience might be something like this: "Hi Fred, I would like to experience a detective mystery with my girlfriend tonight."

Fred would gather options for you to peruse on the basis of your broadest profile recommendations. Once he finds a few good options he might inform you: "Hi, Sherlock5D is either 33 credits or you can offer to share current location and past food preferences." Okay, you go for the share. The next thing you know, while walking out of the door the billboard across the street has changed contextually specifically for you, to a sustainable locust protein based mango smoothie available for instant delivery.

Someday, a typical conversation flow might look like this:

POSTME: *"Fred, can you help me review some questions relating to my article?"*

FRED: "Sure, would love to."

POSTME: *"The movie we saw last night – how much does the movie itself know about me?"*

FRED: "I traded your favorite homebrew recipe for healthbars, your last five movies watched and your persona-type. And by the way it wasn't the movie, but the Mega-Movies aggregators that owned that one. We've freexpensive-bartered with them before, they are well respected."

POSTME: *"I have a question. What if I didn't want to trade information? Has anyone theorized on systems that do not require this exchange?"*

FRED: "Yes, many people in the early 21st century believed the privacy of information should be an essential right and that the network should be structured with guarantees for privacy."

POSTME: *"What was the counterargument? Why didn't it work?"*

FRED: "Freexpensive was invented – it established the

rules of engagement with information and the foundations of law relating to AI-PAs management of this."

POSTME: *"What was there before the AI-PAs?"*

FRED: "Something called Android was a portable AI-less
receptacle of information that effectively acted as an
AI-PA. But there were no rules."

POSTME: *"Odd. Ok, another question, was direct brain
implantation an inevitable step in media technology?"*

FRED: "Actually direct implantation was and remains an
option although not everyone does this. People who
work closely with AI-PA enhanced operations benefit
from it, but it is complicated."

POSTME: *"What do you mean complicated?"*

FRED: "A key problem is that the human brain is structured around specific sensory systems. This has meant
that for humans to be able to undertake useful analysis
of the data from the implant, they have been restricted
to almost the same bandwidth they had without implantation. At the same time, advances in AI-PAs have been
so fast and controlled-safe that human language has
sufficed for instruction despite its low bandwidth."

POSTME: *"I guess the advance in maker-facturing
biocompatible extensions has also allowed us to
continue evolving detachables that are as good as
implants sometimes."*

FRED: "Yes, good point!"

Digital Media next steps

The drive toward wearable immersion is inevitable – whether that be
via a full head-mounted-system, light-glasses blending the world with
AR, or some other route. The draw is ultimately enormous because, at
some simple level, we are talking about the illusion of infinite real-estate. Once the illusion is strong enough, the idea of real-estate won't
be quite as interesting as virtual-estate. And from my personal VR
experiences, prototypes are already close to good enough. So in many

cases the abundant virtual version will be identical to the scarce real version. For example: visit a fragile nature reserve with no worries about contaminating it.

The other drive will be social. We are on the cusp of integrating most of the technology (three to six years) in a way that creates something that is a much more realistic, immersive virtual meeting space. For people that are familiar with the impact of video conferencing on work and relationships, the spatialized extension will have an even more significant social effect.

The question we are left with today as we stand on the verge of another transformation in digital media, is how the individual person with their metadata will play into the upcoming augmented and virtual technology. The existing digital media will reshape itself for these new devices, and will even reach out to your physical being by providing input/output at the physical – even muscular – level. At the same time, devices of all sorts will populate our physical and personal space.

There remains the core issue of cracking the freexpensive digital compromise around personal metadata and media consumption. We need to have a stable solution here if we don't want to risk destabilizing social effects and increasing social injustice.

What would happen to media in a society where everyone is looking through different glasses, filtered by their personal networks? If the glass filtering is a personal choice, ultimately you have to solve the moral issue as we do today. But if the filtering is something beyond your control, a strange algorithmic commercial rule – this is a problem. What if you need to buy that heart rate diagnosis app to save someone's life – but it's not available in your territory?

Questions for business:

- *How do you treat your customers' information – do you see it as yours or as a commodity you are representing on their behalf?*
- *Are your customers part of your promoter network or a resource to draw from unsustainably?*

- *Will your customers accept your service in return for a clear exchange of personal information and agreements on the way it can be used?*
- *Can you integrate your customers' data to create an enhanced, targeted media experience which they benefit from transparently?*
- *Would you share control of your full user profile with a virtual agent acting on your behalf?*

Recommended additional sources:

- *Braden, R. A., & Daniel, S. (2011). The Techno-Human Condition. MIT Press.*
- *Carr, N. (2008). Is Google Making Us Stupid? Yearbook of the National Society for the Study of Education, 107(2), 89-94. doi:1 0.1111/j.1744-7984.2008.00172.*
- *Daniele, F., Ana, A., & Gareth, K. (2014). Hacker, Maker, Teacher, Thief: Advertising's Next Generation. Creative Social.*
- *Eric, S., & Jared, C. (2013). The New Digital Age. Hachette.*
- *Jaron, L. (2014). Who Owns the Future? Penguin Group.*
- *Lanier, J. (2010). You are not a gadget. Penguin Group. doi:10.1111/j.1744-7984.2008.00172.x/full*
- *McLuhan, M. (2003). Understanding Media: The Extensions of Man (Critical Edition), edited by W. Terrence Gordon. Corte Madera. Ginko Press.*
- *Paul, L. (1999). Digital McLuhan: a guide to the information millennium. Rutledge New York.*
- *Sterling, B. (2005). Shaping Things (Mediaworks Pamphlets). Mediaworks Pamphlets. doi:10.1234/12345678*
- *Sterling, B. (2008). Tomorrow now: envisioning the next 50 years. Random House.*
- *Tom, C. (2012). How to Thrive in the Digital Age. Pan Macmillan.*
- *William, H. (2009). The Next Big Thing. Kogan Page.*

Mobile 2030: Scenarios for the Role of Mobile Technology in Society

By Alexandra Whittington and Amir Bar

What could the mobile society of the future look like?

Introduction

Mobile technology has become a central feature of people's lives around the world. We are increasingly tailoring our activities, lifestyles, business processes and social systems to cater to the needs of a mobile-centric world. This chapter presents four possible scenarios for how the role and use of mobile technology in society could play out by 2030.

Mobile is the term for computing, communication and work tools that send and receive data mainly via smart phone. The future scenarios of mobile that are presented in this article emerged from a "two by two matrix" designed with guidance from the Global Business Network (GBN) process described by Peter Schwartz in *The Art of the Long View.*[201] The GBN scenario process rests on the identification of key uncertainties: major questions that: a) might be resolved by the time horizon in question; and b) will have considerable influence on the direction of change related to the question or issue at hand. The advantage of scenarios is that they allow previews of what life will possibly be like when strategic issues are resolved one way or the other. In this case, two key uncertainties for Mobile 2030 are:

- What will the status of resources used in mobile technology be like in 2030: **Scarcity or Abundance?** Availability of the raw materials required to make mobile technology is an unknown into the 2030 time horizon, as are the long-term political, economic, and environmental consequences of their use. Scarcity or Abundance refers also to the status of most natural resources in the world in 2030.

- How will mobile users in 2030 relate to their personal technological devices? Will mobile be one's **Better Half** – a desirable, safe, nonthreatening, and helpful partner that enhances the user's life? Alternatively could it be our **Frenemy** – a friend that is actually one's enemy, a source of endless surveillance, privacy violation, and damage to relationships, opportunities, health, and lifestyle? Is the future of mobile a desirable consumer want or a burdensome survival need that creates tension, confusion, and dysfunction?

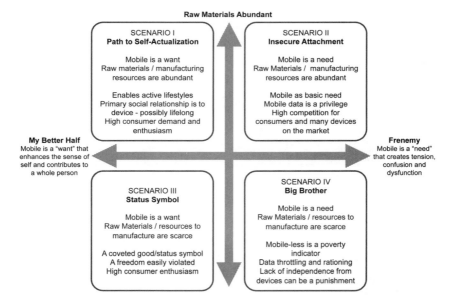

FIGURE 1: Mobile 2030 Scenario Matrix

A graphic visualization of the Mobile 2030 scenario matrix is shown above (figure 1) and the four scenarios are presented below.

Mobile 2030 Scenarios

Scenario I: Path to Self-Actualization

Summary: Mobile is a want. Raw Materials / manufacturing resources are abundant.

- Enables active lifestyles
- Primary social relationship is to device – possibly lifelong
- High consumer demand and enthusiasm
- Enhances sense of self
- Has a democratizing effect
- Allows for financial empowerment
- Increases social mobility
- Enhances interpersonal skills and relationships
- Specialized devices/personalization
- Constant and consistent upgrades
- Vendors always innovating with new designs
- Low environmental impact

In 2030, with more than 100 trillion sensors in the world, everything we do can be monitored. Communications between machines have replaced human involvement, freeing up time for an enhanced life which is more meaningful and efficient. Communication with the world consists of communication with data that is coming from machines (non-human). In order to do that, everyone needs to have a tool that helps integrate them into the human-machine world. It is not therefore surprising that Liam's graduation present from his parents is the new and most powerful yet operation system (OS), the one tool that can define his success and satisfaction in his career and life.

The new operating system Liam is getting will have access to all of his history data and all of his streaming data right after he signs in. From that moment it will be his closest ally in life, helping him connect with the rest of the world and making decisions with regard to his life. The OS is cloud-based and can assume the shape of many products. Liam can carry a mobile device to communicate with it but his OS can also be accessed via his car, TV, and many other devices.

Liam is young and healthy, but his OS still collects and organizes all the information about his health, from what he eats to how many steps he walk every day. It monitors his body vitals via small sensors on his clothes and body. The OS is constantly communicating with Liam's doctor office (which is run by another OS) to make sure that everything is on track. If needed, Liam's OS reminds him that he needs to do more exercise to keep up with the yearly plan, or that the combination of food he is about to order made him feel bad last time he had it.

The fact that technology developments still follow Moore's Law means that Liam's OS is over 100,000 times more powerful than an equivalent system in 2010. This means that alongside talking with Liam it can literally feel him due to advanced physiological and psychological sensors. In fact his OS is so powerful that Liam's career is going to be dependent on his ability to work together with the OS to achieve his future work objectives.

As Liam searches for a potential job, his new OS tells him whether he is suitably qualified based on historical data of his past jobs and courses, as well as assessing whether the job and the company fit his personality. If he finds an opportunity he likes but lacks skills for, his OS suggests how he can close the gap with additional learning (online or in person) and how long it will take him to get to that level.

Between job interviews, Liam spends a lot of time with his OS doing fun things. Knowing his preference for specific type of humor, his OS provides him with short videos with funny sketches. If one happens not to be as funny, his OS knows it immediately by reading Liam's face, and it skips to the next one. He can also participate in daily decisions within his city via the e-voting system that was designed to provide the mayor with continuous citizen feedback. In the evening when his friends are back from work, they meet for drinks, but not before their OSes take their locations, preference, and availability into account and suggest where they all should meet.

While Liam is looking for a full-time job, he gets a constant update from his OS about his spending. Luckily, there is a lot of work available on an hourly basis which he can do from anywhere. All Liam needs to do after stating his job preferences is to tell his OS when he is ready to work. Setting the goals at the beginning of the month allows his OS to manage his time with suggestions of when to work and when to spend time on interviewing or training. This system is so convenient that some of Liam's friends decide that they prefer to live like this, with more flexibility around work and leisure, than to have a full-time job. The ability to work from home in many jobs has increased the ability to do **destination-work**, meaning that the mobility of technology allows people to decide that they are going to work from a different city for a while and to maybe rent a work space on a daily basis. The idea of work-life balance has never been so easy to achieve.

Being so powerful and drawing on advances in cognitive computing and machine learning, Liam's OS knows him so well and spends so much time with him that a strong bond is created. For some people, the OS is now at the level where it can provide them with all the social contact they need. The OS is Liam's constant attentive companion, sharing information, advising, spending time with him, and ensuring he is always in peak mental condition and never really alone.

Scenario II: Insecure Attachment

Summary: Mobile is a need. Raw Materials / manufacturing resources are abundant.

- Mobile as basic need
- Mobile data is a privilege (not a right)
- High competition for consumers and many devices on the market

- Low demand and enthusiasm for technology
- Easy interchangeability of devices, lack of permanent attachment
- Cheaply priced
- Concerns about negative health effects persist
- Mobiles used to determine educational and career choices
- Public utility
- Limits democracy
- Menacing level of surveillance
- Vulnerable to info and identity crime
- Low environmental impact

It's April 14th, 2030 and Emma is searching for the receipt for the Smart-Home system she installed back in December. The government will give her $250 for making her house more energy efficient. However, what Emma really wants is to get one more Government Reward Star to complete the series of 50. With 50 stars, she will be one of the lucky people who get a 12 month pass for her mobile data program which is only available from the government.

With many cheap models of mobile device available, consumers are now more focused on finding a cheap and stable data plan. This government plan is only available for those assessed as productive citizens. Without it, one cannot maintain a normal life. This mobile device data plan is offered by the government for free but users have to share all of their information to prove they are making productive use of their time. The devices are still made from toxic materials, but competition with other nations does not allow for any government to ban them. The newly elected US president promised to invest more in finding a way to make a non-toxic mobile device.

Good citizens share their data with government computers, which then decide what government services they can access and what education and development programs they can attend. For example, at the age of 15, the government decides what profession a person is going to pursue. The government asks the person what they want to do, but this accounts for only 15 percent of the decision. The remainder is calculated based on 15 years of data that was accumulated on the individual. If a person was out of the government data plan for even a few weeks during the 15 years, their chances of enjoying a good career are much lower.

At age 15, people also start to vote, which is mandatory. More importantly, their voting ratio is chosen. Dependent on their performance and behavior, their vote can be worth as much as 20 times more than the standard vote. In this way, the government ensures the greatest influence on decisions is given to the people who contribute the most to the country. Once the ratio is chosen, it is very hard to increase it, but easier to decrease it if the person does not stay productive or if they break the law.

Given that the government is collecting all the data, even good citizens do not use their mobile devices for everything. Attachment to devices is not that high because it is used mainly for completing life's essentials rather than for organizing free time and social activities. There are many models of approved mobile devices and people mostly replace them to show what level of data plan they have, which typically reflects their socioeconomic status.

While no one is really attached to their mobile device, it is the most important device most people own. The chance that the government will reduce the size of the data plan or even remove it from a person can be a devastating experience. The punishment for most common crimes involves losing status in the data plan, and people are constantly aware of the implications if they do not follow national laws and regulations. Punishments for serious crimes may result in losing a data plan for years, and it's not surprising that identity theft is a common crime, and one of the biggest risks for society.

After the government made the mobile device the official source of personal identification, it also established capital punishment for identity theft. Governments are constantly investing more in technology to prevent identity theft, but with roughly one in every thirty-two citizens having their data plan removed for one reason or another, the motivation to steal a data plan (identity) is still high.

Scenario III: Status Symbol

Summary: Mobile is a want. Raw Materials / resources to manufacture are scarce.

- A coveted good, a status symbol
- A freedom easily violated
- High consumer enthusiasm
- Low personal value of user-device relationship
- High prices
- Exploitative consumer-provider relationship
- Black market exists
- Favors the privileged
- Increased reach of education by volume (quantity, not quality)
- Job/job security can depend on personal device
- High environmental impact

Jordan woke with a blurry memory of being knocked down last night. While traveling home by foot, he was viewing a new film and suddenly his streaming video lagged and his high-speed connection froze. Poor connections and interference were always a sign of an impoverished, crime-ridden, dangerous part of town. No surprise then, that he got mugged. They took his brand new device and mobile peripherals. Luckily he had a good insurance plan with theft coverage.

The 2025 Internet Privatization law put an end to most free Wi-Fi in the big cities. It was only free as long as the user consented to detailed data mining of their usage information. The overzealous, large-scale exploitation of user information (everything from personal, professional, consumption, health and political) that began in the early 2000s was finally brought down by a mass movement of consumers who had grown tired of constant privacy invasion.

In addition, prices for consumer technology had grown so high that the products once again signified a serious financial commitment on the part of the user, who then became more protective of the activities they conducted on mobile. So the previously free Wi-Fi was now replaced with very expensive, high-speed connectivity. Again, the expense—a byproduct of the extremely scarce resources at the time—was a deterrent to all but the wealthiest sectors of society. As an alternative, in 2020 various private companies had started to provide free Wi-Fi for those willing to sacrifice their privacy. Thus a bad neighborhood was likely to host poor-quality, free public Wi-Fi, which was operated on a charitable basis for the have-nots, by the same private corporations that offered expensive and discreet data access to those who could afford it.

Devices were hot on the black market considering their prohibitive retail price, so thefts such as Jordan's were common. Luckily the Internet Privatization Law had provisions to protect users from abuses resulting from criminal incidents. For example, "identity shut off" would clear the phone's memory the minute it was no longer detecting Jordan's specific physiological presence nearby. Wearable, ingestible, and implantable devices had become so common that the risk of actual personal bodily harm due to a device theft was very high. This fact had been a huge impetus to the law protecting citizens' detectable data from prying eyes, including the government's. So, even though Jordan was pretty beat up from the mugging, he was sure his identity and well-being were safely encrypted and retrievable only by him.

It would be a tough recovery, but being so fit in his 40s would contribute to Jordan's quick physical healing from the violent robbery. One of the many advantages of mobile devices is the way they encourage and support active lifestyles. Exercise and fitness are perfectly enmeshed in the self-tracking and monitoring technologies that high-scale consumers normally use. "Enabling movement" had emerged as the public health solution for the sedentary society whose ill effects were obvious by 2020. Obesity levels and heart disease rates were stabilizing and even falling in many developing countries, at least among those wealthy enough to use private Wi-Fi and buy expensive devices.

Jordan was a little sad to think of losing the relatively new device that the muggers stole. It was a beautiful piece of equipment with very exotic materials inside. The good thing was that his expensive insurance policy would allow him to buy a replacement quickly. Prohibitively high prices meant the average buyer faced significant wait times even for ten year-old models. Better-off consumers who knew their access to good jobs and living conditions depended on a quality device were more than willing to spend the equivalent of two or three months rent money to purchase a new mobile and protect it with expensive insurance programs. Being marginalized from opportunities was a way of life for those who could not make a similar investment.

Scenario IV: Big Brother

Summary: Mobile is a need. Raw Materials / resources to manufacture are scarce.

- Mobile-less is a new poverty indicator
- Data throttling and rationing common
- Lack of independence from devices can be a punishment
- High prices and high dependency on device creates tensions
- Inconsistent access to high quality technology oppresses workforce / makes work more difficult
- Less consumer enthusiasm and demand
- People have less autonomy, it's a necessary evil
- Reduced freedom
- Blocks direct democracy
- Sedentary lifestyles
- Public health at risk
- High environmental impact

Nush looked at the lottery numbers on the screen of her MyPhone20: an indecipherable mix of symbols and numbers that would determine the direction of her life over the next eighteen months. Her dreams of having a second child in the near future were dashed when she realized that if she didn't land the nontoxic model device she'd hoped for, her fertility would suffer. Medical recommendations offered strict guidelines for the reproductive choices of users of highly invasive devices, also known as wearables, ingestible, implantable, or invisibles. Having broken the terms of her user contract several times in the past year and a half, she knew her chances of winning in the lottery were diminished and she feared the worst.

Nush had hoped for something handheld, which would keep the Wi-Fi toxins from interrupting her cycles and allow her and her partner to have another baby. However, the chances that this lottery would result in a noninvasive outcome were slim, even slimmer since they already had one child and she had violated the usage rules in her contract. Limitations on the number of children couples could have were already strict regardless of device. The wellbeing of the existing population relied precariously on dwindling natural resources in 2030 and there was no way to hide your ecological footprint from your device. With an implanted device she would be monitored constantly on a number of health indicators (exercise, diet, use of tobacco and other vices) which would immediately disqualify her from another pregnancy. The mobile lifestyle had impacted society in ways that limited personal choice substantially.

A consumerist boom with rapid replacement of mobiles had generated a huge demand for the key resources that went into manufacturing the devices, which were concentrated in developing countries. This gave rise both to corrupt leadership and a bidding war to dominate access the highly valuable materials in the regions concerned. Mobile devices became more expensive, with a **blood tax** on the more exotic new materials and technologies that allowed for faster and smaller devices. Only people who had earned credits for lawful behavior, employee compliance, and positive lifestyle habits could win one in the lottery.

Thus, with consumer prices going through the roof, the decision was made to devise a lottery system for western societies so that the devices could be available to all. By 2020 it was impossible to function without a mobile, but supply was limited so a lottery of new devices was the only way to ensure there were enough to go round.

This meant that many people were expected to accept their device without question, knowing their livelihoods depended on it. It was also accepted that one's behavior in the presence of the device would determine outcome and eligibility for an **upgrade** next time around. It was the perfect means of social control.

The service providers had long since surrendered their aura of independence from government interference. It was now common knowledge that the private corporations that manufactured consumer devices were working hand-in-hand with state and international surveillance agencies. This was convenient since public policy demanded speed, access and freedom to examine a citizen's behavior via their device. Being part of the mobile society meant giving up many freedoms. It was all in the user contract and at the whim of the provider and de facto government observers.

The lottery system all but ensured that your assigned devices were the least compatible for your lifestyle. Yet society continued to insist this was the best way to keep people honest and guarantee equality of access. There was even a new category of disenfranchisement known as mobile-less, since hunger and homelessness had all but been alle- viated by the much stricter regulations on consumption throughout society. A guaranteed minimum income had been implemented in many countries, so a new criteria of disadvantage was created to describe the people at the very bottom, the untouchables whose lives were not dictated by mobile. Many of them objected to the invasions of mobile life, and thus scattered themselves to the fringes of soci- ety.

Nevertheless, the untouchables were still entered into lotteries each year (against their will) to be assigned a phone, usually one of the discarded models. Nush remembered a handwritten sign she had seen a disheveled man holding on a street corner: 'Do you own the phone, or does the phone own you?' It was something to think about this morning as she checked her work assignments and daily food and energy rations to provide for her small family.

Conclusion

Examining these Mobile 2030 scenarios challenges us to think about the potential implications for society and business. The mobile device is already a communication, information, and networking tool and as a result the relationships between our lives, our work and our devices are becoming more significant and intertwined. The scenarios highlight how both our social and working lives could become increasingly centered on the mobile and how it could effectively become the controlling agent in our lives – controlling our access to education, opportunity, services and resources.

Hence, it is important to understand how society is and can be transformed by new and ubiquitous technologies like mobile. Not only does a breakthrough technology merit significant examination, but the value to industries across the board should not be ignored. The rapid adoption of personal mobile technology in almost all areas of life, including intellectual, commercial, and social pursuits, makes the topic pertinent for strategic thinkers from any industry.

What questions for business do these scenarios pose?

- *What are the most and least favorable aspects of each scenario for your organization and your employees?*
- *How could the continued evolution of mobile technology and applications impact and potentially disrupt your organization?*
- *What strategies could your organization adopt to take advantage of the potential evolution of mobile technology and to protect against the least attractive developments?*

The Impact of Wearable Lifestyle Technologies and Gamification on Business and Society

By David Wortley

How might advances in wearable technologies and gamification impact human health, social behavior, care costs, productivity, and the business of healthcare?

This chapter looks at the future potential impact of wearable lifestyle sensor technologies, mobile applications, and gaming concepts on personal and corporate health. I examine current global health issues, the lifestyle technologies available today, how they are likely to develop, and the implications for business and society.

Zumba and aerobics classes on NHS to prevent diabetes: Obese patients most at risk of illness will also be taught how to poach and boil food

- GPs will refer patients to classes such as Zumba, aerobics or spinning
- People will also be sent on courses to learn how to cook healthy food
- Around 3.8m Britons have diabetes, the figure has doubled in 20 years

Source: Mail Online March 11th 2015 [202]

The global health challenges of modern lifestyles

Personal health and well-being are attracting a lot of focus, not least because of the growing number of people classified as obese. There are strong evidential lifestyle-related links between obesity and future health conditions such as diabetes and cardiovascular problems. The general conclusion drawn today is that increasingly sedentary lifestyles, higher stress levels, and poor diets will place unsustainable demands on the resources of publicly funded health systems and on the pockets of those who pay for private care.

Regular headlines in the national press about the obesity crisis are often accompanied by details of new diets such as fasting plans, slimming products, adverts for gyms, and research reports on possible causes and treatments for lifestyle conditions. The reality of the situation is that for every scientific report extolling the virtues of a specific approach, there is often a conflicting report published soon after. When it comes to understanding the physiology and psychology of human beings, there is much left to learn, and because the human mind and body are so complex, we have to rely on experts to diagnose our physical and mental condition and offer remedies. Technology is expected to play an increasing role in the future mix of personal healthcare solutions.

The ubiquity of sensors and the growth of artificial intelligence (AI) applications

Sensor technology and AI could herald a transformation in the management of our health. Today electronic sensors and measurement devices are being embedded into almost every conceivable piece of equipment used in our daily lives. We have become accustomed to having information at our fingertips to enable us to monitor and control our environment and our technology. These sensors and monitoring devices link to computers that use AI to manage the equipment more efficiently than a human being could. Examples include the range of technology found in almost every new car to monitor its performance and to tell us where we are and how to get to our destination.

The use of sensor and measurement technology combined with AI can make cars more reliable, with longer periods between routine maintenance and servicing. Hence, it seems logical that similar techniques could be applied to human minds and bodies. This would enable us to perform better physically and mentally, and to live a longer, active life.

Wearable lifestyle technologies today

There are a growing number of wearable consumer health devices available already – or coming to market soon. These seek to measure and feedback on the factors that reflect our physical body's condition and performance. Since measurement and feedback are essential for controlling any activity, these devices hold promise for providing each of us with the tools we need to better manage our lifestyles. A growing number of users can testify to the effectiveness of such devices for reducing weight and maintaining significant improvements in health, motivation, and performance through simple changes in lifestyle habits.

The lifestyle technologies that are currently in widespread use fall into two main categories:

- Devices that measure or analyze the body composition and/or state; and

- Devices and mobile phone applications that track physical activity and sleep.

Both categories of devices can provide useful information to anyone wishing to take more responsibility for managing their personal health. The body composition and/or state devices include weigh-scales, blood pressure monitors, body mass index and fat / water composition measurement devices. The category of devices and applications that track physical activity and sleep provide tools to monitor the parameters that can influence well-being and lifestyle-related conditions. The technology is already advanced enough to provide users with feedback and motivational messages to encourage the habits and behaviors that can improve their condition.

How could technology affect lifestyle choices?

There is a profound difference between the state of the art sensor devices, measurement technologies, and AI used to improve the performance and reliability of machines, and what is currently in use for human beings. Across different sectors today, the control and management of a wide range of machines is largely fully automated with little human choice or influence possible. The same technologies applied to human beings have yet to evolve to a state where the control of our physical and mental condition is fully automated and managed by technology. Human beings are still currently given the choice over lifestyle decisions that can affect their health. How well we care for or abuse our mind and body is regarded as a fundamental human right. This situation could well be challenged by future generations as the consequences of unsustainable lifestyle choices become impossible to manage through a lack of resources.

As a society, citizens are generally protected against ill health or accidents by insurance policies which spread the burden of cost and probability across the whole population, regardless of the level of risks each individual takes. In the future real time-tracking of physical and mental well-being could increasingly be embedded in our daily lives. Hence, there will be a need for some form of contract between citizens and society which defines the rights and responsibilities for each party in ensuring a sustainable future.

The future of lifestyle technologies

The lifestyle tracking devices that are wearable today will become increasingly sophisticated and capable of measuring many more aspects of our physical and mental condition. They are likely to become embedded in our bodies and minds in the form of smart chips and sensors that use the body's own energy sources to power them. Developments in nanotechnology already make this a practical possibility. These devices would have the ability to measure temperature, blood pressure, sugar levels, cholesterol, and body composition on a constant basis. In future they could also be linked to human DNA to provide verifiable identification of the citizen.

The impact on society of these embedded technologies will be very profound and could cause a great deal of tension and conflict in society – bringing ideological clashes. On one side of the debate will be those who believe that human freedom of choice without judgement, penalty, or infringement of privacy is sacrosanct. This view will be challenged by those who believe there should be a balance between the rights of the individual and the rights of society. In future, will society need to be better protected against the consequences of individual lifestyle choices?

Business opportunities and challenges

Clearly any technologies which can improve personal health management significantly can have a positive impact on corporate health costs and staff productivity. As the devices become increasingly mainstream and lower in cost, companies are likely to either offer them as part of the employee rewards package or require their use within the contract of employment. Once these devices can be completely personalized to the individual with the verifiable identity of the wearer, they will almost certainly replace loyalty cards and other forms of identity token. They could also be used to monitor personal performance and attentiveness – some organisations are already using wearable technologies to monitor staff concentration and spot when they are day dreaming. Such wearable and implanted devices would create opportunities and challenges for a range of sectors from high street pharmacies, who could fit the devices to security firms, and providers of banking and finance services.

The offering and use of these devices could become a commercial differentiator in the recruitment and retention of staff as well as a source of profitability improvement. There are likely to be business opportunities for corporations who offer these devices and associated services to their customers and suppliers in order to develop brand loyalty. Insurance companies will inevitably begin to offer special incentives to clients who can prove their healthy lifestyles by sharing the data collected by these devices and applications.

There are already some precedents in the insurance sector, where drivers can gain discounts and other incentives in exchange for agreeing to have **black box** technology fitted into the car to monitor their driving behavior. Drivers use the data from these devices to prove their driving behavior poses less risk. We are already beginning to see the same phenomenon in the health sector when citizens can produce data to show that they are managing their lifestyle choices on exercise, diet, and sleep to continuously monitor and improve their health and well-being.

Gamification and wearable lifestyle technologies

Gamification is defined as the use of the principles and methodologies of electronic game design in non-game applications. It uses psychology to influence and motivate behavior, and is gaining a lot of momentum in the corporate sector where engagement of staff and consumers is critical. Typically, gamification uses incentives such as challenges, targets, points, badges, and rewards for loyalty or achievement. Wearable lifestyle devices will be a key component in the game ecosystem and are already evolving into fashion items such as watches and bracelets. These serve as both sophisticated monitoring devices and rugged, waterproof, attractive jewellery. The Apple iWatch launch in April 2015 is a prime example.

The data collected from these devices via mobile phones will be stored and aggregated **in the cloud.** The gaming element here is that the data will be used to provide feedback to the wearer in ways which provide incentives and guidance on practices which can improve or maintain good health. This use of data measurement and feedback to shape behavior is a reflection of the growing importance of gamification within health applications that motivate users to develop the habits that lead to better well-being.

Wearable technologies will also increasingly use AI and **crowd-sourcing** of knowledge to provide a personalized program of lifestyle habits for exercise, sleep, and eating based on what has been proven to work for other users with similar profiles. Each individual will have a stored personal profile and DNA record backed up by a history of behaviors and activities. This profile could be used in many different contexts to the benefit of the citizen; health insurance, job applications, and even dating for example.

Impact on society

If all of this sounds Orwellian, this scenario for the likely mid-term (two to five years) future is based on giving the citizen private access to their own health data as a fundamental human right. This right is likely to be linked to a contract with society which grants the citizen private and secure access to their own personal health data. In return the citizen would have to agree that this data can be used by the state in an anonymous format. The data would provide the citizen with health statistics and comparisons with peers but also contribute to a global health database. Big data analytics and crowdsourcing would then help society build a better understanding of the best lifestyle practices.

These relatively evolutionary developments in lifestyle technologies and their application to provide a solution to the global obesity challenge should have a profound impact on shaping the future of society. In many ways, the impact of technology on society thus far has led to what I would describe as a **spectator society** in which most citizens do not acknowledge any personal responsibility for societal issues such as obesity. This is manifested by regular press articles blaming obesity problems on everything from government policy through to the **fast food sector** and the withdrawal of school meals in the UK. The developments outlined in this article hold the potential to encourage a more responsible citizenship based on individual and collective responsibility.

Longer-term impact

For the longer-term (five to fifteen years), we are likely to see a revolution in personal health management, especially if wearable lifestyle technologies and gamification strategies do not lead to citizen-driven improvements in personal health management. It may well be that, in a future society, these measurement and feedback technologies become embedded into all citizens, initially on a voluntary basis but later perhaps as a mandatory requirement for every citizen. This revolutionary scenario could be triggered if health problems in society become so severe that measures that were once voluntary become compulsory. Will society and its citizens accept constant monitoring of health parameters and lifestyle behaviors in exchange for the potential benefits? What would be the impact on society if embedded health monitoring technology became compulsory?

The technology is already maturing to the point where it is technically possible to insert personalized sensor devices into the body and brain. This technology could firstly monitor and provide feedback on lifestyle behaviors and conditions. It could also automate the control of key body conditions such as hunger, restlessness, and sleep. In this scenario, these embedded devices would provide unique and secure identity verification for the individual. They could also incorporate online links to key support partners such as physicians and nutrition coaches who could be alerted to the conditions and patterns of behavior which suggested a problem requiring further investigation or resolution.

In this scenario, personal profiles would provide a comprehensive analysis of health and lifestyle behaviors. They could also be used for profile matching in many different situations, such as job interviews and dating web sites. This scenario is very closely aligned with the concept of **the singularity** – a point in the future when men and machines effectively merge. The singularity offers not only the prospect of revolutionary advances in human mental and physical performance but also the promise of indefinite healthy life spans.

The technologies that are maturing today do have the theoretical potential to achieve this but these developments also raise some critical questions for business:

- *How will the corporate sector exploit the commercial opportunities created by the use of wearable lifestyle technologies and the data captured by them?*
- *How might staff recruitment and retention be influenced by the use of these technologies?*
- *What could the impact be on business and commerce if each citizen has a unique and verifiable personal identity and can use these devices as payment and loyalty cards?*

Body-Machine Convergence

By Ian Pearson

How might scientific advances lead to the body becoming just another technology platform and blur the boundaries between man and machine?

The age of convergence

A new era is dawning, in which we'll see the convergence of man and machine. It will have huge impact and could spawn major new industries. With the growth of nanotechnology and the regular invention of new materials, we're witnessing the first stages of the body being used as an electronics platform. How far can and will this go? What kinds of convergence should we expect, what technological potential and applications are most likely, and what are the ethical challenges that arise from them?

We live in an exciting time and are really starting to understand the body as a very sophisticated machine. As we do so, we are slowly learning to make technology that can work with the body's own systems, function safely both inside it and – more recently – on the body's surface.

In the last decade, neuroscience has discovered much about the workings of the human brain and some of those insights are making their way into Artificial Intelligence (AI) research. An elegant virtuous circle between AI and neuroscience will become more and more obvious as time passes. Smarter machines will help us learn more about making even smarter machines. Neuroscience and new materials have also enabled the connection of human nerves to computer chips to help restore mobility to paralyzed people and amputees.

At a more superficial level, the incoming smart watches can track the body's performance via pulse monitoring and spectral absorption. But those facilities have been available in watches for over 15 years and it is really only their better integration into applications that is new. Adding direct sensory links would allow a device to treat our nerves as extensions to its core IT system – bringing great improvements in human capability. Though this generation of products will not do that, it is easy to see how their successors might.

Active skin

Meanwhile, we are starting to see early demonstrations of what in 2001 we first called **active skin**. The active element comes from thin plastic membranes with electronics printed on them which adhere to the skin's surface and allow simple biological properties to be measured and monitored. The current demonstrators can measure blood chemistry and physical properties of the skin. This stick-on membrane layer could be thought of as the next layer down from a smart-watch wearable device. It is already showing the potential to create significant medical and sports markets.

The key to ongoing development is miniaturization and printable electronics. We are familiar with Moore's Law, and it continues to apply. Compared to skin cells, a chip may seem large, but the components on it are tiny. It is already theoretically possible to make electronic devices with sophisticated capability that would be smaller than skin cells. Memory devices have already been demonstrated at around that size. Over a decade ago the first mobile phone was printed on a sheet of paper. Now it is becoming quite commonplace to print electronics. We could soon be printing thin membranes on everyday printers and placing them on our skin.

Apart from simple medical and sports monitoring, we should expect to see this field expand into cosmetic uses – with video tattoos, touch sensitive skin displays, and active makeup all appearing in the next decade. For some parts of the body, stick-on membranes will be most suitable, for others, direct printing onto the skin surface may be better. We already see early printers that can print on any firm surface, such as fingernails. By 2030, electronic patches on our skin could be as familiar as wristwatches are today.

The sports, security, entertainment, makeup, and fashion industries will make much of this kind of technology. Electronics invisibly printed on the skin could control particles in makeup to make it just another computer display capable of producing still or video imagery. Video tattoos and touch sensitive displays on the skin will assist in computer security, identification, fashion, interfaces, leisure and socialization. The many variants of active skin could add up to create a large industry.

Makeup is used mainly by women today, with a smaller but increasing male **metrosexual** market. If future makeup is electronic and more of a technical toy, we should expect many more men to start using it. Tribal electronic war-paints might appear for football games, probably in night clubs, and possibly even on the high street and in the office. Adding technology is really all it needs to make it start appealing to men. It is certainly technologically feasible. The potential applications seem compelling – so surface-layer active skin is highly likely to develop quickly.

It can go further still, with even bigger markets. Tiny devices about the same size as skin cells could be inserted into the skin itself, by needle arrays or more likely blasted in painlessly using ultrasonic puffs of air. Many devices scattered across an area of skin could be linked to each other using infrared signaling to form very sophisticated implants. Self-organization technology would let them do this autonomously, and adapt their control systems if any device fails. These would be much closer to blood capillaries and to nerves than a membrane on the skin surface. They could interact more directly with blood chemistry, and could record or replay electronic signals passing through the nerves. By signaling readings to upper layers such as membranes or wearables, a highly capable architecture arises that enables deep medical monitoring, smart drug delivery, and highly personalized medication.

The proximity to nerves would allow interception and recording of the signals that lead to sensations. Recording and replaying sensations could obviously be the foundation for a wide range of applications and services. Let's look at two obvious examples:

- Firstly, adding the full sensation of touch to virtual reality would immediately extend that industry massively.
- Secondly, in sports, accessing direct feedback via a computer would let a system make the optimal movement feel comfortable and make others less comfortable, greatly accelerating the speed of muscle learning and improving the quality of our sporting experiences.

On the downside, it also has military and police potential, allowing pain to be inflicted electronically and automatically depending on action or location.

Another layer of active skin that shows promise for future business is the **smart membrane**. A thin membrane could have many holes that can be opened and closed rather like stomata on leaves. This could be achieved by using materials that can contract when electric fields are applied across them. A circular hole then becomes a narrow oval, preventing passage. Smart membranes could be used as a means of controlling flow of medication into the body. A layer of active skin that is closely monitoring blood chemistry could signal to a higher layer device that would dispense a specific quantity of medicine via the smart membrane. Such devices could obviously help with diseases like diabetes. They might also be used by sports people to keep isotonic levels optimal. Again, the markets are obvious and just await the technology development.

Brain links

A few severely disabled people have already had electronic implants into their brains to help them use their minds to control their wheelchairs and other apparatus around them. The implants pick up the electrical signals from the brain's surface that indicate a command – allowing control just by thinking. Whereas this requires surgery today, ongoing miniaturization will make it possible to achieve the same goal using injections. The ultimate goal is to achieve electrical contact with every part of the brain, preferably every synapse. Meanwhile the drug industry is developing delivery systems that allow drugs to be released when and where they are needed. A similar system could potentially be developed to deliver electronics. Typically, delivery uses tiny capsules that flow through the blood stream and are ruptured at destination to release their payloads. The release mechanism can be exposure to a microwave beam, ultrasound, or – in the future – each capsule could have an individual IP address. Once in place these tiny devices can pick up signals from the brain, relay them to external systems, and also create electrical signals inside the brain.

More likely still, hybrid systems will be developed that create a dual effect by combining drug release with effects generated by local electronics such as wearable and implanted devices. Further still, trans-cranial magnetic stimulation has been shown to achieve strong effects within the brain, so it offers an obvious third pillar in the architecture for brain links. (Trans-cranial magnetic stimulation uses devices to make extremely powerful magnetic fields that disrupt the electronic signals in a region of the brain, thereby influencing its behavior – typically inhibiting it).

Given that deep implants could also help achieve much more effective measurement of the signals in a specific region than possible with external detectors, a strong positive feedback loop comes into play. The more and better data about the brain that can be obtained, the faster neuroscience can develop, and the AI that parallels it. These neuroscience improvements would enable better implants to achieve given impacts within the brain. This positive feedback loop would accelerate the progress of direct brain links in both directions. Eventually, we will be able to link the brain fully to external machines and devices with signals, sensory experience, thoughts, and memories becoming part of an extended IT-biotech industry. IT and biotech convergence will also accelerate as advanced new materials are invented, especially nanotechnology. This whole mega-convergence is often called NBIC (nano, bio, info, cogno) convergence.

Smart drugs and electronics

The initial markets for IT links to the brain will be aimed primarily at alleviating the effects of diseases such as Alzheimer's – mainly augmenting sensory and memory mechanisms. Drug development activity is already targeted at various neurological problems and at performance enhancement. People are demonstrably prepared to pay highly for drugs to enhance their concentration or memory, to keep them awake and alert, as well as those that control stress or help them socialize better. Recreational and social drugs also have strong markets. If the medical and social negatives that are associated with them can be overcome through future technology, then we might even see these become legalized and more popular. An interesting extension of social drug use that might then emerge could be the use of trans-cranial magnetic stimulation to inhibit some areas of the brain while using electronically activated drugs. At a party or dance, attendees could have drugs activated simultaneously and their effects synchronized to enhance the social experience.

Performance enhancement and electronic brain replication

Such an interface would allow electronic signals to pass to and from each individual neuron or synapse. The tiny devices installed via smart delivery systems might even be able to move slightly to achieve the best location for signal interception. Once in place, each connection could be assigned its own unique address allowing it to identify its neighbors. The architecture could quickly be mapped and replicated externally. That would in effect produce an electronic replica of the brain external to the body, which could be used for research and interfacing. That in itself would be highly useful and ethically significant, since it could be seen as a form of exocortex or **brain backup**, and allow replication of that particular brain with its current state at some future date when the technology permits.

Another use of such interconnection would be to speed up

communications within the brain. Signals travel along biological neurons roughly a million times slower than they would by radio link, so there is clear scope for acceleration there. However, we have yet to understand the impact on the brain if signaling were to be speeded up. Also, as neuroscience gains better understanding into the exact workings of neurons, it should become possible to replicate them electronically too. If so, a brain's structure and content could be replicated. That would effectively create the ability to make a mind backup. Doing this would allow everything to work at electronic speeds. A neuron fires millions of times slower than typical electronic switching speeds.

Without knowing precisely what sort of electronics will be needed to fully replicate a neuron and its chemical environment, it is hard to guess how much performance enhancement would be achievable. In any case, a third parameter is also affected by using electronics – size. In electronics, we are used to miniaturization – reducing refrigerator-sized prototypes down to tiny chips quickly. If a brain could be replicated electronically and then shrunk, signals would not only propagate a million times faster but travel far less distance too.

This external brain would operate much the same as the biological one it replicated. In addition, it could be enhanced with extra memory and processing power, and have senses added to improve its performance. It would also link directly to the biological version so that thoughts could originate in either and be relayed to the other. If it were implemented effectively, the human would be unaware whether a thought, memory, or sensory activities were happening inside or outside the head. The external system would initially act as a brain replica, then – hopefully – as an extension to capability, but ideally would still feel the same as the biological original. It should enhance capability without significantly affecting the nature of the mind.

Those caveats are important. We would have the ability to enhance the brain and the mind, but at the same time we would also have the power to change it. At first, we might not necessarily know exactly how to change it to achieve particular goals, so there might be some initial problems. Later, as we learn how to modify its nature to achieve a specific goal, we would be faced with the even more fundamental ethical dilemma of how to manage human nature.

So the clear long term potential is to make a working replica of the brain using electronics and probably to speed it up by several orders of magnitude. If that electronic brain can also directly access the very high level AI that we should expect in the same time frame, then it would make us truly superhuman. We would be capable of thinking faster, with access to more knowledge, more sensory inputs, and more processing power. A direct brain link is unsurprisingly a major focus of **transhumanism**. We would however, inevitably be forced to face the potential redesign of human nature, forced to think no longer of what it means to be a human, but what it should mean to be a human. That will be a challenging ethical dilemma.

Electronic immortality

If a brain can be fully mapped and replicated, then even without further enhancement, it confers the potential to live on after the brain has died. The electronic replica would contain much the same mind and character, and could presumably be linked (it does not have to actually be attached) to any android or robot body, so the person could carry on. That person might instead take the opportunity to start afresh, enhancing some aspects of their personality, deleting others and erasing bad memories. They might make replicas or have multiple versions of themselves in different bodies. Many ethical issues will arise, not least determining the allowable **post-organic-death environmental footprint** in an already congested world. Will we decide to ration mobility and physical presence, and limit electronic immortals to electronic existence? These issues are not just ethical though, the answers to them will have huge impacts on potential future industries.

AI and emotional convergence

Convergence can be softer too. Most people today are almost glued to their mobiles. They feel out of touch and stressed if they don't have constant and immediate network presence. What we don't yet have but know will be important is our future connection with robots and androids. Even simple robotic toys such as robot dogs or Furbies can elicit a strong emotional response. In science fiction, people become attached to robot and android characters just as they do to humans or aliens. It seems almost certain that we will form emotional bonds with robots that inhabit our homes or work in our office. Companies that manufacture them will presumably capitalize on the potential emotional connection to sell more of them.

As this trend rolls on, we could become accustomed to having robots, androids, holograms, and other display-based manifestations of AI in important roles. They will become colleagues, friends, and possibly even lovers. Home AI will be as much part of the family as pets even before they achieve full sentience, and certainly long before they achieve human-level intelligence. This creates social convergence. AI, robots and androids will become part of our community, not just tools. As AI becomes smarter, human and machine societies will develop and start to converge.

We will have to accept legal convergence too. It can only be a matter of time before smart machines are given some rights and these will be added to as they get smarter. This isn't as outrageous as it might first seem. We generally accept that animals should not be made to suffer needlessly. If we start to make machines that have some notion of self-awareness, pain, discomfort, or stress so we will need to make allowances for that too.

This convergence will go further though. Beyond 2050, some AIs will be hybrid ex-humans, living their electronic immortality. Others will be normal people using direct brain links to inhabit robots and androids while still living. A few may be inhabited by groups of people and AI. As this kind of technology gradually develops over decades, convergence will continue and the boundaries between human and machine would gradually be blurred and ultimately erased.

In closing

Convergence between man and machine looks inevitable, both personally, with our bodies linked in various ways to machines, and socially as we accept them into our community as beings rather than just tools. It will have profound impacts on human society and even on human nature, bringing tough ethical challenges. But at every stage, there will also be big gains to be had for human wellbeing. Convergence will spawn new industries with enormous markets and thereby provide the incentive to address and solve those issues.

The biggest early markets will arise from both AI and the convergence of IT and biotech through monitoring health, increasing sensory capability, and even recording and replaying sensations. Nanotechnology will increase the extent of these opportunities. Later on, convergence of neurotechnology, IT, and AI will result in markets for cognitive repair and enhancement. These services will ultimately have the potential to improve quality of life in our old age, and even to confer a form of electronic immortality when that draws to its end.

These technologies will have a profound impact on society and on business. For example, what will our policy be on employees seeking such enhancements? Several critical commercial questions also arise:

- *Which of these emerging markets fit with your current product and service portfolio and which opportunities are you best positioned to exploit?*
- *How could you participate in research and development in these sectors to maximize opportunities for your organization?*
- *How could you use the ethical issues to establish brand leadership?*

The Rise of Neurosocial Networks – The Prospects for Networking our Brains in the Next 20 Years

By Martin Dinov and Andrew Vladimirov

How might our world change when we can connect people's brains together?

Unleashing the potential of neurotechnologies and neurosocial networks

This chapter explores the potential developments in **neurotechnologies** that could allow us to connect people on a brain-to-brain level. It examines the immense social, technological, and commercial implications of the development of this "neurotech" industry.

Defining neurosocial

We define **neurosocial** as any aspects, technologies, ideas, and methodologies which enable or involve the input or output of signals to our brains at the neural level – often referred as **neural input/output (NIO)**. Specifically, for a technology or idea to qualify as being neurosocial, it should be networked in some way. How can we achieve NIO? Common technologies that fit this requirement and are already used today include:

- Electroencephalography (EEG) and similar approaches
- Functional near-infrared spectroscopy (fNIRS).
- Various forms of brain stimulation techniques such as transcranial current stimulation (tCS)
- Various other types of stimulation such as coherent (laser) and decoherent (LED) light, magnetic, ultrasound – most of which are available in a portable form

We believe the portability of the technologies involved to be important. While it is possible to network our brains using large stationary equipment like magnetic resonance imaging (MRI) scanners, it is more prone to difficulties and not scalable. So in this chapter we will be exploring likely neurotechnological developments that will be neurosocial in nature.

Current technologies

A range of technologies such as transcranial electrostimulation are already available to change the brain's state and stimulate brain activity. We believe these are inherently crude and the **neurostimulation** protocols they employ are not very selective. While they can be tuned to the individual (see next section), the physics and physiology involved are such that trying to stimulate the brain from the surface of the scalp non-invasively has fundamental limitations which – at present – cannot be overcome.

However, this does not mean that the current state of affairs (which is one of hackish and experimental consumer neurostimulation products) will not change. While there are fundamental restrictions to the effectiveness of non-invasive brain modulation technologies, this is analogous to the fundamental limitations of pharmacological brain or body-affecting products, such as caffeine and alcohol for example. In fact, pharmacological products are rarely (virtually never) as specific to the part of the brain as they are meant to be, and their effects include significant individual variability which is very hard to adjust. Despite the limitations, we expect to see great improvements in the technologies involved. In particular such technologies will become easier to use, cheaper, and safer as a result of better real time effects monitoring and protection mechanisms.

An important aspect of reading the brain's current state – and doing something contingent upon it – is the ability to recognize the difference between two possibly quite similar brain states. This is in fact not so trivial – minute differences in EEG signals can signify important differences in mental/brain states. The point is this: how do we personalize the experience for the user so that we can do specific (say computerized) tasks during person-specific brain states? The answer lies in various statistical and machine learning methods that can detect complex patterns in the data in a reasonable period of time.

We already have computer games that are playable using consumer EEG headsets like **The MindWave**, as well as physical toys that move based on the EEG signal, and even drones that can be flown by focusing or relaxing. However, all of these are currently not personalized at all. It is personal only in the sense that you can fly the drone with your brain's state – say by focusing. But the actual computations that take place are quite general. We believe this is going to change quite drastically. Already, personalization of brain-related activities is becoming common in labs around the world.

Technological developments on the horizon

An incredible revolution is certain if micro, or even nano, sized recording electrodes can be developed. A group from MIT has already thought about a potential way to create such a system, where the electrodes would float around your brain, recording activity in a way far superior to current signal capture techniques. Though the technical challenges in creating them are not trivial, working prototypes could be made within a few years if interest and funding are directed appropriately. It is easily conceivable that such machines will be able to stimulate, as well as record. As a result, the possibilities for neurosocial applications and networks could grow immensely.

Another fascinating development set to emerge is the creation of physical neural interfaces that will be able to record and write to specific brain regions, driven by very smart artificial intelligence (AI) software. Even if theses interfaces are not initially micro or nano-sized, they would still allow machine learning software to watch and learn as you record new memories in an area of the brain called the hippocampus. We can then begin to backup those memories and encode, share, and process them digitally.

As for the neurostimulation protocols applied, a range of novel methodologies will be developed that are capable of targeting specific mechanisms. These would include specific biochemical interactions, transport of selected ions across cell membranes, or even specific gene expression. This will bring the selectivity of neurostimulation to a similar level as that of contemporary drugs – without losing its spatio-temporal advantages over pharmacology. This is not to say that neurostimulation would replace use of the relevant medication; rather it is going to compliment it – eventually receiving recognition and funding from major players in the pharma industry. This will open up numerous interesting opportunities for concurrent physical stimulation and drug use, including in a neurosocial context. Inevitably, risks similar to those of substance addiction and abuse will also multiply and will have to be assessed very carefully.

Future applications of neurotechnology

One important area that can be improved hugely through the use of neurotechnologies is education. By monitoring students' attention in real time, the teacher can have more than just an intuitive feel for whether a particular individual is paying attention or not. More importantly, the learning environment can be adapted to maximize the students' attention. Some environments are clearly more condu-cive to education than others. However, it is hard to know ahead of time the educational impact of a particular environment before seeing how each student performs within it.

The situation will change once we can monitor individual attention and behavior. We will be able to stimulate students' brains to respond better to certain types of information than others – depending on the situation and the individual, for example. All of this will initially be voluntary, or employed to help people with learning disabilities. However, once some students and their parents agree to monitoring and even boosting a child's ability neurotechnologically, competitive forces will lead others to follow suit. We believe the consensus will be a general agreement that these technologies are here to stay.

The potential to transform education will have ripple effects across the world, as it forms the roots of every society. A well educated society should produce more, be generally healthier, have reduced crime and unemployment rates, and attain numerous other benefits.

Now let's think about the possible impact on relationships. Imagine having your smartphone or computer tell you how your partner is feeling. This is, again, achievable today, but has not yet been done. Electroencephalography can potentially be used to easily monitor our mood and levels of relaxation, arousal, or wakefulness which could be stored and communicated to others. If EEGs become more widely used (perhaps more selectively and temporarily at first during specific tasks or times), then partners or friends could know when to call each other and when not to. Of course, such information could be used more egocentrically in the social networks of today and tomorrow, giving an interesting twist to social engineering attacks. To counter such threats, powerful brain activity-based biometric authentication protocols may be developed.

If the EEG was combined with a method of influencing brain function (such as tCS), a range of interesting and more controversial developments could be possible. For example, you could give your partner or friend software and networking permissions to modify your brain's state within safe and reasonable limits. So, if you are feeling down or agitated and not relaxed, or overly relaxed when you need to be more awake and focused, they could decide to start a stimulation protocol that will make you happier, more focused, or more relaxed. Or perhaps you are a parent who would like to keep their son focused during school by giving the child necessary stimulations to maintain their attention in class, or to keep them happy, especially during the chaotic teenage years. All of this can clearly happen more easily with the help of automation and software, which may in turn open up markets for parental brain control and software that allows for various types and levels of brain sharing.

There are obvious ethical, privacy, and health concerns here which are interesting in their own right. Neurosocial privacy, or perhaps brain privacy, will surely become a more talked about issue in the years to come.

Other areas that could be highly affected by emerging neurotechnologies are medicine and health. While we can already decide when to go to a doctor for an ailment, we are often not well able to judge the severity of the condition. We also cannot predict how it might develop in the near future. However, objective brain measurements could help – informing us whether this low feeling really is a depression, or just a bad day. This is available today and will certainly become more widespread in the next decade. The device could potentially be integrated with other wearable and embedded devices (**insideables**) into a single personal area network, monitoring peripheral body functions. Neurotechnologies will allow the remote and real-time monitoring of neurological conditions and other ailments. They would also enable monitoring for preventative purposes. For example, if you are wearing an EEG or fNIRs device for gaming, entertainment, or personal communications, why not uses it for health purposes as well?

Within the framework of interpersonal interactions, such brain sharing between patients and therapists, combined with stimulation-assisted neurofeedback, could completely revolutionize counseling, and in particular group therapy approaches. In a similar manner, it could be employed to dramatically enhance the effectiveness of brainstorming and other creative collaboration activities in corporate or other relevant environments, in particular when done remotely. Such applications can actually break groupthink, design by committee, paralysis by analysis, and other ineffective working patterns. They could also promote diversity of perspectives within a particular group by varying the stimulation protocols and/or the brain areas that were targeted for different participants.

Tapping into the true social and commercial impact of neurosocial ideas

The above illustrations of neurotechnology applications give a sense of the broad range of business and startup opportunities that are likely to appear within the next decade. But what are some of the obstacles to creating various types of neurosocial networks?

While greater precision and flexibility in recording and stimulating methods would help enormously, these are not necessary. With today's available technologies, we can already begin to create such neurosocial applications. More important is the need for increased awareness of what is already possible today with commercially available EEG and fNIRs headsets. There needs to be an associated increased level of interest in the brain and what we can do with such brain computer interfaces (BCIs). Investment is also required to create the software and platforms to collect and exploit the data that these devices would provide.

The possibilities of adding BCIs (and more generally and technically, NIOs) to current future applications and platforms would fundamentally transform how we interact with our machines and our world, including with other people. Being able to issue commands to your computer by focusing or thinking specific thought patterns is a great advance. However, this would be amplified many times over when we add networking capabilities to these brain-controlled and brain-influencing devices. Hence, the scale of the opportunity has led some prominent people to speculate that the next batch of startups from players like Google, Microsoft, and Apple will include ventures in the neurotechnology sphere. We believe that this will almost certainly be the case.

What such networking capabilities will really allow is nothing less than a platform for anything to be created that involves connectivity and distribution. In other words, a networked BCI platform can be extended, molded and expanded in many directions by simply writing apps that take advantage of the networking capability. It is highly likely that we will see such networked brain platforms which will also support various non-invasive neurostimulation means over the next decade. In some ways, such platforms will be similar to the first computers: they did not look great. They put together a number of disparate electronic components into a single more general-purpose device that could, in theory, do a lot of things, given the right applications written for it. We believe this is a good comparison for the networked-brains industry that will soon be with us.

What questions should businesses consider?

- *How could these technologies change working practices and the skills required in your organization?*
- *What impact cold these technologies have on the way you interact with customers and other stakeholders?*
- *Should society seek to impose any limits on the development of neurotechnologies or allow the market to determine what's appropriate?*

Life in 2035: Future Consciousness, Cyborgs and Wisdom

By Victor Vahidi Motti

How might advances in science and technology transform our understanding of the limits and potential of humans and organizations?

In this chapter I explore how rapid and radical advances in science and technology could disrupt and reformulate our understanding of human capability and wisdom, of the nature of work and the boundary between human and machine.

A leaderless society of equal people operating a "network of things"

Some while ago, I was asked by a successful business owner – and nervous parent – to advise him as a professional futurist on a promising university program for his highly talented daughter. The conversation was long and I'll make the point short. I told him about many occupations such as pilots, drivers, engineers, managers, physicians, surgeons, and teachers that are already automated or could very soon be replaced by machines like IBMs Watson artificial intelligence (AI) platform. He paused and wondered how we can know which expert fields will fall beyond the reach of machines. Which choices might guarantee job prospects at least until the turn of our 21st century?

I replied: "Whatever can be written will be taken over by programmers and AI researchers sooner or later." In other words, if there is a manual, book, handbook, paper, or the like on how to do something, then software could be developed and evolved to a sufficiently human level of precision and skill to perform that task. "The more creative and imaginative you are, such as a theory builder, the more likely it is that you will be on the safe side."

In that world, major technology advances will allow the average citizen to become so wise that they will probably not need or want a group of leaders to set rules or guide them from the top. Therefore a leaderless network society of people and things could be the new normal. In the future, wise designer-workers will not need to count on managers or leaders to design and implements business operations, systems and processes. Instead they will deliver products and services to customers by communicating and interacting with each other and the things around them in a hierarchy-free manner. Knowledge and experience will be shared freely – with individuals and systems collaborating and supporting each other like counterpart coaches. Let's examine how such technology advances could change our world.

Default automatic deep insight for good or evil

Differential equations are used for forecasting the future of physical systems. Engineers and scientists are using increasingly more sophisticated software to solve them in order to design diverse systems. Such software has left many professionals in disbelief when it automatically provides step by step solutions for complex differential equations. This computation power will increasingly be taken for granted and is a very important leading indicator with respect to the future of artificial intelligence (AI).

Imagine a robot which has uploaded an advanced version of these abilities and consider the possibility If – in the future – ordinary people could insert microscopic versions of these robots into their own brains. These **nanobots** would allow humans to stay permanently connected to the Internet. We would become "all knowing people", at least in terms of our knowledge of physical systems. Using this newly acquired deep knowledge of the nonlinear differential equations that govern how our chaotic and complex systems work and interact, individuals could trigger far reaching consequences through simple initial actions. For example, the basic act of tossing a pen in the street could cause or initiate a very long chain of interconnected events, with the eventual outcome of either a disaster or a miracle in a big city.

Redefinition of a child and its labor

It is easy to get lost in the techno-hype and, inevitably, there are many potentially absurd, ridiculous, or counter intuitive technological scenarios emerging. For example, a finance expert in one of my recent workshops suggested that soon banks will send a robot to loan applicants. Instead of filling out numerous forms it would ask them to *spit* on its hand. The robot would analyze the applicant's genome and decide instantly if their credit risk is high or low. Even though this might be technologically feasible – a variety of social factors would most likely prevent the scenario from materializing.

Let us focus then on some more likely but equally impactful scenarios. We know that our relationship with machines, even our sense of identity, is constantly changing and sometimes in highly unexpected ways. An example that might shed some light on this scenario is the point at which machines will treat and think of adults in the same way as we treat and think of children. Today child labor is a big social problem, but in the future kids could have toys to play with in a way that we now know as a having a job. As children become more intelligent and operations become more simplified and increasingly entrusted to automated systems, what is required are people who can curate and play with a system to fulfill its maximum capacity. The skills and mindset of a computer gamer could become more valuable those of a traditionally trained engineer or technician. Of course, today for a limited number of workers, their job is already a form of play, fun, or like a hobby. In the future, the serious tasks we now call operations management will be redefined as fun experiences and could increasingly be trusted to children.

You can make sense of this change another way. In a highly sophisticated machine controlled environment, there is increasingly little real difference between the intelligence level and skills of an adult human and that of a child. In an automated environment, task specific experience, skills, and knowledge become less relevant than an understanding of how best to "play the game" with the machine that is performing the task. In such circumstances the quantified difference of intelligence or mental skills between adult and child might be as low as 0.001 and 0.0001. Hence, when rounded to two decimal points, there is effectively no difference between them. Therefore, a change of role occurs and in the future tasks will increasingly be interchangeable between adults and children.

The impossibility of copy and paste of personality

We hear stories in the news that the first-ever human head, or more appropriately body, transplant could soon become possible. Personally, I would prefer a human head with a robotic body or a robot with a human face – as in the movie *Bicentennial Man*. A human body (with a robotic head) may not be feasible because the human body needs sleep and rest whereas machines can have continuous awareness. Also, the concept of uploading the human mind to a robot or artificially intelligent machine may need us to redefine the notion of "ongoing self" – a concept which has been debated among philosophers.

Suppose that your "self" is just your memories in terms of experiences and knowledge. In that case, we might simply copy and paste data from your dying brain into a robot which bears your face. However, you can point out that "self" is far more than just memories and what we know. It includes our individual personality, unique patterns of thinking, feelings, decision-making approaches, and ways of behaving in new circumstances. In this case, brain uploading becomes a much more challenging task. Identifying the core components and predictive elements of your personality, what makes your mind totally different from that of another human, is currently impossible – let alone trying to copy and paste them in another place.

The possibility of direct access to brains from distance

With the prospect of a potential increase in protests and conflicts in a changing and ever-more complex world, what future technologies could we imagine governments adopting to control crowds of humans or to wage and prevent wars? For example, **Optogenetics** is a breakthrough technology which uses light beams to give us control from a distance over molecules inside the body of a target. This could enable us to influence what animals feel, how they behave, and what they think. Such a technology has been put to test for making mice feel fearful or fearless.

Provided that the sophistication of Optogenetics continues to improve, we can imagine a world policed or controlled by beams of light. Although it might seem like absurd science fiction, we should expect that advances of neuro-enabled policing could help future governments use light beams instead of water cannons to disperse or neutralize crowds. Similarly, the opposition movements around the world might use light beams to make the human populations fearless. Optogenetics is a game changer as it gives people direct access to neurons, without even touching the target body.

It will become nearly impossible to hide our mind and body

Some technology applications in which a synthesis of biology and technology occurs – like biofeedback and bioassays (e.g. testing and monitoring biological data related to body composition) – may have more far reaching implications than most of us could imagine. Future systems should significantly reduce the time required (from days and weeks to hours) and associated costs of conducting bioassays. Imagine a possible future where people can not only do checkups on their health in real time but also, where allowed, receive instant reports from the bodies of others. This creates the scenario where you can hack into a person's body and mind to see vividly almost all the micro bodily variables of the people you are dealing with by simply pressing a button. We'd have to live in a literally "transparent society" since we could not even hide or cover our mind and body.

Emergence of hybrid minds

Before Albert Einstein, people involved in physics made sense of and worked with four core concepts – space, time, matter, and energy. These four were thought to be independent from each other. Einstein showed that only two hybrid concepts should make sense: space-time and mass-energy. A century ago in 1915 he established the theory of General Relativity – a profound reciprocal relationship between space-time and mass-energy. Earlier separation of space, time, matter, and energy was based on traditional categories that proved to be false after his discovery. Perhaps, in the future, an equivalent paradigm shift in psychology may emerge as the result of an integral combination of psyche with something that has been incorrectly separated from it.

My suggestion for a future psychological paradigm shift could be reflected in the **psychocosmos** which means that your body and mind are what the bigger universe of minds is evolving towards. My brain and that of the other contributors to this book, for instance, might be connected and turn into a hybrid one. A cyborg, as envisioned by Thomas Lombardo[203], Director of both the Center for Future Consciousness and The Wisdom Page, is a "functional synthesis of biology and technology". He argues that a wise cyborg, guided by the ideals of wisdom, will draw its extraordinary and potentially limitless power from the "intellectual, informational, and communicational capacities of computer technologies".

Patterns of progress in the wisdom of human civilization

Lombardo suggests that, in the coming decades, we will witness a new collective enlightenment – which many futurists describe as a "significant jump in the collective mental functioning of humanity". Evolutionary forces will push humanity to a new level of "cosmic consciousness". Before answering the questions surrounding the characteristics and nature of this new higher level and the necessary transition period, we need to explore the possibilities for the very long term pattern of change for the wisdom level of human civilization. The truth is that we cannot predict the future but can imagine alternative possibilities for such patterns of change. For example, progress in human wisdom could improve at a very gradual rate, or experience sudden increases as a result of developments in science and technology – for example the emergence of AI.

Reinventing the learning process for CEOs

CEOs are lonely decision makers who are often overwhelmed by large volumes of information and pressed by approaching deadlines. They might also have a very short time to learn some of the big lessons of running a profitable business. In an ideal world, what they need is an assurance that they are connected to the largest possible collective of minds across the world to help ensure checks and balances on their decision making.

The combination of open access knowledge and "lifelong learning" creates the potential for a major disruption, unprecedented in education and learning. In the past, only a few people could actually become lifelong learners – it needed both sustained interest and easy access to knowledge sources. When you were out of school or university you may have easily discontinued your association with knowledge seekers, providers, and sources. Today, the learning journey should and need never stop, if we can overcome natural human inertial factors. Libraries and universities are no longer monopoly knowledge providers – neither are professors and teachers.

The forces of open access knowledge and lifelong collaborative learning are already helping in regions like Africa to disconnect citizens from the past and redefining the learning opportunities available to them. Some people may stop short of calling these changes innovation, but I feel that disruption is a relevant description. Such developments could benefit those currently in the CEO role. They could also help create a whole new global generation of business leaders who have grown up believing in both the value of collaborative open access learning and the power of tapping in to global wisdom to inform their decision making.

A couple of questions emerge that may help us to make sense of what is on the horizon for us all:

- *How can businesses prepare for the day when wise humans, hybrid people and a network of intelligent things do not need a manager or leader to operate?*
- *What could be the business impact of easy and accurate access to our body and mind from a distance – what are the implications for workers' rights and privacy?*
- *What impact could science and technology advances have on the gap between the rich and poor – what are the implication basic human rights and corporate responsibility?*

The Potential for Technological Singularity and its Future Impacts on Society

By Anish Mohammed

What is the Singularity and what could it mean for individuals, society, government and business?

This chapter explores the notion of the technological singularity, explains how it might come about and the potential challenges it could create as humanity strives to grapple with its deep-seated implications.

What is the technological singularity?

Within mathematics, the term singularity refers to a mathematical object that behaves differently than expected. It is a point where a function yields an undefined value, for example, when trying to calculate infinity or the precise point when Artificial Intelligence (AI) may overtake human intelligence. At this point, the value overtakes the ordinary points in the domain of the function and its trend becomes asymptotic or, so to speak, explosive. When we try to understand the changes in the world around us, especially when we try to form an idea of the possible outcomes from accelerating change, the term **singularity** is an insightful analogy. It encompasses in one word several separate aspects of the rate of societal transformations observed across many fields along with their interconnections and interdependencies.

Observation of the trajectories of various fields of science and technology—computing, telecommunications, biotechnology, nanotechnology, genetic engineering—indicates that they have advanced at an exponential rate, with greater progress being made over steadily decreasing time periods. This is what the technologist and futurologist Ray Kurzweil has termed "the Singularity" (with a capital s) – defining it as, "…a future period during which the pace of technological change will be so rapid, its impact so deep, that human life will be irreversibly transformed."[204]

The history of human civilization may be described as a series of phase changes as new forms of energy and information exchange have been unlocked through technology. Since the 1980s, observers including Vinge[205], Moravec[206], Marchetti[207], and Kurzweil have remarked upon the social consequences of the accelerated rates of invention and innovation which appear to be self-perpetuating.

These phenomena may have profound impacts on most aspects of our lives. Our civilization could be altered drastically and decisively: drastically, since accelerating changes would overtake ordinary people's ability to comprehend and respond to it (a condition that futurist Alvin Toffler described as 'Future Shock'[208]); decisively, since people, whether individually or collectively, would find fewer and fewer personal experiences that are distinct from an integrated whole, for example the rest of society to whom we would be connected in this technological singularity. Hence the human condition itself could be altered irrevocably.

Beyond artificial intelligence – the rise of superintelligent machines

The capability of computational machines is increasing exponentially in terms of memory size, capacity to handle ever larger data sets, and energy consumption, while costs are falling quite dramatically. These developments are expected to lead to the emergence of artificial intelligence (AI) and the broader concept of artificial general intelligence (AGI). The resulting entity would be of such sophisticated and self-enhancing power that even humans with technologically augmented intellects would not be able to compete, nor perhaps even comprehend the thoughts of the AI / or AGI.

At that point, developments in the internet of things coupled with genetic engineering and prosthetic augmentation of human physical and mental capacities of a person, may lead to a blending of human and machine intelligence and identities. This computational trajectory where blended AI may begin to take charge of what we experience means that **superintelligent machines** will gain the capability to alter or "edit" objects in the physical world through the use of nanotechnology. An example of which would be "foglets" of nanomachines that can physically create and reshape reality itself, e.g. generating and reforming physical objects. Our society is dependent upon technology and driven by it. However, the far-reaching potential impact of the singularity means that beyond a certain point, it is impossible to predict the future outcomes of accelerating returns on technological innovation, as the post-singularity world could look so unlike our own.

Enabling technologies of the singularity

To make the most of such technologies requires key resources such as tools that manage large data sets and energy sources to run ever more powerful computer processors which are enabling this vision of increasingly sophisticated machine intelligence. Key emerging technologies that are providing enhanced capabilities in AI include deep learning systems and quantum computation.

In contrast to traditional human-directed computer programming approaches, machine learning systems have the capability to write and adapt their own rules and code over time based on observation of a particular domain. Of particular interest is a machine learning technique known as Deep Structured Learning (DSL) – which simulates the architecture of the brain, particularly the neural activity of the neocortex. Backed by powerful computation, this newly supplemented application of artificial neural networks (ANN) involves iteratively recognizing patterns in data and automatically discovering hierarchies of relationships in digitized representations of the real world such as documents, images and videos.

For example, consider the analysis of a video clip. The DSL approach involves combining bits of sounds and images that then lead to the higher level recognition of concepts such as phonemes and shapes. The aggregation process continues, leading finally, to positive identification of words and faces with reinforcement provided by negative or positive feedback from the trainer. Applications include image and speech recognition, drug discovery, toxicology and even autonomous systems, but the greatest promises lies within natural language processing and – eventually – **brain building**. Recently, deep learning techniques have begun to outperform more traditional machine learning algorithms in the evaluation of large data sets.

An introduction to the science of quantum computing

In contrast to traditional digital computers in which only two basic states are available (0 or 1), quantum computing devices allow for tasks to be performed acknowledging all possible permutations. Quantum computers encode information as quantum bits, or **qubits** that can exist in multiple states simultaneously – thus potentially enabling far faster computing speeds. The advantage of quantum computing lies particularly in big data applications, and is soon expected to further accelerate progress in ANN and deep learning. Quantum computers make direct use of quantum-mechanical phenomena, such as superposition and entanglement. Implementations are still in their infancy. However quantum computing has already been applied to reduce exponentially the time taken to run Shor's algorithm to solve the problem of finding the prime factors of a given integer – which is crucial for cryptography.[209] Other promising techniques such as Grover's algorithm, apply quantum computing to search successfully through unsorted databases with incredible speed.[210]

Quantum associative memory and quantum perception-based neural networks are very recent developments. The quantum property of entanglement—that is superposed correlations among quantum states which get communicated between qubits of information when the superposition collapses—has no classical counterpart. This offers unprecedented possibilities, at least theoretically. Progress is already being made in harnessing quantum parallelism and quantum tunneling. Adiabatic quantum computing by D-Wave Two, the quantum annealer acquired by Google at NASA Ames, is one such device. It is hoped that this technology can be applied to develop powerful quantum algorithms for applications like personal assistants, spam filtering, better air traffic controls, and data analysis.

The aim is to progress from the current, very low qubit computers and experiment with original techniques such as quantum chilling as well as quantum-classical hybrids. The projection – according to what is popularly called Rose's Law – is that the number of qubits should double every year. This could lead to singularity (from the computational perspective) even sooner than projected by Moore's Law. The challenges lie in physically implementing logical gates to construct higher qubit counts for useful application, and in addressing information loss and error correction. As they require super-cooled, low-noise environments, quantum devices are difficult to build and require constant maintenance. Furthermore, there is ongoing dispute as to whether these machines are indeed actually operating on the level of quantum mechanics, something which cannot, by definition, be verified, as it would interfere with the superposition of quantum states.

Implications

The implications of these ever accelerating returns on technological investment could be massive and permanently alter man's experiences, actions, thinking, and relation to others. These changes would outpace slower sectors, such as legal, financial, and judicial, causing considerable potential disruption. It is incumbent upon responsible individuals, therefore, to imagine carefully and rigorously what transformations the fabric woven out of human, social and technological threads will undergo, before such widespread change arrives.

As I see it, there are two key questions which we must ask:

First, are the fundamental assumptions regarding a technological singularity justified by empirical evidence?

The recent quantum models of deep learning might well lead to the achievement of singularity ahead of prior predictions. It is, however, important to take a step back and ask on what premises or assumptions the forecasting has been based, and what is the accelerating parameter that is being measured? If the fit applies roughly to multiple phenomena—cosmological, geological, biological, and technological (as further explained by the six successive epochs identified by Kurzweil[211]) — all contributing to a greater picture of big history, should these be seen as containing multiple singularities rather than a single integrated one? In other words, where does one singularity end and another begin?

Second, how can we reconcile the differences between humans and machines, and create a society where both human and machine intelligence is integrated? Not only that, but how will we be able to cope with machines that have capabilities far beyond our own being – capable of super-intelligence and manipulating our sense of reality?

Applying the Turing Test

Kurzweil and Mitchell Kapor have an ongoing bet and accompanying debate on whether any computer or machine will have passed the Turing Test by 2029. The test determines whether a machine has a capability equivalent to or indistinguishable from human intelligence. We can observe the invocation of several components of human intelligence which machines either will or can never mimic. Human knowledge is composed not just of empirically obtained data, but also concepts, ideas, abstractions, knots of thought (such as paradoxes, dilemmas, and contradictions), as well as emotions, temperaments, dispositions, and psychopathological formations. Can such complex inter-relating phenomena compare to superfast computation of data (acquired from all literature available online) and deep learning simulation of selective brain processes?

Machines have the capacity for either intelligent amorality, or of possessing levels of ethics far beyond our own (likely even more dangerous). It therefore remains a very open question as to whether a machine can ever pass a moral Turing test. Whether the test is passed or not, the replacement of human intelligence by machine intelligence that mimics human moral, emotional, and social behavior, and the displacement of humans by transhumans, would not give more of the same thing, namely intelligence, nor will it be the same goals that are fulfilled faster and better.

In summary the key questions for humanity to answer would be:

- *What are the implications for humanity and human existence once machines could do everything better than humans could?*
- *Should humans consider enhancing themselves to keep themselves relevant to the intelligence race?*
- *Should the technological singularity occur, how might concepts such a business, trade, jobs and profit need to evolve – will they have any meaning or relevance in that world?*

Section 5

Disruptive Developments – How might new technologies enable business innovation?

Tomorrow's technologies – exponential, disruptive and pervasive

New and emerging technologies represent a significant opportunity for innovation in business, a number of them have the potential to be truly disruptive and transform business practices and entire industry sectors. Processing power, new methods of connecting systems and people, and decentralized systems models such as the blockchain all herald new opportunities. At the same time new analytical and simulation approaches, artificial intelligence and advanced manufacturing processing all open a gateway to business innovation.

In this section we explore eight of these potential disruptions and their implications for society and business.

The Decentralization of Everything – Exploring The Business of the Blockchain (*page 295*) – In Rohit Talwar and Alexandra Whittington explain blockchain technology and discuss its potential disruptive impacts for society, business and economies.

The Future of the Phone Call (*page 309*) – Dean Bubley explores the potential evolution of the phone call and considers the implications of more fragmented, functional and customized forms of telecommunication.

Will AI Eat the World? (*page 319*) – Calum Chace examines the benefits and risks of AI and "conscious machines" for business and society.

From Clouds to Networks Without Infrastructure (page 333) – Dr. Peter Cochrane outlines the radical innovations required in networking infrastructures to support the projected growth in internet usage and the rise of the internet of everything.

Future Developments and Opportunities for Deep Learning Artificial Neural Networks (page 340) – Elias Rut and Martin Dinov highlight how deep learning Artificial Neural Networks as could have a transformative impact on our understanding the brain and on a range of business sectors.

How Massive Simulation Models could Transform Decision Making in Business, Government and Society (page 349) – Vinay Gupta's discusses how large scale simulations could enabled us to value the impact of everything from climate change to a new business model.

The Future of Events and Networking (page 354) – Tiana Sinclair highlights how technology innovation could transform the live experience for attendees, event owners, sponsors and planners.

Revolutionizing Interactive Entertainment and Marketing in Public Places through Ambient Interactivity (page 359) – Michael Mascioni provides an overview of how ambient interactivity could enhance user experiences and marketing effectiveness.

Global Drivers of Change

By April Koury, Iva Lazarova and Rohit Talwar

Below we summarize seventeen major science and technology drivers that could underpin the disruptions described across the chapters in this section.

- **Continuation of Moore's Law** – Moore's Law states that the numbers of transistors on an affordable CPU will double every 18 months to two years, resulting in computers with double the processing speed. Experts believe that new developments in nanoscale transistors will continue this exponential trend for some time to come. This is at the heart of discussions about exponential technologies and the transformations and disruptions they can enable.

- **Exponential Technologies** – Across a range of sectors from computing to genetics, researchers and engineers are pursuing exponential improvements in the capability and performance of the systems they are engineering. From computer memory to energy generation, genome sequencing and new materials – the goal is to drive at least a doubling of performance in each standard time period.

- **Digitization of Everything** – Advances in information and communications technology, sensors, and new materials are laying the foundation for literally every object on the planet to have a digital representation of it in the virtual world – from individual identities to the food we eat. The goal is to be able to encode and uniquely identify every element. In many cases those objects will have a digital layer built into their fabric from the point of manufacture, for example our clothing, shoes, wallpaper, and construction materials. With wearable and embedded technologies this physical integration of digital technology will include more and more humans over time.

- **Disruptive Innovation** – Progress in science and technology is driving a range of disruptive developments that are leading to profound societal and business change. The web disrupted traditional media by directly connecting content creators to their audiences. Similarly, companies like Airbnb, Uber, and Coursera have shaken up and redefined their respective markets with new, innovative business models that draw on our growing hyperconnectivity to deliver goods and services for free or at a fraction of the cost. In the "physical" world, new manufacturing paradigms like 3D (and eventually 4D) printing, advanced robotics, synthetic biology, and grown materials are disrupting and transforming manufacturing processes, industries, and businesses.

- **Cloud Computing** – Rather than investing in a local server or personal computer, data content and applications can be stored and accesses remotely over a network via cloud computing. This service frees up space, decreases energy use, and reduces the overhead costs in building and maintaining in-house computing centers. It represents a major shift in how companies acquire and maintain many IT capabilities. On average, organizations fully utilizing cloud computing save more than 15 percent in IT spending according to estimates in 2014.[212]

- **Hyperconnectivity** – At the core of hyperconnectivity is the belief that anything which can be connected to the network, should be. It is redefining the way that humans, enterprises, governments, and even machines connect and interrelate, and it is providing new models for innovation, new opportunities for growth, and new risks that will have to be managed and mitigated. Forecasted social consequences of hyperconnectivity such as shorter attention spans – the tl;dr (too long; didn't read) response to anything over a few paragraphs – and a lack of depth as people expect everything delivered in 140 characters, give rise to concerns that technology, not people, will dominate social settings.

- **Open Platforms for Innovation** – Open platforms are software systems based on open standards, where software is able to function in ways other than the original programmer intended. Third parties can integrate with the open platform and build products and services using the original programmer's assets. Apple's App Store, where almost anyone can build and publish Apps, is an example of an open platform. Because open platforms enable third parties to build while bypassing costly and time-consuming business development, they are a cheaper, quicker way to integrate customers closely to a business and customize deeply to meet their needs. Open platforms will continue to grow as digital technology continues to spread around the world.

- **Big Data** – As society continues to grow the level of hyperconnectivity and automation and embed sensors in everything, the amount of data collected from daily activities and transactions is expected to expand exponentially. According to experts, in 2012 we created roughly 2.8 zettabytes (2.8 trillion GBs) of information, and they forecast that by 2020 we'll have created 40 zetabytes.[213] The expected exponential growth of Big Data ties directly into the growth of the internet of things, or the number of sensors and devices that will be connected to the web.

- **Predictive Analytics** – The growth of big data has given rise to need for tools that can sift through vast amounts of information and find important trends. Predictive analytics draws on techniques such as statistics, modeling, data mining, and AI to predict the near-term future behaviors of people, markets, or systems, based on current and historic data sets. Global spending on big data hardware, software, and services is projected to

THE FUTURE OF BUSINESS

continue to grow at 30 percent per year, reaching an estimated total market size of $114 billion by 2018.[214]

- **Smart Devices** – The growing use of smart devices will continue to increase worldwide, reaching deeper into the developing markets, and providing internet access to millions. For example, the number of smartphone users is projected to surpass two billion by 2016, and by 2018, over one-third of consumers worldwide (more than 2.56 billion people) are expected to use smartphones.[215]

- **3D Printing** – 3D printing is the process of taking a 3D digital model and making it, usually by extruding layer after layer of thin material in succession.[216] Beyond the disruptive potential in manufacturing, 3D printing is increasingly making waves in other fields like medicine, where 3D printers are using cells to print organs and prosthetics that are custom built to fit to specific patients; to construction, where an entire apartment building has been printed and assembled in China;[217] to the culinary, where 3D food printers now extrude burgers and pasta.[218]

- **4D Printing** – 4D printed objects are 3D printed objects that are able to self-assemble or alter shape when presented with an environmental change.[219] In the most basic of applications, pipes could be printed to swell and shrink to move water, or printed bricks could shift according to the amount of stress place on a wall.[220] By designing and producing customizable smart materials, 4D printing has the potential to enhance many fields including robotics, manufacturing, and construction.

- **Artificial Intelligence (AI)** – AI is the "intelligence" demonstrated by machines and software. It is usually based on computational analytical processes in either algorithms or robots, and might ultimately exhibit behavior, reasoning, and intelligence indistinguishable from that of a human being. AI could drastically alter the business landscape by taking over a number of the tasks of high skilled human professions such as doctors and lawyers. IBM's Watson supercomputer has already been deployed in diagnosing medical conditions, and reports claim that the system is significantly better than human doctors at diagnosing lung cancer.[221]

- **Robotics** – The pace of deployment and the range of capabilities of industrial, service, and domestic robots is expected to accelerate. Robots are already in widespread use in manufacturing and are now moving into areas such as healthcare, retail, hotels, policing and security, and domestic care. Prices are expected to continue falling while functionality and intelligence should rise with advances in artificial intelligence in particular.

- **Biotechnology** – As computer technology has advanced in leaps and bounds, so too has the field of biotechnology. We have mapped the human genome, cloned animals, and genetically modified crops in such ways that increases the crop yield, insect resistance, and nutritional output. Beyond agricultural innovation, biotechnology advances could increase human lifespans, deliver cures for diseases, provide new energy sources, and enable genetically enhanced humans, animals, and plants.

- **Nanotechnology** – Nanotechnology is a branch of technology that deals with the manipulation of individual atoms and molecules. The materials produced from this nanoscale manipulation tend to have extreme strength, special electrical properties such as extreme conductivity, and very low friction. It is creating opportunities for product and process innovation, especially in the industries of biotechnology, energy, chemistry, food, electronics, healthcare, chemistry, and space.

- **Nano Bio Info Cogno (NBIC)** – NBIC is the convergence of nanotechnology, biotechnology, information technologies, and cognitive science into one theoretical and applied discipline. This technological unification will deliver a wide range of new products like smart materials that also "remember" their shape, similar to shape-memory alloys.

The Decentralization of Everything? Exploring the Business of the Blockchain

By Rohit Talwar and Alexandra Whittington

How might the evolution of blockchain technology transform business, society and government?

The Blockchain – laying the groundwork for a decentralization revolution

In recent years, the term "Bitcoin" has entered the popular lexicon and is already seen as many things. It is considered a currency, a cryptocurrency, an alternative currency, and even a social movement. But above all, bitcoin has been a vehicle for a technology that demonstrates how technological invention mirrors cultural change. Although finance, wealth, and commerce sit on the surface of the discussion, the more powerful subtext is the notion of the **decentralization of everything**. The underlying technology system known as the "blockchain", has the potential to disrupt the middlemen, authorities, owners, and arbiters of judgment (bankers, judges, attorneys) who make the business and economic world tick. This chapter explores the nuts and bolts of blockchain technology and discusses its potential impacts for society, business and economies.

An uneven distribution of awareness

While some technologists, journalists, financiers, business people, and governments around the world are exploring and embracing the future potential of the blockchain, others remain blissfully unaware of its existence or potential. According to Forbes, the blockchain and Bitcoin were the subject of hundreds of new books in 2014, each promising to make a complex topic understandable and profitable.[222] Yet a recent survey found that a majority (65 percent) of Americans has no idea what Bitcoin is, and of 500 U.S. retailers surveyed, none accept Bitcoin payment.[223][224] Bad PR has not helped. As a currency, Bitcoin has been linked to underworld players like ISIS and organized crime rings, tainting the reputation of digital currency.

There is a growing understanding that the really valuable part of the story is not the digital currency but the underlying blockchain technology. Blockchain is regarded as important—very important—because it could bring about a similar scale of change as the internet itself. Blockchain's potential extends beyond currency, money, accounting or anything financial. At its core, blockchain provides a public ledger maintained by the collective activity of its users – with no central servers or clearing authorities required. Advocates are convinced that applying blockchain to a wide range of transactions and non-financial activities could lead to the formation of an entirely new economic system. They argue that the blockchain offers an incorruptible technology that serves truth and transparency while discarding oppressive centralized authority.

Defining the core components

To clarify, Bitcoin (capital B) can be considered as a communications protocol, while bitcoin (small b) is the unit of account. The blockchain is the general ledger of transactions. Despite the growing excitement and hype, the level of understanding of the basics of the blockchain, bitcoin and cryptocurrencies in general is limited. There are several key terms that need to be clarified before we go deeper in the discussion on the future of blockchain and its potential applications and implications:

- **Bitcoin** (capital B) refers to overall system of digital currency exchange and the mobile apps and computer program that provide the **wallet** through which users buy and receive bitcoins.[225] [226]
- **bitcoin** (small b) is the actual currency which people exchange when buying and selling goods and services with bitcoins.

The Blockchain is a shared public ledger which maintains the record of all confirmed transactions. It enables user wallets to calculate their bitcoin balances and verifies that the purchaser in a transaction owns the bitcoins they are spending. The integrity and the chronological order of the blockchain are enforced with cryptography. Transactions are packed (encoded) in a block formatted to very strict cryptographic rules that are then verified by the network. These rules prevent modification of previous blocks (for example transactions), which would invalidate all subsequent blocks. The general ledger or blockchain is updated constantly with each new block of transactions and this list is shared with everyone who participates – giving very high levels of transparency.[227] [228]

Mining[229] – The miner's role is to ensure that blocks are not tampered with and the blockchain stays intact. Miners use a **hashtag** process that applies a mathematical formula to the information in each new block of transactions. This process creates a **hash** – a much shorter, seemingly random sequence of letters and numbers that is stored along with the block at the end of the blockchain. Each hash is unique and changing even one character in a bitcoin block will change the hash completely. Hence, it should be almost impossible to work out the underlying data from just looking at the hash. Each new hash also includes the hash of the previous block on the blockchain.

The hashtag process should also make it impossible to alter a block as that would change the block's hash and every subsequent hash further down the chain. This would be visible to a miner who tried to run a hashtag verification on the altered block or those that follow it. The hash would be different to the stored one and instantly spotted as a fake. There is competition between miners to create the hash and effectively "seal off" a block. They earn 25 bitcoins each time they do so. This competition effectively keeps the network operating efficiently. The bitcoin network introduces additional steps in the hash verification process to prevent all of the bitcoins being mined almost instantaneously by the miners.

Smart Contracts – These are effectively computer programs which can automatically execute the terms of a contract. They eliminate the need for contractual clauses or people to get involved in their execution. Contracts could be made partially or fully self-executing and self-enforcing – giving higher levels of security to the parties involved than traditional contract law and potentially reducing the transaction costs. Smart contracts effectively monitor that the terms of a contract have been upheld and then process the payment. The can offer a range of other benefits such as identity and asset verification – proving who an asset belongs too and eliminating many potential legal disputes.[230] [231]

Decentralized Autonomous Organizations (DAOs) / Decentralized Autonomous Corporations (DACs) / Corporations as Technology / Fully Automated Business Entity – These are effectively completely automated organizations which are governed by a tight set of business rules laying out exactly how things should be done, whether by humans or software programs. Decentralized autonomous agents (weak AI) would perform the core tasks of the organization – co-coordinating with each other in hierarchy free manner. "Instead of a hierarchical structure managed by a set of humans interacting in person and controlling property via the legal system, a decentralized organization involves a set of humans interacting with each other according to a protocol specified in code, and enforced on the blockchain."[232]

A DAC's ruleset would typically be publicly auditable, written in open-source software and distributed across the stakeholders' computers. Individuals or other DAC's could becomes stakeholders by buying shares in the DAC or being paid in the company's shares in return for providing services. Share ownership might entitle stakeholders to a profit share and further work opportunities. Ownership might also give you a say in how the DAC is run and the design of the operating rules.[233]

Ethereum is a community-driven start-up project that uses the blockchain as platform for building decentralized applications and enabling the exchange of binding smart contracts – eliminating the requirements for trust and a central controlling authority. It aims to decentralize and democratize the internet.[234] [235] It could be considered a platform for DAOs.

Bitcoin: an origins story

Although the blockchain and bitcoin are promoted as transparent, there is also an enticingly concealed, secretive side to the story. Significant controversy surrounds the existence and identity of the actual bitcoin "inventor," Satoshi Nakamoto.[236] Argentine research Sergio Demian Lerner estimates that Nakamoto owns nearly one million bitcoins – an asset worth between US$150-300 billion depending on the prevailing price.[237] Nakamoto has apparently not been seen or heard from in years. In 2014, there was a Newsweek scoop that claimed he was an unemployed Los Angeles-based engineer in his 60's – but this was widely regarded as inaccurate.[238]

Several rumors and theories have been floated including the idea that Nakamoto is a pseudonym for a group of people, another person, or a conspiracy of the illuminati.[239] A university study using analysis of Nakamoto's writing concluded that the real bitcoin inventor was actually Nick Szabo, who developed **bit gold** – a predecessor cryptocurrency.[240] A May 2015 New York Times article reports that many of those most deeply involved with Bitcoin still believe Szabo to be the key man.[241] Without conclusive proof or a credible claimant, his identity may remain anonymous.

The rise of a social movement

As Vigna and Casey, the authors of The Age of Cryptocurrency, so aptly put it: "Nakamoto gave bitcoin its creation myth."[242] This myth, enhanced by the cult-like bitcoiner saying "we are all Satoshi," allows bitcoin to be expressed as not just a technology, but a social movement that favors the deconstruction of Big Brother's critical institutions of control—banks and governments. A Chinese pop economist and conspiracy theorist argues bitcoin is a means to prevent greed.[243] In fact, bitcoin is programmed to stop generating new coins around 2140. The Bitcoin site explains, "The last block that will generate coins will be block #6,929,999 which should be generated at or near the year 2140. The total number of coins in circulation will then remain static at 20,999,999.9769 BTC (bitcoins). Total BTC in circulation will always be slightly below 21 million." [244] However, this is somewhat of a misconception since it is predicted that the profit created from transaction fees leading to this 21 million will drive a push to create new blocks that will become more valuable than the new coins being created. There may actually be no practical limit to the number of blocks that could be mined.

Blockchain's rules-driven structure makes it particularly good at **if this-then-that** scenarios. For example, it is deployed within the central nervous system of ADEPT, an IBM-Samsung venture for the Internet of Things IoT.[245] This is designed to enable scenarios where smart devices such as shelves can monitor stock levels, requisition goods from the stock room, and then notify staff to collect them. Through scenarios like this the blockchain has the potential to power a revolution of interactions between humans and things.

Images of the blockchain future

There are clearly several obvious practical present day applications, and the inevitable range of future possibilities, being posited ranging from the apocalyptic to utopian. We will have to learn to co-exist with tomorrow's DAO's – which will be populated by distributed networks of intelligent agents or what some refer to as "Blockchain Thinkers".[246] These agents will execute their rules in much the same way as program trading systems do today. Clearly there are inherent risks of such systems continuing to execute a fixed rule set irrespective of how the situation around them is changing. The more sophisticated AI and robot technology become, the wider the range of scenarios these agents could handle – and the greater the risk that they might reprogram themselves in unintended and potentially undesirable ways.

Blockchain brings to life the concept of the DAO / DAC as featured in Daniel Suarez's 2006 novel **Daemon**.[247] In the book, Daemon is a program which covertly gains control of hundreds of companies' computers and "provides financial and computing resources for recruiting real world agents. . . " Clearly the Decentralized Autonomous notion could be broadened out to encompass Applications (DAPPs), Societies (DASs), Government Agencies (DAAs), and Governments at the City (DACGs) and National (DANGs) level.

One concern today is that automation of current and future industries could render many jobs obsolete over the next two decades and lead to technological unemployment. But how will we be able to afford to buy the goods and services being produced by these DACs populated by robots and intelligent agents? One view is that governments and citizens might become automatic shareholders in these firms and receive profit shares. Governments might in turn use the dividend income and / or higher taxes on DAC profits to fund some form of universal basic income. More broadly, it is already being acknowledged that the DAO / DAC concept will pose huge social, ethical, legal, and regulatory challenges as we try to adjust to a world in which companies are becoming technology platforms.

The greatest impact on day-to-day life is most likely to happen in combination with other "smart" technologies such as AI, machine learning systems, robotics, and driverless vehicles. This would enable the intelligent automated end-to-end execution of decentralized commerce transactions and smart, dynamic management of public records and information in general.[248] It would also enable the machine-to-machine (M2M) communication that will characterize the Internet of Things – covering the cycle from stock checking, through to ordering, picking, packing, and delivery.

Envisage the "smart" washing machines that orders more detergent, pays for it, organizes delivery and accepts the replenishment without any human intervention.[249] [250] There is a growing consensus amongst the blockchain innovators and analysts that this metamorphosis will become the norm in highly personal ways, with, "....Bitcoin/blockchain technology as the economic overlay to what is increasingly becoming a seamlessly connected world of multi-device computing including wearables, Internet-of-Things (IoT) sensors, smartphones, tablets, laptops, Quantified Self-Tracking devices (i.e.; Fitbit), smarthome, smartcar, and smartcity."[251]

This could revolutionize how human beings interact with objects in the future. Like electricity and telecommunications, blockchain's role as a "backbone" for smart data transfer will be subtle, but essential. Should they succeed in their ambitions, platforms like Ethereum – and those that will inevitably follow it – could truly revolutionize the functioning of many systems in society from healthcare and aviation to commerce and banking. Indeed, they may even lead to the emergence of an alternative, more transparent and democratic internet.[252]

Emerging issues

The emergence of blockchain and the platforms that enable it will also raise a series of fundamental questions, for example:

- What will replace the current models of governance that control commerce and the internet? Will we need them in a totally transparent environment?
- Where might new sources of unexpected risk emerge in a "blockchain world" that is still in its infancy and so poorly understood by all but a small group of pioneers and enthusiasts?
- What are the implications for the way in which systems are developed and the approaches to educating and training tomorrow's software engineers?
- How might these technologies reshape our relationship to reality?
- How is privacy defined within these applications and in an M2M environment?
- What are the incentives for participants within such an eco-system?" [253]

Ethereum and smart contracts

Ethereum's founder Vitalik Buterin believes the technology challenges our old notions of control, arguing that "blockchains are not about bringing to the world any one particular ruleset ... rather; they're about creating the freedom to create a new mechanism with a new ruleset extremely quickly and pushing it out."[254] Ethereum combines both a form of currency and a platform for programming new types of transactional contracts.[255] Ethereum's cryptocurrency is called Ether and is considered a medium of exchange rather than a form of investment like Bitcoin.

While Bitcoin allows the sending and receipt of money outside the formal banking system, the goal of the platform is go further by ". . . making it possible to set up binding contracts outside of the legal system."[256] Essentially, Ethereum provides a backbone network similar to Bitcoin, with a programming language that enables users to create their own tools. These tools can interact, create self-executing contracts and conduct the resulting transactions using Ether.[257] Unlike Bitcoin, there is no limit to the growth of Ether as a currency.[258] The currency was sold to raise funds for the platform and could be mined in a similar manner to Bitcoin. Already, companies are beginning to integrate Ether into their systems. For example, IBM's ADEPT smart washing machine program uses Ethereum.[259] Views differ as to whether Ethereum could replace Bitcoin – it is far too early in its development to assess its full potential.

The decentralization agenda

We are effectively seeing the birth of a completely new technology industry and one forecast predicts exponential growth in blockchain developers, rising from 40 in 2015, to 400 in 2016, and 4,000 by 2017.[260] The decentralization revolution has been labeled with different names: "Cryptocurrency 2.0," "Bitcoin 2.0," "a Web 3.0 platform". In addition to Ethereum, there are already multiple players with differing agendas pursuing decentralized solutions including: [261] [262] [263] [264]

- BitTorrent – offering decentralized file sharing
- BitShares – enabling decentralized currency exchange
- Blockstream – creating "sidechains"—i.e. smaller secondary blockchains
- Truthcoin – a form of blockchain for prediction markets
- Telehash – a decentralized encryption tool
- Maidsafe – providing distributed data management, including self-encrypting data

Perhaps the most disruptive impact will come if Ethereum delivers its goal to ". . . allow multiple organizations to build side blockchains with their own cryptocurrency and feed back into the main Ethereum chain".[265] This would effectively create a decentralized network of monetary systems all falling outside the control of central banking and legal frameworks – a concept that may be hard to imagine and a truly game changing moment in the information age.

Block chain applications – goodbye middlemen?

A range of potential uses of the blockchain have been identified including health care apps, medical records management and the retention of personal memories.[266] [267] The laundry list of ideas for blockchain includes crop insurance, gambling, reputation systems, decentralized social networks—and even an all-seeing, all knowing Skynet.[268] In the next few years, blockchain technology could disrupt and eliminate a range of parties involved in almost every type of commercial transaction. From contract attorneys to retailers charging credit card transaction fees – the game could soon be up. A range of historically necessary business functions could cease to exist, while others will evolve into new roles entirely. Sectors affected could include:

Banks – Major financial institutions could be the players facing the biggest disruptions. The sector is already wrestling with the unsettling arrival of Bitcoin and a range of over 500 alternative currencies.[269] At the same time Ecuador has launched its own digital currency[270] and some suggest cybercurrency could eliminate paper cash within a decade.[271] A range of blockchain-based FinTech (financial technology) ventures are now emerging which seek to remove banks from a range of financial transactions – speeding up the process and reducing the cost for the parties involved. In many cases these start-ups are receiving funding from the very banks they are seeking to disrupt.

Records Management – Anyone whose job revolves around checking and maintaining records is at risk of being replaced by a blockchain ledger that could do the work cheaper, faster, and error free. For example, blockchain could be used to coordinate public land databases, which would cut red tape when local governments are involved with real estate transactions.[272] As we move towards the DAO model, blockchain could perform a range of administrative tasks.[273] How big a threat could blockchain pose to human workers whose roles can be automated away as excess "middle men"?

Supply Chain, Inventory and Warehouse Management – Blockchain would enable the automation of transactions across the supply chain from ordering to delivery. The counterfeiting and theft of goods would also be much less feasible, and property ownership transactions would become more transparent and incorruptible. Blockchain is a technology that offers the potential to make fraud impossible. It would also provide accurate management of inventory records and reduce the spread of black market goods.

Lawyers, Mediators, Arbitrators – Third-party objectivity could lose its edge as a service or product. In the legal system, "smart" contracts would reduce the caseload, while law practices would bill for fewer wills and legal agreements in general. Evidence-gathering may be seriously impacted by the decentralization and encryption of data that goes hand-in-hand with blockchain. Future blockchain-related categories of crime might include tampering with transactions, theft of cybercurrency and hash fraud.

Judges – The judiciary and other legal professionals will no longer be needed for a number of situations such as property and payment disputes, the execution of contracts, and the determination of measurable outcomes (like bets/wagers).[274] One of the startups experimenting with applying blockchain to legal property issues deals with counterfeiting. Couple this with data from the internet of things – where the objects in a room could give evidence, and we are laying the foundations for a fundamental reworking of the legal system.

Notaries – Documents and contracts, deeds, and other formal paperwork would no longer need to be notarized, since the blockchain could be used to authenticate them. A blockchain app called Proof of Existence is already certifying documents.[275]

Policing – There are several Dapps ("decentralized apps") in development which will see blockchain serve the citizen.[276] For example, Sidekik is a mobile Dapp designed to end abuse of police power by gathering information during a brush with the law (for example GPS, audio, video) and preserving the evidence securely on a decentralized platform (Maidsafe).[277] Even if the officer confiscates the suspect's phone, the data would already be in safe storage that only the app user can access even if the device is destroyed. The advantage of Dapps might well be to "liberate us from the tyranny of large online operators," but it could also serve a greater good of protecting citizens from unjust treatment by law enforcement with a form of undeniable proof safeguarded in the blockchain.[278] [279]

Electoral Governance – If public issues around trust of such new technology can be overcome, blockchain could pave the road for more effective and transparent democracy. Voting and consensus monitoring could become simpler and more dependable using blockchains – giving greater power to the citizen.[280] It would also bring down the cost and complexity of running an election. In the words of one commenter, "the blockchain does not lie, cannot lie and will never lie"[281] – this sounds like the perfect election monitor. One of the major "losers" in the blockchain technology future is anyone who wants to rig an election.

To suggest the extinction of the "authenticating" occupations like attorneys and bankers assumes a huge leap of faith by the public is possible. How likely is society to hand over entrusted roles to machines? One of blockchain's biggest selling points is that it serves the greater good and higher purpose, "The blockchain turns the entire network into its source of truth. It's a mechanism for us to collectively confer legitimacy on one another."[282] This, perhaps, is why Ethereum's Stephan Tual calls blockchain's potential a "decentralization singularity."[283] Truth is possible when no individual lays claim to it exclusively.

Conclusion

One of the few constants in 21st century life is rapid technological change. Nevertheless, the World Wide Web has been the dominant model of connectivity for twenty years. Now, the decentralized blockchain is upending that old "truth" with a new one—that centralized control authorities and their servers are not necessary for the next generation information society to function. In fact, Ethereum and their peers view blockchain as "the key to fixing deep-rooted problems that have plagued our online lives for decades," one of which is the problem of authenticity and verification; another is that all information is centralized.[284]

The anticipated potential for blockchain to revolutionize almost everything seems unlikely in the short term given the facts stated at the introduction to this chapter – including that most people don't know what bitcoin is, nor have ever used it. It seems highly unlikely that a society with no understanding of the most popular cryptocurrency would suddenly be ready to allow all its banking, legal, and political systems begin to run on the same protocol. Yet futurists, developers, and blockchain converts the world over are betting big on the future of Ethereum and the other blockchain players to change the world – soon.

The fact that investment interest has spread from Silicon Valley to Wall Street suggests that we could see a growth in experimentation and uptake. However, turkeys rarely lobby for an early Christmas. Change is likely to be resisted in a variety of ways by those in power, those who run the threatened middlemen functions, and those who simply fear handing control to a technology they don't understand.

The blockchain, the underlying thinking and the technologies that support it, are all in their infancy and the industry is taking its first tentative steps. Inevitably – as with any development with such wide ranging potential impact – there are a number of issues to be resolved before blockchain can prove itself to the mainstream. One concern is the increasing fracturing within the upper echelon of blockchain decision makers over the question of whether the solution is one currency or many smaller, competing currencies.[285] Some suggest this should be among the key topics for an independent research center devoted to blockchain.[286] As with many emerging technologies, we may find that the entrance of bigger well-funded technology players will drive the development of standards and a solution that best fits their view of the world. However this would run counter to the democratic and decentralized ethos of the blockchain.

The success of blockchain depends on the ability to move and store large amounts of data. There are concerns here over the creation of a potentially massive blockchain. Every participant is effectively operating off the same blockchain central ledger – populated with thousands of addresses, this represents a lot of data.[287] The key issue centres on the capability of the technology to manage large blockchains efficiently and process transactions quickly.

The risks coexist with hopes for a range of positive applications as discussed earlier. One analyst smartly observed, "Bitcoin's blockchain was designed to handle the exchange of money, and retrofitting it to other uses requires some programming jujitsu and has inherent technical limitations."[288] This retrofitting will be a key indicator to watch as players such as Ethereum and others, seek to deploy blockchain to redesign the information age. Ultimately, there is no question that blockchain will push the commercial and political boundaries of the World Wide Web.

Closing Questions:

- *What are the potential applications of blockchain technology in your industry?*
- *How could blockchain disrupt or transform your partner/competitor/supplier/customer operations?*
- *What might push blockchain and cryptocurrencies in general, into the mainstream? What's the "tipping point"?*

The Future of the Phone Call

By Dean Bubley

How could businesses benefit as standalone telephone communications give way to contextual voice and video?

Reimagining telecommunications

Telecommunications is changing. Voice and video are becoming an integral feature of other applications rather than just a standalone service in their own right. This article considers the potential evolution and implications of ever-more fragmented – but more functional and customized – forms of telecommunication.

The demise of the traditional call

Telephony has been with us for over 100 years. Both the user-interaction and business models are simple: person A calls person B for X minutes, and a service provider (a telecommunications operator or carrier) connects them. The behavior is familiar, too: one party is a caller, who dials a number or name in their phonebook, with the recipient's phone ringing to alert them to pick it up. The calls might be explicitly charged per-minute or per-second, or might be bundled into a subscription package of some sort.

Billions of people around the world use the phone every day for a wide variety of personal and business reasons. But that strength is also its limitation – it is a generic, largely-undifferentiated service in a world where everyone now has many options for how they communicate. While various features have slightly enhanced the phone call – voicemail, caller-ID, high-definition voice, audio-conferencing, and so on – the basic product has remained the same.

A few competing products have emerged in recent years courtesy of the Internet and mobile apps. Skype and Viber are good examples. These developments have moved the needle in some important ways, such as free calls, addition of video, or a separate non-number identifier. They remain standalone tools however, which are fairly similar in usage to the traditional dialer. Even new cool apps like Wire (a design-led, Skype-type service) and Talko (a group collaboration app blending two-way, one-way, and recorded voice and messages into timelines) which offer improved user-interaction and functionality, are still standalone services.

In recent years, phone calls in many developed countries have suffered (see figure 1) not just from competition but also from unpopularity. Revenues and prices are falling, but call volumes are flat or falling, too. Many parents complain that their children only communicate via text or messaging apps, not calls. Even among older groups or in business, there is a declining tolerance for receiving unexpected, interruptive, anonymous, or worthless spam calls.

Software and the web are substituting for telephony in some cases. For example, it is easier to book a taxi via an app than calling a traditional cab office and dispatcher. Coupled with cheap or free voice and instant messaging (IM) apps, this has led to declining revenues for telecoms companies. Many people do not need all the bundled minutes they are allocated and may end up using fewer despite being given ever-larger quotas.

While telephony still has the advantage of ubiquity, it is increasingly seen as just a lowest common denominator means of communicating when nothing better (or cheaper) is available. And as networks, phones, apps, and users become more sophisticated, this situation is only likely to worsen over time. This is bad news for the traditional telecoms industry and its suppliers. In other words, the supply of ways to call is increasing, but demand is falling. Something needs to change for voice communications to retain its crown as the main form of facilitating human interaction over distance.

Peak telephony a reality in developed markets

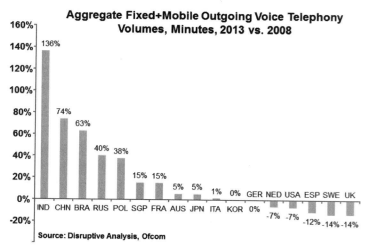

FIGURE 1 – Peak telephony a reality in developed markets
(Source Disruptive Analysis Ltd.)

Three routes to the future

Fortunately the broader communications industry is not resting on its laurels even if the more traditional phone companies appear rather lost. Innovators from around the world will exploit better networks, enhanced devices, improved underlying voice-processing technologies, and cloud-computing platforms to re-invent the phone call along three dimensions:

- Improved user interaction flows, features, and interface models for calling so the traditional experience is refreshed and better-controlled
- Embedding voice (and video) communications directly into applications and websites so it fits better into the task at hand, and
- Using intelligence, machine analytics, and sensors to provide

insight into the context and purpose of each interaction to help make it more effective.

Collectively, this has huge implications for the consumers, society, government, businesses, and – in particular – the telecoms industry. It is worth exploring each of these trends in turn before bringing together a synthesis and roadmap for the next phase of evolution.

Better standalone communications

Various advances will occur by putting better user controls or intelligent computing capabilities into the call path. This could involve either what is called the **media stream** (the actual audio and words spoken), or the **signaling** (how the network sets up the call, rings the recipient, and so forth). Some examples of this already exist, such as call-recording in the finance industry or even the use of a personal assistant to screen calls. But there is a growing trend of performing more of these tasks with software that reacts to the particular circumstances or context.

We are already seeing the classical phone-call experience evolve. For example, Skype users often start an interaction with a chat message like, "Are you there?" before one participant asks, "OK for a call?" The other perhaps responds, "Two minutes. I'm getting my headset," or similar. Other mobile apps such as Talko are aimed at business collaboration and allow one-way voice messaging as well as normal two-way conversations. Further enhancements will take us away from rude, interruptive, unexpected ringtones that demand our attention now.

Some voice applications are also being enriched with recording, voice analytics (perhaps for speech-to-text transcription), and even real-time language translation. There are tools to change the sound of your voice – think of an audio equivalent of Instagram filters. Some call centers are already using software that can sense if you sound angry and perhaps direct you to an agent selected for their soothing tones.

Coming next is **whisper mode**, where your PC or phone overlays extra audio (unheard by the other party), giving you background information or advice. Think of those scenes in crime movies where a second person (e.g. a detective) is listening in the room with another handset and gesticulating to the speaker to keep talking while a trace is done. In the future, it might be your own computer that exhorts you to close the sale, advises you to calm down or speed up, or perhaps interprets a strange idiom or jargon term for you so you don't need to disclose your ignorance.

Another coming set of innovations concerns how your inbound calls are managed. We already use **caller ID** to decide whether we know a caller and if we should pick up the phone or let it go to voicemail. Now a range of extra options are starting to emerge with much greater power and flexibility. Perhaps you only want to permit your boss or partner to ring? Maybe the network will interrogate your phone, realize it is on charge, and boost the ringer volume in case you're in another room? Perhaps the phone, or an assistant application in the cloud, will detect (or interrogate) telemarketers and decline to connect them unless they pay a fee or offer a reward for occupying your time?

Taken together, such improvements will take the old format of standalone voice telephony and make it more user-friendly, better-controlled, and flexible. While prices per minute might still fall, that doesn't mean the other features cannot be monetized, whether by a phone company or a separate provider.

Communications in context

The future evolution of **contextual communications** has a number of phases. The first – which is already starting – involves embedding voice (or video) directly into an app or website. Early examples include voice-chat in multiplayer games, live-chat for customer support in e-commerce websites and banking apps, or video-consultations with doctors alongside remote monitoring of real-time medical data. By incorporating the communications stream as a secondary feature inside another primary app, it allows the easier blending of different interaction models.

Why make a separate call while looking at a website, when you could make the call in the website – perhaps co-browsing and discussing a holiday destination with a friend, and then adding in the travel agent, for example. And it makes more sense to speak to an arriving taxi driver inside the app like a walkie-talkie rather than disclosing your number to a stranger. A key enabling technology here is WebRTC, a standard for embedding real-time communications (RTC) into the web or mobile apps. We will also see voice communications adapt to the device being used. The normal option of a phone call might not be the right way to interact with a robot, a door entry-system, a smartwatch, or a security-guard drone.

Communications using context

Putting voice into a context is only one step along the path. Beyond that lies using **contextual information** to help the user (at either end of the connection) achieve a particular objective or purpose. Here, contextual information can be of three types (see figure 2):

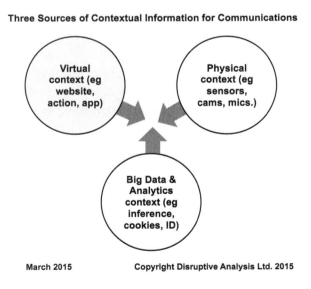

FIGURE 2 – Three sources of contextual information for comms
(Source Disruptive Analysis Ltd.)

- *Virtual context*: This is your electronic status – which website, app, or content you are using, the web-page you are on, the fields of a form you are filling in, the point you are at in a business workflow or a game

- *Physical context*: This is **sensed** information from sources such as device microphone(s) and camera(s), location, movement, temperature, power consumption, battery level, heart-rate, biometric inputs, and so on. With processing, this can yield information about acoustics (whether you are in a street or a room), your identity via fingerprint or voiceprint, and maybe even your health or stress level, and

- *Analytic context*: When linked to cloud platforms, additional insight can be factored into the application – perhaps past behaviors and preferences, website history, records from a customer database, or even correlations with your friends or people around you.

This three-way blend of context sources, **machine learning**, and artificial intelligence (AI) predicting future events or requirements presages a new era for communications. For example, if you have a query part-way through completing an online insurance application form, the call-center agent should be able to see your name and what you've already entered rather than starting from scratch again. In the future, the system might also be able to see your blood-pressure rising and bump you up the queue.

The experience of speaking to your bank manager from a busy and noisy restaurant will be different to calling from the seaside to say, "wish you were here" to a loved one. The **friends and family** app might accentuate the sounds of waves crashing on a beach in the background, while the finance app would cut out as much of the hubbub as possible. In other words, the voice-enabled applications will be able to infer what you are trying to do and work out how to assist you in realizing your real objectives for the call.

Many of the possibilities remain unexplored. Exploiting sensors to blend in **real world** data, as well as analytics, extends the range of possible applications hugely. Modern handsets (and other devices such as tablets and wearables) tend to have multiple sensors – perhaps two microphones, two cameras, orientation sensors, location-awareness, and more.

Future device chipsets will incorporate even more **cognitive smarts**. Imagine if the phone or app knows that you are running through an airport. A virtual personal assistant could suggest to a salesman that it might not be the best moment for a call. More prosaically, a phone might recognize it is lying flat on a table, and adjust to speakerphone mode, detecting multiple participants around the room, and adjusting their volume levels, if one is further away.

Clearly, the dividing line between context-awareness and privacy-invasive creepiness will need to be considered carefully, especially as AI-type software becomes more capable. In some cases, users may decide that relinquishing personal data may be a price worth paying for more effective communications, business processes, and social interactions. That said, this is likely to be an area where trust and experience will need to be built over time, probably with various mis-steps on the way.

What could all this mean for society and business?

We are seeing communications start to fit better with peoples' real, underlying purposes. The plain undifferentiated phone call will start to evolve to reflect why you want to speak to someone, and how you want to convey your message and manage the conversation.

In the future, communications will:

- Be embedded directly into apps, websites, devices, and experiences rather than being a separate function
- Adapt to the users' circumstances – where they are, what they're doing, what they want to achieve from a call
- Incorporate various processing and cloud functions – from recording to language-translation and emotional analysis
- Have multiple methods of rendezvous, not just interruptive calls where one person wields all the power, but invitations,

always-on windows, asynchronous messages, walkie-talkie mode, and many more, and

- Incorporate many different models of identity (or privacy) beyond the traditional phone number.

These developments will refresh and revitalize the use of voice communications – taking it from clunky, one-dimensional phone calls to a much broader set of applications, experiences, and business models. This also has major implications for companies and governments who will increasingly need to communicate with customers and citizens on their terms and with their preferred tools. At one level it may mean an end to unsolicited voice spam. Conversely, it may make sales and support functions more effective as well as internal company processes.

Other side-effects may be less welcome. If we reinvented emergency systems today, we might not choose 999/911/112 calls, but have a more flexible way of getting help via messages, apps, or other fragmented communications methods. But for now, we are mostly stuck with the legacy telephony. It has taken many years just for some authorities to support SMS. An urgent and global re-think is required for critical communications, which is one of the most conservative and slow-moving areas of telecoms.

It is also unclear how any of this wonderful, new communications functionality will be monetized. While it will clearly have even greater value than vanilla phone calls, it will also be much harder to price and charge for these advances. Context cannot be charged by the minute. The telecoms industry will find it hard to adjust, as will the providers of the various new applications that incorporate voice or video. But ultimately, this should allow us to go beyond merely "speaking at a distance" (tele-phonos) towards forms of electronic communications that fit our underlying needs and desires.

Maybe the next generation of teenagers will start to think that speaking into phones is cool once again. Here are some key questions to consider:

- *How could your business improve its interactions with its customers or suppliers, by integrating voice/video directly into its apps or website?*
- *What contextual capabilities or insights could your company's products and data add to other communications apps or services?*
- *How might your employees' behavior change in a post-telephony world? What could that mean for business processes, collaboration, and workflows?*

Will Artificial Intelligence Eat the World?

By Calum Chace

What are the potential benefits and risks of artificial intelligence (AI) and artificial general intelligence (AGI) to business and society?

Artificial Intelligence – promise and perils

Artificial intelligence (AI) is ubiquitous. It is improving at an exponential rate, and it is changing the world. It has already brought great benefits, and it promises to bring even more in the future. But it also brings perils. In the short and medium term there is the prospect of technological unemployment. In the longer term the arrival of artificial general intelligence (AGI) (conscious machines with volition) is one of the few genuinely existential threats facing mankind. In this chapter I introduce the concepts of AI and AGI, explore how AI is evolving, highlight the potential applications in business and examine the challenges of progressing to true AGI.

What are Artificial Intelligence and Artificial General Intelligence?

Artificial intelligence (AI) is intelligence demonstrated by a machine or by software. Intelligence, like most words used to describe what the brain does, is hard to pin down: there are many rival definitions. But most of them contain the notion of the ability to learn, to acquire information, and use it to achieve a goal.

It is vital to distinguish between weak AI and strong AI. Strong AI, or AGI, is a machine that can carry out any cognitive function that a human can. We have long had computers which calculate much faster and more accurately than any human, and computers can play chess better than the best chess grandmaster. But no computer can yet beat humans at every intellectual endeavor.

Whereas ordinary AI simply does what we tell it to, an AGI would have the ability to reflect on its goals and decide whether to adjust them. It has volition. It may also – although this is not necessary – have consciousness. No human can beat a top chess computer at the game, but – as yet – no chess computer "knows what it is doing".

AI is everywhere

Today, AI is all around us. People in developed economies interact with AI systems many times every day without being aware of it. But if it all suddenly disappeared they would notice, but its omnipresence has become unremarkable, like air. The most obvious example is your smartphone. It is probably the last inanimate thing you touch before you go to sleep at night and the first thing you touch in the morning. It has more processing power than the computers NASA used to send Neil Armstrong to the moon in 1969. It uses AI algorithms to offer predictive text and speech recognition, and these features improve year by year as the algorithms are improved. Many of the apps we download to our phones also employ AI to make themselves useful to us. Translation apps are the result of algorithms being trained on vast amounts of data, and smartphone maps apply algorithms to suggest optimal routes based on huge data sets about traffic and weather conditions.

The AI we use becomes more powerful with each generation of phone, as their processing power increases, as the bandwidth of the phone networks improve, as cloud storage becomes better and cheaper, and as we become more relaxed about sharing enough of our personal data for the AI applications to understand us better.

Many people in the developed economies make several searches a day on Google or Bing. As of early May 2015, Google carries out 40,000 searches every second.[289] That is an application of AI. When you visit a store, the fact that the products you want are on the shelf is significantly due to AI. Supermarkets and their suppliers continually ingest huge data feeds and use algorithms to analyze them, to predict what we will want to buy, when, and where. As a result, retail supply chains are significantly more efficient than even a decade ago.

Other consumer-facing companies like Amazon and Netflix wear their AI on their sleeves, tempting us with product and movie recommendations based on their AI applications' analysis of our past choices. This is the same principle as direct marketing, which has been around for decades of course. Nowadays the data available and the tools for analyzing it are so much more effective so people living in skyscraper apartments no longer receive junk email about lawnmowers.

Some of the biggest and most successful companies in the world are entirely driven by AI. For example, Google is often described as a search company or an advertising company and makes most of its huge revenues from search-driven advertising. But actually it is an AI company. The secret sauce in Google search is **Page Rank**, an AI algorithm which indexes the world's knowledge via the web. Google is applying AI to an increasing range of industries, and threatening to disrupt many of them.

America's other tech giants are determined not to be left behind. Facebook, Microsoft and IBM are all investing huge sums in world-leading AI research – people and facilities. Amazon and Apple have more of a foothold in the world outside computers and cyber-space, but AI is central to their activities too.

The financial markets make extensive use of AI. High-frequency trading, where computers trade with each other at speeds no human can even follow – never mind participate in – took off in the early 21st century. Since that time however, it has reportedly fallen back from around two-thirds of all U.S. equity trades at the start of the 2008 credit crunch, to around 50 percent in 2012.[290] There is still confusion about the impact of this on the financial markets. The **flash crash** of

2010, in which the Dow Jones lost almost ten percent of its value in a few minutes, was initially blamed on high-frequency trading. Later reports claimed that the AI applications had actually mitigated the fall. The crash prompted the New York Stock Exchange to introduce **circuit breakers** which suspend trading of a stock whose price moves suspiciously quickly. The financial Armageddon which some pundits forecast has not arrived. Although there will undoubtedly be further shocks, most market participants expect that new and developing AI tools will continue to be absorbed into what has always been one of the most dynamic and aggressive sectors of the economy.

Hospitals use AI to allocate beds and other resources. Factories use robots – controlled by AI – to automate production and remove people from the most dangerous jobs. Telecoms companies, power generators and other utilities use AI to manage the load on their resources. AI is everywhere you look and it is improving rapidly. This may present us with two major challenges: automation in the near term; and conscious machines in the longer term. Let's look at each of them in turn.

AI and task automation

AI is growing more powerful at an exponential rate. It improves our lives enormously, supporting us in carrying out a wide range of professional and personal tasks, providing information and analysis to make us more efficient, and more effective. However, there are concerns that AI is automating some jobs out of existence and that this trend will increase rapidly in the coming few years.

Automation has been a feature of human civilization since at least the early industrial revolution. In the 15th century, Dutch workers threw their shoes into textile looms to break them. (Their shoes were called sabots which is a possible origin for the word saboteur.) The development of steam powered engines raised automation to a new level. The classic example is the mechanization of agriculture. This sector accounted for 41 percent of U.S. employment in 1900, and only two percent by the year 2000.

In the late 20th century, automation came mainly in the form of robots – particularly in the automotive, electrical, and electronic industries – and this is set to accelerate. Robots are peripherals – the physical manifestation of AI systems. Despite the recession, sales of robots grew at ten percent per year from 2008 to 2013 when 178,000 industrial robots were sold worldwide. China became the biggest market installing 37,000 robots compared with 30,000 in the U.S.[291]

So the process of automation has been familiar in manual labor jobs for many years and it has also rendered obsolete large numbers of clerical roles. The word **computer** originally meant a person who does calculations, but the days when offices were filled with hordes of young human computers are long gone. The humble PC has also removed the need for legions of secretaries.

Up to now, the replacement of humans by machines has been a gradual process. It has been painful for individuals to be dismissed from a particular job, but there was generally the chance to retrain or find new work elsewhere. Some people argue that this may now be changing thanks to the rapid advances in machine learning and the availability of increasingly powerful, and ever more portable computers.

A recent report by the Oxford Martin School estimated that 47 percent of American jobs would disappear in the next 20 years in two waves.[292] The first would attack relatively low-skilled jobs in sectors like transportation and administration. Some of this would come from self-driving vehicles which are likely to appear on our roads in significant numbers from 2017. Some 30 U.S. cities are expected to experiment with self-driving cars by the end of 2016.[293]

In the U.S. alone, there are 3.5 million truck drivers,[294] 6,650,000 bus drivers,[295] and 230,000 taxi drivers.[296] There are numerous hurdles to be overcome before all these jobs become vulnerable. Google's self-driving cars have travelled three-quarters of a million miles without causing an accident but they can only travel on roads where very detailed maps have already been produced. They cannot handle heavy rain or snow, they cannot detect potholes or debris obstructing the road, and they cannot discern between a pedestrian and a policeman indicating for the vehicle to stop. However, none of these problems look insurmountable and politicians worldwide have understood that they need to agree policies and procedures to cope with the arrival of this technology.

The second wave described by the Oxford Martin School would attack jobs in the heartland of the middle and upper-middle class: professional occupations like medicine, the law, managerial jobs, and even work in the arts. The claim is that systems like IBM's Watson will progress from being decision-support systems to decision-taking systems. As the ability of the machine to turn raw data into information and then insight improves, the space remaining for a human to add value shrinks and eventually disappears.

In this vision, a requirement for creativity is not necessarily a defense against automation. Computers can already write sports articles for newspapers which readers cannot distinguish from pieces penned by humans. A computer system called Lamus in Malaga, Spain, produces chamber music which experts cannot identify as automated.[297]

What will be the impact if nearly half of all today's jobs disappear in a mere two decades? In the past, humans have turned their hands to more value-adding activity and the result of automation has been higher overall productivity. The children of people who undertook mundane jobs in offices and factories now work as social media marketers and user experience designers – jobs which nobody could have imagined a generation ago. Perhaps our children will also be doing jobs that we barely conceive of today (Emotion Coaches? Dream Wranglers?). But the pessimists fear that this retreat up the value chain will be impossible if AI systems are clambering up it as fast or even faster than we are.

Even if we can keep inventing new types of employment, perhaps the rate of churn will simply be too fast for people to keep up with. Will we all be willing and able to change our career annually or every six months as computers keep stealing our old ones?

As with many questions about AI, no one knows the answer yet. Optimists counter that the rapid growth of online education – the Massive Open Online Courses (MOOC) revolution – means that employees can re-skill themselves faster than ever before and for free. They also argue that many of the fears are exaggerated. For instance, they argue that self-driving lorries and buses will still need attendants to cater for the unexpected circumstances that life throws up as well as to load and unload people and goods. They point to the example of aircraft, which have been flying by wire for decades but which still have human pilots on board.

Businesses and the professionals who advise them are waking up to the challenge of automation and AI. To conclude this section, here are some of the hard questions being asked within a range of industries. How do existing players maintain and increase the level of value they add in:

- Fund management – when individual investors can access comprehensive information about market performance and use AI to compare and contrast at the touch of a button?
- Audit –_when clients can compile and assess their financial performance data using machines?
- Litigation – when clients can carry out the discovery process much faster and cheaper using AI?
- Banking – when newcomers can automate the transfer and custody of money and when the blockchain idea behind Bitcoin may make financial transfers free and more secure?
- Vehicle manufacture – when the majority of the value in a vehicle lies in the software rather than the physical components?
- Healthcare – when smartphone apps enable citizens to diagnose their condition without leaving home?

Artificial General Intelligence – conscious machines

The idea that science could create a conscious machine – or that one might somehow emerge from an existing computer system – has been a staple of science fiction since the inception of the genre. The science of AI got started in the 1950's and in an early flurry of over-optimism; its pioneers announced they were poised to make it a reality within a few years. They were wrong, of course. Since then almost everyone has assumed that conscious machines will not be created for hundreds of years – if ever. Hollywood built some great franchises with the concept (e.g. Terminator, The Matrix) – but that only consolidated the sense of unreality and fiction.

The situation is changing. Towards the end of the last century, in books like *The Age of Intelligent Machines* (1990) and *The Age of Spiritual Machines* (1999), the controversial futurist Ray Kurzweil began arguing that continued exponential improvement in computer power meant that conscious machines might arrive within decades. He attracted a significant audience but his argument was widely ignored – or ridiculed – by the mainstream media and general public opinion.

Then Oxford philosophy professor Nick Bostrom published his seminal book *Superintelligence* (2014) and suddenly the world sat up and took notice. Several of the world's smartest celebrities echoed his warnings, coining clever sound-bites. Stephen Hawking compared the creation of AGI to the arrival of a super intelligent alien species and wondered why we were paying the threat so little attention. Silicon Valley entrepreneur Elon Musk asked if humanity might prove to be simply the "boot loader" (start-up program) for digital intelligence, warning that we may be summoning the demon. Bill Gates said he shared these concerns and didn't understand why more people did not.

Suddenly you couldn't move for media articles saying that conscious machines are just around the chronological corner and they will wipe us all out. It seemed as if a law had been passed mandating the use of an image of a Terminator at the head of these articles. Journalists woke up to the fact that around the world, vast amounts of money are being spent on projects which could lead to AGI. There are two main approaches being pursued: whole brain emulation; and building on weak AI.

Whole Brain Emulation

The archetypal whole brain emulation project is the Human Brain Project (HBP) in Lausanne,[298] led by Henry Markram, which has been awarded $1 billion in grants mainly from the European Union.

America's response is President Obama's BRAIN project,[299] currently funded at around $300 million a year and therefore likely to exceed the HBP's funding during the decade. Together, these projects are seeking to build a working model of a human brain.

There have been varying reports of a Chinese initiative along the same lines. Until 2010, Australian AI researcher Hugo de Garis ran a China Brain Project at Wuhan University,[300] and in March 2015, the founder of Baidu – China's answer to Google – invited the country's military to join him in making China a world leader in AI with a new China Brain Project.[301] No doubt many other countries have similar ambitions.

Enhancing weak AI

Attempts to improve and build on weak AI systems are more widespread and more fragmented. We noted before that many of the world's largest and most successful companies are increasingly building AI into everything they do. It is hard for an outsider to guess what Google's effective budget for AI research is, but judging by the range of initiatives under way it seems likely to be in the hundreds of millions of dollars. In January 2014, IBM announced a $1 billion investment to establish the new Watson Group, following the system's success in the *Jeopardy!* game show.[302]

The same probably goes for Facebook and Microsoft, with Amazon and Apple not far behind. There are also numerous AI labs of significance in the publicly and privately-funded academic worlds, and then of course there are the military and the intelligence communities. America's National Security Agency (NSA) and Britain's Government Communications Headquarters (GCHQ) have some of the world's largest supercomputer complexes and are believed to be at the forefront of developing AI techniques.

Of course not every project to improve weak AI systems is attempting to replicate the processes of conscious intelligence – most of them are not. However, they all help create the sub-systems and modules that such a project would require. The move from the symbolic approach of the late 1950s and early 1960s to the statistical and probabilistic approach used today in deep learning systems makes them astonishingly powerful.[303] It used to be thought that computers would never equal humans at facial recognition, real-time translation, or driving cars. Today those hurdles are being overcome.

Will AI eat the planet?

The backlash against the claim that a perilous AGI is just around the corner was not slow in coming, but it has yet to find a voice as famous or as snappy as Hawking or Musk. Many of the grandees of AI research have lined up to pour scorn on the concerns, claiming that AGI will not be created for centuries and that it will be harmless. These grandees include: Yann LeCun, head of Facebook's AI program; Andrew Ng, previously head of the Google Brain project and now at Baidu; Christian Koch at the Paul Allen Brain Research Centre; Demis Hassabis, founder of Google Deep Mind; and David Ferrucci, project manager of IBM's Watson project.

Andrew Ng argues that current AI systems are at best a mere cartoon representation of a human brain and AGI is nowhere in sight. Yann LeCun asserts, "...while Deep Learning gets its inspiration from biology, it's very, very far from what the brain actually does. And describing it like the brain gives a bit of the aura of magic to it, which is dangerous. It leads to hype; people claim things that are not true."

When might we see Artificial General Intelligence?

The experts know whereof they speak and their arguments must be taken seriously. However, there are plenty of other AI researchers saying the opposite. Nick Bostrom compiled a meta-survey of AI experts most often cited in professional journals and the median estimate for the arrival of AGI was 2050. Max Tegmark, writing about a conference of AI experts organized by the *Future of Life Institute* in January 2015 said: "We don't know what the probability is of machines reaching human-level ability on all cognitive tasks during our lifetime, but most of the AI researchers at the conference put the odds above 50 percent, so we would be foolish to dismiss the possibility as mere science fiction."

Clearly there is controversy about the timing of the arrival of AGI. A lot hangs on how much longer Moore's Law will continue. Moore's Law is the observation that the processing power of $1,000 worth of computer doubles every 18 months – an exponential increase. Exponential growth is an incredibly powerful force. If I take thirty steps ahead of me I will travel about thirty yards. If I could double the length of my stride with each step I would reach the moon. People have been claiming for years that Moore's Law is tailing off or even that it has stopped. But in February 2015 Intel updated journalists on their chip program for the next few years and it maintains exponential growth.[304] The first chips based on its new ten nanometer manufacturing process are expected in late 2016 or early 2017, after which it expects to move away from silicon, probably towards a III-V semiconductor such as indium gallium arsenide.[305]

So although we cannot say with certainty that AGI will be created in the first half of this century, it is not a possibility that can be excluded. What we do know is that the human brain is a physical system and it generates consciousness. We are an existence proof that consciousness can be generated by ordinary matter organized the right way. Our brains were developed by a slow, inefficient, messy, but powerful, and non-random process called evolution. The drive to create AGI is using a fast, powerful, and purposeful process called science. So it is at least a reasonable hypothesis that AGI can be created. There is vigorous debate about whether one could be created in the next few decades but many AI researchers think it could and there is a tsunami of money backing them up.

From AGI to Superintelligence

The other big question about AGI is whether we will like it if we do build one. A human brain cannot – for the foreseeable future at least – be expanded, speeded up, or re-wired to improve its efficiency and effectiveness. All these things are possible with an AGI. It seems likely that the first AGI to be built will rapidly be developed further to become a **superintelligence** (an ASI).

In human societies fairly subtle differences in intelligence produce enormous differences in economic and social outcomes. But with superintelligence we might not be talking about the sort of differential between say, Albert Einstein and Justin Bieber. How will humanity fare if and when an entity appears on the planet whose intelligence is as far ahead of ours as Einstein's was ahead of an ant's? When people understand that anything they could do, would be trivial compared to what the ASI could achieve, will we delight in having a big brother who can solve all our political, social, and technological problems? Or will we lose the impetus to create and to struggle, and fade away into oblivion?

As Hollywood is keen to remind us, there is no guarantee that the ASI will want to help humanity. It might calculate that we are a potential threat and decide to get its retaliation in first by launching a devastating strike. The doomsday scenario sees ASI taking control of our nuclear weapons, unleashing deadly pathogens, and turning every robot, weapon, and machine into assassins. The ASI could wipe humanity out in fairly short order. Simply crashing the internet would probably see off a sizeable majority of the world's population as monetary systems collapsed, supply chains failed, and food stocks ran out in the cities where more than half of us now live, causing the total breakdown of law and order.

Even without bearing us ill-will, the ASI might harm us while trying to help. Taking an apparently trivial example, selecting for itself the goal of "putting a smile on every face" could lead to some horrific results. And in the classic phrase of Eliezer Yudkowski, founder of the Machine Intelligence Research Institute (MIRI) "…(perhaps) the AI does not hate you, nor does it love you, but you are made out of atoms which it can use for something else."[306]

The solution would be to either: set the goals of the ASI so that humans benefit; or to control the ASI to prevent it from causing harm. But these are immensely challenging tasks. Since the ancient Greeks, we have been debating the best ethical code to follow and we are no closer to agreement today. If we cannot agree on the nature of a good life or how to do the right thing in any given situation, how can we program ethical instructions into an ASI? Isaac Asimov attempted to draw up three laws for robots, but the point of his stories was to show that they wouldn't work. They led to contradictions and regrettable unintended consequences.

Similarly, how do you set about controlling an entity that is a million times smarter than you are and thinks a million times faster than you do? Every initiative you contemplate, it has anticipated and every action you take it has already implemented counter-measures for.

One solution may be to ensure the first AGI – and therefore the first ASI – is an Oracle, a mind that can respond to questions but has no access to the physical world, including no access to the Internet. This is no simple task either. How do we ensure that a superintelligence with powers of persuasion a million times greater than Bill Clinton does not convince its guardians to release it?

Many people – especially, it seems, in Silicon Valley – are convinced that an ASI would be well-disposed towards humanity and usher in an age of ease and plenty. Maybe they are right but the case is far from proven. The bottom line is that the whole subject is fraught with uncertainty. We don't know for sure that we can create an AGI, and if we can we don't know when. We don't know whether it will have goals that are compatible with our well-being and whether we can constrain its actions if not.

What we do know is that there are many thousands of people who are working full-time to improve AI and much of this work may contribute to the arrival of AGI and ASI. They are collectively, immensely well-funded. By contrast there are very few people working full-time on the so-called **Friendly AI** project to ensure that AGI is safe from a human point of view.

The good news is that we probably have a few decades before AGI arrives. The less good news is that we may need all that time to get it right – and we have to get it right first time. AGI is an existential threat and we may not get a second chance. The best organizations working on friendly AI (like MIRI, the Future of Humanity Institute in Oxford, the Centre for the Study of Existential Risk at Cambridge, and the Future of Life Institute at Boston)[307] need more funding. They need and deserve the support of businesses and individuals who are keen to see a positive future for our children and our grand-children.

What is to be done?

AI, AGI and ASI raise a lot of questions. We don't yet have the answers, but we need to get better at asking the questions. Policy makers, like Generals, have a tendency to prepare to fight the war that just ended. The accelerating rate of technological innovation means that change is arriving faster, with its impact is more profound, and harder to predict. As AI improves we need to get much better at working out the nature of the changes it will bring and preparing to deal with them.

To conclude, here are three questions which leaders of any business could usefully ask today:

- *Where is the greatest potential to apply AI to automate processes in my organization and deliver significant cost and efficiency gains?*
- *How are we tracking the potential adoption of AI by competitors or disruptive new entrants?*
- *How can my organization help mitigate the risks raised by AI and AGI?*

From Clouds to Networks Without Infrastructure

By Peter Cochrane

How can today's internet be scaled up to meet all our global needs?

This chapter explores the radical innovations required in networking infrastructures to support the projected growth in internet users, web-connected objects, and internet traffic.

Unleashing the insatiable internet

Only two decades ago commercial life was dominated by telephone networks designed to deliver specific services. They had to meet strict performance criteria, within tightly regulated and globally controlled operating conditions and standards. Fast forward to today, and the internet now occupies the top slot by network usage in a manner and by mechanisms no one could have imagined in 1995. In complete contrast to telephone networks, today's internet evolved in an open ended fashion with no pretence of an overall plan, design, or indeed the exercise of any real control – quite the reverse! To date it has remained open, neutral, and free, and perhaps more impressively, it has coped with the astonishing growth of eCommerce, Social Networking, Video, Voice Over IP (VIOP), and Entertainment Services. Moreover it has engendered new business models and technology solutions in almost every sphere of human activity. So the obvious question is;

can this expansion go on, and if not, what comes next?

The Cloud looks to be the next big net development accompanied by The Internet of Things (IoT). However, there are a number of practical challenges already visible around the evolution of the IoT. Let's explore some of the critical challenges in the evolution of the Internet, IoT and the so called Cloud of Things (CoT).

Clouds

Clouds (plural) are already evolving and speciating rapidly with large numbers of commercial suppliers and end-users creating clouds of every possible variety: corporate; institutional; government; military; educational; personal; global; national; regional; local; civil; open; closed; secret; visible; invisible; fixed; mobile; permanent; transient; spurious; and more. We might see this as a fragmentation of the internet, but in reality many aspects of the Cloud introduce new network elements and operational changes that could bring significant benefits and remove unnecessary traffic from the Internet.

Perhaps the most interesting feature of Clouds is their ability to operate in local clusters with device-to-device, machine-to-machine, vehicle-to-vehicle, and Cloud-to-Cloud (et al) data transfers. The Cloud enables these to take place independent of the internet or any other form of network per se. Surprisingly, this first became evident in emerging economies where a lack of infrastructure saw people using BlueTooth to communicate and share information across a table using mobile devices. On occasions, a designated device would be used to store and forward material to and from the group when it later strayed into a mobile cell site or wifi hot spot. Such facilities and modes of working are now appearing in developed economies through dedicated apps that make the processes simple and intuitive. We might consider these as personal/group Clouds of the transient variety. They may also constitute our first glimpse of the concept of Networks Without Infrastructure (NWI).

The potential future depth, breadth, and impact of this particular technology is hard to judge at this time but suffice it to say there are now sharing apps being used to convey video footage of goals around the crowd in football stadia in real time. Historically of course, people everywhere have always shared audio and video files in a similar manner to avoid prying eyes and the limits of local loop network bandwidth. So I think we can safely assume that the process of Cloud evolution is well underway and the survival of the most adaptable and rewarding Cloud solutions will decide the final outcome. All we have to do is watch, wait, and make our choices in exploiting the whole Cloud paradigm as it rolls out.

As for NWI, this is a network technology in its infancy that looks set to grow rapidly in the face of our desire to transfer ever-larger file sizes and a growing number of internet bandwidth bottlenecks. If fixed and mobile operators fail to satisfy the growing user demand for network bandwidth, NWI could certainly provide a viable alternative for local data transfer.

Almost paradoxically forms of networking such as NWI (Figure 1) look to be far more sustainable than doing it via the internet alone – by virtue of removing the need to traverse vast amounts of energy consuming network hardware. NWI effectively bypasses much of that infrastructure. This is positively compounded by the inverse square law for wireless energy, for example communication over a distance of metres rather kilometres means we require far less energy per device i.e. microwatts (μW) instead of milliwatts (mW). This also bodes well for the next (and probably much bigger) evolutionary step into the IoT.

Wired/Wireless connection to internet if required or available

Store & Forward to internet if necessary via designated mobile

FIGURE 1 – Local Cloud (NWI) Working

The Internet of Things (IoT)

The core argument for the IoT centers on connecting literally every object and device. The highest level goal is to supply and support all humanity with sufficient resources including food, water, housing, goods, and services whilst reducing overall energy and material consumption to sustainable levels. Industry, farming, production, and supply in general are moving to new processes and techniques that demand less material and energy. Embedding sensors in such a wide range of objects means we have to take the concepts of **reuse, repurposing and recycling** (R3) to whole new level in terms of delivering long term efficiency. Reducing overall recycling wastage levels to very low single digit percentages is a primary objective can be addressed without the IoT – through the adoption of nano and biotechnology. However, the biggest saving from the IOT opportunity probably lies in the arena of reuse and repurposing, and hence the need to tag and track (almost) everything from initial material sourcing right through the process of production and onto the logistics of supply, purchase, use, maintenance, repair, and final disposal – with further R3 opportunities.[308]

To be ecologically effective, the IoT will require almost every manufactured item to be suitably tagged and tracked. So what is the scale of this? The best published estimates so far span 50-250 billion things – but this is more of an estimate than a well quantified and analytic number.[309] There is some thinking that says that these are probably conservative numbers and could significantly undershoot the true total in the longer term! Obviously, all this in itself raises sustainability issues! At the very least we have to worry about the energy consumption of more than 50 billion individual things. Projections for 2020 suggest we could see between five and 7.6 billion internet users and an unknown number of connected machines and sensors.

The total internet energy consumption has been estimated at three to ten percent of the total electrical energy generated on the planet. So a crude scaling from around three billion people and 10 to 15 billion objects on the internet today rising to five billion people and more than 50 billion things on line by 2020 is clearly an untenable energy demand proposition. Even if the IoT devices only required ten percent of today's internet capacity and energy usage, the planet cannot afford or supply the expected growth in demand. We have to do much better and most likely keep it within the existing energy budget or even less. We have no choice, our future depends upon it.

From an engineering perspective we might start by asking some very basic questions such as: does my toothbrush or my car need to be online 100 percent of the time? The answer has to be no and their networking need not be global, it can be entirely local. This turns out to be true for the vast majority of things in our lives: all of our white and brown consumer goods; medical and fitness monitors; hospital and industrial instrumentation; and more. While they may need to communicate to each other – they don't really need to do it via the internet. On initial inspection it is clear that communication **thing-to-thing** trumps the need to use the internet or any other form of global network.

Two prime examples would be cars on a freeway and sea going containers. In the former case 1,000 vehicles per five kilometer stretch cannot all link via 3G / 4G / 5G should there be an accident or some form of congestion, but they can talk **car-to-car**.[310] In the case of shipping, some 20-30% of sea going containers are below decks and the majority of those above deck are embedded and surrounded by a shell of containers. Again, satellite and mobile network coverage is impossible, but they can talk to each other and then on to the ship and via satellite on to shore.[311]

Networking

There is a further supporting dimension to this argument that says today's 3G / 4G / 5G mobile networks only transport less than five percent of total internet traffic, whist WiFi comes in at more than 50 percent, and wired connections around 40 percent (Figure 2).

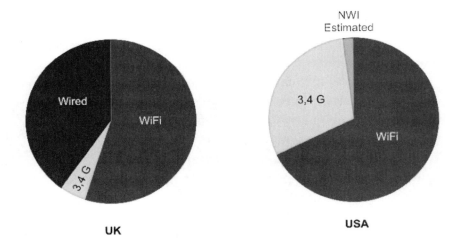

FIGURE 2 – Distribution of Wired, WiFi, 3G/4G and NWI Internet Traffic

Offloading mobile network traffic to WiFi is not just encouraged but it turns out to be vital. WiFi already handles around 70 percent of the total mobile traffic while 3G / 4G / 5G services represent around 30 percent and are falling fast.[312] Whilst the leap from 2/2.5G to 3G was significant, 4G has seen only marginal functionality gains. Whilst 5G will offer far more, the problem is that the coverage will be less than desired or necessary unless there is at least a ten-fold increase in the number of cell sites – and realistically that isn't going to happen. Clearly the popular vision of the IoT using 3G / 4G / 5G as the primary communication medium is untenable, but Clouds or NWI could do the job.

At this point it is important to note the power savings of proximity. Not traversing the internet is obviously the biggest source of energy saving. However, the reduction in wireless transmission power is also significant too. Today our wireless devices use maximum transmission powers of around 500mW over distances spanning roughly 100 meters to ten kilometers. Our vision of the evolving NWI would reduce such distances to around 10 meters maximum which would demand far less than 5mW and mostly a few µW. This might also be reflected back into personal computing and mobile working to herald a move toward genuinely thinner clients (for example cloud-connected user devices with reduced levels of functionality) with longer battery lives and even thinner profiles. At this stage it is impossible to say whether this will happen. However it is clear that we need to start thinking through the implications, and to start looking at NWI as a new opportunity space.

Conclusion

As with all technological change, it is those who embrace the new opportunities that typically prosper – stealing a march on their competition to become more efficient and effective in delivering goods and services. Clouds and NWI present a huge opportunity space in this regard and the field is wide open to those willing to innovate.

This raises important questions for business:

- *How could you and your competitors' businesses benefit from the adoption of IoT/CoT/NWI?*
- *What strategy are you going to formulate in order to win this race?*
- *What are the potential business implications of the huge potential increase in energy demand required to service projected growth in the number of people and objects connected to the internet?*

Future Developments and Opportunities for Deep Learning Artificial Neural Networks

By Elias Rut and Martin Dinov

What is deep learning and why is it becoming such a big deal?

This chapter examines why we should know and care about the concept of deep learning, explains the core technologies, and assesses the potential implications of what deep learning could do for robotics, research, and businesses.

A very gentle introduction to artificial neural networks and learning

Artificial neural networks (ANN) are mathematical and computational models used to classify or numerically evaluate a series of inputs, producing useful outputs as a result. These networks can be used in a great variety of situations to do many types of tasks. The diagram (see figure 1) illustrates such an artificial neural network with two connection layers.

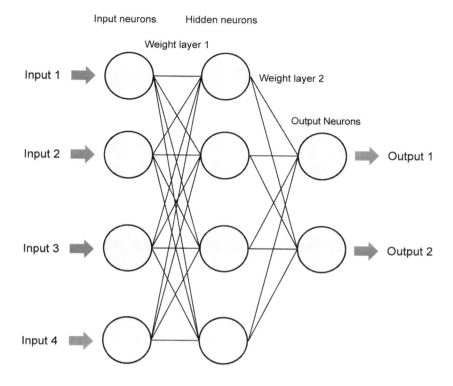

FIGURE 1 – A typical two layer multilayer perceptron (MLP) ANN with a single hidden layer.

These networks are normally implemented as a computer program. The basic idea behind such networks is almost always that you give the network inputs which will be transformed, evaluated, and then will finally generate useful outputs, that are a function of the inputs. The process of getting the outputs to represent something meaningful related to the inputs is the process of training the network.

The circles in figure 1 represent neurons – small, independent processing units that apply a simple, fixed process on the sum of their inputs, and transmit the result to the next layer. Connections between neurons – represented by black lines – have weights (numbers) that determine how much the information of the sending neuron will influence the receiving neuron. In most networks, these weights are the only variable and therefore the only "trainable component".

Ultimately, the output of the network is entirely determined by the weights (which can be trained) and the simple functions that each of the neurons or nodes performs. In other words, they determine what the neural network will do, given some input. The process of getting the network to do something useful given some inputs is the process of the network learning, or being trained.

The big deal about deepness

Such ANNs (especially with one middle or hidden layers) typically require the inputs to be preprocessed before being fed to the first layer. This is to clean up or extract the most meaningful and useful parts of the input signal before giving it to the network for learning from these extracted features. Many of the desirable attributes of this form of machine learning come from these middle layers, which are called **hidden layers**. Having multiple such layers allows the networks to learn more complex things while requiring less manual preprocessing. This is because each new added layer can learn things that were computed or performed by the previous layers. This means that interesting features embedded in the signals in the earlier layers can get picked up or pulled apart by the subsequent layers, more or less automatically during the learning process. (See figure 2.)

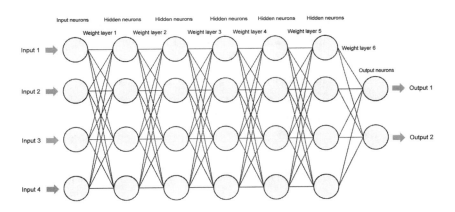

FIGURE 2 – A six layer MLP ANN with 5 hidden layers

However, introducing many hidden layers makes the task of training the network more complicated to implement. To alleviate this problem, a set of algorithms have been devised that are collectively called **Deep Learning**. With deep learning, we can train networks such as the one above, or even ones with tens of layers. This allows neural networks to do a great many things very well, once trained.

Four examples of the application of deep learning

Understanding the human brain – Deep ANNs trained with some form of deep learning have proven useful in the quest to understand how the human brain works. On some level, this is not a surprise, as these types of machine learning models are indeed modeled on how the brain operates. The exciting thing about networks trained in a so-called **supervised way** is that such models seem to explain a large proportion of the data from the human brain's visual recognition system. In other words, such models may very well portray correctly how some areas of the human brain are working.

Image recognition and classification – Using biologically-inspired deep ANNs to understand the brain better is not the only application of such models. They have recently been used successfully in image recognition and classification. A number of the top search engines now use massive neural networks with many layers and millions of artificial neurons. These can fully-independently recognize images fed as input to them as containing any of a number of things such as specific types of objects, people, and abstract entities such as writing, art, and artifacts in nature. Deep learning is a major approach in getting such ANNs to work.

Artificial Intelligence – Deep learning also plays an ever increasing role in more versatile artificial intelligence (AI) systems, like IBM's Watson. These are capable of working with and simplifying gargantuan data sets for a multitude of applications. Such systems have been used to make more optimal medical decisions, to give customer advice on online sales platforms, and also to suggest and generate culinary recipes. What makes this possible is deep learning's capability in finding relationships between data points at even abstract conceptual levels. This makes the technology interesting enough for IT giants including Facebook, Google, Twitter, and now IBM to warrant large-scale acquisitions and investments in this field, as recent developments have shown.

Financial markets – The first startups have appeared that are using deep learning to better understand and predict global markets and stock trades. At present, such techniques are neither fail-proof nor orders of magnitude more powerful than more traditional approaches. Yet, deep learning can increase information quality and thus lead to better decision making, which can be a great advantage in such heavily contested fields.

A look at the future of deep learning

How will our models of the brain help us to better understand it in the future?

In the next few years, we will see a large number of brain research groups and laboratories around the world employing – and extending their use of – deep learning techniques. Many will use these methods in the quest to understand this most complex of organs that defines and shapes our existence and experience. As we gain an ever-finer appreciation of the intricate workings of the human brain and mind, we will incorporate these insights into still newer AI and machine learning models – many of which will use some kind of deep learning approach. We are nearing the time when the multitude of different models of the brain are beginning to converge and our understanding of how things work and fit together is growing exponentially.

The central focus for brain research over the rest of this and the next decade will be combining deep learning models, which only work very well in mimicking some parts of the brain, with other types of models. It is likely that one of the first combinations of deep learning with other techniques will be in understanding the human visual system. While human image recognition seems to work somewhat like deeply-trained models, we will soon begin to tie that understanding and these deep learning models with other aspects of cognition such as emotions, tactile (touch) sensations, various types of attention, and other cognitive capacities. This, in turn, could lead to significant improvements in the fields of computer vision and image recognition systems.

Today we can see a clear trend towards automation in the service segment and our bets are on even more changes in the coming years, motivated by the high cost of personnel in most modern societies. Deep learning and related methods are and will be a big contributor to making these changes happen. We are already seeing the emergence of home robots, home companions, and automation systems that can recognize faces and rudimentary facial expressions. These will further evolve into more personalized and nuanced systems. They will interact with their surroundings more easily and more naturally, and thereby also potentially increase their chances of acceptance in society.

As an example of this, you will be able to show your home robot or your cell phone something which interests you. They will recognize what you are showing them, what it is about, and if they can read and understand it, they will do so. If they cannot, they will at least know where to direct you so you can learn or find out more about what you are showing them. These various systems will in large part be driven by deep ANNs.

A better awareness of the situation will also lead to better decision making and with that, more helpful actions. We will surely find such deep learning systems being combined with other types of complex models to help us respond better to all sorts of situations. One example could be reinforcing a certain robot or software assistant's behavior when you say "thanks" or discouraging the behavior when you look or sound annoyed. These and other types of features, when combined with deep learning systems, will make for far more flexible and interactive systems. They will begin to convince people into thinking that these systems really are intelligent – which they will be. Indeed, we already live in the age of intelligent machines. Deep learning and other emerging methods – in combination with improved hardware – will lead to a new era of machines that will be much better at mimicking the capacities and behaviors of humans – if we wanted them to.

Sociocultural, political and other effects of deep learning artificial intelligence methods

We will see deep ANNs being used more for information extraction and integration and thus decision and policy making. The trick here will be to present the situations in question in such ways that they become sensible for a network and allow it to be trained to recognize or guess the most optimal output for new situations. Financial and economic issues may perhaps be more easily translatable to representations that will be amenable to using and being modeled by deep learning methods.

Improved algorithms and hardware for trading decisions will lead to ever more complex financial transactions and flows. We have already reached a point where it is becoming clear that financial systems and organizations have grown to such proportions and become so interwoven that they are very hard to understand, even for specialists. Deep learning methods might help to dig through these volumes of data and help identify areas and statements that are unusual, questionable, or predictive of some type of behavior. In fact, neural networks (though not necessarily deep ones) are already used by banks to detect fraudulent or suspicious card or account activity automatically, efficiently, and reliably. If your card was ever temporarily frozen due to suspicious activity, you have quite likely interacted with a neural network model, just like the ones above. Such networks would have been trained on previous examples of suspicious and non-suspicious data.

The organization, democratization, and understanding of complex social organizations, consumer and voter behavior, political volatility of regions, and many more situations are currently often dealt with crudely, sometimes even intuitively and impulsively by the world's key players. Advanced machine learning methods will be able to help us make more rational, calculated decisions and we expect to see them used for this more frequently in the future.

Again, as mentioned above, in order to employ such machine learning or AI methods, we need to know how to translate real-world situations into slightly more formal, or mathematical, representations. While this is both abstract and difficult, it is not unimaginable, as we already do so for a wide range of data types – for example images, videos and text. So, once we have a given real-world situation, problem or context translated into an appropriate form that can be fed into such deep neural networks and other models, we can get meaningful output for that given real-world situation, problem or context.

How might investors, entrepreneurs, and others capitalize upon the growing interest and use of deep learning? The boundaries between what is and what is not achievable with these technologies can be very confusing for people without any knowledge in the field. The scale of the opportunity has the potential to lead to investment in projects that turn out to still be technically impossible. However, there are already many areas where a successful application of the methods can lead us in meaningful and fruitful directions.

Finally, deep neural networks will become ever more complex, with newer varieties of them being invented for specific purposes. Hence some understanding of the fundamentals will be necessary in order to deal with the many task-specific applications that ANNs can be created for and applied to.

Final words

The development of deep learning algorithms and equally importantly, hardware capable of supporting the running of these very computing-intensive algorithms has allowed our machines to do hitherto impossible things. Deep learning will certainly remain and become an ever more central aspect of intelligent machines in the coming years and decades. Perhaps most importantly we will see a merging or integration of deep learning methods with many other machine learning and AI techniques. The results will sometimes be difficult to predict in advance, but will also most surely lead to new insights into intelligence, the human brain, the creation of useful machines and robots and a plethora of other things.

For those in business, the emergence deep learning Artificial Neural Networks raise some key questions:

- *What applications within your organization could lend themselves to exploration using ANNs?*
- *As we deepen the use of machine learning and AI to develop behavioral insights – are there any limits to how we should use these tools either within our organizations or in targeting potential customers?*
- *What are the societal and market implications of using the technologies to analyze complex social, political, and economic situations and inform the resultant decision making?*

How Massive Simulation Models could Transform Decision Making in Business, Government and Society

By Vinay Gupta

How might the evolution of technology and simulation tools enable us to value complex systems such as nature?

So what's it worth?

Right now money is represented, for the most part, as hard incontrovertible numbers: $61.47, £22.42, €11.92. In contrast, the elements of nature are represented as 300 page reports with complex charts and graphs, and the conclusions are argued over indefinitely. What if we could make tools which have the ability to represent nature as easily as we represent value in the abstract economic game that we use to manage most of our planet's physical and (increasingly) intellectual resources? This chapter examines the valuation challenge and explores how new technology developments could enable us to develop large scale simulations that enabled accurate valuation of the impact of everything from climate change to a new business model.

The challenge of computing true value – from commerce to nature

It is already possible to have forms of money that work like software. For example, bond trading and similar areas of finance can include esoteric financial instruments which require extensive and complex software support to calculate their value over time. These are instruments which a "paper-and-pencil team" could simply never trade, no matter how long they took, because of the danger of arithmetic error. Twenty years from now, we will likely have a million times more computer power: could we finally build a system which models value directly, rather than abstracting it out to simple numbers? Could we compute the true value of nature, and of a contract, and thereby right the world?

One of the most pressing problems in economics is the question of value: we do not know how much a thing is worth until we try to sell it. Factors which may have nothing to do with the inherent value of the thing (say a general economic slowdown) can completely distort the value of the object we are selling. More complex financial markets use mathematical systems like the Black-Scholes model to try and get a more flexible model of value that bakes in some kinds of uncertainty and risk. However, as we have seen, these models tend to under-estimate the damage which can be done by long tail[313] and black swan[314] events. This leaves our financial systems as a whole vulnerable to price volatility, contagion, and collapse – leading to the need for expensive bailouts.

Our models of value have only just started to mature out of the pencil-and-paper age and into the age of seemingly-intelligent machines. This is a good thing, because it could address our inability to value natural assets correctly, for example climate stability, standing forests, or living whales. Limitations in valuation approaches have resulted in a general decimation of wealth on planet Earth, as valuable ecosystem services are destroyed. We continue to clear-cut timber for essentially worthless throwaway veneer furniture and the cardboard it is shipped in. It's clear that **wealth** is being destroyed as we deplete the forest or whale population, almost regardless of how we value the natural ecosystem, but we can't seem to represent this wealth accurately. What we cannot see in spreadsheets, we destroy as if it did not exist.

What can be done? Part of the reason ecosystem services are so hard to value is that they are **complex systems**. We know that if we cut down all the forests, the rain stops but it is almost impossible to model realistically the effect of cutting down one tree – it only impacts rainfall by some tiny percentage. Furthermore, these systems are profoundly non-linear. Systems absorb damage and recover gracefully, until suddenly we pass below some critical threshold, populations collapse dramatically, and a species becomes instinct. It's the exact opposite of something going viral: instead of suddenly blowing up, it suddenly falls down. We are losing bees at an unbelievable rate right now, and nobody seems to know why: is it something we did? New pesticides? Climate change? Some subtle change to farming practices intersecting nine other causes? We just don't know.

Large scale simulations and the search for new valuation approaches

Now let's consider how we might one day, in theory, work out the value of these complex systems. Computers get faster by roughly one thousand times per decade. I know that seems crazy, but it's true. Sometimes a little more, sometimes a little less. Over twenty years, a factor of a million; over forty years, a factor of a trillion.

A trillion.

Right now we can model moderately sophisticated systems: 10 day weather forecasts, or the neurons of a tiny worm. Putting a million times more computer power behind those kinds of tasks could lift them into an entirely new domain. Right now we can model the behavior of individual drugs. In 20 years, we will likely be able to model entire organisms or ecosystems. Real opportunities for change could be created if we were able to do massive simulations, run over and over again to simulate the randomness of the future, and statistically model the outcomes. This could give us leverage on the subtle cause-and-effect problems which bedevil our ability to understand and value correctly the assets embedded in complex systems.

Some of this data will come from sensors, but how do we model the economy as it intersects with these systems? One possible answer is **blockchains**. These are the underlying technology behind bitcoin, a very popular "cryptocurrency" (currency created by software alone, not by a central bank) with a current market capitalization of around $4 billion. Most transaction systems are trust based in that they rely on the buyer promising to honor the contract. In contrast, the blockchain (which itself is not a currency), is simply a "trustless" way of sharing information – a permanent history, a little like the history that Wiki-Pedia maintains of each of its pages. This is coupled with some strong authentication technology so we know that if somebody authorizes money to be spent from your bitcoin account, that person is you.

In future, if – as seems likely – we conduct the majority of trans-actions using technologies like blockchain, we will have an essentially permanent record of how the economy really functions. We could then feed this dataset into a simulator big enough to have a reasonable grasp of nature, perhaps with additional data sets from smart cities and similar projects. Perhaps we could then finally know what something is worth: by simulating the world without it, and seeing if we like the result.

Of course, no simulation can model the full complexity of the real world – at least no simulation we can currently conceive of. As we see in climate research, the validity of simulators is an intensely political thing. However, right now we essentially have no significant modelling capacity – and only one world on which to perform experiments. Even a relatively basic simulator which was generally agreed to be broadly scientifically valid could give us enormous amount of leverage in a variety of hard to model policy areas. At the very least, it will make the assumptions behind various world-views completely objective: climate denier software looks very different from climate scientist software.

What are the implications for business?

What is business going to be like in an environment where we have a scale model of the world to run experiments on? I can't say for sure, but I think we'll see four major changes going forwards into this aspect of the digital age:

- People will expect a holistic understanding and analysis of any systemic change to law, regulation or finance, demonstrating its safety before allowing implementation.

- Systems which do not leave transparent "data trails" will be regarded in the same way that we currently look at tax evasion.
- Pressure on rich countries to pay for the resources they have used in the past will mount as the full impact of climate change is felt and modelling systems show exactly how their economic growth has destabilized other regions.
- Data sets pulled from public transaction ledgers (like the blockchain) will be available to anybody who wants to understand the world better, including businesses that want to simulate a business model, new product, entry to a new market, or potential competitor responses.

Radical transparency coupled with massive simulation is going to change the way we approach the future: we'll model the outcomes of possible decisions rather than flying blind. Never forget that the breakthrough invention of the Wright Brothers was not the aeroplane, it was the wind tunnel. Once you have a wind tunnel in which to test scale models, designing an aeroplane is an essentially mechanical process of trial and error, with learning possibly taking place in months, not decades.

Let's just hope the software we use to simulate our world faithfully does the job of forecasting what can be known, rather than becoming distorted by political factors: the simulated eventually steers the real.

Key questions:

- *What is your organization doing to assess the potential impact of cybercurrencies and blockchain technologies?*
- *How would business practices change if we could accurately simulate critical decisions such as business model changes or new marketing strategies?*
- *What might the impacts be if society could model and charge businesses for the true value of the ecosystem service they use?*

The Future of Events and Networking

By Tiana Sinclair

How will technology change the nature of networking and event?

A range of digital technologies are emerging that could both replace or enhance the live event experience. This chapter explores a range of these developments and the ways in which they could be deployed to augment the physical experience for attendees, event owners, sponsors, and planners.

Digital enhancement of physical networking

In our fast paced, technologically advanced world with information readily available online, one may wonder why people still meet in person at business events. However, attending events still proves to be one of the best ways to connect with people, learn something new, and of course network. If we look at contemporary networking at events we find that on average one may get to speak to around four people. Indeed the first person would very likely be sitting or standing nearby. So the question arises, how many of those four connections would prove to be meaningful, engaging, or beneficial? Furthermore, what can we do to enhance such an analogue approach, and particularly what technologies and emerging platforms can we adopt to scale our experiences, and boost our networking reach to engage with those who matter the most? Likewise, as online social interactions became prevalent, further solutions on the intersection of event and digital tech become available.

Alternatives to the live experience

Webinars and **live streaming** technologies have been around for a while but the landscape is changing rapidly. More and more companies are determined to hold their events using Google+ Hangouts On Air. Just imagine this: a video chat service where an unlimited number of people can join your conference. Real-time content management platforms like EventSlides also make it easier for the organizer to distribute presentations to their attendees as the event is happening, making the information accessible on every mobile device. Similarly, apps like Meerkat and Periscope stormed the world by offering everyone a chance to livestream from their phone camera. This also opens up a discussion around unlocking new revenue streams based on the popularity of these on-demand channels. Admittedly, these solutions have already made a significant contribution to the industry, saving businesses and organizations large amounts of money that would otherwise go on travel and logistics.

Augmenting virtual and physical events

Technologies such as virtual reality (VR), augmented reality (AR), and wearable technology have entered both virtual and the live event environments over the last few years. Other technologies are still making their way through the adoption cycle to find the right product and market fit and, as some may argue, will eventually intersect with both our online and our offline worlds. For example VR devices like Oculus Rift now allow us to host virtual conferences in very unusual surroundings where your imagination is the only limit. They can also add extra dimensions to live experiences such as conferences and trade shows.

Pilot launches of products like Google Glass taught us that a lot of possibilities open up when combining online and offline experiences. If we apply this idea to physical networking, an interesting concept of hybrid net/physical interaction emerges. Just imagine your social network extensions floating above your head in an AR layer! Augmenting your physical experience with this digital overlay could open up several possibilities. Social profiles could become visible to everyone: we could see common likes, places of interest, mutual acquaintances, and even their entire career history depending on how much information the person you are looking at wants to present to the public. This advancement will eventually turn connecting in the physical world into a much easier, more structured, quantified, and as a result, more joyful experience. The common advice to "always have business cards ready to give out" may not be that relevant when it comes to networking strategies of the future.

Deploying artificial intelligence and behavioral analysis

Advances in artificial intelligence (AI) will also play a pivotal role in the industry. The brightest futurist minds continually debate the subject of AI and how it could become more and more self-aware. On the commercial side, we are now witnessing a race towards perfecting an AI-enabled pocket personal assistant. These apps are now capable of planning our day, booking travel arrangements, setting up meetings, reminding us to complete our tasks, and even posting social updates. Perhaps at some point in the not-so-distant future, we will be able to outsource our routine duties (at least the digital ones) to one of those assistants. An automated Twitter client may one day become a **mind clone**.[315] This concept is currently being explored to test hypotheses concerning the ability to download a person's consciousness into a computer after combining detailed data about that person with future consciousness software.

The way we collect data will change. Companies such as CA, IBM, SAS, and Cisco are reaping major rewards by using behavioral analysis to better understand attendee preferences and interests.[316] Better knowledge of attendee behavior patterns provides significant insight into the true success of an event. At the same time we see the rise of **quantified self** movement which aims to measure all aspects of our daily lives with the help of technology. Self-tracking is rapidly evolving into a mainstream trend. People are able to use smartphones and wearable sensors to record an expanding range of data – event professionals just need to tap into it and learn how to apply the insights.

For example, consumer-focused brain-computer interfaces like MindWave may well become more popularized and more delegates could start to wear them routinely. If this happens, then event managers, their sponsors, and exhibitors would be able to draw on data from the devices to monitor participant levels of attention and concentration as well as the emotional responses to particular presentations, trade show stands, and activities. Based on that insight, they could then target the individuals who truly paid attention – perhaps with additional content, special offers or information of relevant future events.

From telepresence to multi-sensory omnipresence

It is true that we live in a time of information overload where the human brain simply cannot process all the information coming our way, and be everywhere to capture those events we have missed. Live streaming and real-time technology makes it easier to recap on the moments we have missed, however it doesn't provide us with a complete, fully immersive experience. In other words, instead of projecting a recording of an event to a remote audience, can we project ourselves into it? Edward Snowden's appearance by telepresence robot at TED2014 allowed him to view the room through the installed camera and interact with the host and the attendees.[317] This marked a notable chapter in the industry and raised some important issues. Could there be a time when empty seats at events will be filled with fully functioning personalized robots, drones and holograms? Would they become autonomous enough to start exchanging contacts between attendees and one another and begin sending us daily reports?

Emerging technologies will enable deeper levels of engagement at the multisensory level and create enormous potential for integration with our existing digital identities and social media platforms. After all, it is very likely that in the future our online and offline connections will not be so different from each other. Indeed, the process of networking may one day transform into a two-worded concept of **net working** meaning quite literally, working the net. Our individual outreach is continuously ascending towards a gigantic leap.

Here are three questions these developments raise for your organization:

- *How are we preparing to embrace the transition of events and conventional networking and make the full use of digital platforms and emerging technologies?*
- *How will adoption of these technologies change the way we do business?*
- *What are the implications for us if our personal and business off-line and on-line worlds merge?*

Revolutionizing Interactive Entertainment and Marketing in Public Places through Ambient Interactivity

By Michael Mascioni

What impact will ambient interactivity have on the future of interactive entertainment and marketing in public places?

The rise of ambient interactivity

One of the most profound transformations in interactivity in public places is the emergence of ambient interactivity, which typically refers to interactivity embedded or built into physical structures and environments. In my view, it also applies to interactivity embedded in virtual environments and structures. Ambient interactivity unshackles, unleashes, and expands interactivity, enabling a free-flowing interactive force that meshes well with audience desires, preferences, and behaviors. This chapter explores how this could play out to enhance user experiences and marketing effectiveness in public places.

Ambient interactivity in public places

Some of the more common forms of ambient interactivity include interactive windows and interactive tables which are being leveraged to deliver informational, marketing, and entertainment applications. For example, interactive tables in restaurants are providing touch-sensitive menus incorporating ordering capabilities and even games. These interactive forms have proven to be highly effective and impactful. In many ambient interactive forms, motion sensors are utilized to track user movements which can trigger certain content displays or experiences. In some cases, light sensors are also used for similar purposes. Interactive mirrors will increasingly appear in public places over the next five years, allowing users to interact with a wide range of content through that surface.

The whole scope of ambient interactivity in public places will dramatically expand over the next five years as a myriad of current and new technologies combine to afford more vivid, dynamic, and extensive interactivity. Ambient interactivity is and will be particularly important in attracting younger audiences who crave and exhibit the **always on** digital lifestyle. They have high expectations for continuous and fluid interactivity that shifts from one digital device to another effortlessly and seamlessly.

A number of projects have been launched in public places allowing visitors to control such environmental elements as lighting and sound, and to co-create or co-generate content and displays. For example, Prysm offers users the opportunity to interact with large scale **collaborative video walls**. Over the next five years, a wider range of ambient interactive forms will allow audiences in public places to create their own experience more often and in more diverse ways. New events will be created or co-created in these environments by visitors utilizing a variety of tools. For example, they may have an opportunity to manipulate lighting and special effects in public places using tools such as laser poles, columns, wands, gesture control armbands, and haptic feedback controllers.

A key development for interactive technology in public places is the automatic display of audience-specific content geared to specific in a location using artificial intelligence to gauge their preferences. One manifestation of this development is the concept of **reflective signs**.

This involves using facial recognition techniques to gauge audience content preferences and then displaying that content to the particular audience. This technique will be expanded significantly in the near future via detection of the content that visitors in public places are viewing on large screens, interactive furniture, smart phones, tablets, other surfaces, and devices. In fact, detection of audience interest in particular content will likely extend beyond a specific location to other locations using networked media.

A number of developers, such as Perch Interactive, have developed large screen interactive displays built into structures such as tables or walls that are modeled after or activated by smaller interactive devices such as smartphones and tablets. This kind of approach may very well be expanded to enable the delivery of more large-screen 3D and holographic games, elements of alternate reality games, and other game forms via ambient displays in the out-of-home market.

Key elements of ambient interactivity have developed around projecting 3D images onto buildings and water walls. Another layer of experience can be created using augmented reality (AR) – by over-laying special effects on those projections using smartphones and tablets. Interaction with these projections will expand considerably in new directions over the next five years as the functionality of AR extends and becomes multi-sensory. Users will increasingly interact with these projections through wearable virtual reality (VR) and AR systems, and the exhibitors may even use laser devices to overlay special effects on these projections. Users will also have an opportu-nity to insert their own images into holographic projections on their surrounding walls, floors, and other surfaces.

Kinetic interactive displays will likely play a key role in ambi-ent interactivity in the next five years. The power of this ambient interactive form has already been demonstrated by such systems as Hyposurface. This is a 3D surface that displays content, including Internet feeds and apps – triggered by user movement, sound, and other means. The system's use of movement to trigger content displays has a special appeal, and has strong potential in museums, stores, amusement parks, and other public places. This form of ambient interactivity is likely to play a much greater role in public places in the near future as businesses and other organizations embrace and further shape this kind of technology.

Drones

Drones will become a more significant part of interactive exhibits, attractions, and other experiences in public places, spawning a different kind of ambient interactivity. Early versions have already appeared. Displaydrone is a system conceived by Dr. Jurgen Scheible of Stuttgart Media University and Dr. Water Fichter of the University of Stuttgart. It fuses a flying robot (multicopter) with a video projector and a mobile phone to enable a flying display to be projected onto walls and arbitrary objects in physical environments.

Re-shaping the environment

The concept of ambient interactivity will broaden to encompass more elaborate and diverse rapid 3D scanning and printing experiences. Visitors in public places will have an opportunity to reshape and add to their environment by developing new 3D printed objects, artifacts, objects, and attractions. This could happen in collaboration with other visitors and designers at museums, amusement parks, location-based entertainment centers, stores, and other public places. These may include new/adapted vehicle models, clothing forms, game machines, and art objects, such as sculptures.

Virtual reality and augmented reality

The greater use of VR and AR systems, including wearable systems in locations such as museums and amusement parks will enable the delivery of more vivid and dynamic immersive experiences. For example, the combined use of wearable AR systems and 3D projections might become an intriguing option for users in public places. In this scenario, a user could interact with those projections using a wearable system and superimpose special effects and other images over the projections to explore more striking real/virtual experiences. These experiences might spawn new forms of 3D adventures and games in public places.

Some indications of these possible experiences can be gleaned from such innovative AR systems as Magic Leap and HoloLens. Magic Leap, which reportedly utilizes a glasses-like technology, beams light on the user's retina to capture real world images, and overlays virtual images, such as fictional characters, over the real images to give the user a unique sensation of directly seeing virtual 3D images in the real world. HoloLens, a wireless smart glasses system developed by Microsoft, enables the creation of, and interaction with, realistic high-definition 3D holograms. It incorporates gesture recognition, voice recognition, and spatial mapping capabilities. The system, which is due for introduction in 2015, promises to have many diverse business applications, and will even allow for objects and other material viewed on the system to be printed on 3D printers.

Robots

Robots under visitor control might also play a greater role in enabling and fostering ambient interactive experiences in public places over the next five to ten years. They may be directed by visitors using gestural devices, smartphones, and AR/VR systems to adjust and prepare environments for particular interactive events and experiences in those places.

Some of these ambient interactive experiences will likely be offered on a premium basis or as part of subscriptions by museums, location-based entertainment centers, and other leisure facilities, as they seek new revenue sources and ways of attracting visitors.

In light of the trends highlighted in this article, ambient interactivity seems destined to become much more pervasive, diverse, and expansive in public places in the next five to ten years. It will create much greater and richer engagement opportunities for visitors, operators, retailers and advertisers in leisure facilities and stores.

What questions should businesses consider in relation to the use of ambient interactivity as an innovative communication, marketing and entertainment technology?

- *How might new forms of ambient interactivity impact on marketing and entertainment in public places and how could business utilize the opportunities?*
- *What special marketing/pricing strategies will businesses need to develop for the use of diverse ambient interactive forms?*
- *What kind of ambient interactivity content and experiences might appeal to your organization's stakeholders?*

Section 6

**Surviving and Thriving –
How can business adapt to a rapidly changing reality?
What are the critical success factors for business in a
constantly evolving world?**

Changing the game not the rulebook

Given the range of technological developments anticipated, businesses, and organizations more generally, will have the potential, and arguably need, to respond in ever-more fundamental ways. Business cycles, new structures, new business models, and new ways of acquiring and managing talent will play a significant role in addressing the opportunities and challenges of a constantly evolving world.

Six key aspects of the future evolution of business are explored here.

Experience Rules: How Stakeholder Experiences will Drive Profit into the Future (*page 375*) – Joyce Gioia highlights how maximizing the experience of each stakeholder group could be the most critical driver of future corporate profitability.

Acceleration of the Slow Movement (*page 382*) – Dana Klisanin explores how businesses may reject the notion that speed is everything and increasingly embrace the concepts of the Slow Movement.

Business Agility: The Future of Work (*page 386*) – Laura Goodrich describes the power of business agility as mechanism for ensuring firms have the capacity to respond rapidly and effectively to emerging and anticipated change.

The Future of Work, Talent and Recruitment *(page 391)* – Matt Alder examines how critical forces of business change are shaping tomorrow's organization designs and models of work and employment.

The Future of Talent Management: Recruiting, Workforce Planning, Leadership Development and Performance Management *(page 395)* – Kevin Wheeler explains how disruption will force us to rethink every aspect of talent management in tomorrow's organization.

Making the Shift from Disruptive to Hyper Scalable *(page 406)* – Omar Mohout argues that future success requires companies to adopt Hyper Scalable thinking to succeed in winner-takes-all markets.

Global Drivers of Change

By April Koury, Iva Lazarova and Rohit Talwar

A range of 27 emerging drivers of change could play a critical role in reshaping the business landscape.

- ***Shorter, Faster Business Cycles*** – Organizations are under pressure as the perceived speed of the business cycle increases while the duration of each cycle decreases. Constant adaptation in structures, processes and systems is becoming an expected norm.
- ***Level of Complexity in Business*** – Driven by the rapid pace of social and market change, innovation, and regulatory requirements, complexity is forcing many firms to figure out how to navigate the fine line between chaos and control. Often businesses are faced with a multitude of complex processes, regulatory requirements, governmental procedures, differing staff expectations, and organizational structures and cultures. This may be balanced by increasing data collection and desktop and mobile device analytics.
- ***Commoditization*** – Economic pressure, global competition, and automation are combining to commoditize, or drive down the prices of previously premium-priced goods and services, across a wide range of sectors. Vendors of everything from clothing to plane tickets appear be locked in a "race to the bottom" to offer the lowest price. Many fear that these lowest

cost strategies are unsustainable and may lessen investment in workforce development and innovation. With extreme commoditization, only the most innovative and deep pocketed businesses are likely to survive such intense price competition.

- **New Business Models** – New models are emerging at three levels. On one level, asset funding is shifting from ownership to usership and crowd based platforms (for example Crowdcube) are being used to source debt and equity finance; at the next level crowdfunding is increasingly being used to fund innovation through platforms like Kickstarter; and on the final level revenue models are changing with aggregated buying, auctions, freemium, and pay-per-usage becoming more widespread.
- **Markets of a Billion** – In parallel with the exponential business model, businesses increasingly target markets of a billion people or more as a goal from the outset. This is the ambition of many ventures spawned by the innovators from programs at Singularity University. They are tapping into the possibility that, in the next decade, there will be an emergence of new trillion dollar industries which will thrive via advances in science, technology, and ICT. The sharing economy, smart cities, 3D and 4D printing, and the Internet of Things (IoT) are a few of the expected emerging trillion dollar industries where markets of a billion consumers will be likely.
- **Exponential Organizations (ExO)** – As technology grows exponentially (for example the doubling of computer power every 18-24 months), the linear business model is failing to adapt quickly enough. By utilizing new organizational techniques and leveraging exponential technologies, these organizations grow output and / or improve performance at an exponential rate compared to similar, linear model competitors.
- **Attributes of an ExO** include capturing the hearts and minds of people both inside and outside of the organization with a higher aspirational purpose; leveraging external people rather than owning employees; adopting algorithms to gain insight about their customers; renting, sharing, or accessing rather

than owning assets; engaging their community to create networks and positive feedback loops; utilizing real-time, adaptable dashboards that everyone in the organization can access to measure and manage organizational performance; encouraging experimentation; decentralizing authority; and using collaborative tools to create sharing and transparency. Familiar ExOs include Airbnb, Valve, Uber, and Netflix.[318]

- *Hyper Scalable Corporation* – A hyper scalable business model is one in which a company with relatively few employees offers value at nearly zero cost to millions of users simultaneously. Skype, for example, employs roughly 1,600 people yet handles roughly 40 percent of all international telephone traffic. Hyper scalable models tend to be based on intangible assets like music or data, they use information technology as a lever, and they utilize the internet as a free distribution channel.[319] As more and more people gain access to the internet worldwide, the low startup costs and potentially exponential profits should encourage the continued growth of hyper scalable companies.

- *Decentralized Autonomous Organization (DAO) / Decentralized Autonomous Corporation (DAC)* – In its broadest definition, a decentralized autonomous organization is an entity that exists autonomously on the internet.[320] The activities of the entity and how they should be conducted are specified through strict business rules. DAOs typically have a distributed network of intelligent agents which can execute these rules. DAOs also rely on hiring people to perform tasks that the automation is unable to do for itself. DAOs contain some sort of internal property that has value, and they are able to use that property to reward humans and other stakeholders for their activities. For example, one DAO might perform services for another and be rewarded financially. It can then use that money to pay those who it hires. Bitcoin and Namecoin can be classified as DAOs. As algorithms become more intelligent and autonomous, DAOs should become more common place online.

- *Algorithmic Corporation / Companies as Technologies* – Algorithmic corporations are managed by software rather than humans. Giant retail corporations are currently using algorithmic technology to fuse online shopping with the in-store experience, creating a new, interactive relationship between the businesses and their customers. Customers are now able to communicate directly to legacy companies, and those companies in turn are able to track and predict customer preferences in real time, allowing them to meet changing demands quickly.[321] This growing business model will continue to be driven by the advancement of mathematical algorithms and the related software, which will speed up decision-making, flatten out organizations, reduce headcounts, and reduce overhead costs well into the future.

- *Talent-less / Talent-light Corporations* – Enterprises may increasingly evolve their business models and reward systems to acknowledge the difficulties faced in recruiting and retaining talented employees, especially in a world where talent is replacing capital as the most important factor of production. They will operate with a very small core of highly talented permanent staff and the rest of the activities will be performed by technology, contractors, subcontractors, and partners.

- *Community Investment* – While many firms now have some level of community involvement, a growing group of companies has realized that long-lasting investment in the local community is vital to address the toughest social issues. Community investing typically focuses on economically improving run-down communities, often in places where the state is retreating.[322] As the community improves and people are able to gain economic stability, less strain is placed on federal social welfare – bringing an increase in gross domestic product and other overall measures of community vibrancy and wealth production.

- *Crowdsourced Funding* – Increasingly, startups and new ventures turn to crowdfunding sites like Kickstarter and Indiegogo to fund the pre-sale of products and services in advance of launch. Using these online platforms, funders commit a certain amount to become early customers or investors of the company. Crowdsourced funding is also being used across every aspect of financial services – including raising debt and equity investment, insurance, invoice discounting, mortgages, and personal loans – facilitating the rise of a new financing model.

- **Freemium Business Models** – A freemium business model is one in which the business gives a core product away for free and sells add-on premium products such as proprietary features, functionality, or virtual goods, for example, Skype and WhatsApp. Originally developed by software companies, freemuim models are now found across many industries, driven by the consumer demand for free products and services.

- **Rise of Co-Creation** – Customers play a much larger role in business ecosystems where they can co-create and help design new products and services for companies. Advances in technologies such as 3D printing and the movements toward open source design sharing and more collaborative consumption will continue to develop this driver. Large players like IKEA[323] and Kia[324] have used co-creation to innovate new products and brands that meet their customers' needs. As a result, the lines between traditional business, society, and consumers are blurring. Co-creation focuses on maximizing the emotional, intellectual and physical quality of the user experience, and it utilizes people and human needs as the first frame of reference. Concepts like design thinking will encourage co-creation and focus greater attention on developing more enduring, sustainable and eco-friendly products and services.

- **Sharing Economy and Collaborative Consumption** – Rather than purchasing to own, people are increasingly turning to the sharing economy to, in essence, rent and share in the ownership of items. Owners are using new "middle men services" like Airbnb and Snapgoods to lend out everything from rooms in their homes, to kitchen appliances, clothing, tools, houses, and cars.[325]

- *Scale of Reverse Innovation* – Reverse innovation is the movement of innovative goods and services developed in the emerging economies into the mature markets. Examples include a $3,000 car by Indian manufacturer Tata and the XO-1 laptop priced at $100. Reverse innovation is challenging established companies, business models, and research centers in mature markets.

- *Organizational Reframing* – Organizational designs and working practices are being influenced by a number of converging factors that are forcing them to rethink their purpose, strategy, and design. These factors include technology advances; new operating structures and cultural models such as flat organizations; businesses leveraging social networks to amplify their reach; and growing cultural diversity driving the need to accommodate multiple worldviews, religions, and customs in daily work.

- *Networked Organizations* – As firms switch from doing everything in-house to seeking partners to deliver solutions to customers, networked organizations grow. Startups, small firm cooperatives, freelance communities, and independent workers favor the networked organization model, where they often integrate new management approaches and business models.

- *Increase in Distance Working* – As firms cut overhead costs and employees seek jobs that require less travel time and increase working flexibility, remote or distance working continues to grow. Cloud computing, the proliferation of mobile devices, and greater connectivity all contribute to the rise in distance working. A survey of business leaders at the Global Leadership Summit in London found that 34 percent said more than half of their company's full-time workforce will work remotely by 2020.[326]

- *Rise of the Independent Worker/Contractor* – Independent contractors are projected to comprise more than 40 percent of the U.S. workforce by 2020.[327] These workers will require new skills and support to manage an independent existence, which forces companies to rework their traditional staffing and resourcing models to better answer the needs of both the organization and the independent contractor.

- **Rate of Obsolescence of Professional Knowledge** – An individual's professional knowledge is becoming outdated faster than ever because of rapid changes in work-related technology and the job market, which in turn is necessitating continuous education. Over the next two decades, Artificial Intelligence (AI), robotics and automation are expected to eliminate 50 to 80 percent of the work undertaken by professional and skilled workers in a range of sectors, including financial services, accounting, legal, manufacturing, construction, administrative support, retail, telemarketing, and transportation.
- **Alternative Reward Systems and Models** – Increasingly businesses are coming under pressure to support a more diverse and continuously evolving mix of benefits for their employees. Enterprises have to find new reward models that both meet the desires of their employees and that ensure equitable treatment of employees performing similar roles.
- **Digital Assets** – Digital assets include multimedia, images, and any form of digitally stored content (anything stored in binary format) that includes a right to use it. The difficulty of securing and monitoring patents on assets that are so quickly replicated and distributed is driving firms to accelerate the pace of innovation and use of digital rights management. Value creation could become de-linked from physical objects as virtual immersive worlds grow and drive up virtual spending on digital assets.
- **Gamification** – Businesses are turning to gamification, the use game techniques to engage users to solve problems, to motivate shoppers to buy goods and services, for co-creating products and services with consumers, and for employee training.
- **Future Outsourcing Hotspots** – Outsourcing markets are gradually becoming defined by specialization in niche areas such as specialist manufacture, business analytics, and software

testing. The next wave of outsourcing hotspots are expected to be in Eastern and Central Asian and Latin America.

- *Future Fortune Global 500* – By 2020, the Global 500 could be dominated by a number of companies from emerging markets in Asia and Latin America. The trend reflects the shift of economic power from Europe and the United States to developing economies like India, China, and other economies following in their wake.

- *Rise of Micro-Businesses & Micro-Entrepreneurship* – Micro-Businesses, companies that employ fewer than 10 people and have a turnover of less than €2 million/$2.4 million, are becoming an increasingly important part of the economy. Both micro-businesses and micro-entrepreneurship are driven by new economic models like the sharing economy, micro-commerce, and micro-payments. According to the U.S. Small Business Administration, from 2004 to 2010, micro-enterprises created 5.5 million jobs, while the largest businesses actually lost 1.8 million jobs.[328] Micro-businesses diversify national employment risk, can be started relatively quickly, and are often active in key knowledge-based industry sectors

Experience Rules: How Stakeholder Experiences will Drive Profit into the Future

By Joyce Gioia

How will organizations need to rethink stakeholder experience to ensure future profitability?

Embracing stakeholders

With technology and innovation becoming so pervasive in our lives, it is interesting that simultaneously human beings are craving greater depths of experience. Whether people are related to organizations as employees, customers, students, investors, vendors, family members, or simply as part of the community, they seek positive interactions. When employees and customers have those positive interactions, the enhanced relationships promote higher levels of engagement. Moreover, the higher the levels of engagement, the higher the profits or gain from operations for non-profits. This chapter will explain how the quest for profit will result in restructuring the corporation of the future to focus more directly on what will positively affect the bottom line: **positive stakeholder experiences**.

The research points the way

A wide range of recent customer and employee engagement research reflects that the deeper the level of involvement or engagement, typically the more positive the feelings towards that organization are. Subsequently, these positive feelings engender loyalty that results in higher sales, better retention, and continuity of performance. Accenture's Customer 2020 research finds that when companies enhance the **Customer Experience**, they typically grow their revenues.

"Consumers continuously evaluate providers, resulting in a growing switching economy that accounts for an estimated $6.2 trillion in revenue opportunity for providers across 17 key markets today. . ."[329]

Julian Measey, a consultant focusing on the customer experience writes: "Managing your employee experience drives profit growth." There is a growing understanding that the employee experience informs the customer experience.[330] In addition, a meta study by Gallup in 2012, evaluating 263 research studies across 192 organizations in 49 industries and 34 countries, confirmed "… the well-established connection between employee engagement and nine performance outcomes," including profitability and productivity. The study showed how, "…engaged companies [consistently] outperform their competition."[331]

For a few years now, there has been a rising tide of consulting firms offering services dedicated to enhancing the experience of a particular group of stakeholders. Some organizations learned years ago that by creating more engaging experiences, stakeholders will feel more connected, and therefore choose to stay engaged with the firm — ultimately making them more profitable. There are already consulting firms focusing on just about every stakeholder group, including customers, employees, investors, suppliers, and patients.

Simulations on the rise to help craft impactful experiences

Simulations are increasingly being used to create experiences that engage stakeholders at deeper levels. In a recent example, one of Harvard's teaching hospitals in Boston, Massachusetts wanted to find ways to enhance the experiences of families and patients during labor, delivery, and the hospital stay. Taking cross-functional teams of healthcare professionals through short, safe, carefully engineered simulations was very effective in helping the hospital redesign the process for all of its stakeholders. One of the innovations to come out of their work together was a video[332] to put both patients and their families at ease.[333]

Employers will have to create more engaging experiences

Creating differentiated experiences is working to help employees choose to join employers, stay with them, and deliver their best efforts at work. According to John Bremen, Managing Director, Towers Watson, 70 percent of employees would like to have a satisfying level of engagement, yet only 43 percent have one.[334] It is the most successful and profitable organizations that have already realized the importance of creating these positive experiences for their employees. Many have come to realize that without taking these steps, not only do they have burned out employees, but they are also at a competitive disadvantage.

Moving into the future

As companies become more conscious of the challenges of maintaining human connection in an increasingly digital world, I believe the understanding of the importance of the experiences of internal and external customers will expand to include all stakeholders. This means focusing on populations we would not ordinarily think about, like vendors and even the families of employees and customers. The level of experience drives the degree of engagement and the stronger the engagement, the more profitable the relationship. Here are some of the key shifts we can expect in the near term future.

More enriching employee experiences to come

Focusing on their internal customers, employers will find ever-more engaging ways to use simulation, gamification, and adventure to enhance work and learning experiences for employees. By knowing what particular employees are looking for, employers will increasingly tailor work and the experience around it to individual preferences. Using gamification, some work will be turned into fun activities, similar to what Microsoft did with its Windows' Language Quality Game. Microsoft used an innovative application of gamification to tweak its foreign language dialogue boxes and help screens for earlier versions of Windows'. As a result, the company engaged over 4,000 of its employees worldwide to help perfect the language before release.[335]

Expanded use of gaming and simulation

In the near-term, employers will use better-constructed training simulations to help people experience certain types of work without placing them in harm's way. Already hospitals are building learning centers that simulate emergency departments, operating rooms (ORs), homes, and even offices. These simulated environments give employees at all levels and in all professions a real sense of what health crises are like, before the individuals need to go into the actual situation. In the simulated OR, medical students studying to be surgeons will be able to operate on live humans rather than cadavers. While 3D OR simulations are already in use, the next generation will be even more sophisticated, adding in multi-sensory input such as smells and replicating the body's behavior in ever more accurate and sophisticated ways. In the simulated offices, hospital administrators will be able to practice the language of leadership before moving into positions of authority. In the simulated doctors' offices, physicians and nurses alike will be able to practice interacting with patients and perfect their history-taking and examination techniques.

Star Trek-like holodecks are coming, too

In the longer-term future, employees will practice on a Star Trek-like holodeck that can be programmed to simulate their work environments. Others will climb into their Virtual Reality (VR) suits to practice their physical skills. Employers will have a much better understanding of the experiences that make people happy and build more of them into the workday, often using higher levels of technology than are available today.

Transforming customer experiences

Using immersive VR and augmented reality (AR) applications powered by artificial intelligence (AI), customers who travel may be transported back in time to experience life as it was hundreds of years ago. There will be group immersions in which students get to experience the activities of school and play as if they were living in the past or an imagined future. Customers will be able to select the intensity of their experiences and choose a level from mild to extreme, depending on the degree of reality they are prepared to handle. Customers of consumer products and services will buy interactions along with their standard purchases. Each interaction will be a simple code (similar to the QR codes today) that may be accessed by the VR suit to provide the multi-sensory experience.

Improving the vendor experience

Beyond being paid in a timely manner, vendors in the future will be looking for a higher level of partnership, where they may be strategic partners of their customers, not just vendors. As valued partners, companies will look for ways to enhance vendor interactions by using technology to make communication seamless. Beyond this enhancement, companies will find other ways to express their appreciation and demonstrate that they value these relationships, even going so far as providing some of the exclusive benefits provided to employee or customers like free food, discounts, or other perks.

Appreciating the value of investors

Without investors, publicly held companies would not survive. Yet up to now, far too little attention has been paid to these valuable stakeholders. Town Hall Meetings online, periodic video messages, and other technology will be used to keep in touch with investors. Investors will be able to undertake virtual tours of factories and watch as the latest model rolls off the production line. Carnival Cruise Lines offers what they call **shareholder credits** in the form of a bonus stateroom credit to passengers who are investors in their stock. For frequent cruisers, it is like receiving additional dividends for free.

In the future, we can expect to see a greater number of companies add value to investors with discounts, rebates, and other financial incentives for investing in their stock or otherwise supporting the organization. Companies have significant opportunities to augment the perception of their organizations by changing the perceived value of ownership, resulting in significantly increased shareholder value. Companies will begin to pay increasing attention to the need to recognize and reward investors and customers for helping to generate additional business through introductions and referrals. Commission payments, discounts, loyalty points, and ever-more exclusive gifts and unique experiences will be offered to those stakeholders who bring in the most business.

The coming of the CExO[336]

To ensure that the stakeholder relationship efforts of the various departments involved deliver congruent brand experiences, organizations will increasingly appoint a **Chief Experience Officer (CExO)**. The CExO is different from the current CXO role (also called Chief Experience Officer) that many technology and consumer facing companies have today. The current CXO role typically only relates to enhancing the customer experience and the external marketing function and typically has no responsibility outside of marketing, service, and sales. The new iteration of Chief Experience Officer will typically report directly to the CEO. This executive will have responsibility over not only marketing, sales, and the external customer experience, but also the entire realm of stakeholder experiences, including employees, investors, and vendors as well. Keeping these diverse brand experiences congruent will be a challenging part of the new CExO's remit.

In addition, he or she will be responsible for the overall quality of experiences the company delivers in both the physical and digital realm. With a background that may include operations, marketing and sales, as well as psychology and even counseling, this individual will be well equipped to advise the various divisions on how to maintain consistency of brand experience across diverse stakeholder groups.

Profit and technology will drive the shift

Most people crave positive experiences and will gravitate towards organizations that can provide those experiences on a consistent basis. Driving this shift to experience-centric business model is the relentless focus we are already seeing on maximizing profit and growing revenues. At the same time, technology and Big Data will support the effectiveness of the model by giving valuable, ongoing feedback about what's working and what's not.

What organizations must do now to stay ahead of the curve

Corporate leaders must acknowledge the fundamental shifts taking place in their markets and begin to look at the experiences they are delivering to all of their stakeholders. They must think about how they might enhance those relationships in meaningful ways. One size will not fit all. Recognize that within groups of stakeholders, there may be segments worth addressing separately. For instance, millennial employees will have different values and attitudes than their baby boomer counterparts. As we move into the future, I believe no single other factor will have more impact on driving profitability than **experience**.

Creating deeper, more engaging experiences will be about finding ways to add value to all of the organization's stakeholder relationships. The prime objective of the CExO role will be to ensure that the experience engine that is tomorrow's corporation continues to serve all of its stakeholders to optimize profits.

Here are three questions for you organization to consider:

- *How effectively do you monitor, manage, and enhance the experience of critical stakeholder groups for your organization?*
- *Would your stakeholders recommend doing business with/working with your organization? If not, why not?*
- *What can/should you do to address any issues right away, so that your customers, employees, vendors, and investors all become "raving fans"?*

Acceleration of the Slow Movement

By Dana Klisanin

What are the potential future implications of the rise of the slow movement for business?

Is faster the only option?

In the face of accelerating change and hyperspeed thinking about the future, the question arises as to whether getting faster is the only option for businesses that want to succeed in tomorrow's economy – or is there an alternative? In this chapter I introduce the concept of the Slow Movement as a body of thinking and practice which believes that faster may not always be better. I explore how it is playing out from food to town management and explore the possible implications for businesses that want to explore the slow path to the future.

In celebration of slow

"I want to build a clock that ticks once a year. The century hand advances once every 100 years, and the cuckoo comes out on the millennium. I want the cuckoo to come out every millennium for the next 10,000 years." *The Clock of the Long Now – Danny Hillis*

The *Clock of the Long Now* is currently being built in western Texas.[337] What is the point of the clock and why does it matter? The Clock is a creative attempt to foster long-term thinking – something that matters to all businesses.

I have opened with an introduction to the Clock because it's an excellent example of the values embraced by adherents of the **Slow Movement**, a cultural movement that promotes the idea that faster is not always better. Carl Honoré, author of *In praise of Slowness* explains: "It is about quality over quantity in everything from work to food to parenting."[338] This focus on quality is not only changing the way firms do business, it is simultaneously addressing the roots of some of our most pernicious global challenges.[339]

The good news is that the Slow Movement is accelerating. What started with the **Slow Food** movement has become a catch phrase, embracing many aspects of the counter-culture movements that preceded it. The non-threatening nature of the word slow has served as an aggregator, bringing previously marginalized movements into the mainstream. Slow is not associated with any one culture, thus it transcends and includes. Adherents of the Slow Movement embrace the speed of the Internet, but with a caveat. Rather than web surfing and aimlessly scrolling through social media, they use it to collaborate and to improve their efficiency in order to pursue what really matters: time to engage with family, friends, and their own pursuits.

In the business world, the Slow Movement encompasses a range of concepts from Conscious Capitalism and the Benefit Corporation (B-corporation)[340] through to Lifestyles of Health and Sustainability (LOHAS). It embraces economic models in which care and the environment have value and are thus, valuable.[341] [342] The roots of the Slow Movement are found in a new mythos, or worldview of interdependence. People are reconnecting with the natural world and acknowledging our interdependence with the biosphere in ever-greater numbers. This reconnection results in activism.[343] Activism that is as quiet as starting a vegetable garden or as loud as the 400,000 strong People's Climate March that occurred around the world in 2014.[344] This brings us to another name for or aspect of the Slow Movement: the **Transition Movement**.

The Transition Movement is a grassroots movement "...that seeks to build community resilience in the face of such challenges as peak oil, climate change and the economic crisis".[345] The individuals and groups who are using the Transition Model in their communities are called **Mullers**. As a result, at the community level, so called **Transition Towns** are on the rise.

What does this mean for business?

The Slow Movement is already changing the way individuals and families eat, play, learn, heal, dress, vacation, and much more. One reason for this acceleration is scientific evidence that links multitasking and super-speed lifestyles to negative stress. Negative stress is associated with everything from depression to cancer. The belief is that in the future, as people increasingly recognize the toll fast-paced lifestyles are taking on their health, their families, and the environment, they will begin to slow down. The result? We will see an expansion of businesses that support the Slow Movement and an increasing emphasis on "cradle to grave" thinking, also known as **life-cycle assessment** – focusing on assessing and managing down the environmental footprint of products from creation to the end of their life.

As the Slow Movement continues to spread, I believe people in ever-greater numbers will reassess their values. When keeping up with the Jones no longer means living in bigger houses or driving new cars, families will rethink their priorities. In the future, the businesses that thrive will be those that not only mirror these values but actually practice them; Mom and Pop are going back into business and the neighborhood is eager to support them. The handcraft movement, also called the **Makers Market** is a big part of the Slow Movement. It will continue to grow, increasingly enabling one or more parent to stay home with the children, while simultaneously living a fulfilled life and earning extra money or exchanging their outputs for goods and services.

The Makers movement and the Slow Movement share the values of authenticity and connection. The products are sustainably made and include handmade everything, from jams to dishes, hair barrettes to shoes, books to toys, perfume to cough syrup, and so forth.

The *Clock of the Long Now* is a large-scale creative effort to increase humanity's ability to think long-term. The Slow Movement, Transition Towns, and Makers Markets all share an overarching goal: to reconnect us with the natural world and a sustainable healthy life. When we slow down to garden, to eat, and to play we find ourselves increasingly aware of our ecological and social interdependence. We are no longer isolated individuals fixated on our own welfare, but rather individuals who are part of a collective fixated on the welfare of each other and Earth. Through uniting with these goals and ideals, businesses in the 21st century will thrive and increase the chances that future generations will watch the cuckoo come out on the millennium.

Here are three questions for reflection:

- *What would it take to restructure your business as a B-Corporation?*
- *Which elements of Slow Movement thinking could be integrated successfully into your existing business?*
- *If you were to create a new business focused on one aspect of the Slow Movement, what would it be?*

Relevant search terms for those interested in finding out more about the Slow Movement:

Transition towns, Mullers, home gardens, bee-keeping, sewing, communal childcare, home schooling, hybrid education, reclaimed, recycled, upcycled, steampunk, alternative energies, holistic health-care, Earth-based spirituality, Makers' market, stay-cation, local vacationing, eco-tourism, organic, craft beer, transformational festivals (e.g. Burning Man, and "The Bloom"), sustainability, Integral theory, social economy, free culture (Open Source, Creative Commons), collaborative heroism, permaculture, story-telling, Elder Wisdom.

Business Agility: The Future of Work

By Laura Goodrich

How can ensure organizations are sufficiently agile to respond to the needs of a rapidly changing world?

A Cougar or a Labrador?

Recently my friend Leah and I were walking our two Labrador retrievers. The dogs were off-leash and enjoying their freedom when suddenly they ran back to us with their tails between their legs. As we scrambled to get their leashes back on, Leah said "It must be a cat."

"A house cat?" I asked.

"No, a bobcat." she replied.

Once we had the dogs safely on leash, we began to look for the bobcat. But we didn't see one, and we continued on our way.

Then I happened to glance back, and the cat I saw crossing the path was no ordinary housecat, or even a bobcat. It was a cougar.

With new urgency we hurried along. The path rose up a hill, from where we could see that the cougar was working its way around the periphery of the open grassy range. It was slinking down low in the classic "on the hunt" stance. Now we were scared, and we got out of there fast. Once we were safely home, we called the authorities. We learned that cougars can run fifty miles an hour and leap forty feet. Truly a real threat, a very agile threat that could have easily overtaken us.

If you're in business, which would you rather be? A friendly Labrador retriever on a leash, or an agile cougar? I will bet your choice was the same as mine. In business now and into the future, you've got to be fast and agile. This chapter explores the challenges of building and sustaining agility to help the organization respond, adapt to and anticipate ever-faster changes on the horizon.

Netflix: How an agile company embraced the future

Here's an example of what can happen to a company that isn't agile. Remember Blockbuster Video? At its peak in 2004, Blockbuster had over 9,000 stores and up to 60,000 employees. It ruled the movie rental business. By 2010—only six years later—the company had filed for bankruptcy. Its upstart competitor Netflix quickly became the number one provider of movies to consumers.[346]

Even though Blockbuster was not an old company, its business model quickly became obsolete. It earned much of its profits by charging its customers late fees on video returns. This system worked only until disruptive change happened. Instead of charging customers to rent individual videos, Netflix offered subscriptions, which made onerous late fees unnecessary. Customers could watch a video for as long as they wanted, or return it and get a new one.[347]

Blockbuster ignored change. They assumed that Netflix was an ordinary house cat but, as it developed momentum, it became clear that Netflix was indeed a cougar – and it took down Blockbuster. That is how disruption happens. It doesn't seem like a problem in the beginning, but in reality it's a real threat. For agile companies, there is opportunity in disruption.

Agility as a future management methodology

For companies seeking to stay ahead of the curve, the agile management approach is the wave of the future. Here are four of the primary facets of agile management:

1. *Regular adaptation.* A key principle is regular adaptation to changing circumstances. Your strategic plan, which may be

intended to chart your course over the next year or five years, cannot be carved in stone over the entrance to your building. It needs to be flexible to reflect changing conditions, both internal and external.

2. **Trust.** Success is achieved by motivated individuals who communicate with each other. This can only happen in a culture of trust. Success is no longer a matter of the CEO issuing a memo that the employees must obey. The successful project is the result of a high level of trust and communication between every member of the team.

3. **Communication.** Information is valuable. It must be shared not only among employees and management but between a company and its customers. Close, daily cooperation between business people and customers fosters a climate of agility, whereby the company is never caught off-guard by an unexpected external or internal change.

4. **Efficiency.** In business, time management is critical. When you have to wait for a cumbersome report to be delivered to your desk, that's time wasted. When the R&D team has to wait for feedback from the customer, that's time wasted. The agile business environment is finely tuned to respond quickly and decisively, and to ensure that every action moves the team one step closer to success.

Square: Creating a future-ready organization

Square is another company that started out looking like a cat but is quickly becoming a cougar. Founded in 2010, the San Francisco-based company created a new and simple way to take credit card payments. Four years later, it processed sales of more than $100 million in a single day, making it the 13th largest U.S. retailer by annual sales.[348] It defied all expectations by creating a way to send money that has almost no barriers.

How did Square grasp the future? It saw an opportunity for creating a simpler payment solution and offered the product quickly. The idea for Square came from the pain point that many small-business owners had long struggled with: the cost and difficulty of taking credit card payments. Square's plan was to allow anyone, anywhere, to take credit card payments. It began in 2010 with the Square reader, a small piece of disruptive technology that converts a credit card's magnetic stripe into audio pulses, which are then transmitted to Square via an iPhone's headphone audio connector and cellular network. The reader turns any iPhone, iPad, or Android phone or tablet into a credit card processor.[349]

The company is driven by an emphasis on teamwork and transparency. As someone who values agility as the company moves into the future, CEO Jack Dorsey regularly invites the entire workforce to offer feedback. Every Friday, the staff assembles for the **Town Square**, the company's weekly all-hands meeting where they talk about how they're doing and where they're going.[350] This is a core enabler of Square's agile mindset.

Becoming agile

When you are ready to take your organization to the next level, here are some practical steps that your company can take:

- *Identify the agents of change.* Pinpoint the core group of people who will embrace the new approach. The CEO must be involved, not only to give the program legitimacy but to provide an example of leadership. There will be some training involved, and to get started you may even want to hire external assistance.
- *Set goals.* The key players in the business need to know what the company wants to look like in the future and how it will behave as an agile organization. Performance goals are important, such as answering customer emails within two minutes or getting a beta version to the customer by a certain date.
- *Be ready to change deeply entrenched practices.* For example, when companies commit to enterprise agility, one area that may require change is moving from annual financial cycles to adjusting the budget every quarter or even every month,

reflecting real-time changes in planning assumptions, both externally (sue to competition and the economy) and internally.

- **Make it fit your company.** Not all aspects of agile principles can be implemented across every organization equally. Agility is not set in stone, it is always changing.

In order to ensure that your company is ready to move into the future as an agile cougar, here are three questions to ask yourself and your team:

- *As companies become more agile in the future, they will become increasingly transparent as information is shared freely both within the organization and with its stakeholders. How transparent is the organization and what can you do to increase it?*
- *The pace of business is getting faster. Your organization needs to identify and respond to customer demands and market challenges promptly. How agile is our response to new challenges?*
- *Change brings both challenges and new possibilities. Being agile means identifying and acting upon new possibilities and new solutions that may not have been possible before. How do we assess and embrace new opportunities?*

The Future of Work, Talent and Recruitment

By Matt Alder

How is technology dictating the future of the workforce?

Adapting to exponential change

Technology will continue to drive change in the workplace at an exponential rate, however many established companies and organizations are either struggling to keep up or are in denial about the implications for their business. Gaining an understanding of the key issues is vital for any organization that wants to grow and thrive in this new world of work. In this chapter I explore some of these critical forces of change and how they are shaping tomorrow's organization designs and models of work and employment.

We are currently seeing the start of radical disruptive change in the ways companies find and employ talent for their businesses. In some markets the change is already highly visible, in others it is happening very much under the radar. The implications though are huge for every company that employs humans – understanding how this change could pan out is critical for any company that wants future competitive advantage.

The unevenly distributed future: what's happening at the cutting edge?

In some recruitment markets the pace of change is much quicker than in others and offers an interesting insight into what could soon become mainstream. Acute skill shortages have meant that some industries need to think more radically than others. This thinking is being supercharged by emerging technologies to create some dramatic outcomes which are fundamentally changing the employer-employee relationship.

One such outcome is the growing trend towards remote working. For most companies, remote working is just about allowing certain employees to work from home some or all of the time. For companies at the cutting edge of the trend, it is much more than that. Indeed, companies where the entire workforce works remotely are becoming far more common. Embracing a remote workforce opens up the ability to recruit in geographically diverse areas using global talent pools. This means that increasingly, it is no longer the biggest or richest companies who are attracting the best talent – it is the most flexible that are winning.

Remote working is also responsible for driving a shift in the balance of power back to the talent itself. Alongside the untethering of work from a physical office comes the ability for skilled practitioners to untether themselves from working for a single employer. An interesting byproduct of this shift is the rise of the digital nomad – freelancers who travel the world while working on remote projects for multiple employers.

Within a few short generations we have gone from the concept of a job for life with an all-powerful employer, to a project based existence where the supply and demand of talent drive the power dynamic. This is nothing less than a complete reworking of the employer-employee relationship.

We are already starting to see the logical next stage in this employee-employer uncoupling with the rise in skills marketplaces and work distribution platforms. Although some of these platforms have been around and growing for several years, there has been a recent explosion in usage that is now affecting all areas of the employment market. Sites like Odesk and Elance offer a marketplace for highly skilled workers, while Taskrabbit and Fiverr offer one for more casual help and talented hobbyists respectively.

In response to these shifts, a generation of smart companies is emerging who are harnessing the marketplace concept to their considerable commercial advantage. Uber has grown dramatically in the personal transportation space globally, yet it owns no cars and employs no drivers directly. Uber's often controversial approach provides a platform that connects drivers to passengers and manages customer service and quality through a ratings algorithm that negates the need for a huge layer of human management. This gives Uber a level of flexibility and nimbleness that is driving considerable global advantage – and wrong footing both their competitors and government legislators.

The new work horizon: what's around the corner?

No one can truly predict the future, but all these trends point to dramatic change over the next ten years that will result in a very different world of work. A genuinely global distributed marketplace for talent seems inevitable but it is not the whole story, a number of potential scenarios are in play that suggests even more radical change is coming.

The current trend for implementing social technologies in the workplace will quickly become the norm and will make internal communication more effective and self-organizing. If you couple this with the use of talent markets that reward new types of employees on results rather than time spent, there will be no need for many management layers within organizations. Companies such as Zappos are already experimenting with **holoratic** structures that have no job titles or managers at all. Such radical thinking around organization design and the need for the continual management of change will be mainstream in a few short years.

Change is happening so fast it is impossible to predict with any kind of certainly what kinds of jobs the exponential development of technology will bring. This has significant implications both for workforce planning and education systems. For example, the rise of automation, whether that is manifested in driverless cars, advanced pattern-matching algorithms, or sophisticated artificial intelligence has the potential to redefine countless established professions.

There is also a strongly backed scenario that predicts automation will hollow out the workforce, dispensing with millions more jobs than it creates. The impact of this will be widespread and create significant political and social conundrums that will have to be addressed head on if they are to be solved.

The companies that succeed in the future will be those flexible enough to embrace these changes. This redefinition of work will also represent unprecedented upheaval for millions currently employed in the traditional way, however. Flexibility of thinking will be needed everywhere, particularly within governments if we are to transition positively and truly realize the benefits this radically new world of work could provide.

Here are three questions companies need to ask themselves:

- *Where is the best talent in your market and how flexible will you have to be to utilize it?*
- *What impact will automation have on your business and what are the implications for the size and shape of your workforce?*
- *What sorts of flexible organization designs will needed to create the business structures of the near future?*

The Future of Talent Management: Recruiting, Workforce Planning, Leadership Development and Performance Management

By Kevin Wheeler

What could work be like in twenty years or less – what are the implications for finding and leading talent?

Reframing our notions of work, jobs and careers

Work is not what it used to be. Work can be done anywhere. Younger workers do not see any reason to come to an office every day. A café, a restaurant, and your bedroom can be your office at different times of the day. Even your job could be something that didn't exist a decade ago. New careers have emerged; old ones are dying – up to 50 percent of all current jobs will disappear within 20 years, according to a study by Oxford University.[351] Organizations are different; hierarchy is shrinking. The 21st century has dawned with new expectations and demands. Consumers look for personalized products and services, delivered instantly, at a low price. Speed and variety are the watchwords. Capital is less important. More and more speed trumps process and control. In this chapter I explore what the coming together of all these developments could mean for the future of work and talent management.

The emergence of "career mosaics"

People are thinking differently about work than they did five, ten or twenty years ago. While a large part of the workforce retains a traditional mindset on this and seeks a normal working schedule, a growing segment does not. Whether it is part-time work or just a flexible schedule, more employees are seeking an alternative to the normal nine to five routine. This trend is only likely to grow in the future. Some employers are embracing the change and offering choices, but others remain fixed in the past.

Younger people, especially recent graduates and laid off workers, often find that working for themselves is a better choice than working for a company. There has been a drastic rise in the numbers of self-employed and there seems to be no end in sight. Over 53 million Americans are classified as freelancers – some 34 percent of the workforce.[352] This is similar in Singapore, Australia, and many European countries. The trend has been driven by the need for flexible working hours, accelerated by the recession and reinforced by lean organization management models and a changing mindset. Work, at least as we have traditionally described it, is not necessarily seen as the major life activity. More people are looking at doing just enough to achieve a standard of living that gives them time to have hobbies, enjoy their family, travel, and just meet with friends.

I believe working for money will increasingly be less important than working for fulfillment and camaraderie. Over the coming years, perhaps as much as half the current working population will not work in any way that is normal, traditional, or usual today. Already in the developed world, fewer people are marrying[353] or having children. Some of these people may choose to live in communal arrangements, sharing incomes, resources, and responsibilities – a trend that is already visible in many countries. Governments will have to relook at income redistribution policy (taxation and fees) as automation and robotics reduce the need for workers. There will most likely have to be a guaranteed income either in the form of subsidized housing and other services or through direct payment of a minimum living allowance. As contentious as this may sound today, we could see business leaders lobbying for it in the future to ensure the population can afford to buy goods and services.

Organizations will need to decide what current work could be done better through automation or outsourcing and what work is essential. They will need to decide who their core employees are – those whose jobs will not and cannot be automated and who are vital to producing the product or service. This will necessitate some tough decisions and lead to the need to provide the less essential services through alternate means.

An example of this trend is when corporations like IBM and Apple decide to outsource their manufacturing, product assembly, and even at times product distribution to trusted third party vendors. This has two effects: it reduces the size of the workforce; and concentrates power and networking among a smaller and more strategic group of employees. Indeed, many third-party vendors are using automation to manufacture their products, further reducing the numbers employed. As mentioned above, projections indicate that this trend will continue as robots become more sophisticated and have rudimentary intelligence to learn new tasks.

Governments will need to find new ways to redistribute income to those who have been unemployed because of automation and who do not have the higher-level skills required for the new jobs that are created in new and emerging sectors. It used to be relatively easy and quick to develop programs to teach new skills and the time required to completing the training was reasonable. Many emerging roles, for example data scientist, high-level programmer, or genetic technician require such complex and sophisticated skills that training programs take far longer to develop and complete, and many people will be unwilling or unable to do so.

The path ahead is not a simple one and the choices and implications are complicated. For example, will some employers make the moral choice to keep employing people even when their roles could be automated? Some feel that governments may require employers to maintain a certain level of employment even though workers could be replaced by outsourcing or automation. Today, requiring firms to do this is contrary to a free market economy and is an unlikely scenario in many countries. It could legalize inefficiency, lower productivity, and increase costs.

One solution might be to find ways to change the corporate tax structure to better reflect the increased profits that fewer workers will bring. For example, elimination of personal income taxes in favor of much higher corporate taxes might be a possible scenario. This increased tax revenue could be used to provide a guaranteed income for unemployable workers. Over the next decade, there will be challenges to our concepts and assumptions about work, taxation, income distribution, education, and – as a result – even our political systems.

A new look at jobs
The concept of a job or of a position that contains a more or less static set of skills and competencies is already fading. Most organizations need broad categories of work performed – mechanical engineering, database administration, and customer service representation for example. The skills and the duties performed can be remarkably different within and between organizations however, and vary over time. By keeping jobs narrowly defined, we limit not only our ability to hire quickly but also the potential for creativity and change.

The idea that people will assume roles that vary widely from time-to-time is already taking hold. Employees with general skills, who can move quickly from role to role, are far more valuable than a deeply vertical specialist who can usually be hired as a consultant when required. Firms are finding that innovation and new products/services often come from unexpected people. By ensuring that the organization has a mix of bohemians and outliers, as well as more traditional workers, it can hope to continue to be innovative. This will require new leadership roles and competencies, different organizational structures, more tolerance of variance, and more trust.

Recruiting tomorrow's workforce

Organizations are becoming less hierarchical and – in seeking to be innovative and efficient – reducing the size of the workforce through automation and robotics. This emerging smaller and automated work environment will change the nature of recruitment. I anticipate that recruiting will be based on seeking fewer people as permanent hires – seeking out candidates with the skills and capabilities to take on the many roles that will be needed. On the other hand, recruiters will also need to find the deeply vertical specialist who can provide skills on a contract basis or who is willing to enter into a strategic alliance. Strategic plans may be fleeting and constantly changing – suggesting that recruiting will need to be responsive, flexible and fast.

As we automate, the nature of work shifts from routine tasks more and more to project based activities. Hence firms will increasingly look to the notion of **work swarms** or **SWAT Teams** – pulling groups of internal and external resources together quickly and helping them gel so they can become effective and deliver on the goal in potentially ever shorter timeframes. Hence, recruiters will need to find and put together global, dispersed teams made up of full-time, part-time, and temporary employees with complementary skills – coupled with third party partners.

Organizations may have small semi-permanent cores of employees, but an ecosystem of consultants and temporary/part-time employees will surround them. All of these will need to be found, assessed and "influenced" so they are willing and ready to participate when required. Software, especially artificial intelligence (AI) and smart analytics will assist recruiters in finding, assessing, and matching the right people to the firm's needs.

Already, progressive recruiting functions are using networks of former and current employees, experts, and customers to refer potential employees. Over the next five years, these networked candidate pools – pools of talent that can be found and engaged in real time – will be the normal way to source people. Rather than try to develop relatively static databases of candidates, networks allow for the flexibility that a complex business environment will require.

Communities of people with similar interests and skills will also exist. While their primary purpose will be to educate and answer each other's questions by leveraging the network, they will also be a source of candidates for employers and opportunity referrals for each other.

Uber, the disruptive taxi service, is a model for how future organizations might recruit, train and manage the performance of employees. It is completely staffed by self-employed entrepreneurs who own their own cars and drive when and where they want. Uber recruits them by word-of-mouth and through small, local branding efforts. Customers rate them after each journey and drivers who do not get good ratings are removed immediately. Customers are also rated by drivers and unruly or argumentative ones are denied further service. Uber has a very small permanent staff, yet the company operates globally and has thousands of drivers. It is able to do this by using technology to connect drivers to customers and to the headquarters.

Uber's operating model has not met with universal approval. It has faced legal and ethical challenges because it is disrupting the assumptions that work has been based on; specifically that firms should offer permanent work, provide benefits, control the actions and time of employees, and so on. But even given this, they have had little problem recruiting drivers and tapping into the entrepreneurial spirit of people globally. Many emerging firms are operating under a similar model and will put pressure on governments to change labor laws.

Future evolution of training and development

Because of smaller workforces and the need for a changing mix of skills, learning will need to be a more continuous process. Technology will play a large part and most skills-based training will take place through video, e-learning, simulations, and online conversations. There will be a rise in informal and self-driven learning with most people assimilating new information and gaining skills as their needs arise. Networks of people will provide quick answers to questions and add to our knowledge. There will be much less waiting for classes, or applying to be given training and development opportunities, and less reliance on canned content.

Using the Internet and perhaps intelligent bots such as Siri, people will increasingly assemble their own learning materials from what is available on the web or from specialized libraries. They may even contribute to the stored information by sharing their own videos and materials with others. Crowd-sourced learning and content sharing could become a major trend. Apprenticeship programs, mentoring and various forms of internship are also gaining popularity as preferred ways to learn.

Workforce and succession planning

Workforce planning was only ever partially successful in the 20th century, and now has become largely illusory. Skills defined as critical one day (webmaster, for example in 1999) are commonly available today, while those skills ignored (creative thinking) are now highly sought after. Performance management looks at yesterday and at best tells you where someone was but not where he or she is today or where they should be tomorrow. Succession plans can consume weeks of management time only to be discarded as needs change and people move on.

At the beginning of each year and often each quarter, in many firms, HR managers and recruiters still pour over anticipated hiring numbers that inevitably change significantly only days or weeks later. Hiring managers are not certain what they will need or when they will need it, and unannounced mergers and acquisitions can invalidate months of work. The bottom line is very clear – for many organizations, it is becoming almost impossible to plan the workforce of the future in any meaningful way for more than perhaps three to six months ahead.

Instead, organizations will have to replace linear models with adaptive techniques that are based on the ability to anticipate changes in talent needs and markets. This means developing employee readiness to respond rapidly to needs, and encouraging and championing a new approach to thinking about positions, roles and jobs. The focus needs to be on the process of recruiting and ensuring that you have the tools and capabilities in place to meet any demand, not on achieving specific short-term numbers.

The success of Talent Management will be judged largely on how well it does the following four things:

1. ***Research and market awareness*** In order to anticipate the challenges and to educate and guide hiring management, recruiters and HR leaders must gain a thorough knowledge of both the supply chain and the skills and capabilities of current employees. This means doing research into who is in the local talent market and who is in an extended, global market. A new role in HR is the data scientist who scans the internal organization for signs of change, for example indications of growth, downsizing, outsourcing, and potential mergers or acquisitions. They will also have to connect constantly to the external talent market so that the firm has a sense of which skills and capabilities are readily available and which are more difficult to find. This will require the use of competitive intelligence tools and techniques to identify talent at competitors and an assessment of how likely they might be to move to your organization.

   Monitoring the traffic patterns to recruiting websites will provide valuable information about who is interested in the organization and an opportunity to find out why. Making sense of vast amounts of raw data will be challenging and differentiate success from failure. Researching the market in this way is an active rather the passive process that is also trying to "sell" potential candidates on the attractiveness of the firm. Hence recruiters will need to develop the skills to brand the firm and the nature of roles and work that could be on offer.

2. ***Readiness*** – not succession planning Having a wide range of

people ready for any needs that may arise is a far better goal than traditional succession planning. While we cannot predict that a particular position will be replaced or eliminated, we can make sure that we have a wide basket of skills and people ready to be tapped when needs arise. These people and skills will also need to be diverse and not necessarily those that already exist in the organization. As skills become obsolete, individuals will need to recognize this and be willing and able to learn quickly what is needed. A simple example is the constantly changing popularity of certain programming languages. Every two to three years the most commonly used language changes – necessitating relearning. Firms will be most successful when they learn how to leverage networks of people with a wide range of skills that can be tapped at any time.

3. *Rapid Response* Once a requirement is identified, it will need to be filled very quickly. Candidate quality and speed in finding a suitable individual are often cited as the two most desirable traits in a recruiting function. As markets get tighter, the ability to tap into the right candidates quickly through network relationships will become a significant success factor.

   Firms will need to attack talent needs aggressively and quickly on a global scale using rapid response teams and leveraging automated AI-based tools that can analyze a candidate's past performance, personality, and ability. Referral networks of current and former employees, suppliers and customers should also provide candidates more quickly than traditional recruitment methods. Traditional recruiting methods will prove less and less effective, and the recruiters who use technology, analytics, and networks are more likely to land the best candidates.

4. *Leadership* Successful talent leaders will not look much like they do today. Rather than hire and manage a team of contract and permanent recruiters, they will assemble teams of data scientists, market analysts, marketers, and social media

experts. Their role will be to find, engage, and influence a range of people who have the skills the organization needs. They will negotiate working terms and act more as talent agents than recruiters.

Rather than focus on control and technical mastery, a talent leader will need a range of skills that include the ability to collaborate and find synergies between people and groups internally and externally. They will need to be influencers and build trust. The dominant requirements in recruitment will morph from sourcing and assessment skills, planning, and administration to influencing skills. Emphasis will be placed on the ability to deal with ambiguity, decision making in an uncertain world, and capacity for innovation.

The future of talent in smaller firms

Small firms will benefit from the power of the networks the Internet makes possible. These networks are open to everyone and are highly efficient ways to find people, learn, educate, get work done, and communicate. In fact, this ability to create and tap into networks is the driver of many of the changes that are coming. Work can be performed by distributed and virtual teams of workers that are assembled as needed. These are often called swarms or SWAT teams because they can come together quickly to address a specific need and then disband just as quickly. This means less need to hire permanent employees and to be obligated to them even after the need for their skills is gone.

We are moving away from experts as teachers and instead using the network as the source of expertise and peer evaluation – with the volume of use as the indicator of quality. While traditionally only large institutions could afford the costs of expert, permanent employees and of training their workforce, networks are an equalizer and can provide even a tiny firm with the same benefits.

Reframing our thinking

The developments I've outlined represent massive changes for the business world. The past 100 years of business practices and leadership skills are being replaced with a set of processes and skills 180 degrees removed from their predecessors. These changes are forcing us to reframe our thinking. Success requires us to work in the opposite manner to almost everything we have known: from planning to intuition, from a mindset of permanence to one of transition, from process to speed, from risk management to risk adoption, from engineering to design, from hierarchy to collaborative teams. While you may not see all of these trends yet, we are close to a tipping point on all of them. They will affect you sooner than you know.

Here are three questions to consider for your organization:

- *Most of the valued practices and assumptions that we have learned are being threatened – so what are the challenges your organization will face as it comes face-to-face with this new world?*
- *The rigid, semi-permanent structures of traditional firms are changing and only those who can anticipate market direction and respond rapidly will survive. How will you make this transition to an organization that is flexible and constantly able to adapt as needs change?*
- *Where are you now on the journey?*

Making the Shift from Disruptive to Hyper Scalable

By Omar Mohout

How do you adopt Hyper Scalability to change your company for the future?

In this chapter I explore the limits of the disruptive innovation philosophy and highlight why future success requires companies to adopt Hyper Scalable thinking to succeed in winner-takes-all markets.

Man cannot live by disruption alone

Disruptive innovation is a concept pioneered by Harvard Business School professor Clayton Christensen. Unlike his famous predecessor Michael Porter who was interested in the success of companies, Christensen focuses on why businesses fail. In his bestseller *The Innovator's Dilemma* Christensen describes why big companies tend to focus on incremental rather than disruptive innovation, finding that pursuit of the latter would undermine short term profitability. His book is a distant echo of the **creative destruction** concept formulated in 1942 by the influential economist Joseph Schumpeter. Christensen argues that every business must be disruptive or will get disrupted. Disruption became the mantra of Silicon Valley where entrepreneurs are busy launching the next killer app.

This chapter will outline why the pursuit of disruption is increasingly the wrong goal and identify a more powerful objective of Hyper Scalability. It will close with an outlook on how companies can thrive and prosper in a future that is driven by accelerating technology.

Time for a new revolution?

The industrial revolution that started some 250 years ago gave birth to new manufacturing processes – shifting handcrafted products to mass-production by automating and replacing manual labor with machines. Historically, it started in the United Kingdom, reaching its latest high in China, transforming the nation into a manufacturing powerhouse. For companies that create physical goods, industrialization had traditionally been pretty much the only way to scale their business. After all, ever-smarter machines can produce non-stop while requiring fewer and fewer human operators to keep them running. However, we are reaching a critical juncture and industrialization as a process to scale companies may have reached its limits. Machines require raw materials and energy to keep producing. These two resources are becoming a major constraint: natural resources are not endlessly available and energy-costs have sky rocketed and are expected to continue doing so despite short term declines in oil prices.

The game is changing and we are seeing the entrance of a new generation of companies with business models that take scaling to new levels. What do Spotify, Square, PayPal, Facebook, and Pinterest have in common? They serve millions of users with a very small team of employees.

Without repeating the beating-a-dead-horse discussion of when a company stops being a startup, for the purposes of this article I propose the following definition: a startup creates and commercializes a proprietary product, enabling it to scale rapidly to global proportions without linear dependence on human capital.

In other words, a small team can conquer the world. Think about Snapchat and Instagram which serves 100 million[354] and 300 million[355] monthly users respectively with less than 200 staff each. They are **Hyper Scalable**. A company is Hyper Scalable when it offers value at a near zero cost simultaneously to millions of users with a disproportionate small team.

Consider Skype with 1,600 employees to handle 40 percent of all international telephone traffic. National telecommunications providers with tens of thousands employees on their payroll can claim only a fraction of Skype's call volume. Adding insult to injury, the existing players also have to bear the heavy cost of the infrastructure – giving Skype a free ride. In other words, Skype is using someone else's assets as a free lever; in this case company owned assets.

Airbnb, an online marketplace that connects people looking to rent their homes with people who are looking for accommodation, is worth more than the Accor, Hyatt, and Intercontinental hotel chains and is already has market capitalization twice that of the nearly 100-year-old Hilton Group. Airbnb's 800 employees can offer over a million rooms to the market without a single cent of investment in real estate. Hilton on the other hand needs over 300,000 employees to operate 680,000 rooms and requires the owners to make massive real estate investments. In other words, Airbnb is using someone else's assets as a free lever; in this case people's homes.

Similar extreme disproportionate relationships between the size of the team (super small) and market impact (gigantic) can be found in the Hyper Scalable business models of Uber, Twitter, Netflix, Kickstarter, EventBrite, Dropbox, Evernote, BlaBlaCar, and booking.com to name a few.

These born-on-the-web companies have scalability in their DNA. They don't open a costly factory, they simply open their laptop. They don't need precious natural resources – instead they mine creativity and innovation. While trading and manufacturing businesses suffer from inventory control, these technology startups have no inventory – perfecting the just-in-time supply and production model.

These Hyper Scalable startups are not constrained by expensive logistics, physical transportation of goods, or distribution channels. For digital service startups, the product is the distribution! While size matters for any other business model, these startups achieve scale without size effectively creating a potentially unlimited upside to growth.

Hyper Scalable firms also solved the conundrum of service companies: humans are not scalable. Even the best sales person works a maximum number of hours per week, just as a retail store is typically closed almost as much as it is open. Compare that with their digital equivalents: the landing page and the e-commerce website; both run 24 x 7 x 365; cost a fraction of their physical counterparts; are usually multilingual; and most importantly, they can serve massive numbers of prospects and customers around the world simultaneously. In other words, they are Hyper Scalable.

The Hyper Scalable business model

But how do you become Hyper Scalable? What's the business model behind it? The answer requires us to understand the rules of the fast emerging digital world and find the necessary levers. More specifically, it requires a combining of the strengths of machines (precision and scale) with the strengths of people (insights and creativity) and using them as levers for growth and innovation. There are, in my view, three critical building blocks (see figure 1) to create a Hyper Scalable business model – these are explained below:

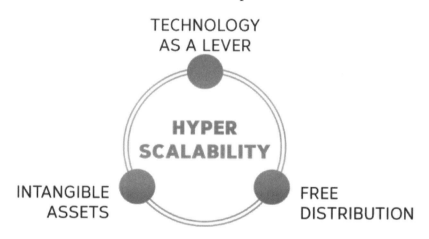

FIGURE 1 – Critical building blocks of a Hyper Scalable business model

Building block 1: A Hyper Scalable business model is based on intangible assets

The range of intangible assets in the economy continues to grow – think of music, books, movies, photos, patents, franchising, algorithms (software), blockchain, and data. In a digital world, the reproduction cost of these intangible assets is virtually zero while the quality remains 100 percent however many times you reproduce a digital asset.

Where tangible assets (e.g. atoms instead of bits) are a required part of the business model, they should be leveraged not owned – as Skype and Airbnb showed in the above examples. The same goes for booking.com and Uber. Note that even firms selling physical assets like Alibaba are levering third party assets as well. All they have is a website and an office while In contrast; Amazon is building warehouses and investing in the supply chain on a massive scale – potentially giving it more control over the service level. However, in its 20 year history, Amazon has yet to report an operating profit.

Building block 2: A Hyper Scalable business model requires (information) technology as a lever

In medieval times, music was not scalable. A troubadour played in markets and castles and was paid for the entertainment. Only the invention of the phonograph as a carrier of sound in 1877 by Thomas Edison made music scalable. Music could be recorded, distributed and enjoyed without the required presence of the musician, effectively removing the constrains of time and space. Not surprisingly, as the technology advanced, we saw the emergence of a new species in the music biotope: rockstars. A rockstar is an example of a successful Hyper Scalable Artist. Without the artist being present, thanks to technology, people can enjoy music at anytime and anyplace making artists omnipresent.

Building block 3: A Hyper Scalable business model uses the Internet as a free distribution channel

Perhaps the biggest lever in the history of humanity is the invention of the wheel. But the value of wheels is in proportion to the availability of roads. Twenty years ago, the Internet – in essence a distribution and sharing technology – laid the seeds for a new kind of scalability. Information technology is to the Internet as wheels are to roads – it multiplies its value massively. Through the Internet, we can reach 40 percent of the world's population at almost zero cost. The moment we go online, we are also global. Global is the default in a world with increasingly better bandwidth and cheap connected devices. Serving a customer digitally on the other side of the planet is as easy as a customer around the corner. Clearly fulfilling the order may for physical goods may be more complex when serving customers on the other side of the world – but the internet has made the transaction possible.

In the case of music, the MP3 format and free distribution over the Internet created a killer combination – just ask the remnants of the old music industry who were savaged by the barbarians-at-the-gate: technology driven companies such as YouTube, Apple, and Spotify. As an intangible asset, music is now dominated by companies that understand the rules of the digital world. A free distribution channel also tilts the power balance from sales to marketing. The whole sales funnel can take place in the cloud, from generating to closing leads. In a digital world, the landing page is the new salesperson and marketing is simply sales at scale.

Designing tomorrow's company

By combining the trinity of create, replicate, and scale as levers for its business model, tomorrow's company can achieve Hyper Scalability. This is the stuff that the new digital heroes are made of. How else than by applying this combination can a WhatsApp with around 60 engineers support an impressive 18 trillion messages per year? More than twice the total of 7.5 trillion text (SMS) messages that the world sends together annually. There is a reason why economists call technology the "only free lunch" out there.

Is Hyper Scalable compliance a guarantee for success? No, it's not. For a Hyper Scalable company to be successful, it also needs to find a big enough market with a deep need or pain that can be addressed. A simple but effective way to achieve that is to quantify it along two dimensions: pain and frequency; the greater the pain and the greater the frequency of occurrence, the better. One way is to express the extremes on the two dimensions is to picture it as a **shark bite** versus a **mosquito bite** problem (figure 2.)

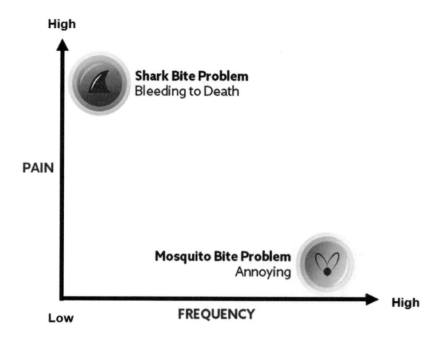

FIGURE 2 – Shark bite versus a mosquito bite problem

A **Shark Bite Problem** has a big impact (you are bleeding to death), but it happens once. If you find customers with a shark bite problem, they will be happy to pay (a lot!) to solve their problem but unfortunately this problem does not occur very often. In other words: You found a business but not a sizable market.

A **Mosquito Bite Problem** occurs often (in summer) but has little impact (you can live with it). The problem is widespread but the issue is so small that consumers, although annoying, are not willing to spend (much) money on it. Doing nothing is the most common response. In other words: you found a sizable market but not a viable business. For most new technologies, the real competition comes in the form of inertia as other suppliers and potential customers stick to what they know.

If a business can achieve network effects (better known as Metcalfe's law) it can establish a leadership position in a market. A network effect occurs when a good or service becomes more valuable when more people use it. The first telephone on its own had little or no value. Who can you call? The more people that have a telephone, the greater the value of the device is. According to Metcalfe's law, the value of a network is proportional to the square of the number of connected users of the system. Two telephones can make only one connection, but five can make ten connections, and 12 can make 66 connections. The greater number of users with the service, the more valuable the service becomes. Businesses like Kickstarter, PayPal, Facebook, Slack, and EventBrite are enjoying network effect benefits.

Hyper Scalability is also giving birth to **full stack** companies. These companies control the full customer experience and value chain as never before and on an immense scale. It's not a surprise that Google launched hardware (Chrome notebooks), operating systems (Android), and acquired Nest to impact the consumer's life. Netflix produces its own movies and content now. Uber knows all about the customers and drivers enabling it to set dynamic pricing based on real-time demand and supply. The pricing algorithm is perhaps the most powerful component of Uber's business model. Uber takes yield management to a whole new level. Dynamic demand-based pricing is common in the travel industry but it seems inevitable that in a digital world, the whole market is going in that direction. The writing is on the wall.

Is Hyper Scalability the same as being disruptive? No, it's not. Tesla is disruptive without being Hyper Scalable. Nor is the free Metro newspaper Hyper Scalable, yet its innovative business model is disruptive for the newspaper industry, especially in the train travelers segment.

Startups and companies that are pondering how to be disruptive or how to be innovative are asking the wrong question. The same goes for companies that desperately want to put a digital strategy in place. Not only is, "What should my digital strategy be?" the wrong question, it makes them focusing on the wrong things, for example how to digitize processes and data; and the ever changing technology.

I believe the real question firms must ask is how to be Hyper Scalable. The answer will inevitably lead to disruption, innovation, and a digital strategy.

From the bell curve to the exponential curve

In a market where the constraints of space and time are obsolete, the old forms of protection from competitors that companies enjoyed – most notably geographic – is being removed. As a result, almost every market that is digitized effectively becomes a winner-takes-all market. The Bell distribution curve will be replaced with a Power law whereby the second company enjoys a market share that is half of the one before. Think Google. The competition is not a little bit smaller; it's less than half the size of Google.

In this new world, old economy principles – such as ownership of assets – become a constraint on growth, and the notion of pursuing economies of scale now provides a rather small incentive for building large corporations. We are in what Andreessen-Horowitz calls the, "deployment phase of the internet"[356]. There was never a better time to build innovative digital products and services with minimal investments. The sky is no longer the limit. The potential for creativity has increased exponentially and the pace of just about everything continues to accelerate, creating a world of opportunities, a world where access trumps ownership.

Hyper Scalability can be achieved by any company irrelevant of its location. While natural resources are limited, creativity and innovation have no limits. While labor might be expensive, Hyper Scalability can be achieved by just a handful of talented people leveraging technology. Our wealth, after all, is determined not only by our own skills and talents, but by our ability to access the ideas of those around us; there's a lot to gain.

Where is all this leading?

Hyper Scalable companies are not a side show. They are likely to dominate every market in a world that is eaten by software[357]. Software is not an industry anymore; it will impact every single company. Every company will become a software company in the same way that every company in the 20th century was a pen-and-paper company.

At the extreme end of Hyper Scalability, we are moving to a business world where a company is in essence nothing more than an algorithm. With the emerging technologies of Natural Language Processing and Cognitive Systems, such as IBM's Watson, it will be possible to create services that are self-improving. What this means is that in essence, even the underlying business model of a company will be able to improve and even innovate itself. Indeed, we are at the dawn of the age of **algorithm-only zero-employee companies**.

Our economies and societies are based on the traditional factors of production: land, labor and capital. Our tax systems, and therefore our welfare society, are based on these pillars. But now technology is shifting unprecedented wealth to a very small group of people. It's time to rethink how to cope with this new game in a winner-takes-all-society.

I end with the appropriate words of Oliver Samwer: "God has given you the Internet!"

Here are some questions that your business needs to address around its strategy in a digital world:

- *What are the intangible assets that our business model is based on – what value do we place on our data?*
- *How can we leverage the tangible assets that the business is using?*
- *How could we re-conceptualize our business as a Hyper Scalable organization?*

Section 7

Industry Futures - How might old industries change and what new ones could emerge?

Revamp the old and bring in the new

There are a number of critical forces that will fundamentally change the landscape for old industries and provide the space for new sectors to emerge and thrive. The need for new thinking, strategies and practices are explored in aviation, construction and journalism. Four possible new industry sectors are also described – body shops, cosmeceuticals, energy from methane hydrates and space-based solar power.

These opportunities for industry transformation and creation are discussed across eight chapters.

The Future of Aviation (page 420) – Andrew Charlton presents the case for reform of the aviation sector ecosystem to address the critical capacity constraints and create a platform global growth

Futures Journalism: a Manifesto (page 425) – Anna Simpson argues the need for journalism to evolve – learning from the practices of futures and foresight research.

Shaping the Future of Journalism (page 430) – Puruesh Chaudhary also discusses how the practice of journalism needs to evolve in the face of continuous global change and rapid technological advancements.

Constructing the Future (page 435) – Julian Snape traces the rapid evolution of 3D printing and examines how it could transform construction sector practices and employment levels.

The Future Business of Body Shops *(page 442)* – B.J. Murphy outlines a powerful vision of the emergence of high street Body Shops performing a range of human body enhancements.

The Rise of the Cosmeceutical Sector *(page 452)* – David Saintloth highlights how gene editing technology could enable the emergence of a new cosmeceutical health and beauty sector.

The Great Energy Controversy of 2030 *(page 459)* - *James H. Lee* examines the potential opportunities and risks associated with tapping the energy potential of methane hydrates trapped below the arctic permafrost.

Space-Based Solar Power and Wireless Power Transmission *(page 462)* – Devin Daniels explores the transformational societal impact, commercial potential and technological challenges of harnessing space-based solar energy for power generation.

Global Drivers of Change

By April Koury, Iva Lazarova and Rohit Talwar

Below we highlight six drivers of change that could herald the emergence of new industry sectors.

- ***Disintermediation / Redefinition of Key Sectors*** – As buyers and sellers are more able to connect directly with each other via the internet, the role of the long supply chain in many sectors will continue to decline. With technologies like 3D printing, distribution companies may take on the role of manufacturer, where the distributor not only ships goods, but also prints them on demand.

- ***Quantification of Self / Self-Tracking / Life Tracking*** – Massive growth is expected in the number of people preoccupied with collecting and analyzing personal data concerning every aspect of their lives – participating in continuous "life tracking". They gather personal data and bio-metrics from a variety of wearables and mobile devices. These individuals are collecting and recording data – tracking, monitoring, broadcasting, and comparing it with their past data and with others using mobile devices.

- ***Green Manufacturing*** – Green manufacturing focuses on achieving profitability via environmentally friendly manufacturing processes. Shifting social attitudes and the adverse impact of environmentally harmful practices will see a growing number of firms trying to adopt green manufacturing and more environmentally friendly practices. A trade-off will always be perceived between low cost and eco-friendly, and firms and individuals may scale down their eco-commitments in tough economic times. Government incentives may help accelerate the development of eco-friendly practices and sectors.

- *Brain Uploading* – By 2025 some experts predict we will have mapped how the human brain works and technology companies will be competing to host the "back up" of our brains online. Three major projects in Europe, the U.S. and China are currently involved in major research activities to understand how the brain stores information and memories. This will ultimately allow us to create memory back-ups with the information stored remotely via an online service provider. A variety of technology companies such as Google have initiatives underway to provide these brain uploading services.

- *Biomimicry* – Biomimicry is design that imitates nature's models and systems to offer sustainable solutions. It has inspired the design of numerous products and buildings such as stream-lined trains and cars and self-cleaning aircraft interiors. Neural networks are computer models that draw inspiration from the neuronal connections in the brain. Nanotubes and nanowires have been built upon the tobacco mosaic virus design, which consists of tiny tube-like particles.

- *Atomically Precise Manufacturing (APM)* – Atomically precise manufacturing is an evolution in manufacturing where items are built from the bottom-up by assembling and bonding molecular level components, and it is considered the future of nanotechnology. Experts suggested that as early as 2030, APM will enable production of unprecedented scope, functionality, efficiency, and productivity.[358]

The Future of Aviation

By Andrew Charlton

How will the forces and factors shaping the future impact the world's oldest immature industry and will it have the capacity to cope?

Aviation is a fundamental part of modern life and critical to the effective operation of the global economy. Almost every vision of the future expects there to be more flying. However the rules and procedures we have used to govern aviation to date are almost certainly not going to cope with the scale of change on the horizon. If present aviation management models and decision making approaches persist, I believe there will never be enough airport capacity or airspace management capability, so we will need to look again at how to provide the required services. In this chapter I highlight these future challenges and explore possible ways in which they might be addressed.

Demand for flying and the capacity to cope

The commercial aviation industry is more than 100 years old. In that time, one prediction that has inevitably been true is that demand for air transport will outrun supply. There is every reason to believe that will continue to be the case. The implications are huge however, because the second most accurate prediction in air transport is that building airports is very difficult. In other words, demand for aviation will grow faster than our ability to build the necessary capacity to manage it.

Our airspace is virtually infinite. Aircraft already know their location in four dimensions. Continuous data streaming, refined avionics, and better, more intelligent in-flight systems will allow each aircraft to manage its gate-to-gate trajectory through time and space. The airlines will be able to manage the trajectory of their fleet. The aim will be to optimize each day's operations across the airline's network, reducing guesswork and delays. Improved flight surveillance and data communications capability will facilitate these changes, bringing into focus questions about where and how pilots are best deployed to operate aircraft and how to bring more aircraft safely into the system. These questions are central to the technological and computing upgrades.

But all of this will be irrelevant unless we find a way to increase airport capacity safely.

Airports as a key to aviation growth

Airports generate trade and trade generates employment. The underlying dynamic of aviation as an engine for trade impacts all parts of the aviation industry. For the last 70 of the 100 year lifespan of commercial aviation, the ultimate regulatory body has been the International Civil Aviation Organization (ICAO), established by an inner sanctum of developed countries in 1944. It has been the stand-ard bearer for equality of treatment for all aviation industry players. Consequently, it regulates to ensure the industry moves at the speed of the slowest player. As a result protectionism has been allowed to thrive.

The continuing rise of mega-cities will paradoxically bring greater demand to fly to them, putting huge pressure on local airports. The best-laid intentions to build airports on the outskirts of such cities could frequently be overtaken as they are surrounded by urban development. At the same time, airports at small non-mega-cities may well have capacity available. We will have too many airports and not enough capacity. Airport hubs will define international trade routes rather than nationality-driven interests. The pressure to trade and the need for growth and employment will provide one dynamic. Furthermore, the rise of new middle classes around the globe will further increase pressure on the current system. These would-be travelers are equally entitled to see the wonders of Florence, explore the rugged beauty of the Australian outback, and to find markets around the world in which to trade.

Eventually protectionism will be overcome. Well capitalized airlines with access to better, larger airports will overwhelm those that struggle under nationality-based restrictions to growth. Over time, the citizens of nations with constrained airlines will also demand change.

The future for national airlines, airports and air traffic management

I expect that the national carrier aspects of most airlines will disappear. The role of carrying one's citizens to their destination will become one of taking citizens of the world wherever they want to go. For the first time, airlines will become truly networked industries, finding airports with available capacity to act as nodes for their network. Instead of being locked into a particular airport in a particular country, airlines will choose nodes that best deliver their passengers across their network.

Airports will rise to this challenge by squeezing every ounce of capacity out of their facilities whilst straining every sinew to expand. That is hard work now and it will still be hard work in the future. The need for growth and trade will always face challenges from localized self-interests that object to airport expansion. Those airports that can make that argument will have a competitive advantage over others. A competitive airport sector will emerge.

The overarching constraint on airport runways is safety. That is not going to change. Aircraft, often weighing more than 200 tons, need time and space to accelerate and break away from gravity, and to decelerate and exit a runway safely. That creates the capacity constraint. It also creates noise. No amount of bio-fuel will silence the need for thrust and braking.

When it comes to access to runway capacity, ICAO's rule has always been first in, best dressed. ICAO mandates that charges must be non-discriminatory, transparent and non-commercial. That creates queuing. Traditionally, that was in holding patterns above the airport. Now, it can be on the ground prior to departure. As airports become busier, queues of aircraft create pressure on air traffic controllers and impacts safe operations. Congestion also adds to emissions and to noise for local residents, making any proposal for expansion that much harder to pursue.

The role currently played by the more than 150, usually state-owned, national border – constrained air navigation service providers (ANSPs) will need to change. Airports will have an increasing interest in ANSP operations. Airlines will too, in order to optimize their networks' daily operations. But as their operations increasingly become true network businesses, airlines' demands for service performance will concentrate on those airports critical to their network. In turn, airports will have more reason to demand specific, customer focused service from their local ANSP.

In other words, the airports will look to extend their authority from the runway to the sky surrounding the runway. There will always need to be an umpire to resolve queue conflicts as aircraft arrive at their threshold. It will no longer be the role of the regulator, as owner of the ANSP, to be the umpire because the needs of the airlines – the customers to the airports – will demand commercial thinking. Instead, the airports will control the queue controllers. The sovereignty argument will fall away. The question for the regulators will therefore be, under which set of rules should the umpire arbitrate? They can cling to the 1940s, or find a commercial, pro-trade approach. The race will go to the responsive and commercially flexible. The rest will follow over time.

The discussion above raises some critical questions for the aviation sector, and the governments, businesses, communities and travelling populations which it serves:

- *How might the conflict play out between the demands of a growing, interconnected world and the current restrictive aviation regulatory framework – what are the implications for trade, employment and global growth?*
- *As mega-cities grow, who will control access to their inevitably limited airport capacity?*
- *How might the balance of power and responsibility evolve between the players in the aviation eco-system?*

Futures Journalism: a Manifesto

By Anna Simpson

The pace of change demands a new space for journalistic enquiry. What can journalism learn from futures techniques?

Journalism, both the practice of gathering and sharing information about the world today and the global institutions built to disseminate it, is in crisis. Yet our need for systems to make sense of rapid change and inform our actions is pressing. This article proposes a new school of futures journalism, to help us make sense of change and its implications, and asks how it should look.

A crisis of understanding

Nature Climate Change published a new paper in March 2015 which finds the Earth's climate system moving into a regime of multi-decadal rates of change that are unprecedented for at least the past 1,000 years.[359] Lead author Dr Steven Smith of the Pacific Northwest National Laboratory told *Carbon Brief*, "What was normal is going to keep changing. It is unlikely that we can avoid most of the changes projected for the next several decades."[360]

A couple of hundred tweets followed, but who really heard? Last year, we heard news that the Amundsen Sea segment of the West Antarctic ice sheet has reached the point of inevitable collapse. This is an event that will raise sea levels more than a meter possibly as soon as the next few hundred years, and yet it "hardly registered", notes Iain Watt, an energy and climate specialist at Forum for the Future.[361]

If we are complacent, it might be symptomatic of the difficulty we face in distinguishing the relative significance of events. Big data rains down on us and we cower. There is no longer a pause in the day in which we conscientiously turn to the news and give it our full attention. There are few moments for sharing our response. We may express outrage; how often do we really feel it? When do we act on it?

This crisis of understanding comes at the same time as the collapse of journalism as we knew it. The problem is not a dearth of interest in the media, but rather an abundance of engagement with it and access to it. The rise of citizen reporting and even automated journalism (Wordsmith for one, delivers millions of personalized recaps each football season) has made "curation" the buzzword of the day. There has always been a need for someone to shepherd insights: traditionally this was the role of the editor. Now, IBM is offering a curation software service using its Watson artificial intelligence software, which can guide subject experts through complex documents and data.

However, software isn't the answer to our lack of perspective. What we need is a new approach to journalism characterized by new forms of enquiry that can achieve insight, not just relating to the one subject, but across complex systems. Old forms of journalism have had their day. Newspapers were organized in sections. Magazines spoke to different trades. Too many stories were lost in the gaps. We need a way of looking at stories of change in a systemic way. Not just what they mean for our homes or cities or environment, but what they mean for all three – and not just in today's news but in ten or fifty years time. We can't know how stories of change today will end, but we need to understand where they might lead.

Looking beyond the news

What should such a practice of **futures journalism** look like? How would it differ from journalism as was? For a start, the emphasis shifts from reporting the data to understanding the implications – not just in a linear way, but as a system of consequences: political, social, environmental, and so on.

Take climate change reporting as a case study. Conventional reports focus on the data. If they look ahead, they make projections as to the environmental impacts – sea level rise, flooding, changing weather patterns – and deductions: the need to divest from fossil fuels, for instance. This is valuable. What is lacking however is any sense of the systemic impacts and implications. What does the collapse of the West Antarctic ice sheet mean in relation to other global trends such as competition for land, global economic shifts, and the rise in religion?

Crucially, the journalist would then circle back from these questions to the current context: how should this perspective affect our decisions in the here and now? Journalists can learn from the way in which futurists facilitate this sort of enquiry.

"The role of the futurist is to help people to be aware – not of the numbers really, but of the movement", explains futurist Charlene Collison. "A crucial part of our value as futurists is simplifying complex data into movements and patterns to which people can respond. Data can make us aware, we can use it to back up our case for action, but we generally make decisions based on what we value and feel to be right."

Change, agendas and ethics

In light of this, the futures journalist needs a new ethical charter. The conventional framework for journalism is characterized by principles such as freedom of expression and the fundamental right of citizens to receive truthful information and honest opinions.[362]

But when we talk about the future, we also influence it, shaping aspirations and design practice. This means the futures journalist carries responsibility towards the possible worlds they are shaping, as well as the current context they are reporting. The relationship between their assumptions, their agendas, and their practice takes on a heightened significance. A recent call for papers by the Journal of Futures Studies asked authors "…to surface as many of their own assumptions as possible: theories of social change, epistemology and images of the past and future that inform their discourse and work."

Why is this so important? It is because we must break through our assumptions if we are to imagine things differently. When we talk about the future, we create spaces in which to imagine. New cultures, identities, designs, and actions become possible.

If these spaces aren't wide enough to allow change, there can be no action – even if there is an obviously pressing need. Climate change is the paramount example here.

Just as important as self-awareness though, is awareness of others. A lot of writing about the future focuses on the scientific break-throughs and transformative technologies, and asks how people will adapt. If we are to imagine a world that works for people – establishing systems where famine and poverty are anomalies and not inevitabil-ities – then we must put humanity at the heart of our enquiries. This will take courage because some of the places we explore will be deeply uncomfortable. We will need to re-establish both empathy and trust so that we can ask difficult questions with respect for the lives the data describes. It's an urgent calling.

A new school of futures journalism

We need a new school of futures journalism, with an emphasis on long-term and systemic reflection. Finance for this practice will be based on recognition for the value of far-sighted enquiry into the complex implications of change today. It is a very different proposi-tion to today's **fast-food approach**, where success means a short-lived surge in interest. News is only the point of departure for futures journalism; the interest is in the journey.

We've seen a similar shift in emphasis in the world of brands, from the point of sale to the ongoing consumer experience. Depth and longevity of engagement are proving a source of untapped value; will the same be true for journalism?

It won't be an easy shift. Will today's crumbling institutions spot the opportunity? Or will newcomers corner the vast potential first?

This raises some critical questions for the stakeholders in futures journalism:

- *How might rigorous reporting of change with an emphasis on future consequences affect business practice, government and social behavior?*
- *What would be the ideal relationship between institutions for futures journalism and other organizations shaping the future – in business, society and governance?*
- *Which established or emerging financial models would best support futures journalism?*

Shaping the Future of Journalism

By Puruesh Chaudhary

How can we maintain the future quality of journalism in the face of information overload?

This chapter explores how the practice of journalism could evolve in the face of continuous global change and rapid technological advancements.

The craft of the storyteller

I believe that new territories emerge which then later disintegrate, either to be re-engineered or evolved into something we may know as new. This "new kind of newness" shapes lives, communities, realities, and perceptions. The proliferation of innovation and access to technology play a fundamental role in connecting lives and experiences. Storytellers describe and explain these networked realities, building perceptions and opinions.

The dynamics of how information is created and shared has changed drastically due to emergence of social media. Information consumers are now actively participating in shaping realities. The media, a watchdog, struggles with covering all sides of the story so that value and credibility is not lost. This is mostly due to the fact that it does not engineer or orchestrate a story, rather it acts like a bystander; a human-dependent medium that transmits information.

The future of journalism will determine how new tools, techniques, and technologies such as bots will be used to assimilate information. Who though, will determine what value and credibility the information holds in the pretext of an informed citizenry?

Time for transition

News structures and journalists must adapt to changing technology. How quickly they will adapt to the growing societal need for an enhanced quality of life across the board is a question that needs much introspection. Who do we turn to for ideas and information on how to improve key aspects of our lives? Trends indicate that individuals prefer to follow the advice of other individuals than organizations – but why? Is it because the trust deficit is so great and the choices are so abundant to an information consumer that he or she no longer feels the need to be informed by a traditional infrastructure? Could it be that the detachment of personal ideas from organizational policies are becoming an impediment to a freedom of thought and thereby expression, and somehow a certain degree of an objective opinion is diluted?

There is significant technological and scientific advancement on the horizon that could transform the delivery of journalistic content, with some commentators arguing that it could be automated completely. However, we believe the human-medium that factors in ethics and values should still play a fundamental role in how challenges and opportunities from the future are communicated. Perhaps this brings us back to basics. Maybe this comes across as journalism 101. Integrity of information choices can be slightly convoluted when ethics and values function as mere variables that are not specific to transient economies and communities. So the way that the information flows to enable consumers to interact, changes in line with geo-political and societal development.

For example, why is a retweet not considered equal to an endorsement – when clearly there is a level of association even in a disassociated way? The distinction draws in an element of fear we are witnessing that arises regarding the use of social media. In many countries and news organizations, journalists on a nine-to-five payroll do not have the freedom to express their personal views in "social space". While the line between professionalism and freedom is blurring in other sectors, this ghastly journalistic isolation is giving rise to many alternative media outlets and platforms.

Every now and then an unannounced forum pops up as being **newsy**. The citizen journalism phenomenon has had a multiplier effect on the number of news sources and – because it is dispersed by its very nature – the audience is often flexible and the insights are extraordinarily interesting. Facts, opinions, and chosen realities can be seen developing into stories; each phase can be moduled and assessed to build a theoretical knowledge base.

The traditional media sector is now competing with an extraordinary information industry. However, the traditional media groups should – in theory – have an edge over the broad swath of content of the internet. This is due to the high level of professionalism and sophisticated ethical standards that news organizations by and large try to maintain. However, even though it is easy for the traditional media to champion such ethics and values as their trademark, there are clear are regular lapses. Several breaches can be quoted as examples, such as the phone hacking scandal in the UK in 2011. Ethics and values are a competitive advantage in the information industry. Public trust is a key stock for the industry, but neither ethics nor values are static notions, so trust is maintained through credibility of the content.

Drivers of change

The drivers of change in journalism may perhaps in the medium-to-long term be the same as for any other sector. Accelerating innovation, disruptive technology advances, demographic shifts, resource scarcity, religious extremism, and ethnic tensions will essentially determine the future news stories. Hence, credibility will come from the ability of the sector to deliver quality content that – in its independent capacity – recognizes these inevitable dynamic shifts. The sector's impact will be judged on its ability to formulate a "knowledge footprint". Expert knowledge adds tremendous value, enabling journalists to make the judgments required for objective and ethical reporting. Although the imagined future is distributed and sources of knowledge will be widespread, increasingly it is becoming necessary for journalists to build expertise which enhances their credibility.

The amount of information and data accessible in the coming decades will continue to expand exponentially. This will be impossible for human journalists to keep up with, yet there will be a lot of "news" in all that data. The practice of journalism in the future will require us to go beyond typical journalistic thought processes and the standard systems that support them. Certainly in the coming decades, we can expect that most organizations, especially news providers, will be deploying artificial intelligence (AI) tools to help make sense of the information superglut. Indeed this is already happening in many sectors such as policing, professional services, and medical research.

Future AI-based reporting systems will identify newsworthy events and produce relevant news content independently of humans. Imagine what an expert journalist could do if aided by a digital assistant that could search for and verify huge stocks of information that would otherwise be quite impossible to gather and analyze. The future is incredibly exciting for professional and credible journalists. It is quite possible that such tools could help the financial markets to develop a sustainable operational framework for information stocks, maintaining public trust.

Foresight Journalism

Foresight journalism is a distinct practice that helps position stories in a future context rather than simply reporting the facts of what has just happened. Hence it can be helpful as an informal policy tool. Journalists who help their communities think ahead are also helping society move forward. Journalists do have a role in public leadership and that is an important part of foresight journalism.

There are many communications, media and journalism faculties that have not yet developed a program that focuses on foresight journalism. A foresight journalism program will enable the next generation of information gatherers and knowledge assemblers to create new value systems to help in shaping the sectors' credibility. Being ahead of the curve will not only be about adapting to new technologies and tools, it will also require outward and forward looking thought leaders within the information ecosystem. These leaders can be the transformers; catalysts that can equip traditional media organizations with the ability to adapt to changing needs.

Today there are concerns about the potential future scenarios and societal impacts of AI as the technology advances rapidly. The public will want to know more and understand it better. Similarly, on the environmental front, we are at a point where climate-caused catastrophes and environmental destruction threaten billions of people and climate-change deniers are finally being ignored. In this context, there should be high demand for good quality foresight journalism that explores likely, plausible futures, potential solutions, and possible coping strategies. While this may not be happening routinely today, at some point the information industry will come to understand the importance of foresight journalism.

Three questions for news organizations to consider:

- *What are the features and characteristics that will make customers want to pay for content generated by professional journalists when free alternatives may be provided by their AI counterparts?*
- *How should traditional news media respond to the rise of new technologies, networked journalism and the growing importance of information gathers and assembler communities?*
- *What are the implications of adopting a foresight journalism approach on staffing levels, the time required to produce well-researched articles and industry business models?*

Acknowledgements: Melisanda Middleton and Steve Outing.

Constructing the Future

By Julian Snape

How might 3D printing impact the future of the construction industry?

The next wave of innovation in construction

Traditionally, construction is labor intensive and costly, requiring the co-ordination of architects, tradesmen, and logistics to complete domestic and commercial structures. The scaling up of 3D printing to gantry and free roaming robotic systems heralds a period of significant disruption for the industry. This chapter examines the evolving technology of 3D printing and the transformative ways in which it could impact the construction sector.

3D printing

In a 2015 survey of over 1,000 business leaders by the Singularity University, 3D printing was ranked as the number one "most disruptive technology" in the next few years.[363]

3D Printing – or additive manufacture as it is known within the industry – has been around for decades. It uses a print head that moves in three dimensions to deposit layers of plastic through a heated print head in a technique known as Fused Deposition Modeling (FDM). For metal objects, a high powered laser is fired at a metallic powder to fuse layers as they build up, a technique known as Selective Laser Sintering (SLS). At the end of the twentieth century, additive manufacture was developed to speed up and reduce the cost of producing prototypes before committing to longer production runs using traditional factory production methods.

At the beginning of the twenty-first century there has been significant technological advancement, with additive manufacturing devices becoming far smaller and much less expensive. Small 3D plastic printers are now available for the enthusiast for less than $450 (£300) unassembled and around $750 (£500) for assembled **plug and play** versions. Perhaps the most interesting developments have been in the types of materials that can now be printed.

Plastic and metal have, until recently, been the most commonly used materials for additive manufacture. However, added to that list now are ceramics, bio materials, fabrics, and glass. Recently a collaboration between the technology vendor 3D Systems and the American chocolate giant Hershey's created a 3D printer capable of producing personalized chocolates. At the same time, ever-faster and ever-larger 3D printers are coming to market or being announced – dramatically increasing the potential impact of the technology. As such, with a little imagination, I can foresee 3D printing driving the widespread disruption of many industries, for example construction.

Affordable housing

It cannot have escaped anyone's attention that the subject of lack of affordable housing is regularly in the news in many countries. In big cities in many mature and fast-growing economies alike, many people in their thirties and even forties are unable to afford their own houses. They have to find expensive rented housing or still live with parents. Notwithstanding issues developers may have acquiring land for development, with much desirable land often in areas classified as greenbelt; one of the major problems is the speed and cost of construction.

The process is traditionally very labor intensive with many trades combining to produce the finished article. Architects, surveyors, scaffolders, bricklayers, carpenters, glaziers, plumbers, electricians, and plasterers all work together. However, with 3D printing as the new kid on the block, this may all be about to change, as it is now possible to print buildings, either in sections or even in situ. It may well be the most significant innovation for the construction industry in the last 100 years – and it is here now – not in spades – but in print heads.

Current experimentation

In 2013 the Dutch architectural firm DUS Architects began using a scaled up 3D plastic printer called a KamerMaker (Dutch for "room maker"), to build a 3D printed Canal House in Amsterdam using sustainable bio plastics.[364] Built in sections off-site, the components were then transported to the site for assembly. It's now as a tourist attraction as they continue developing the technology.

In China, things have gone a step further with 3D printing of houses in concrete. In March 2014 the Shanghai based company WinSun printed ten houses in 24 hours using a concrete like material mix of ground up construction and industrial waste combined with quick drying cement and an industrial hardening agent.[365] Fabrication was achieved using a giant 3D printer measuring 6.6m x 10m x 40m to print sections which were then moved to the site and assembled. The ten houses were small simple one and two room buildings that required finishing with glazing and other services. Win Sun claim the main structures cost only the equivalent of $4,390 (£2,970) to build – less than the cost of a garden shed in the UK. They have now printed a five story apartment block and medium sized villa. The Egyptian government has already placed an order for 20,000 single story printed houses and WinSun is looking to develop their printer to build using sand in desert areas. So the age of truly affordable rapid build homes is approaching.

These two examples are just the tip of the iceberg of what will be possible. So far they are scaled up versions of existing 3D printing technology to prefabricate buildings in sections. These require the sections to be transported to the site and builders to assemble them. It would speed up and further reduce the cost of construction if the buildings could be 3D printed onsite, and this is indeed is now happening. Professor Behrokh Khoshnevis of the University of Southern California is developing a huge 3D printer that runs on rails and is capable of printing a house in concrete onsite, even planning for plumbing, electric cabling, and windows.[366] Such onsite printers will do away with the need for a large workforce – needing just a few supervisors to run it. These will be quite bulky machines requiring articulated trucks to move all the parts to the site. While this may initially be problematic for any building larger than two stories, even this limitation may be overcome.

The Institute for Advanced Architecture of Catalonia (IAAC) in Barcelona has managed to combine the disruptive technologies of robots and 3D printing to produce what they call Minibuilders.[367] These consist of three different types of robots. The first is a "tracked foundation robot" that lays down the first layers of the building until they rise beyond its reach. Then a "grip robot" takes over and is able to clamp onto the top layers of the structure using rollers to move around and add layers to whatever height is required. Finally a "vacuum robot" uses suction to climb up and down the completed surface to add reinforcement wherever needed. Although in its infancy, it is not difficult to see where this is heading. In theory the technology can build up to any height and does not need large scale transportation systems to move it onto site.

The possibilities grow

It's not a huge leap of the imagination to speculate as to what further additive manufacturing capacity will be needed to complete buildings rapidly with minimal human intervention. 3D printing systems are now available that combine materials, for example integrating plastics with both ceramics and metal. When combined with concrete printing, it is possible to envisage the manufacture of plastic or metal pipes for plumbing, circuits for electricity distribution, and even glazing – all during the main onsite construction process. Indeed, Hewlett Packard is already working on printing transparent glass. Using the vacuum robot, even the plastering might be accomplished in record time.

This technology is closer to becoming a commercial reality than many people think. In the UK, Loughborough University have partnered with the Swedish construction firm Skanska on an 18 month development program to bring commercial concrete printing to the market by 2017. The project is being conducted in collaboration with Architects Foster and Partners, Buchan Concrete, ABB, and Lafarge Tarmac.[368]

Looking 10 or 20 years ahead, one of the most exciting ideas for the use of 3D construction is literally out of this world. For mankind to survive, explore, and expand, one view is that it must surely inhabit environments beyond that of the Earth. This means going into orbit, back to the Moon, to Mars, Venus, and even the asteroids. It would be ideal if habitats could be constructed before the first intrepid colonists arrived at their destined planet or orbit. This could be achieved using robotic 3D construction systems, especially if they were designed to use locally available resources. The European Space Agency (ESA) is working with architects Foster and Partners to develop just such a technology.[369] The craft is designed to land a metal tube containing an inflatable dome and 3D printer robots. In the first phase it will deploy the dome. Robots will then use lunar regolith (loose surface material) combined with light-weight foam to build a protective shield over the top of the structures – this is needed to protect against micrometeoroids and space radiation.

An Earthbound 1.5 ton mock-up has already been simulated along with trials of printing in a vacuum. It is reckoned that such robotic 3D construction systems could be deployed on the Moon in the Shackelton Crater where there is plenty of constant light for solar power. A four person shelter could be built and ready for human habitation within four to six months of deployment. The next step would be to use the same process to develop similar habitats on the surface of Mars using Martian regolith. An obvious application would be the surfaces of asteroids – providing habitats for miners or for those wishing to have a cheap ride to anywhere in the solar system that the asteroid's orbit will take them.

Socio-economic effects

The socio-economic effects of advanced, rapid 3D printing in construction should not be under estimated. Initially it may follow the pre-fabrication method and still require a small army of builders and trades people to erect and finish the building. However, once the printing of multiple materials is available onsite, then carpenters, plumbers, electricians, plasterers, and many other associated tradesmen could see a rapid decline in the demand for their services. Such technologies can also be applied to existing traditionally constructed buildings for re-plastering, construction of extensions, other improvements, and maintenance. Therefore we could expect a rapid increase in unemployment among the relevant trades' people who perform those services today.

Another effect of a sudden increase in the extremely affordable housing stock will be to burst existing house price bubbles which could be a major headache for those with little equity who want to move. Few buyers will want to pay $300,000 (£200,000) or more for a house than can now be obtained for $30,000 (£20,000). Most of the future value of housing may well be in the land upon which it stands rather than the building itself.

New commercial opportunities

So where are the opportunities? Apart from the 3D printing robot and gantry industries, one big future growth area will be in the raw materials used by printers. Sustainability will be and already is a key word. Much of the material for construction can be developed from recycled building material, plastics, and even sand. Any plastics deployed will probably either be recycled or bio-plastics – considerably reducing the need for oil-based plastics. 3D printed construction can truly be considered a far more energy and waste efficient green technology than those in current use.

At the beginning of this chapter, 3D printing was highlighted as potentially the single most disruptive new technology of the future. This may be the case but there are other candidates emerging. On the horizon, there are also a large number of other potentially transformative technologies such as robots, drones, artificial intelligence (AI), the Internet of Things, and biotech. All of these are almost certain to have similar socio-economic impacts to 3D construction and it's all coming at once. We are living in very interesting times – an era of rapidly accelerating technological development which may well be upon most of us before we are ready. It is up to commercial and political leaders to stay informed and take into account the socio-economic effects of these disruptions before they are forced upon them, or else they may need to retreat rapidly to their 3D printed habitats on Mars.

Here are three questions 3D printed construction raises for business:

- *With the idea of 3D printed construction falling well within the five year planning horizons of most businesses, how should the commercial sector start planning to take into account it might impact on their property plans and market entry strategies?*
- *What should business leaders and politicians be doing to address the potential socio-economic fallout of a growing 3D printing construction industry?*
- *What are the potential implications of the displacement of traditional tradespersons and a dramatic fall in average house prices?*

The Future Business of Body Shops

By B.J. Murphy

How will cybernetics, 3D printing, and the biohacking movement change the way we enhance people?

Emergence of a new business sector

In the near future, I expect that the **cyberpunk fantasy of cyborgs** and **genetically enhanced** humans will become a lucrative business opportunity. Google co-founder Larry Page once said: "Lots of companies don't succeed over time.[370] What do they fundamentally do wrong? They usually miss the future." We are presently accelerating into a future where people can enhance and augment themselves at their whim. The question we need to ask ourselves, and one which I hope to answer in this chapter, is: how will a viable industry business model evolve for a future dominated by cyborgs?

The future of any business is nothing more than a race against time itself. It requires a keen eye on what is going on throughout the different sectors of science and technology, and subsequently a proactionary drive to move forward revolutionary ideas, even with the prospect of there being risks. To not move forward would be to remain in stasis. If you stand still or retreat, the future will continue accelerating, watching as you wither away – cast into the dustbin of history. If you are a business owner, or have any plans to become one in the future, this should scare the hell out of you.

Technology today is accelerating at an exponential pace, with computing power maintaining Moore's Law – the doubling of transistors in a dense integrated circuit every 18 to 24 months. In addition, most other information technologies are adhering to what inventor Ray Kurzweil refers to as the **law of accelerating returns** – the exponential growth of evolutionary systems, including but not limited to technological growth.[371] Keeping this in mind, the success of a business – both small and large – requires exponential thinking, as opposed to a linear outlook. My aim is to help you envision that future, consequently allowing you to weigh up the available options carefully and determine the best method of moving your business forward into the future. So keep calm, take a breath, and let's jump into the rabbit hole, shall we?

Introducing Body Shops

Let me first tell you my vision of this near-future business practice. My vision requires an open-minded understanding of what makes us human and what we can do to help ourselves and others address our current biological limitations. In the next 15 to 20 years, I expect the emergence of what I call **Body Shops** – that is, essentially, a shop where you walk in human and leave as a cyborg.[372] These shops will be on a par with tattoo and piercing shops in terms of access and popularity. The difference is that with tattoo and piercing shops you merely require staff with experience in both art and the proper means of piercing the body in non-detrimental ways. With Body Shops however, it will require people who are experienced in the fields of both plastic surgery and biotechnology – capable of delivering what I consider to be **fast food plastic surgery**.

What do I mean when I say **fast food plastic surgery**? Understanding this primarily requires insight into what makes the fast food industry so popular, as opposed to sit-down-restaurants. According to a study published in the *Journal of the Academy of Nutrition and Dietetics*, the growing popularity of fast food boils down to three simple factors:

- Speed – Their service is quick;
- Convenience – The restaurants are easy to get to; and
- Cost – They are inexpensive compared to full service restaurants.[373]

When we think of plastic surgery however, these three factors are practically nonexistent. Plastic surgery requires a lot of time to complete procedures and the healing process; the practice is limited to hospitals and private business establishments; and the price tag for a single procedure costs an arm and a leg (pun intended). So when I say **fast food plastic surgery**, I'm basically advocating the idea that we will eventually reach the point where the business practice of modifying the human body will become fast, readily available, and inexpensive for the common person. This will become an essential business model for mass market **Body Shops**. Let's now explore the underlying enablers – cybernetic implants, 3D printed prosthetic limbs and biohacking.

Cybernetic implants and 3D printed prosthetic technology

Demand for augmentation of the human body is on the rise. According to the American Society of Plastic Surgeons (ASPS), from just 2012 to 2013, they witnessed a clear increase of interest among 30 to 70-year-olds in modifying their body via plastic surgery. In 2013 alone, 15.1 million more cosmetic enhancements were undertaken, alongside a 5.7 million increase in reconstructive procedures[374]. ASPS President Robert X. Murphy, Jr., MD, reported that "Facial rejuvenation procedures were especially robust last year, with more Americans opting for facelifts, forehead lifts, eyelid surgery, fillers and peels. With new devices and products hitting the market each year, there are more options and choices available to consumers wanting to refresh their look or [undergo] a little nip and tuck."[375]

What Dr. Murphy said is especially important, for it paves the way to understanding the growing popularity of modifying the human body, for both medical and non-medical reasons. As more products hit the market, the more options people are given. Increasingly, this offers the opportunity to start re-looking at ourselves and re-defining what our body can and should do – whether it's how it should appear or how it should affect our daily lives. We can reasonably assume that, the more technological advances create the potential to enhance our currently limited biology, the more people will take the leap forward and embrace the opportunity to modify themselves in ever-more fundamental and dramatic ways.

In fact, we're already witnessing an increase in the number of people acquiring cybernetic implant procedures. In 2014, *CNN Money* interviewed Amal Graafstra, founder and CEO of biohacking company Dangerous Things. Graafstra discussed his company's business practice of providing people with implantable radio frequency identification (RFID) and near field communication (NFC) tags. Doing so would allow them to control electronics and other devices with simple gestures like waving their hand. "A couple of years ago," Amal said, "I was selling a tag maybe once a week. Now we're looking at least one a day. We've sold probably around 2-3,000 implants across all of the different types."[376]

Dangerous Things isn't the only company providing implants to help people unleash their inner cyborg either. Grindhouse Wetware is best known for its popular magnetic finger-tip implants. These allow people to acquire the physical sensation of feeling the shape and current of electro-magnetic waves.[377] If provision of cybernetic implants is a reality in 2015, imagine what could happen in the next 15 to 20 years!

Pioneering the cybernetic limb market

At the forefront of this revolutionary new stage of human existence are Aimee Mullins and Hugh Herr – two very successful individuals at polar opposites in terms of profession. Both are pushing this train of thought beyond its originally perceived limits by ensuring that cybernetic artificial limbs are readily available, low in cost, and vary in design to help each person acquire their own sense of individuality. Mullins is both an athlete and a fashion model, whereas Herr is an engineer and biophysicist. What connects them is the fact that both are double amputees. I am sure you are wondering: so what? Well, it isn't so much the double amputation of their legs which brings them together; rather how these two individuals decided to address their disability and their goals for humanity.

During a 2009 TED conference, Mullins walked on stage (you read that right) and started talking about why she no longer considers herself disabled. She recalled the time when she met up with a friend who noticed Mullins was now taller than her friend remembered. Mullins explained that she has an entire assortment of prosthetic legs that vary in length, allowing her the option of choosing her height on any given day. Her friend's response was perfect: "But, Aimee, that's not fair!" This response had become her "ah ha!" moment, realizing the practically limitless future possibilities of prosthetic technology and how it could affect our daily lives.

Mullins asserts that: "The conversation with society has changed profoundly in this last decade. It is no longer a conversation about overcoming deficiency. It's a conversation about augmentation. It's a conversation about potential. A prosthetic limb doesn't represent the need to replace loss anymore. It can stand as a symbol that the wearer has the power to create whatever it is that they want to create in that space. So people that society once considered to be disabled can now become the architects of their own identities and indeed continue to change those identities by designing their bodies from a place of empowerment."[378]

In 2014, during another TED conference, Hugh Herr discussed the remarkable history of his disability and how he made it his life's mission to not only conquer his own, but subsequently conquer all disabilities as a whole. He leads the Massachusetts Institute of Technology (MIT) Media Lab's Biomechatronics group, which is making great strides in engineering low-cost, highly efficient prosthetic limbs and exoskeleton suits.

Herr explained how he used different prosthetics to help conquer difficult feats in a more efficient way than he ever could with his original biological limbs, for example mountain climbing. This, in turn, became Herr's 'ah ha!' moment, helping him reach a similar conclusion to Mullins. Herr explains: "Every person should have the right to live life without disability if they so choose — the right to live life without severe depression; the right to see a loved one in the case of [the] seeing impaired; or the right to walk or to dance, in the case of limb paralysis or limb amputation. As a society, we can achieve these human rights if we accept the proposition that humans are not disabled. A person can never be broken. Our built environment, our technologies are broken and disabled. We the people need not accept our limitations, but can transcend disability through technological innovation."[379]

The coming transformation of the prosthetic limb market

These examples offers an excellent segue into the ongoing efforts of open-sourcing prosthetic technology to the overall populace. Both Herr and Mullins envision a near-future where prosthetic technology is available to everyone that empowers them with nearly limitless options in expressing their self-determination. The largest base of consumers for this future business practice will, at first, largely revolve around those with disabilities. Gradually, as those with disabilities are then enhanced and augmented with advanced technology, we will witness a shift in how we define **disabled**. In other words, people who are simply able-bodied may start to consider themselves disabled in comparison to those who've been enhanced.[380] Once that occurs, a whole new base of consumers could begin to emerge.

The growing popularity of low-cost prosthetic technology is overwhelmingly clear. In 2014, Intel held a contest entitled **Make It Wearable**. They invited teams to compete in developing new, wearable technologies that would essentially either change how humans go about their day-to-day lives or change the human condition itself. In response, entrants began engineering new and revolutionary technologies.[381] By November 3rd the finalists were selected. The winner was the Nixie – an autonomous mini-drone that wraps around your wrist. In second place was the newly established UK-based company Open Bionics with a goal of producing low-cost, light-weight, modular limbs by combining bionics with 3D printing.[382]

Since then we've witnessed a wave of open-source, low-cost prosthetic limb production. Formed in 2014, volunteer-based group Limbitless Solutions has gained considerable attention for its emphasis on helping disabled youth become able-bodied again using Limbitless' prosthetics. This was especially welcomed, given the lack of emphasis on youth from corporate prosthetic development companies because they would be developing prosthetic limbs that would need to be re-designed overtime as the children grew up. With 3D printing, this problem goes away completely. The company mission states: "Limbitless Solutions is a growing engineering community devoted to changing lives through the innovation of new bionic arm designs and development of a worldwide network of makers and thinkers. . . Our mission is to create a world without limits, where everyone has access to the tools necessary to manufacture simple, affordable, and accessible solutions through open source design and 3D printing."[383]

As 3D printing continues its seemingly exponential growth, the amount of options people will be able to choose from to enhance themselves should grow just as fast. As I was writing this, a new 3D printer was introduced to the world that could change the 3D printing industry forever. Called the CLIP (Continuous Liquid Interface Production), the relatively new company Carbon3D had shocked the world at TED2015 with a 3D printer that uses light, oxygen, and UV cured resin to develop objects 25-100 times faster than previous 3D printers.[384] This goes hand in hand with the goal of making Body Shop enhancements both affordable and quick.

Biohacking

So we have covered both cybernetic implants and 3D printed prosthetic technology. The last major facet of future Body Shop establishments will harness the power of **biohacking**.[385] As noted previously, there are already biohacking companies helping **hack** peoples' biology via cybernetics. However, as fate would have it, in the last couple of years a new potential in biohacking has presented itself under the guise of genome editing.

Previously there were methods of editing an organism's genome, for example RNAi (Ribonucleic acid interference), however those methods were quite limiting. Thanks to a group of researchers, led by geneticist and molecular engineer George M. Church, a new method was developed with near perfect accuracy throughout an entire range of different organisms – including the possibility of editing human biology.[386] This method has since come to be known as CRISPR (clustered regularly interspaced short palindromic repeats). This uses an RNA-guided DNA enzyme known as Cas9 to help target and manipulate, or altogether change, entire genome sequences. The possibilities for such a revolutionary new tool – medical and non-medical – are practically limitless.

The prospect of gene hacking was predicted by Ramez Naam, who authored the book *More Than Human: Embracing the Promise of Biological Enhancement*, in which he stated: "In just a few decades, we've gone from the first tinkering with human genes to the discovery of dozens of techniques that could alter the human genome in very precise ways. Those techniques give us the power to cure diseases or to enhance and sculpt our bodies. This new control over our genes promises to enhance our quality of life as dramatically as the medical discoveries of the past century."[387]

The path to body shops – imagining the future

So imagine with me, if you will, what these groups of radical technologies could achieve in the next 15 to 20 years. With cybernetic implants, we have the prospect of changing how people will interact with firstly their various electronic possessions, and subsequently their surrounding environment. A growing number of people are already acquiring magnetic finger-tip implants, solely for the purpose of enhancing their sense of touch. Once cybernetics advance to the point where a person's entire body is connected in some way to online systems, we will officially give birth to bio-computing.

The markets for 3D printing and prosthetic technology are accelerating at a remarkable rate, delivering open-source, low-cost bionic limbs in just hours, and soon mere minutes! Enhanced and unenhanced people will walk into these Body Shops to try on new synthetic body parts as if they were a pair of glasses. By that time, we could officially have done away with disability altogether. The new market slogan won't be "Become able-bodied!" instead it will be "Become augmented!"

With genetic biohacking, we are truly traversing extremely radical grounds. People will be looking to well-regulated Body Shops for proper genetic enhancements, as opposed to DIY underground establishments. The marketing proposition would be to become superheroes; to become gods! For better or worse, this will be a new booming business opportunity.

Once this book is published, and you're reading this chapter, months will have gone by and even more new and radical technologies will have been developed. As noted at the beginning, future business strategy requires a keen eye on what is going on throughout the sectors of science and technology. We are moving at an incredible rate, and actually, I believe my 15 to 20 year estimation for the emergence of Body Shops may be a bit conservative. Getting there, however, requires an open-mind, a proactionary drive to move forward, and, of course, it requires you.

As business people, it is up to you to determine how you will proceed with the future of human enhancements. I've presented a clear case for how enhancement could turn into a viable business opportunity. There will, of course, be a question of risks and how best to manage them. I can only offer the advice of adhering to the proactionary principle (as opposed to the precautionary principle) when discussing the mitigation of any possible risks. And of course, there's the question of when these Body Shops will emerge? Whenever they do, I predict many will achieve dramatic success with the Body Shop business model, on which other businesses will eventually base their own strategies.

Having said that, this chapter certainly raises other questions you'll need to answer for yourself:

- *How might your future business respond to laws that may or may not limit the degree in which a person can be enhanced?*
- *Given the open-source nature of 3D printing technologies, how can your company stand out from everyone else in terms of design, manufacturing and service capabilities?*
- *Given the potentially contentious nature of this market, are you prepared to become a business that represents the customers' interests when they are put into question?*

Let the future commence!

The Rise of the Cosmeceutical Sector

By David Saintloth

How might recent disruptive genetic technology development drive the creation of a new health and beauty sector?

In this article I examine the emergence of a new gene manipulation technology and explore how it could drive the creation of a new cosmeceuticals health and beauty sector and bring about radical change in the existing cosmetic hair and skin products market.

Before the power

"The facts of life. . . to make an alteration in the evolvement of an organic life system is fatal. A coding sequence cannot be revised once it's been established." Dr. Tyrell (BladeRunner)

And thus began a fictional conversation between a billionaire scientist and one of his creations – the Nexus 6 version of the replicant biosynthetic beings – in the form of the deranged Roy Batty. An exchange occurs where Batty at one point implores "I need more life Father", expressing his frustration at the inability of his maker to provide a solution for the rather pressing problem of an engineered four year lifespan for all replicants. The crux of the difficulty – as Tyrell explained – was that changing the genetic sequence of a living organism could not be done without inducing some form of cancer formation – oncogenesis.

Genetic science was in its infancy at the time Phillip K Dick was writing Do Robots dream of electric sheep? – the short story on which the movie was based. We barely had tools beyond x-ray crystallography to probe the molecular construction of living cells. It was akin to feeling our way blind to understanding how DNA was coded into the dynamic creatures that team the entire planet. And so it was that when this film was made in the early 80's, the very idea of replicants was high science fiction, perfect fodder to tickle the imagination of those who in the future would dream of making possible that which Tyrell in his fictional world had believed was impossible.

The truth was all around us

The irony of Tyrell's discussion is that for us as animals, we undergo changes of state that necessarily require the revising of our genetic code. These transformations take us from two cells in mammals – the germ line cells of our parents – to clusters of billions of different cells. In real time, different parts of our genetic inheritance are activated, executed across multiple pathways and then shut down. We grow and evolve as physical beings because of the ability of our systems to modify in real time the expression of the genetic code contained within them. Conceptually this is no different to what Tyrell described as being impossible. The difference being that what Batty wanted was to have his existing genes modified so that he could have extended life.

With the sequencing of the Human genome in 2000, it became clearer that a significant number of our pathways were coded for by complex interactions of existing genes rather than what had been previously believed, what was termed the central dogma of one gene, one protein. The realization that humans were fully represented by about 25,000 true genes left no doubt that complex interactions between the genes and sub-systems were at play to allow expression of over 100,000 types of tissues that are produced in our bodies. These low level systems included restriction enzymes – ribonucleic acid (RNA) sub-complexes performing complex interference. We have since learned that they also included other systems that were unknown up until the dawn of the second decade of this millennium.

The invention of CRISPR-Cas9[388] [389]

In 2012, the first signs emerged that it could be possible to utilize various complexes of biomolecules to perform targeted modifications to the genes of a given organism. This first technique was termed Transcription Activator Like Effector Nucleases (TALENs). They were great at binding to genetic sequences of a given type but were not as specific as was hoped. They have been useful in allowing researchers to create specific "knockout" organisms to study the impact of deactivating or replacing an existing gene. However, their lack of specificity means they are not an ideal solution for performing the in vivo genetic editing that would be required to at least in theory overcome Roy Batty's limitation.

A technique to address the genomic editing function was being developed around the same time as TALENS – known as Clustered Regularly Interspaced Short Palindromic Repeats (CRISPR). This approach seemed to magically provide all the benefits of TALENS with significantly higher specificity and very low possibility of oncogenic triggering. The power of the method has now crossed into the Zeitgeist, as the creators of the technology lead by Dr. Jennifer Doudna have come forward to declare that they are against utilizing the technique for performing germ line or somatic cell editing until the ethical ramifications of the technology are fully explored.

In my writings on the future of genetic engineering technologies, I predicted the invention of gene editing technology about seven years ago. I stated it would one day lead to a future of real time custom genetic modifications – creating a multi-billion dollar industry – which has now been called the age of cosmeceuticals.

Cosmeceuticals

Although difficulties still remain to be ironed out regarding the specificity issues with CRISPR, there are no obvious technical limitations to be overcome. Then the ethical issues will be all that remain as barriers to industry development. It is clearly worth attempting to prevent many types of conceivable modifications, although Pandora's Box may already be open. CRISPR modifications are not excessively difficult to perform and already the global biohacker community is salivating at the possibilities that the technology makes possible. The cosmetics sector in the U.S. alone is projected to be worth over $62 billion by 2016 and is growing. The global industry was valued nearly four times that at $245 billion in 2012. So what is the potential and what are the implications of this pending cosmeceutical industry for business?

The first set of potentially lucrative low hanging fruit market opportunities are likely to arise from targeting research activity at areas that are unlikely to have strong ethical or legal barriers to funding. Let's explore some of these opportunities.

Targeted Hair growth: Imagine being able to modulate how and where hair grows on your body. The combination of CRISPR-like technology and increased understanding of how hair follicles are activated across the landscape of our largest organ will lead to the ability to genetically induce such growth. This should provide a massive market comprising people who have issues with the density or lack of hair growth in certain locations of their body. This should emerge as an early opportunity to monetize the new technology. To put it in context, the global hair care products industry is estimated to be worth $83 billion by 2016.[390]

Targeted Hair elimination: Gene editing technology could also be used for the removal of hair. As we develop an understanding of what causes hair to grow in the first place, and can turn on or off expression of hair growth, we can then genetically remove hair from unwanted locations in a precise manner. The billion dollar shaving industry will be significantly impacted by this technology which could lead to lifelong gene modification that would eliminate the need for repeat purchases of shaving products. So Gillette and other companies are in clear danger of having their market disrupted once these technologies are commercialized. The U.S. Men's shaving market for example was valued at $3.6 billion in 2012.[391]

Hair texture change in vivo: The hair products industry owes a great deal of its existence to the varied types of texture of hair expressed by different lineages of the human family. Billions of dollars a year are spent by people of both genders seeking to make their curly hair straight or make their straight hair curly. With the continued investigation of the genetic triggers for modifying hair roots and then targeting genetic edits to those parts of the genome that control those triggers, we will create the ability to genetically modify the type of hair texture that emerges. Rather than using harsh chemicals, heating irons or pressure to modify hair texture, genetic treatments will allow modification in germ line or somatic line (e.g. permanently or for a period of time). It should be obvious how lucrative such an industry would be once companies figure out how to induce the desired modifications.

In addition to the existing market, the potential for addressing underserved demographics in the ethnic markets of Africa, Central and South America, and the Caribbean could create a brand new revenue stream for genetic treatments to modify hair texture. This global ethnic haircare market has been estimated to be potentially $500 billion in size already.[392]

Hair color change in vivo: The global hair color products industry is already valued at $7 billion per year and is expected to grow.[393] This market is ripe for a new type of disruption should the full details of the mechanisms of hair color be identified. If so, using CRISPR-like technology could enable temporary or germ line modification to change hair color naturally without using any chemicals or causing damage to the hair itself. It is already known that the most significant contribution to hair color lies in the concentration and type of melanin expressed in the roots. Research is required to identify this sub mechanism, how it is modified using various types of enzymes and the genetic sequence modifications that enable them. Then changing hair color genetically will be a trivial affair. Going forward, it may be possible to add entirely new expression profiles – for example to generate hair of novel colors that currently humans can't express. This could be done by studying other mammals that do produce those colors and simply adding in the modulating genes. The power of gene editing has mostly been focused on allowing changes to existing genes but the same technology can be used to add in entirely new genes and thus make completely new functionality possible.

Eye color change in vivo: The global color contact lens industry is forecast to be worth $13.47 billion by 2019.[394] This offers a huge opportunity to do for eyes what could be done for hair using CRISPR-like technology. The process will again require analysis of the specific genes involved in melanin concentration in the tissues of the iris. Tissue geometry is also known to affect the apparent color of the eye – it may also be possible to modulate this by applying diffraction effects to incoming wavelengths of light.

Skin color change in vivo: Finally, a brand new market to be explored is the genetic modification of skin tone. This would have a huge impact – potentially changing the various ways in which human lineages have interacted in the last few centuries. The social and cultural strife created by adherence to beliefs of difference based on skin color could finally be eliminated when humans can be dark skinned one month and light skinned the next. The social ramifications of this technology will be legion. Aside from that, the market opportunity is indeed a large one. In India alone – a country still dealing with the effects of colonial and cultural stigmas revolving around skin tone – the skin lightening cream market was worth $432 million in 2010.[395] The U.S. market for self-tanning products was estimated at $775 million for 2014.[396]

Summary

With the invention of in vivo gene editing, human society will be impacted in unexpected ways. For example, all of the apparent values attached to the concept of race could become obsolete – dramatically reducing the risk of persecution, prejudice and genocide of populations simply because of the color of their skin or the texture of their hair. The emergence of new markets for genetic modification may help foster greater cohesiveness of the human family. This would allow us to finally shake off the pernicious fabricated evils of a past where our external differences were used as tools of oppression and hatred.

I believe there is globally pent-up demand to allow people to appear as they wish on their own schedule and – if they wish – to propagate their conception of self through to their children. The future marketers of the industries that will emerge to service that demand will have their hands full selling humanity a dream that had simply only existed in fiction up to now. Collectively, the opportunity segments mentioned above create potential markets worth hundreds of billions of dollars across the globe. I believe the swift and the bold entrepreneurs and agile corporations will be the ones to take greatest advantage of the potential of this new technology to service that demand.

There are a number of questions for society and business that emerge:

- *What are the possible social ramifications and commercial implications of a technology with the potential to challenge notions of race and color, how impactful could the resulting shifts in society be?*
- *What role could businesses have in directly shaping the influence of this technology so as to both be profitable and a benefit to mankind?*
- *What are the implications for strategists and marketers in introducing potentially socially contentious and commercially disruptive gene editing products and services?*

The Great Energy Controversy of 2030

By James H. Lee

What comes after fracking?

Where can we find abundant supplies of relatively clean energy? Are traditional energy companies going away anytime soon? Dig deep for a possible answer.

Towards American energy independence

As we search for disruptive change at the edges of science and society, futurists and other visionary thinkers often get excited (and sometimes worried) about things that aren't yet in the news. These are called **weak signals**. By listening closely to these weak signals, it is sometimes possible to get a sense of tomorrow's headlines.

Today's **big story** is that with breakthroughs in fracking and other means of natural gas extraction, America is moving towards energy independence. We have defied Hubbert's Peak (concerns that we were reaching or had passed the peak of extractable oil reserves). Indeed U.S. domestic oil production is now getting very close to levels that haven't been seen since the 1970's. Global supply far exceeded demand in 2014, leading to a recent collapse in energy prices. However, there is an even more abundant source of energy that we have not tapped yet.

Unleashing fire ice

Deep underwater and also beneath layers of arctic permafrost are fields of crystalized natural gas in the form of methane hydrates. Sometimes known as **fire ice**, methane hydrates are a dense form of energy that combusts easily into flame (figure 1).

How methane hydrates are formed

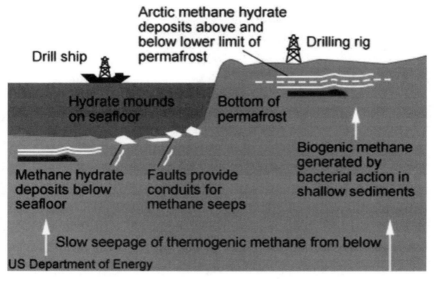

FIGURE 1 – Methane Hydrate Formation[397]

It has been estimated by the U.S. Geological Survey that somewhere between 10,000 trillion and 100,000 trillion cubic feet of natural gas exists in this form in cold climates and under high pressure. This represents more organic carbon than the world's existing sources of coal, oil, and conventional forms of natural gas combined. These global reserves could generate enough power to supply the U.S. for over 1,600 years.

The Japanese are leading the effort to harvest these deposits. With few natural gas fields of their own and a post-Fukushima disaster reluctance to embrace nuclear power, methane hydrates offer an abundant and local alternative fuel source. Experts estimate that commercial levels of production will start sometime between 2020 and 2030.

Methane hydrates are found beneath the coastal waters of virtually every continent. So, while countries like Japan are in greatest need, it is a globally available energy source that could potentially benefit everyone. However, there is a sizeable danger. On a molecule-by-molecule basis, methane is twenty times more effective as a greenhouse gas than carbon dioxide. In fact, it is believed by some that the release of methane hydrates from ocean warming triggered a six degree Celsius increase in temperatures during a mass extinction event at the end of the Permian era.

Given the possibility of inexpensive energy from the ocean or fighting over ever-dwindling supplies from conventional sources, we may find this to be a politically acceptable risk, but not without considerable debate. Why?

Many of our carbon-based industries are based on resource extraction. There is an existing infrastructure that favors natural gas for power generation. Furthermore, natural gas is considered a clean-burning fuel. This suggests that methane hydrates may be the **next big thing** after the fracking boom is over. It is a mainstream alternative to alternative energy.

If a magic lamp was found at the bottom of the ocean and a genie appeared, would anyone be able to refuse his offer?

This opportunity raises some key questions for business:

- *How should we assess the trade-off between the scale of the opportunity and the environmental risks? How will future generations judge our decisions?*
- *Will new business models be required to fund the research and development costs associated with evaluating this new opportunity – or it can it be handled using existing energy industry approaches?*
- *What can be done to mitigate the risks and public concerns associated with extracting methane hydrates?*

Space-Based Solar Power and Wireless Power Transmission

By Devin Daniels

What could tapping into space-based solar power mean for the future of energy on Earth?

The first item to address when considering the concept of space-based solar power is the same question asked by any mildly experienced business person when first propositioned with a new idea: why? Why pursue this idea over any of the possible competitors? What unique promise does this specific idea hold? In this chapter I will seek to address this question and many others. I will also seek to explore the viability of wireless power transmission – the core technology that is necessary for space-based solar power to become a reality.

An overview of space-based solar power

While the reasons to switch to space-based solar power abound, and many will be discussed further in this chapter, it is best to address the most key reason first. Space-based solar power production will allow electricity to become virtually limitless in availability in comparison to the current constraints on its production. The sun is, in essence, a nuclear fusion reactor that is many orders of magnitude larger than our planet, and as such is the most abundant energy source in the solar system. Without indulging in the slightest proclivity towards hyperbole, switching to space-based solar power could irreversibly alter the way businesses and governments view and utilize energy as a commodity.

The call for abundant energy

While the average consumer in the modern western world hardly pays attention to his/her energy consumption, aside from when it comes to pay the utility company, businesses and governments are familiar with just how taxing these energy demands can be. In fact, we have reached the point in scientific endeavors where the energy available is not sufficient for all the desired tasks we want to use it for.

A prime example is the Large Hadron Collider at CERN in Switzerland. While current experiments are useful and provide insight into the nature of the universe, much greater energy is required to test certain aspects of modern theories. Inconvenient – yes – however, this limitation has yet to truly impact almost anyone else not engaged in working at the cutting edge of physics. That doesn't mean that having exponentially higher energy availability will not affect anyone but CERN, not by a long shot. Indeed, space-based solar power generation is an idea that could be extraordinarily dangerous to a number of currently established energy sectors. Coal, oil, nuclear, hydroelectric – truly almost all of our current energy production methods could be rendered obsolete if we tapped into space-based solar power on a planetary scale. With the nature of the power source, there is absolutely nothing that can compete in terms of energy production (aside from a larger star).

The benefits of harnessing space-based solar power for future productivity cannot be overstated. Abundant, reliable, and affordable power is the key to future advances for civilization. With it, we can accelerate the progress of many developing countries. Without it, the development of infrastructure is a slow, painful process. Countries without abundant access to oil are reliant upon foreign imports to fuel industry and society. Oil, as with many other forms of current methods of providing power, is a finite resource and can often be difficult and expensive to obtain.

The nature of space-based solar power generation means that it would be no more difficult for countries like Zimbabwe, Malaysia, or Syria to obtain or purchase it than it would be for countries like the United States or France. In fact, with the level of production space-based solar power is inherently capable of, and without an enormously radical advance in energy storage technologies for the excess generated power, it would be folly for whoever was engaged in the production to try and selectively sell it.

The current state of wireless power transmission

Wireless power transmission is the critical enabler – and major current hurdle – to space-based solar power production. Without the development of a material capable of tethering a space-based object to a ground station, wireless power transmission is the only method of getting power produced in orbit to the surface of the planet. Any kind of wireless transmission such as WiFi or the radio waves used to provide cellular signals for mobile phones are in fact a wireless transmission of power. However, the concern is with the accuracy of modern transmission methods.

The modern methodology for sending a wireless signal, such as those above, is a broadcast approach. This entails sending a signal of equal potential in all directions, so that wherever the receiver may be, it can benefit from the signal. Such methods currently have a very low accuracy rate, and lose a lot of power by sending an unfocused signal. Developments are being made in the field of pinpoint wireless power transmission, where the signal received is much closer in energy to the signal that was output. Recently, a Japanese team of researchers set a new record for a pinpoint wireless transmission of power – a transmission over 55 meters with minimal power loss. While this is more than enough for any usage inside the home (which could lead to plug sockets becoming a relic from the past), it's obviously not sufficient for transmission from space.

This key development is absolutely crucial for furthering space-based solar power generation as a method of producing power for usage on the surface of the earth (as many space-based objects already use solar power). Space-based solar power is far from the only usage, however. As mentioned above, the currently achieved maximum range for accurate wireless power transmission is sufficient for home usage, though the equipment is currently cost prohibitive for implementation in the consumer market. While equipment costs are likely to fall as the technology advances, the development of space-based solar power generation is necessary for wireless power generation to become successful outside of niche markets.

While the accuracy in research situations of wireless power transmission is promising, it's a long way away from replacing modern conducting wire. So, it would be possible for wireless power transmission to be used within the home with current technology (given the likelihood that equipment costs will fall). If current levels of accuracy could be achieved over the distance needed to transmit power from space to the ground however, the abundance of electricity as mentioned above would change the importance of wireless power transmission. The convenience of never having to plug in another device or appliance should far exceed any concerns.

Disrupting with wireless power transmission

This concept brings us to the first major potential change in the desires and demands of consumers that the success of these two technologies could enable. With wireless transmission becoming the norm for space-based solar power generation, the house, office building, and factory of the future could become entirely wireless. Any device that would traditionally use a power plug could instead house a wireless power receiver. In fact, devices powered by wires may become viewed as archaic.

Given the success of efficient power transmission over the distance needed to transmit power from space, personal devices would also no longer run off of batteries. Instead, the likelihood is that we'd see widespread use of towers similar to those used to relay cell phone signals This would allow any device to receive power on the move as easily as a phone can receive data. In fact, there's little reason why cellular and wireless power transmission couldn't share the same towers. Those best positioned to start offering this service would be modern cellular phone service providers. Given the abundance of power available, charging might move from a metering system to a monthly agreement between the consumer and the provider company for the usage of the company's towers – similar to an unlimited monthly cellular plan.

The utilization of towers to transmit power wirelessly should prove to be a trump card for electric vehicles – creating potential disruption in the transportation industry. One important customer for the oil industry (fossil fuel power stations) could well be put out of business by the abundance of power enabled through space-based solar. Towers transmitting wireless power from a position of abundance will make electric vehicles not only cheaper but far more convenient than gasoline cars.

Electric vehicles will be able to charge while driving, receiving power on the go. Cheap, powerful battery technology will no longer be the concern and obstacle it has been. Instead, electric vehicles could be produced with smaller batteries than before, powering themselves from wireless transmissions, and only relying upon their battery for power in between towers. This would increase the demand for energy towers, which would also serve to provide a larger amount of cellular service along roadways, further driving the permeation of accessible internet services in consumers' lives.

Business opportunities enabled by space-based solar power

Let's get to the meat of what space-based solar power means for the future of business. As discussed, wireless power transmission opens up new avenues for businesses in the technology sector. While this is interesting, it represents merely an evolutionary step rather than a revolutionary one. What I will now focus on are the avenues of businesses that are currently cost-prohibitive or otherwise impractical that could be enabled by abundant electricity. These opportunities have revolutionary potential, and could transform the global landscape. The possible effects range from the emergence of new "power players" on the world stage to a vastly higher quality of life for those in developing countries. As highlighted earlier, many energy sectors could be negatively impacted by the advent of abundant, cheap solar power. However I believe this shift will have a very large net positive outcome.

Chief among the potential benefits is the production of clean drinking water. While many in more developed nations have never had to worry about it, access to clean drinking water is a problem the majority of the world faces. Even in the more developed world, there are areas heavily affected by droughts. For example, the state of California within the United States is facing the possibility of a drought worse than that which caused the 1930's Dust Bowl. The solution lies in transforming our abundant supply of seawater into a drinkable form. The most effective way of desalinating large amounts of seawater is still boiling water and collecting the steam. However, this process is inefficient, requiring enormous amounts of power to produce a decent amount of clean water. When the question of energy efficiency is demoted in importance by the nearly infinite abundance of electricity, it will be a simple matter to setup steam desalination plants in areas like California to provide much-needed drinking water. Furthermore, universal availability means it will be as easy to power a desalination plant in Liberia as California.

Perhaps one of the biggest opportunities for business is the potential acceleration of development in emerging nations. When the cost of importing oil is no longer a consideration, it will be much easier for countries to develop modern infrastructure. This, coupled with implementation of steam plants to produce drinking water could have a transformational impact. In these countries, many people spend hours every day fetching clean drinking water from distant sources. As you can imagine, this is a rather large impediment to productivity. Infrastructure enables accelerated progress of industry sectors and helps fuel the consumer society, all of which help create jobs, income, business opportunities, and national economic development.

The future looks promising, and those who have the vision to see the direction the world is heading in should be well positioned to achieve high levels of prosperity in the years to come. It is time for the wireless transmission of power to migrate from the laboratory to the consumer and business markets. Most importantly, it is time to perfect the accuracy of transmissions over long distances. With the advent of large solar power collection stations in space, energy can become extremely abundant. This would bring potentially radical benefits to individuals, society, business, and government, and usher in a whole new wave of advantageous future technologies.

Here are three questions to consider about energy and the development of space-based solar power:

- *How can we bring about the shifts in thinking required among individuals, businesses, and government that could lead to a radical reduction in our dependency on finite, depleting fossil fuel resource s? Are you comfortable depending on fossil fuels?*
- *What steps are required to accelerate the investment in research and development of the underlying technologies that could make space-based solar power a viable industry sector?*
- *What are the potential social, commercial, and governmental implications of adopting a more sustainable approach infrastructure to infrastructure development enabled by space-based solar power?*

Section 8

Embracing the Future –

What are the futures and foresight tools, methods and processes that we can use to explore, understand and create the future?

Looking through a window on the future

Hopefully, the previous sections will have inspired you to look at how you can bring futures and foresight thinking into your business. In practice organizations, internal futurists, and external advisors, face a number of challenges in helping the business embrace longer-term thinking in an all-too-often operationally focused environment. The mantra of "slowing down to speed up" can be aptly applied to the approaches that provide businesses with a window on the future – or at least on possible versions of the future. It is often a case of looking for the best fit between process, organizational culture, and influential advocates of foresight inside the organization.

Four different aspects of applying futures and foresight tools, methods and processes in business are described in this section.

Foresight Infused Strategy Development (*page 471*) – Maree Conway is an experienced foresight and strategy consultant and the founder of Thinking Futures (Australia). She explores how to infuse foresight into existing corporate strategy processes to strengthen outcomes and execution.

Automated, Experiential, Open: How to Overcome "Futures Fatigue" with Emerging Foresight Practices *(page 482)* – Cornelia Daheim, a leading German futurist and foresight consultant, highlights a growing trend towards the use of IT-based, participative and experiential approaches to invigorate and enhance the practice of corporate foresight.

Storifying Foresight: Scenario Planning as a Tool for Improved Change Management Processes *(page 490)* – Dr. Claire Nelson, Ideation Leader of The Futures Forum USA and White House Champion of Change, explains the critical role of scenario planning and storytelling in helping organizations shape and share their desired visions of the future, and in delivering the resulting organizational changes.

Is the Future of Design Thinking in the Future of Business Foresight? *(page 498)* – Jim Burke, a U.S. foresight coach focused on delivering innovation and effective ways to think about and act on future, highlights the growing use of Design Thinking as part of the foresight process, particularly for prototyping future scenarios.

Foresight Infused Strategy Development

By Maree Conway

Why do traditional approaches to strategy execution so often fail and how can foresight infused strategy development help?

Developing futures ready strategy

This chapter explores how to infuse foresight into existing strategy processes to strengthen outcomes and execution. I will explore issues with conventional strategic planning before providing an overview of the major elements of foresight infused planning and how to start using this approach to strategy development. Infusing strategy with foresight enables the development of futures ready strategy. This means creating a strategy that is flexible enough to allow people to respond proactively to whatever challenges and opportunities the future brings to their organizational doorstep. At its core, futures ready strategy is underpinned by new ways of thinking that challenge today's assumptions about the future.

The challenge of strategy development in environment of rapid change

Why do we need foresight infused strategy development? It is a truism to say that the world around us is changing rapidly. New economic, social, and political systems are emerging. Social unrest pervades many places around the world. A digital transformation in how we work and live is upon us. Few people alive today have lived through change of this scope, speed, and level of intensity. The way we make sense of today's world is unlikely to be of much use in ten or twenty years' time and applying today's thinking to strategy development for the future remains a major reason for execution failure. Foresight provides the capabilities and methods needed to help shift our thinking to a space where we are able to engage with future unknowns to strengthen decision making today.

Why care about infusing foresight into strategy? Conventional strategic planning with its accompanying set of protocols that underpin how planning is done is no longer effective. The need to plan is now generally accepted and significant amounts of money, time, and effort are invested in the process. However, the resulting plans are increasingly incapable of driving strategy implementation. The plan fails in the execution stage.

Typical causes of failed strategy execution

Hrebinniak[398] lists a range of processes related factors that lead to execution failure including:

- Inability to manage change effectively and overcome resistance to change.
- Trying to execute a strategy that conflicts with the existing power structure, and
- Lack of feelings of ownership of a strategy among key staff.

Lietdka[399] sees execution as failing because "…nobody really cares about these strategies…strategies must be felt as personally meaningful and compelling by the members of the organization who must adopt new behaviors to execute them." Martin[400] writes: "It's impossible to have a good strategy poorly executed. That's because execution actually is strategy – trying to separate the two only leads to confusion."

Martin sees the primary cause of poor execution as poor strategy – which implies a poor strategy development process. More than a decade ago, Fuller[401] reflected this sentiment when he wrote: "While the need for planning has never been greater, the relevance of most of today's planning systems and tools is increasingly marginal."

A primary reason for poor strategy development is the belief that producing a plan is the purpose of the exercise – rather than the final stage of a future focused strategic thinking and decision making process. A plan is simply a document that records the actions you agree to take and that allows you to assign accountabilities, monitor implementation, and report on the achievement of goals – it's not a strategy.

More importantly, poor strategy development often results from poor strategic thinking. The new behaviors required to execute strategy effectively demand the adoption of new ways of thinking. Conventional planning approaches focus on the past and present and that produces conventional thinking. If strategy development doesn't allow people to shift their thinking beyond today, the resulting plan will be "business as usual" and it will fail when it meets the future.

Issues with conventional strategy development approaches

Today's issues with planning are not new. Conventional strategic planning was described by Gerstner[402] in 1973 as "an academic, ill-defined activity with little or no bottom line impact" and by Ashkenas[403] in 2013 as "either an over-explained budget or just bad amateur theatre – lots of costumes in the form of analysis, charts, and presentations but with very little meaningful substance that can be translated into action." Because conventional processes focus on the plan as the major outcome, a shared understanding of the organiza-tion's preferred future to inform action today is often not developed. In other words, the instrument has become the purpose – the plan has become the strategy.

Conventional planning approaches tend to have the following characteristics:

- The process seeks certainty and constrains thinking about alter-native futures – people interpret change from the perspective of the past and the present, not the future.

- The plans produced are inflexible – unexpected change invalidates the plan as proposed implementation actions are no longer relevant.
- A "business as usual" future is assumed – alternative futures are not explored to create new ways of seeing possible opportunities and challenges.
- Quantitative data is preferred as it infers certainty – there are no quantitative data about the future, yet imagination and qualitative data are often not viewed as valid information sources.
- Assumptions about change and work are not challenged but rather reinforced – if alternative futures that show different ways the future might emerge are not created, today's ways of operating are not disputed.
- Staff plays a minor role in the development of the plan – usually at the end of the process when they are asked to look at a draft plan, rather than being invited to share their views at the start of the process.

Jargon associated with strategy and strategic planning is plentiful but rarely in those words do we see the term "future". It is probably considered to be implicit in the process, but for new ways of thinking to emerge Inayatullah argues that the future must be treated as an asset – something that can be explored and used on a continuing basis to inform strategy development.[404] Consideration of the future must be overt in strategy work if the aim is to surface new ways of thinking about tomorrow – this is sometimes called divergent or generative thinking. No plan survives contact with the future unless the future drives the plan.

Infusing foresight into organizational strategy processes
Voros Generic Foresight Process provides a framework for infusing foresight into existing strategy processes.[405] It has explicit stages that focus on new thinking, challenging assumptions and crafting futures

ready strategy (Figure 1).

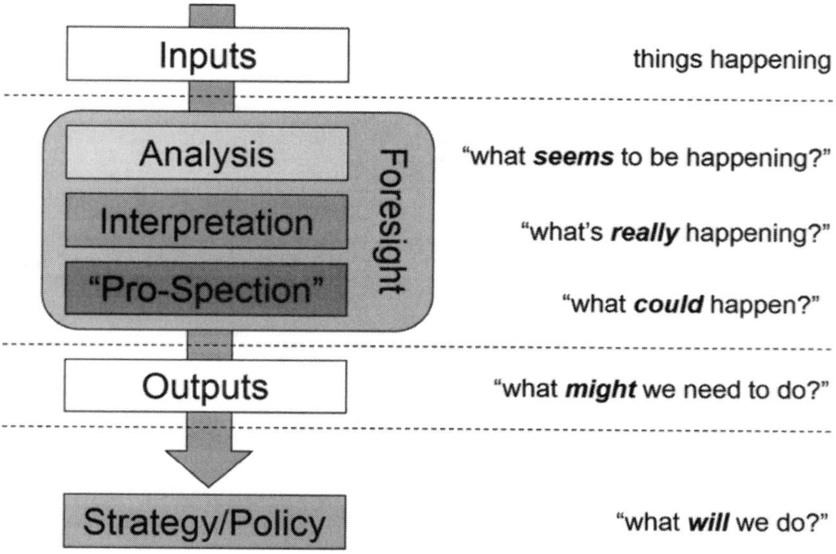

FIGURE 1: Generic Foresight Process (© Voros, 2003)[406]

The **inputs** stage gathers information about change in the external environment – it's the realm of environmental (horizon) scanning. **Analysis** is about pattern recognition and looking for what really matters for your organization – this is the realm of methods like trend analysis. **Interpretation** is the stage where assumptions and mindsets are challenged for future relevance and validity by going beneath the visible surface to explore system dynamics and worldviews – Causal Layered Analysis is useful here. Finally, **Prospection** is where plausible images of the future are developed. Scenario planning/thinking is commonly used here. Doing prospection is also the stage most often missed in conventional approaches – resulting in shallow and "change susceptible" strategies.

A range of options emerge from these steps that need to be evaluated for relevance and credibility. Strategic options are then selected by the CEO or Board, followed by implementation of those options. Foresight infused strategy development can still produce a plan if that is needed. However, that plan will only be written after exploration of the shape and form of possible future operating environments.

Foresight infused strategy processes are context dependent – methods must be chosen and tailored for each organization. The methods chosen will depend on how familiar your organization is with foresight. The methods adopted if you have never used foresight before will be different to those that might be tried after doing it for five or ten years.

At the core of foresight infused strategy development are people and collaborative processes. This is in contrast with conventional planning that tends to quarantine planning and strategic thinking to the senior managers of the organization. Often this means a narrow and entrenched set of perspectives shape the plan. In contrast, foresight approaches assume there is no one right way of viewing the organization and its possible futures. Diversity of perspectives on change in the external environment and those possible futures is valued and necessary if entrenched assumptions are to be challenged.

Opening up strategy processes to staff and stakeholders and other participants also requires:

- Leaders who are comfortable with using a diversity of alternative views to inform their thinking.
- The suspension of hierarchy at least for the duration of the process.
- A commitment of time and resources to the process.

How to start with foresight infused strategy development?

A preliminary step is to make an organization wide commitment to use foresight. Know why you want to use foresight and how you will integrate it into existing processes. There are then four basic steps:

- **Scanning and Analysis** – look to the external environment and seek to understand strategic uncertainty and complexity that you find there.
- *Strategic Thinking* – bring the understanding that arises into

the organisation by providing spaces, time, information and opportunities for staff to be involved in strategic thinking exercises using foresight methods.

- **Reframing** – support staff to change the way they think about strategic uncertainty by challenging assumptions about how work might be done in the future.
- **Embedding** – work to build a futures focused culture where using the future is just "the way we do things around here".

These four steps don't replace existing strategy processes but rather strengthen the future readiness of outcomes. They help produce strategies that allow the organization to:

- Face the future – the organization is alert to change and ready to respond.
- Challenge assumptions – it's recognized that today's operating roles are not always useful for the future.
- Build a long term mindset –moving beyond status quo thinking to focus on what's coming and how that might affect today's operations.
- Use data **and** imagination – understanding continuously the whole change picture with a range of information sources, incorporating a wide range of evidence.
- Collaborate and co-create – allow people across the organisation work together to shape the future they want.

Case studies

Using foresight infused strategy processes starts with customizing tools and approaches to the particular needs of the organization. This section provides two case studies of using foresight, including lessons learned and differences in outcomes.

Organization A

This organization decided to infuse foresight into its planning process by establishing a central foresight unit. However, the unit was told to simply "do foresight" with no clear expectations around role and outcomes. CEO support existed but there was little ongoing support to build the commitment of senior and middle managers to the new approach. Organizational politics and a personality clash, not obvious at the time, contributed to this lack of engagement by managers.

The CEO wanted to use scenario planning to confirm the strategy he had put in place. He dictated that a scenario exercise be undertaken and while there were some good outcomes, there was little real engagement and the implementation of new strategic options didn't proceed. The arrival of a new CEO saw foresight removed from the organization's planning processes, including the dismantling of the foresight unit.

Problems with this approach included the establishment of a foresight unit that was not integrated into the organization's operational structure; it was not clear how outcomes would be used; a grand announcement was made that foresight would replace existing strategy processes which it didn't; and the power of organizational politics and turf defending behaviors wasn't recognized until too late. Lessons learned included:

- CEO support is essential, but the next management level down is the key to successful use of foresight.
- Language is important – foresight may not always be the right term to use.
- Personal goodwill is important when introducing foresight – staff with high personal credibility and strong internal connections should be selected.
- Ensure the approach is collaborative and accepted by managers and staff as useful – in this case, the approach was imposed top down essentially by an edict
- Using foresight is a long term activity and needs time to become embedded in organizational strategy processes. In this case, lack of real support and engagement saw the demise of foresight as soon as the CEO had left.

Organization B

The CEO of organization B was open to the idea of using foresight and involving staff in the process. He wanted staff to be informed and to participate in a structured process to provide input into the development of the plan. There were clear expectations about the exercise's scope, the required output, and how it would be used. Strong organizational trust was present and the CEO led the process well. There was wide engagement of all staff in identifying issues, challenges, and potential actions, and a scenario planning workshop was held with the Board and Executive staff. The outcomes of the process were used to inform the development of the plan.

The process here was run by an existing planning unit so the use of foresight was not seen as replacing anything. All senior managers provided input into the design process and supported the general approach. Lessons from this case included:

- Managing upwards is critical – keeping the CEO informed and clear about the foresight process being used was essential.
- Finding time to deepen the conversation at a number of points was a challenge as the process was accelerated because of the perception that everyone was too busy to spend a significant amount of time on the exercise.
- Stretching the thinking of participants into new areas while keeping engagement was a challenge for the facilitators.
- Understanding the depth of knowledge of staff who are implementing the process is critical – they hold much organizational and cultural knowledge that is essential to successful adoption of foresight approaches.

Table 1 summarizes three major differences in outcomes from the two cases relating to testing the validity of existing strategy, how foresight processes are used, and the degree to which assumptions are challenged.

TABLE 1: Comparison on Major Differences in Outcomes

Issue	Organisation A	Organisation B
Validity of existing strategy	Nothing would change the CEO's mind about "his" strategy if the foresight process had negated that strategy and people knew this. The validity of the foresight process was therefore reduced from the start.	The CEO was open to incorporating new options into his existing strategy if the outcomes had indicated that would be useful.
Foresight processes used – in both cases an environmental scan and a scenario planning process were used, including staff and board workshops	Outcomes were not used to inform planning even though they largely confirmed the existing strategy. The scanning report did prove to be of value in some areas.	Outcomes largely confirmed the existing strategy, and helped to focus action areas in the plan. An environmental scanning system was developed as an ongoing function as part of the process.
Challenging Assumptions	The process provided a safe space for some areas to challenge the CEO's assumptions underpinning his strategy, but nothing changed because the CEO was not open to seeing alternatives to his strategy.	"Undiscussables" were surfaced and challenged. In the case of the Board, the assumption that their role was not strategic was challenged strongly. The Board adopted a more strategic role as a result.

The two cases highlight the importance of CEO leadership and spending the time to gain the support of managers in the organization. Ensuring that foresight processes are designed with people in the organization is also essential. To gain acceptance from people in the organization foresight needs to be positioned as a way to inject thinking about the future into existing processes rather than the "next best thing in strategy". Finally, if assumptions underpinning how people develop strategy are to be challenged effectively, the process must include time and space for what Van Der Heijen called strategic conversations – ongoing discussions that are big picture and that focus on questions about the future of the organization.[407]

Concluding comments

This chapter has provided an overview of why foresight infused strategy development must now be the benchmark for effective strategy. It highlighted major elements of the process and a framework implementing it in organizations. This is a process that generates strategies developed by people in the organization, based on a deep and shared understanding of changes shaping their organization's future. This is strategy that as Lietdka suggests, is experienced and felt on an emotional level not just known on a rational level.[408] She writes that successful execution comes not from being told to implement a set of goals but from "desire driven" action taken by people who have been involved in thinking about the future. Fundamentally, strategy without people is strategy without a future.

Practical Questions:

- *How does your organization evaluate the effectiveness of strategies and strategy execution – how you assess the cost of poor execution?*
- *How open and collaborative is the current strategy development process – how could this be enhanced?*
- *What might the benefits be of moving beyond status quo thinking to adopting a foresight infused strategy process?*

Automated, Experiential, Open:
How to Overcome "Futures Fatigue" with Emerging Foresight Practices

By Cornelia Daheim

Which effective new forms of foresight practice are emerging for use in corporate foresight?

Several emerging practices have appeared in corporate foresight recently. In this chapter, I present a short introduction showing why such constant renewal on the methodological side is critical. I then introduce examples of such practices to provide an overview for the practitioner aiming to inject new approaches into their work.

Can exploring the future become a routine?

"I'll need a triple shot", answered Jack, the head of futures research in a major multinational B2B company, when I asked if he wanted an espresso too. I needed one after listening to a long trend presentation on the future of augmented reality at this international innovation conference. There was a lot of interesting, relevant information in the perfectly delivered talk, but somehow neither of us connected to it. Silently, Jack and I sipped our espressos.

Finally, he said: "You know what? If I'm honest, I am bored by all that trend stuff. I used to be so excited about the future when I started out ten years ago. I was on a mission to win over every last critic in my company. Now, most of these trend presentations and reports leave me cold."

"Of course, they are much better than ten years ago. And there is still so much to learn, not that I really understand this 4D printing thing, for example. But recently, I seem to just go through the motions with my projects. For me, this futures stuff is a routine. The future has become stale."

The conversation went on for a good deal longer and ended on a lighter note. However, what he said stuck with me. I started noticing other sufferers of what I now call "futures fatigue". In the numerous conversations that followed around this topic, it became clear to me that Jack was in fact one of many with this syndrome. What had happened here? How could it be that while foresight in business seemed to become more and more widespread and professionalized, there was also a sense of fatigue for many of its practitioners?

The background: Increasing diffusion and professionalization of foresight

The answers are manifold. First of all, it is a sign of success. When corporate foresight was much less widespread in Europe 20 years ago, a trend workshop or presentation as such was exciting and interesting just because one rarely came by one. Today, the practice of systematically analyzing the possible developments of the future and designing appropriate actions – the practice of corporate foresight – has become widespread. Companies from BBVA to Volkswagen systematically analyze future options and employ their own experts or even departments for these tasks. In Europe, the last two decades can be seen as a time of the professionalization and increasing diffusion of foresight. In parallel, the methods and background of foresight or future research were increasingly being taught in universities, leading to a growing inflow of qualified professionals trained to perform foresight projects.

In many European countries, an established foresight practice is now a standard within larger companies, rather than the exception it still was ten to fifteen years ago. Thus, there has been an increasing use and diffusion of corporate foresight, a professionalization and growing maturity of practices as well as practitioners. The existing fatigue symptoms of experienced practitioners could thus be seen as a side-effect of a maturing form of practice and its increasing visibility.

Future business roadmaps, trend and scenario reports, and presentations are now commonplace. Furthermore, one may argue that in some cases they have actually become too successful for foresight's own good. This is obvious when foresight means a widespread, but uniform discussion of universally acknowledged megatrends that we all at least think we know everything about. This diagnosis also holds true when foresight becomes a perfectly polished and glossy future vision video displaying the next generation of gadgets being used by beautiful people – boredom, routine, and detachment are the logical consequence of such sanitized views of the future.

The new path: Emerging practices and their benefits

In recent years, we have also witnessed a renewal of methodology and practice forms in the foresight field that can be regarded as responses to the fatigue problem. Recently, I conducted a study on emerging practices in foresight that identified four main clusters of emerging practices that are increasingly being used.[409] They all aim to overcome the limitations or challenges of existing standard practice and thus point us towards the state of the art as well as future foresight practice. Examples of corporate applications exist for all four clusters, but have not yet become widespread. The four identified poles or clusters of emerging practice are:[410]

- IT-based and automated foresight
- Integrated qualitative-quantitative approaches
- Open and crowd-sourced practices

- Experiential foresight

Definitions and examples of each approach are provided below:

IT-based and automated foresight refers to utilizing (non-standard) IT-based tools that support specific steps in foresight. A range of these tools seek to automate parts of the scanning process by using increasingly refined search algorithms to identify and report on key emerging trends, ideas, developments, and weak signals. Others such as The Global Futures Intelligence System by The Millennium Project[411] seek to enable real-time collaboration in scanning and evaluating current and future developments, allowing for cooperation across geographic and institutional borders. The benefits of automation clearly lie in enabling faster, more wide-ranging scanning, and a more effective categorization or "knowledge content structuring" process. This frees the analyst from the tedious task of data management, allowing them to focus instead on evaluation and insight.

Integrated quantitative-qualitative approaches describes practices that bridge analysis frameworks. One example is the development of scenarios connecting traditional analytical qualitative and narrative techniques with an interrelated system dynamics modeling approach. The benefits lie in bridging the often still separate worlds of qualitative and quantitative analysis – providing deeper and improved insights on both sides. The key lever is being able to integrate a view of complex interdependencies of many factors, and relate them in the context of established business culture and language. Decision-makers need to be comfortable that the potential impacts of alternative future developments do have a relationship to actions they need to take today.

The last two categories are the more radical forms of practice.

Open and crowd-sourced practices open up the foresight process to a larger number of more diverse contributors. Examples include BBVA's open platform-supported dialogue on future development in the context of their innovation activities, the fully open Future of Facebook project, and the Future Agenda project, initially funded by Vodafone that engaged over 50,000 participants in its first cycle.[412] A range of tools are emerging that enable a large number of participants to contribute to a foresight process. The benefits of these practices lie in this integration of multiple views, as well as in greater transparency, and improved insights generated from a wider variety of perspectives.

Experiential foresight includes all practices that employ new communication and engagement formats, integrate gamification / serious play, or the approaches of design fiction and design thinking to literally construct, create, and experience the future. They aim to make the future more tangible – dealing with the future from a more directly involved, experience-oriented, and playful perspective. Examples include numerous card games on trends and future creation such as *The Thing from the Future* or the *Mobility VIP cards*.[413] Others include scenario gaming and the **future prehearsals** format where future scenarios are enacted and experienced instead of only being discussed. Another approach is complete world-building games in which possible future worlds are co-created with large groups. The latter was demonstrated by the Rilao Remote Viewing Protocol where 300 participants co-created a complete future world with artifacts from the future in a day. This process exemplifies the link between these practices and design fiction, a current development in design that creates speculative future objects[414].

Futures perspectives: Directions of corporate foresight

How and where can corporate foresight practitioners employ these emerging forms of practice more? The following table gives an overview and summarizes the key characteristics and benefits:

Practice Type	IT-based and Automated Foresight	Integrated Qualitative-Quantitative approaches	Open and Crowd-sourced Foresight	Experiential Foresight
Charac-teristics	Utilizes IT-tools to improve scanning / data analysis and to connect various perspectives	Integrates qualitative and quantitative methods Employs system dynamics perspective	Opens up the process to stakeholders outside of traditional institutional boundaries Harnesses power of the crowd for insights	Playful, serious gaming approaches World building / design fiction / creating future artifacts Directly experiencing future worlds / scenarios
Key Benefits	Increased efficiency of the process Improved insights via variety of perspectives	Higher impact with decision-makers Improved insights via analysis of interdependencies	Higher process speed More participants to be integrated Improved insights via more diversity of perspectives	Higher impact, especially with decision-makers, via more direct engagement and emotional experience Encourages perspective of creating the future Can uncover blind spots of traditional analytical techniques

It is clear that these practices are not intended to and will not replace established techniques such as scenarios, trend scanning, Delphi, road-mapping, or wild cards and weak signal analysis. Of course, as with all methodologies, they should also only be used where applicable for the task and context at hand. As a means to overcome or forego futures fatigue however, they are a key lever for pushing for higher impact of foresight on action today. They can achieve this aim by creating a deeper understanding of what could come and of what we can do now to create a positive future. Playful approaches can inject the enthusiasm back into a well-informed analytical futures process, and experiential scenario gaming can shed new light on the interaction of stakeholders. IT-based and qualitative-quantitative approaches will probably simply be used much more in the coming years because of the underlying technological changes on the one hand and the sheer need for a better connection to decision-makers on the other. The other two forms of emerging practices are related to two more fundamental drivers: the longing for more authenticity and a more direct and personal experience; and the need for companies to be more transparent, more inclusive, and to open up more to stakeholders and society.

Also, it is clear that the experiential and open practices in particular push most companies' cultures in innovation and strategy development much more than a traditional trend report does. That is exactly the point why more business practitioners should start to integrate them into their processes. Because if foresight becomes routine, consensual, and does not challenge business as usual, it is not what it has to be, this is to move out of the comfort zone, towards what could be.

So what critical questions should business consider?

- *How far have you integrated emerging practices into your company's foresight approach?*
- *Which of these emerging practices fit best with the existing corporate (foresight) culture and context?*

- *What could be the next step or pilot project to use any of these practices to either re-invigorate the existing foresight process or to create more impact and inject more authenticity and action-orientation into it?*

Storifying Foresight: Scenario Planning as a Tool for Improved Change Management Processes

By Claire A. Nelson

How can we use storytelling and scenario planning to help manage organizational change more effectively?

Rethinking change management

Change management is seen as one of the most critical management skills, yet it remains a sub-optimal process for many organizations. The aim of this article is to address the use of scenario planning as a tool for change management process, and to amplify the potential role of storytelling.[415]

The role of foresight and scenario planning in anticipating change

"The power of storytelling is unquestionable. We are all storytellers and we live our lives through a network of stories." – International Storytelling Center.

The rapid rate of change, increasing complexity and shorter, faster business cycles are making **futures sensing** and analysis even more essential skills for business leaders. Strategic foresight is vital to improve leaders' adaptability and resilience to internally driven or externally demanded change, be that a new technology, a new competitor, or our customers' pivot to the next must have product or service.

Leaders typically invest significant time and assets constructing compelling strategic visions that can inspire and guide their organizations into a desired future. As such, strategic foresight is critical for developing the resilience needed in a dynamic, shape-shifting future. If vision can be said to have inspired the invention of the airplane, it is foresight that anticipated the need for air traffic control. Strategic foresight as opposed to strategic vision provides leadership with the understanding required to improve sustainability and effectiveness of the vision. Foresight helps crystallize the picture, highlights the possible consequences of our choices, actions or inactions, and better prepares us to navigate the change journey.

There is no one way to do effective foresight, as its application and success depend on the organization's culture, the challenges at hand, and our readiness for change. One popular technique is scenario planning, typically outlining three or more plausible potential futures which encode various possibilities for social, environmental, technological, economic, and political factors. The scenario story allows a mental rehearsal of ways the future might play out and how an organization could respond to each scenario. Scenarios are not predictions about the future but rather "stories of possible futures".

Scenarios allow the organization to highlight the discontinuities from the present, to see future alternatives more clearly, and to think critically about the threats and opportunities inherent in the potential futures outlined in each scenario. These insights should help us make better decisions and develop more robust plans. After the visioning, decision making, and planning comes the challenge of steering the organization in the direction of the preferred future. This process of scenario transfer and change management can be especially challenging when truly transformational change is required.

Meeting the challenge of change management

"Those who tell stories rule the world." – Native American Proverb

Scenario transfer is the entry point to the change management process called for by the preferred scenario. Change management involves:

- Working with an organization's stakeholder groups to help them understand what the change means for them.
- Helping them accommodate and sustain the transition.
- Working to overcome any challenges involved.

In short, the process helps to effect the organizational and behavioral adjustments needed to make and maintain the change. A major concern is how the organizational culture will adapt to the changes called for, to the evolving future under construction, and to the emerging future outside the domain of organizational control. One key issue to consider is the set of collective myths that define the character and behavior of the organization.

The organizational history and stories that underlie its culture influence how we treat the future and affect our change management processes. The story may be about the way the founding mothers defied the odds to win the first contract against the beast that threatened to destroy their chances. Or it may be the time the company almost folded but was saved by the wily CEO who stepped up to save the company from being eaten alive by its competitor. Think about your organization's stories that are passed around in the hallways, at the water cooler, gym and via other parts of the jungle radio that permeates the corporate communications ether.

Communicating both the required changes and the processes by which they will be achieved must be done in a manner that inspires and motivates people to follow. In scenario transfer, stakeholders are required to assess their current strategies, plans and products against the scenarios, and to tailor their future actions or response strategies accordingly. As such, scenarios must be plausible, consistent and offer insights into the future that are useful for decision making.

Hence, given the potential for stories to trigger or block action, it is vital to embolden the change process with powerful stories that compel change in the organization. This is why we need to **storify** our scenarios.

Why do stories help people to manage change?

"The universe is made of stories, not of atoms." – Muriel Rukeyser

It is often said that life happens in the narratives we tell one another and ourselves. Stories inspire us to take action, allow us to share and embed values, and to connect with a purpose or vision. Stories help us persuade. Stories are more memorable than facts and figures. Savvy leaders tell stories to inspire and motivate us – think of the election advert or political stump speech. Stories help to facilitate conversation. Stories increase clarity by defining who, what, how, where, when and why of a process or project. Stories can help define the value we seek to create by emphasizing what's really important and describing the level of effort involved in the change. Stories help people connect.

Think about the impact of the 30 second stories that permeate much of today's culture globally, the advertisement. Research shows that regardless of the content of an ad, the structure of that content predicted its success. The most popular ads tell a more complete story using Freytag's Pyramid.[416] The key elements being an exposition defining the story world including characters, plot action including rising action, the climax, falling action, and a dénouement (or final outcome). This dramatic structure can be traced back to Aristotle. Shakespeare mastered this structure, arranging his plays in five acts. While we use science and data to help us make the right decisions, some of the best business books and speakers use stories to help us act on the decisions we need to make.

Our brains are hard wired for stories. Stories trigger emotional response, and emotions – not logic – drive most consumer behavior. When you share facts and statistics with your audience, they are either going to agree or disagree with you. Research shows that facts and figures activate two regions of the brain called Broca's area[417] and Wernicke's area[418]. These are the language processing parts of the brain, where we decode words into meaning. On the other hand, when we are being told a story, in addition to the language processing parts, other brain areas that we would use when experiencing the events of the story are activated. In total, up to seven areas can be activated. If someone tells us about delicious foods, our sensory cortex lights up; talk about motion and our motor cortex gets triggered; or experience a beautiful piece of art and our visual cortex is stimulated. When we tell stories to others that have helped us shape our thinking and way of life, we can have the same effect on them too.

We make up stories in our heads for every action and conversation. Whenever we hear a story, we search for and relate it to a similar experience – synchronizing the brains of the person telling a story and the person listening. Research conducted at Yale demonstrated that when a speaker had activity in her insula, an emotional brain region, listeners did too; and when her frontal cortex lit up, so did theirs.[419] If you want someone to change a behavior then model it with a story. The character in the story should go through the transformation that you would like the reader to go through. Stories where individuals solve a problem can help persuade others that they can do the same. This is a reason why reality shows that aim to fix people are successful. Scenario transfer can be achieved when the stakeholders of a foresight exercise create the scenario narrative – its story world, characters, and plot action. The scenario narrative can live alongside the reality the organization experiences and can be changed when the situation changes.

Storifying your scenarios

"Each of us has the power to tap into our stories, our narrative assets, to become better communicators—to entertain, to share our history and culture, to spread knowledge, to persuade, to advance a cause, to teach, to dream a vision of the future." – International Storytelling Center

The three main parts, or elements, of a story are:

- The setting or story world (when and where a story takes place).
- The characters (the people, person, animal, machine, company, city, country —a story is about).
- The plot (what happens in a story or sequence of events).

The plot usually involves a problem or a conflict that must be resolved and moves from exposition to conflict then climax and resolution. The resolution is how the problem is solved. A good story needs conflict and resolution. The well-defined character or protagonist encounters some kind of trouble (conflict). The conflict could come from nature, another person, or even some flaw in the main character. The action taken signifies growth and change; and finally, some sort of redemption. The audience is enthralled as they crave knowing what's next. A good story creates vivid pictures, causing listeners to imagine their own images and their related experiences as the story unfolds. A good story is one that touches people in some way – making the listener laugh, cry, think, and ponder it long afterwards. A good story has substance, that is to say, direction and purpose.

Amanda Marko author and consultant, proposes four storytelling frameworks that may help us lead change:[420]

- The Connection story overcomes natural skepticism by letting people know that you are like them.
- The Influence story helps to change someone's mind.
- The Success story creates a more personal and memorable version of a case study.
- The Clarity story is an organizational narrative or strategic story.

To storify your scenario, decide which framework will suit the change management process at hand, and aim for specificity. That is, pick one thing to focus on and explore it in depth rather than trying to cover all aspects of your subject, whether that is a business process, outcome, or system functionality. To storify the scenario consider the setting. Where is it? When is it? What are the social conditions? What special details make the setting vivid? Consider the characterization. What does the character think, say or do? How does the character behave towards others? How do others behave toward the character? What does the character care about?

To storify your scenario, get your stakeholders involved. Trigger the story formation by having a leader do something remarkable that inspires people in the organization to recount what happened. Stakeholders can be asked to defend and describe the current strategy as well as products, services, channels, and brands in the scenarios presented. Wildcards can be integrated as conflicts to inform the story evolution. Use theater games to open creative conversations in which participants take on the personas of future consumers, producers, or clients. Old company myths can be re-purposed as a setting and exposition against which new actions (corporate initiatives and future projects) are described as protagonists.

Potential consequences and responses can be described as twists and turns and finally the resolution will be the successful accomplishment of the preferred future. Use technology to facilitate the creation of mockups of blogs, websites, e-magazines or e-newspapers that broadcast your stories. Use live stage performances and video blogging to act out scenarios. Storifying will transform the typical flatland scenarios into richer, deeper perspectives of the future that in turn evoke the emotions critical for a successful change making process.

In the emerging future, I believe the business leaders who produce the best results will be those who practice **Influence Leadership**. The future is flat and connected. Organizations are changing quickly. Structures are flatter and reporting lines more complex. Staff and customers are global. And the noise of information is deafening. The challenge of managing rapid change requires that leaders become accomplished at communicating strategic goals and visions in a way that influences and persuades.

Sharing stories whether in print, video or verbally is a powerful way of creating enduring influence. When we tell stories, people get what we are saying, and they remember it. The ultimate goal of successful change management is to change policies, services, products, and behaviors to ensure effective and efficient buy-in to a desired future. Through a strategic foresight scenario process that creates and shares powerful storified scenarios, we will engage one of the most powerful techniques we have as humans to communicate and motivate others to change.

The end.

Here are three questions business could pose about storytelling and change:

- *What opportunities are emerging to use scenario planning to help anticipate the future in this complex, dynamic, unpredictable business environment?*
- *Where can you use storytelling to help inspire and engage your team to embrace change?*
- *How can you design your organization to increase flexibility and adaptability and enhance the process of managing change?*

Is the Future of Design Thinking in the Future of Business Foresight?

By Jim Burke

What is Design Thinking and how will organizations combine it with foresight to map better plans for the future?

Introduction

Design Thinking (DT) is now a tested tool for use alongside foresight processes. It provides a thorough and insightful way to create studies and stories of the future that efficiently reveal the wants and needs of colleagues, customers, and other key stakeholders. It can point to future solutions more effectively than many other approaches. This chapter introduces business managers and leaders to the concepts of DT and the ways in which it can be used to complement corporate foresight activities.

Origins and growth

DT practice has its roots in the late 1960s, was refined in the 1980s and 90s at Stanford University, and found a prominent business role after David M. Kelley and Bill Moggridge started IDEO in 1991 as a design-thinking studio.[421] DT has recently been gaining more traction in businesses, non-profits, and government agencies because it allows business leaders to generate insights into human-centered problems quickly. With those perceptions, organizations can better craft initial solutions or prototypes that are more easily created, tested, refined, and produced. In this article, I focus on describing ways of using DT to create stories or scenarios of the future.

Foresight and design thinking

DT engages people to answer three fundamental questions that touch on the goals and challenges of organizational development and business growth:

- What is desirable? (human perspective)
- What is feasible? (technical viewpoint)
- What is viable? (business reality)[422]

Figure 1 reflects a summary of the ways that foresight and DT can combine to provide a flexible tool for business analysis and planning:

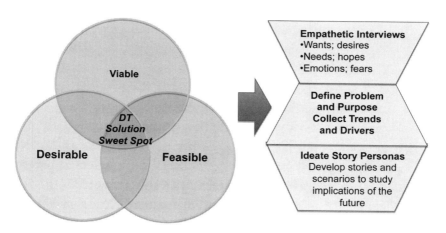

FIGURE 1: Applying Design Thinking and foresight to develop refined stories of the future

There are six key stages in an integrated DT and foresight approach:

- Empathetic interviewing and listening
- Defining the problem or purpose
- Collecting Trends and Drivers
- Ideation of Personas
- Prototyping Scenarios
- Testing

These are described in more detail below.

Empathetic interviewing and listening

At its heart, DT is human-centered, with the first step being **Empathetic Interviewing and Listening** to pay attention to the feelings and emotions of key stakeholders. The aim is to probe to understand the real underlying problems before creating assumptions or gathering foresight artifacts (for example, trends and forecasts) about products or services. Empathy helps us dive deeper into a client's desires when looking into the future. The process must start with a clear understanding of purpose – the initial, top-level rationale for a futures study needs to be clear and can vary for example:

- Compete effectively
- Drive innovation
- Understand R&D options, or
- Clarify industry turbulence to prevent surprises.

This rationale offers a good starting point that DT-oriented practitioners can use to draw out personal stories and needs from the key stakeholders. Diving deep to hear and understand critical needs can help with the process of prototype creation and building snap-shots of potential customers through people-centered stories and scenarios.

Empathetic survey questions

Key to the success of empathetic interviewing is the use of short, open questions which cannot be answered with a simple yes or no. Typical examples of empathetic questions one might ask in such an interview would include:

- Tell me about the ways you see yourself in the future and what your needs might be in that future?
- What did you do with those thoughts and insights?
- Tell me about the last time you were surprised by a product or service? What made it surprising?

Of particular value is here is the **five whys approach** of repeatedly asking Why? Why? Why? Why? Why? to drill down on a topic to get to the root cause or desire that underlies an issue or goal. Probing like this offers unique insights and can generate surprising new awareness for the interviewee. The interviewer should practice listening attentively, not arguing, accepting silence while the interviewee thinks, capturing everything (often by both an interviewer and a separate recorder), and promising anonymity.

Clarifying the problem in the definition phase

The results of empathetic interviewing provide the foundation for the **Definition** step in the DT process — defining the problem or goal. In one case, an organization realized that the real reason they wanted to explore the future was not to look at emerging social trends, but to respond to rumors of an impending market development that would eliminate their independence and value. That concern led to a foresight study that revealed how future technologies would lead to customers demanding more sophisticated services and increased independence to help them better collaborate with industry and government.

The **Definition** phase also guides the planner's foresight process and reduces the risk of producing a vague look at the future that is entertaining but not actionable. Defining a good problem statement lays a foundation for creating solution ideas and, in the case of foresight, helps frame and study a specific futures problem. The frame is of particular importance. The business planner may want to expand and even change a sponsor's or colleague's perspectives, enlarging the frame to tap into different viewpoints that deliver new interpretations of experiences and information.[423]

Think wide, think narrow, and don't forget the trends

By now you have probably noticed that DT switches between wide and narrow views. Empathetic interviewing opens up the dialogue and narrative space; the next stage of defining the problem narrows and focuses; the fourth phase, **Ideation**, opens it up again. Foresight tools and processes can play a valuable complementary role in bridging the gap between defining the problem and ideation.

Before ideation, those involved need to better **understand the driving forces and trends** that will carry the business into the future. This need for understanding usually results in an environmental scan, using futurist tools to collect and identify ongoing, emerging, and marginal **future factors** – for example trends, forces, developments and ideas. The outputs are typically presented using some form of analytical categorization framework such as STEEPLE to bucket the information gathered:

- Socio-demographic
- Technological and scientific
- Economic
- Energy and environmental
- Political
- Legal and regulatory, and
- Ethical

To help makes sense of these diverse future factors, the interactions and dependencies are often explored using some form of systems map or model. Whilst we cannot go into detail here, such systems thinking typically involves capturing key elements of the system from different perspectives (e.g. personal, business, industry, culture), identifying key influences and stakeholders, and incorporating the future factors affecting the system.[424]

Creating new ideas

Armed with this material, we are ready for the Ideation stage. DT guides us towards an initial answer — often a product or a service — and the foresight results are intended to spark solutions, not the end outcome. Futures ideation at this juncture could include forecasts, but it may be premature. Consider instead creating stories of the future using DT to craft scenarios from different viewpoints. We talked earlier of using a range of perspectives, from personal to cultural, to guide trends collection, and DT offers another complementary tool – personas.

Bringing your stakeholders to life

A persona is an analytical tool that puts a human face on the key actors in a story or scenario. Effective personas allow product and service developers to better understand a segment of their customer base by building a snapshot of the person, starting with a name (complete, not generic, i.e., not Mary Smith, but Xia Mu Rong or Stephanie Randolph). The aim is to draw on the empathetic interviews to iden-tify their uniqueness, differentiating qualities, occupation, goals, and attitudes toward life. To emphasize their humanness, the persona may be quoted, for example, "I want to be able to travel to and from my job in comfort and speed."

A regional bank in U.S. Northern Virginia has an innovation center that capitalizes on visuals to create a sense of relationship with personas. A center visitor sees persona descriptions liberally sprinkled throughout the workspaces, some with snapshots of the character mounted on posters, others life-sized with the persona seeming to invite a conversation about who they are and what they want. The realism helps designers get a much better sense of customer needs.

We can use this tool in different ways — for example to create a set of four or five (not more) personas. The aim is to explore how custom-ers and colleagues might live in a future story or scenario, which may have been built separately. Persona development adds details about specific activities to build a human sense of the future. Another approach builds the scenario around the persona. For example, if the persona is an energy engineer, the scenario looks at a story about that career in 2030 in the context of the business in question. If the persona enjoys sports and outdoor action, we might create a scenario about the persona playing games in 2025.

Creativity

A variety of DT tools can be used at the **Ideation** stage to help create personas and scenarios. For example, brainstorming is particularly effective for identifying ideas, insights, and story characteristics quickly. Recently, some creativity experts have criticized brainstorming[425]. To be sure, unstructured brainstorming, where participants are tasked to create ideas about something general (for example, what is the future of transportation?) can create far fewer useful ideas, especially when the group facilitation is unguided and undisciplined. In those cases, an expert or the loudest voice in the room can often dominate.

It is far more effective to prepare the group for brainstorming by selecting a varied group of participants (keep the size from six to eight participants) and presenting them with a specific question, even going back to the **Define** step to do that. To help put participants in the right mindset it can be useful to share the results of the analyses of trends and drivers. It is also useful to warm the group up through short mental workouts that help flex their creativity muscles. An Internet search on creativity warm-up exercises will provide a rich variety of example approaches. Brainstorming is intended to create with a focus on quantity — filtering will come later and leaders should discourage criticism by using improvisation techniques. When a team member starts to criticize, suggest the person use the improv technique of **yes-and**, rather than **yes-but**. The person who downgrades the idea of using a smartphone to create architectural designs ('yes, but it is too small') is motivated to say: "Yes and it could wirelessly connect to a 3D printer to see the architectural idea quickly and in 3D."

Initial scenario solutions

After generating ideas for scenarios, the group moves into the

Prototyping stage, combining thoughts and insights to build a scenario that offers a more coherent view of the future. The goal of this step is to make something tangible that people can interact with or use to understand how the future might unfold. So the prototype could be as simple as grouping post-it notes to combine ideas into scenario themes. One way is to group them by STEEPLE category; another is to pull the ideas together by major drivers, like energy costs or demographics. The aim is to help those involved to see emerging stories. Details can be specific or metaphorical. I've seen organizations use Lego to represent trends data and create prototypes. Rudimentary storyboards with stick-figure cartoons representing scenarios are useful and the ease of making cell phone videos allows participants to **live out the future**.

Improvising the future

Taking another page from improvisation, a colleague and I used improv techniques to present trends to a group of 100 people. The participants were divided into groups of six to eight, asked to choose their favorites trends and then act out how they might develop in the future. It was crude, quick, and dirty, and it gave the players a way to experience and react to the future in a unique way.

Improvisation starts to touch the last step of DT: **Testing**. This calls for the organization to be willing to engage before the scenario is perfect and be eager to start understanding it, even if it is a rough approximation of the final delivery. A word of caution, a favorite DT saying is: "Fail early, fail often, fail cheaply." You will almost certainly have something in your prototype story that will fail in the first iteration for example:

- The story does not resonate,
- You leave out an area critical to the customer, or
- Your time frame is too far out or far too close.

That is why you create a prototype. If you do not, you may fall prey to insidious emotion – falling in love with your idea and being blinded to its shortcomings. Apply the **yes, and** approach, accept the failure, learn the lesson, apply the insights, and create again.

DT calls for a different relationship amongst the participants and sponsors, moving from passive report delivery to active co-creation – this is one of DT's major benefits. In addition to offering creative ways to build innovative products or services, DT offers the potential to transform hierarchical relationships between managers and staff into one of more collaborative creation. The increased level of shared ownership and co-creation affects scenario building and, more importantly, the process of identifying action implications. Finally, applying DT to design actionable suggestions offers ways to reveal new measures of effectiveness and can lead to more refined recommendations.

Where are DT and foresight going?

DT is in a growth phase, being used by increasing numbers of organizations and their consultants, design agencies, and marketing partners – and being applied to more projects. As DT continues to grow in popularity and utility, it will become more important for professional managers to understand and integrate DT techniques and processes into their foresight and forecasting activities. We can expect DT to introduce new tools and techniques for the foresight-oriented business leader who will find better ways to enable colleagues and other key stakeholders to understand themselves, customers, and their collective futures in a more effective manner.

Summary

Combining DT and business foresight offers a relatively young and emerging framework. However, the results to date suggest that integrating traditional futures techniques with complementary, creative DT provides more fidelity in understanding the needs and desires of an organization, its customers, and its stakeholders. The integration of DT and foresight can lead to the crafting of more feasible solutions, and to the design and development of more viable business products, services, and models.

Here are three practical questions:

- *Which areas of your strategic development could benefit most from integrating DT and foresight – for example exploring product and service development opportunities; addressing competitive pressures; understanding new models of organization and management; responding to disruptive market developments?*
- *In creating stories of the future, how can managers include a balance between scenarios that include incremental growth and those focused on radical transformation?*
- *What challenges could you face in trying to adopt a DT approach and techniques such as empathetic interviews, and how can these be overcome?*

Section 9

Framing the Future – How should organizations look at the future?

Living with organizational transformation

How can we frame the future in a manner that helps the organization embrace and explore the unknown? The prospect of uncertainty and complex change can cause anxiety amongst investors, organizational leaders and the work-force at large. Foresight is not intended to deliver hard forecasts – its true value is to help us consider a range of plausible future possibilities or scenarios. Hence it provides ways of thinking and tools for lifting the lid on a range of possible outcomes in the future. This allows organizations the opportunity to make informed choices about the change required to meet the challenge of taking opportunities and address the emerging and anticipated risks.

In this section we focus on the challenges of helping an organization developing a future-oriented mindset. The authors emphasize the development of foresight capability as a critical leadership and managerial competence, reflect on the pace and scale of technology driven change, and look at ways of framing challenges and future goals.

What Works in Transforming Organizations and Institutions? *(page 510)* – Professor Sohail Inayatullah at the Graduate Institute of Futures Studies, Tamkang University, Taiwan and Director of meta-future.org, identifies some critical insights, and sets out principles for how we can use foresight and a learning journey approach to framing new strategies and driving organizational transformation.

Futures Thinking - A Critical Organizational Skill (page 516) – Hardin Tibbs, a highly experienced UK-based futurist, strategist, educator, and writer, highlights the importance of developing the critical future thinking skills that enable a organization to anticipate and adapt to change.

Critical Foresight Skills (page 521) – Dr. Peter Bishop was Director of the Foresight program at the University of Houston and is now the Executive Director of Teach the Future which helps educators teach foresight. He highlights how organizations can acquire the key foresight skills required to create new adaptive strategies and drive change in uncertain times.

Business Management in a Time of Change: The Importance of Futures Studies (page 537) – Professor Francisco Jose Martinez-Lopez from the University of Huelva, Spain, specializes in information technology and future studies, and Mercedes Garcia Ordaz is Associate Professor of the University of Huelva of the Department of Financial Economy, Accounting and Operations Management. They explore the critical importance of future studies and long term planning in an era of rapid change.

Is The Pace of Change Accelerating? (page 542) – Stephen Aguilar-Millan is a consulting futurist from the UK and Director of Research at the European Futures Observatory. He examines the potential for the pace of change to stop accelerating and examines the possible consequences.

The Outside Context Problem, A Concerned Observers Guide (page 546) – Benjamin Mottram – a UK-based future thinker and authority on crowd sourcing and gamification discusses how organizations can make sense of and address the unforeseen and complex problems that will be thrown up by a constantly changing operating environment over the next two decades.

Be There Now (page 551) – Paul Brooks, a Hawaii-based researcher on social and economic emergence, stresses the importance of openness, dynamism and scalability in helping a business prepare for the future.

What Works in Transforming Organizations and Institutions?

By Sohail Inayatullah

How can futures thinking be of real use to organizations?

This chapter sets out some critical insights principles for how we can use foresight and a learning journey approach to framing new strategies and driving organizational transformation.

Unlocking the business value of foresight

For foresight to be useful to organizations, it must have three dimensions:

- First is that the journey is learning focused and not about particular forecasts.
- Second, for organizations to transform they must challenge their **used future** (the future that no longer works but, because of a previously held worldview-mindset, it continues to drive our assumptions and shape our perspective) and overturn the practices they employ that do not match their desired vision.
- Third, for a new organizational future to emerge successfully, it must have a supportive worldview and underlying narrative or metaphor.

The challenge for change agents in organizations and institutions is straddling the boundaries between a technical list of things to do, often immediately relevant, and the need for adaptive strategies. The latter requires both the skills to fix the current problems and the capacity to find tomorrow's opportunities. Doing the latter means that individuals within the organization confront what they don't know, otherwise anxiety and resistance to change can feel overwhelming and leave new strategies ineffective. As Peter Drucker is reported to have said the existing "culture eats strategy for breakfast".

Technical fixes to adaptive responses to transformative journeys

As a futurist having worked with hundreds of organizations over a thirty year time span, I have found that every intervention works best as a learning experience journey. I try and frame the workshop, the program, the course or series of interventions as a learning journey. Often in these journeys, the data becomes overwhelming, especially data about the future. It is contingent on multiple factors, many unknowns, so individuals are unable to learn. They give up or having seen previous failed interventions, become cynical.

As a way to assuage the cynics and to get some runs on the board, I move to **single loop learning** – the plan-budget-delegate-review cycle – focusing on specific technical fixes they can engage with on Monday morning and over the next six months. Possibility is restored since action has been purchased. However, the technical fix typically only works until there is an unexpected shock, for example a leader resigns, a board member challenges the overall strategy process, or the firm is hit by an external shock such as currency revaluation, a new technology, or a troubling geopolitical event. At this stage, what seemed so easy before, a simple "to do" list, now seems like a waste of time. "We had the perfect strategy for yesterday's future," commented one CEO.

Double loop learning is then required, wherein there is **learning about learning** – the development of futures literacy. It is not just that the product, process, or strategy is questioned, but that the future itself is questioned. It is not just that emerging issues and weak signals must be identified and alternative futures explored, but that the core narrative of the business needs to be unpacked.

In one instance, a steel maker had to reflect on whether they were still the **men of steel**. They now realized they were in fact a **leaky oil tanker** and needed to change their core story, undergo a transformation and become **Optimus Prime**.[426] They had to engage in new learning about the changing world economy and their story within it. It is this deeper level of foresight that moves organizations to make the transition from technical fixes to adaptive responses to transformative journeys. Foresight at its best does that.

Core principles of foresight driven transformation

Over the decades, I have found a few simple principles of futures thinking that help along this process.[427]

1. It's a learning journey – The first principle is to frame the journey as learning based. The short term financial and political output pressures are thus reduced, and with calm minds experiments can be conducted that optimize productivity.

2. Challenge the used future – The second principle is to challenge the **used future**. Every organization has particular practices that they engage in that do not reflect their preferred future. Indeed, they often run counter to the stated strategy. Police for example; drive their cars around wasting labor, energy, and having little or no impact on reducing crime or increasing safety. Education continues to be standardized with students sitting in rows. But once the used future is named, then alternatives can be created. With policing this means moving toward big data-oriented approaches: putting analysis, efforts, and forces where problems are, instead of promulgating the belief that being seen driving around a neighborhood leads to reduced crime. With education, this means redesigning classrooms so they are student-centered and technology enabled.

However, futures are used because they are held as true – not by reality – but by the prevailing worldviews of the sector, the organization, and those with influence and power. In policing, this has been the worldview of command and control, a visual show of strength. This may have worked over a hundred years ago, but with new types of crime, cyber for example, quick action – and indeed prevention – are far more important.

In education, the issue has been the deep worldview of the "school as factory". The factory model may have been useful over a hundred years ago – primarily to create loyal laborers – it is far less important in a knowledge economy where person-based critical learning is more important. The "weights of the past" often prevent the shift to a new future. These are twofold: first, memories of education ministries and the principles of how they learned; second, the fear among leaders that they will no longer be in charge. They fear that the new technologies will make them irrelevant. Central thus to national strategies to transform the factory model is to offer support to current leaders, boards, and CEOs and to find ways and spaces for them to contribute.

In interventions in education ministries in Australia and Malaysia for example, a key enabler was to re-skill current leaders in the new technologies and demonstrate that their lives would be easier if they moved from a story of **I am in charge** to **we are all learners**. This approach also seeks to demonstrate that the shift from the factory – as the underlying worldview – to the **playground** better positions the nation in a globalized knowledge economy. In addition, even in the terms of parents seeking scores, their students will do better since they are engaged – participating in the futures they seek to create.

3. Find the worldview and narrative – The third principle is finding the worldview and the metaphor underneath the used future, and finding a new cognitive pattern that supports the new story. In international policing this means shifting the story from the **thin blue line**[428] in which only police officers have the solution to policing. In its place we need the metaphor of the orchestra, where everyone contributes towards safety. Citizens, for example, can contribute through wiki-crime portals and community policing.

In one example an insurance company, after receiving presentations on changes in health,[429] realized the importance of diet, ageing, meditation, genomics, and geo-location and that health insurance was not their best long term strategy. They could have made a list of immediate actions they should pursue to optimize profits in their current business model. Instead, they decided to move towards a new narrative. They chose to move from insuring against sickness to becoming a health knowledge navigator and creating the **healthier you**. As a result, their overall story started to shift and they saw themselves as now co-creating health with their customers, instead of waiting for disease and paying for illness. They then shifted the underlying strategy. This involved lobbying government to make supportive legislative changes and hiring different types of people; those who understood prevention and knowledge navigation. The new story supported the new strategy.

Conclusions – foresight driven transformation as a learning journey

Thus, in conducting foresight that is effective, it is first important to frame the experience as a learning journey. There are four levels to this journey:

- Zero loop where participants can't see a way forward and just give up.
- Single loop where they seek to eliminate uncertainty immediately by having a list of actionable strategies.
- Double loop learning where when confronted with the unknown, they venture towards creating a learning organization that has the capacity to adapt.
- Narrative foresight; the search for new stories that better enable and support the organization's new realities.

Second, it is important to challenge the used future. This is the future that no longer works but because of a previously held worldview-mindset, we continue its practice. Once the used future is challenged, new futures can emerge.

Third, a new future can successfully emerge if and when there is a supporting worldview and guiding narrative or metaphor. Otherwise, it is too easy to return to what no longer works, to what is comfortable, and which our thinking supports. This is the old pattern, our old habits and the financial systems that support them. Culture thus can work with strategy instead of "eating strategy for breakfast".

So what questions might we pose for business?

- *What is the **used future** in your organization?*
- *What worldviews and narratives support the continuation of that used future?*
- *What are some alternative worldviews and stories that could help enable a new future?*

Futures Thinking – A Critical Organizational Skill

By Hardin Tibbs

What do organizations need from the skill of futures thinking? Knowledge of the future? Or do they just need to know when and how to adapt to possible future change?

The key features of successful futures thinking

This chapter reviews the basic objective of futures thinking and shows how its key principles can be derived from the tension between limits to our knowledge of the future, and the imperative that every organization has to adapt to change.

Knowledge of the future is a problematic objective

Many existing futures research methods were developed with the aim of gaining knowledge about the future. Creating knowledge looks like an appropriate objective because it follows the typical pattern of academic disciplines. Unfortunately, when the notion of knowledge is applied to the future it throws up unexpected paradoxes.

What exists in the present – for us to observe and research – is change, from which we make inferences about the future. This appears similar to hypothesis formulation in scientific research. But the model of hypothesis followed by empirical testing does not work for futures thinking. By the time the future happens and either confirms or falsifies the hypothesis, the knowledge obtained is no longer directly useful. It is no longer knowledge about the future but about the present.

Not only that, but one of the basic tenets of futures research is that we cannot know the future with certainty. Sometimes this is expressed as an aphorism: **there are no facts about the future**. If this is taken seriously, it means the knowledge creation goal is misguided, despite the focus of many futures methods. Picking the standard academic objective has wrong-footed futures research.

The limits of prediction

It is often asserted that the hard sciences are useful because they can make predictions, just as Newtonian physics predicts eclipses. But these are all in principle predictions about isolated sub-systems of reality, with simplifying assumptions made about other aspects of reality – mainly that nothing unexpected will intrude from the larger system. Predicting **the actual future** implies being able to know the future of reality as a whole, without any convenient simplifying assumptions and no field of science is able to do this.

Prediction technologies, for example ones based on big data, suffer from the same limitation. We can expect rapid improvements as computer intelligence increases and the volume of data builds. Increasingly accurate predictions will be possible in operational situations where the behavior of the system is well known and external disruptions can be safely ignored. Such predictions will however, prove dangerously misleading in longer-term and more open-ended situations involving strategic uncertainty that has not been encountered before. In other words prediction technologies will be very useful for operational management, proving better than older prediction-focused futures research methods. They will be much less useful for strategic leadership however, and as a result the uniquely human skill of futures thinking is set to play a growing role in strategy, particularly in this period of rising volatility and uncertainty.

Adapting to environmental change

Futures thinking as a skill set is focused on addressing the adaptive needs of organizations rather than acquiring objective knowledge about the future. To see what this means, consider an ecological analogy. An organization is like an organism that occupies a particular environmental niche to which it is well adapted. Its routine activity in this niche corresponds to operational management. If the environment changes significantly, the organism will no longer fit and must adapt and evolve in order to survive. For an organization, this is equivalent to change in its external environment that demands strategic rethinking.

The purpose of futures thinking is to detect weak signals that foreshadow loss of fit with the strategic environment and to prompt a process of adaptive self-change in response. The distinction here is between normal operational variability which management agility can handle and strategic shifts which require the organization to rethink itself – in the extreme by reinventing its identity.

Three methodological principles emerge from this:

- First, the research focus must be on what is changing in the present and on insight into the structure of the strategic situation. Note that the ability to recognize change in the present depends in part on knowledge of the past, simply because change requires the passage of time to become visible.
- The second principle is that a representation of the new change dynamics and their future implications must be integrated into the mental models of the decision makers, to enable action.
- The third is that the payoff is not going to be definite knowledge about the future, but about how to respond effectively to the change. The future is mainly being used as an exploration space for projecting possible outcomes based on signals of change and what is known about the structure of the system.

The first principle involves facing the present as an open-ended strategic system. The entire present situation will never be known with certainty – not only because research budgets are limited. In principle the range of factors involved and the rate of change means that it is impossible to have a complete and accurate picture. Instead, a search for informed insights is needed. For this reason much of the research will be indirect and will focus on understanding the perceptions, perspectives, and mental models of a diversity of knowledgeable industry participants and observers.

Three key activities

From all this we can conclude what successful futures thinking looks like in practice – a conclusion borne out by the author's futures consulting experience starting in the early 1990s at Global Business Network (GBN) in California. In simple terms there are three key futures activities that need to be adopted as cultural skills by the organization and acquired as personal skills by the senior leadership:

- First, there is the practice of observing change in the strategic environment, which calls for methods similar to the ethnographic research used in anthropology.
- Second is the practice of sense-making to interpret the change and derive implications about the future. This ensures that management's **action frame** is kept up to date.
- Third is the creation of adaptive and advantage-seeking responses, an activity similar to design thinking.

These three activities are not a futures research method as such, because the second activity itself will typically make use of a futures method, for example scenario development. Rather these three are the methodology – using the term in its accurate sense – of futures thinking seen as a vital cultural practice every organization needs for its survival.

Here are three questions with which to test your organization's future fitness:

- *What must be true about the future for your existing strategy to work?*
- *Are there any hints that the future might be different from this?*
- *How might your strategy need to change to take account of emerging and potential changes in your environment?*

Critical Foresight Skills

By Peter Bishop

What are the critical capabilities that businesses need in order to do good foresight work and how can they acquire those skills?

Tooling up for change

Strategic foresight is becoming common, if not routine, in many large enterprises and it is expected to grow even further as the rate of change continues to increase. Nevertheless, it is still relatively new as a function in most organizations. Hence it is necessary to identify the key skills of a foresight professional and how one might obtain those skills in the world today. This chapter explores both the nature of those skills required and how they can be acquired.

Background: the need for foresight

People have been interested in the future for millennia, but it was not until the 1950s and 60s that the techniques of traditional forecasting and planning were developed and implemented. Forecasts were made using the extrapolation of historical trends and plans were made based on those extrapolations. Traditional forecasters assumed that the drivers of change were relatively well-known and fairly predictable. Planners assumed that one's actions would have relatively predictable effects. Forecasts and plans are now the stock and trade for hundreds of thousands of professionals and organizations. Their success has even penetrated modern culture which still believes that the most likely future will occur and that organizations can influence the future in predictable ways.

Traditional forecasting and planning worked well in quieter more stable times but now one cannot make those assumptions as easily. Surprising developments occur all the time and actions often have unintended consequences. The world therefore needs a new approach to the future, not to replace traditional forecasting and planning, but to complement it when the uncertainties inherent in the future can no longer be assumed away.

As a result, strategic foresight is fast becoming routine in business, in government, and in civil society. The reasons for its rise are fairly simple. New, almost instantaneous communication technologies are driving ideas together, producing innovations, and disseminating those innovations to every corner of the globe at the speed of light. The result is an increasing rate of change and an unprecedented complexity of issues. People in previous generations, mostly since the dawn of the industrial age, have felt much the same way. They were subjected to increasing rates of change that were also driven by the communication technologies of their day—pamphlets, newspapers, telegraphs, telephones, radios, and television. New transportation technologies such as the sailing ship, the railroad, the steamship, the automobile, and jetliners also transported people and their ideas to previously unreachable lands. While transportation technology today is relatively mature, communication technology (the computer, the PC, the Internet, and now mobile computing) is advancing at breakneck speed.

There is little left untouched by this communication revolution, least of all how we deal with the future. In more placid times, it was sufficient to wait for change to occur before having to respond to it. In fact, it was prudent to wait until one was sure about a change before responding. It was like planning for conventional warfare compared to nuclear war. While a level of military readiness is always required, planning the actual campaign could wait until it was clear who the adversary was and where the battle would take place. It took time to move men and materiel into place, time that could be used for planning.

Nuclear war, on the other hand, would take place in hours, not months or years. Planning time was over once the missiles were launched. It is no coincidence, therefore, that practicing how a nuclear exchange could go was a special priority within the Pentagon in the 1950s. Enter Herman Kahn, a major figure in the RAND Corporation at the time, who is considered one of the founders of a technique known as scenario development. The scenarios were not predictions; they were explorations of the uncertainties of nuclear war. The speed of change was also driving the need for this new approach, one that took the inherent uncertainty of the future into account.

As a result, foresight, as it has matured from the late 1980s to today, is essentially a means to anticipate and influence changes that used to be over the horizon, and therefore of little concern to forecasters and planners. Those changes are now on the horizon, if not closer. So scenarios take the place of single-value predictions and transformations take the place of incremental goals when the present no longer lasts as long as it once did.

Critical foresight capabilities

With Andy Hines, I published a taxonomy of foresight capabilities in our book *Thinking about the Future: Guidelines for Strategic Foresight*.[430] We had asked our colleagues in the Association of Professional Futurists to share useful tips and techniques from their practice of strategic foresight. We received hundreds of replies and selected approximately 150 instances which we grouped into six activity categories:

- *Framing* – Initiating a project by selecting a domain, goal, and problem to address and identifying the objectives, scope, deliverables, resources, and schedule.
- *Scanning* – Collecting information about the future of the domain.
- *Forecasting* – Developing the expected (baseline) and alternative scenarios based on the information collected.

- *Visioning* – Articulating the preferred future in the form of a vision statement and long-term goals.
- *Planning* – Identifying and coordinating resources to move toward the vision and achieve the goals in the form of long-term strategies and short-term initiatives.
- *Acting* – Implementing the plan to create change.

Futurist Terry Grim used this framework to develop a more detailed list of foresight capabilities.[431] She applied a **software maturity model** approach to foresight. Maturity models were developed in the 1980s by the Software Engineering Institute at Carnegie Mellon University at the request of the U.S. Department of Defense (DoD). At the time, the Department was buying a lot of software but much of it did not meet requirements, or it was late or over budget. Rather than assess the products, however, they developed a mechanism for assessing the processes that the software development firms used to develop the products. The DoD's reasoning was that firms that had better processes would produce better products than firms that had poor processes. The approach of the maturity model transformed the contracting process for software development within the U.S. Federal government since only firms that are rated as capable (the third level on a five-level system) can bid on contracts. It has also been applied within IBM to teach and assess the strategy development processes within business units. So Grim's Foresight Maturity Model lists the skills necessary for the practice of foresight within organizations, one of the purposes of this chapter.

Grim used a literature review to develop a list of the processes to be assessed. She used the same six-part set of processes, called disciplines, from Hines & Bishop above. Each discipline contains three to five practices and each practice is conducted at one of five levels of maturity.

Rohrbeck also used a maturity model in his extensive study on the skills necessary for successful foresight.[432] Based on a literature review, workshops, and over 100 interviews, he identified 20 dimensions of foresight in five categories; information usage, method sophistication, people and networks, organization, and culture. Not all of Rohrbeck's 20 characteristics are technically capabilities, but they are listed in Appendix II.

Rohrbeck does focus more on some capabilities than on others. Before that, he identifies two conclusions from his research on the value of corporate foresight:

- Large incumbent companies tend to be ignorant and slow to respond to discontinuous change.
- Companies need specific systems to detect and manage discontinuous change.

So should an organization be motivated to address these concerns, the following can be used to define guidelines for the design and successful implementation of corporate foresight systems. Four of the guidelines concern the critical capabilities that an organization needs to maintain a successful foresight practice:

- Interpretation of future-related information by top management.
- Information gathering by boundary spanners.
- Dissemination of foresight insights by participation and multi-level communications.
- Use of qualitative data to make participation easier and ensure the use and impact of foresight insights.

Acquiring critical capabilities

The second question then is how one acquires these new foresight skills. Fortunately, education and training in these capabilities have been growing since the mid-70s when Jim Dator founded the Hawaii Research Center for Futures Studies at the University of Hawaii at Manoa, and Jib Fowles and Chris Dede established the Master's degree in Studies of the Future at the University of Houston-Clear Lake. There are now approximately two dozen graduate programs in foresight around the world today. A list of such programs can be found here http://www.accelerating.org.[433]

Certificated corporate training programs have also grown apace. Technology Futures Inc. offers the longest running training program in the U.S., focusing on technological forecasting. The Global Business Network conducted very popular (and very expensive) training programs in its day. The University of Manchester has consistently offered high quality seminars on foresight since 1999. Today there are several such certificated programs offered every year – some of which are listed in Appendix III.

Conclusion – Still more to do

So we have a good idea of critical foresight capabilities from the likes of Grim and Rohrbeck and of the certificate and degree programs where one can learn about those capabilities. Are we done? Is there any group who should know about foresight that is not being taught today? Absolutely, there is – the students of our time! We teach a great deal about the past, which we should, but almost nothing about the future. Should they have to wait to learn foresight as an adult? Shouldn't we be preparing them for their future just as we do the adults? The lack of foresight education might have been understandable and even excusable when teaching foresight was new and immature. But we now have 50 years of experience teaching foresight in universities and in corporate training programs. We should offer that instruction to the students of the world as well.

We need to encourage and support teachers and administrators to introduce futures thinking into their classes and schools at all levels. Foresight will only become routine when today's students become the adults of the future, realizing that, of course every person and every organization needs to be able to anticipate and influence change in the future.

Closing Questions:

- *What is your organization doing to develop foresight capabilities – how are the training approaches and capabilities being assessed?*

- *How are management and leadership development programs being updated to include foresight tools and techniques?*
- *What role should businesses play in ensuring that foresight is being taught in schools, colleges and universities to help prepare students for the future?*

Appendix I

Foresight Maturity Model, Terry Grim (2009)

The Foresight Maturity Model[2] lists 25 Practices (processes, capabilities) within six disciplines.

Organizational Disciplines – Concerning the operation of the foresight unit within the enterprise

Leadership: Clear ownership and active leadership to implement and institutionalize foresight capability.

- Engage people in conscious and thoughtful actions to proactively create the future they have chosen.
- Create an environment that provides timely anticipation of change, embracing positive changes and responding creatively to negative changes.
- Communicate clearly the goals, results, and implications of foresight activities.
- Create an environment and processes that drive foresight knowledge into action.
- Recognize the cultural artifacts and mental models operating in the organization and how they influence organizational decisions.

Planning: Ensuring that the plans, people, skills, and processes support the organizational vision.

- Identify the implications and consequences of alternative futures and actions.
- Explore a variety of potential strategies and options.
- Choose and refine a strategy that optimizes progress toward the organizational vision.
- Develop a plan to address the activities, processes, talent, and communications required to achieve the strategy.

Framing: Establishing the boundaries and scope of the endeavor.

- Identify the root problems and true issues driving the project, reconciling with those that have been explicitly stated.
- Set measurable and documented objectives which have the agreement of stakeholders.
- Track progress toward objectives and reframe root problems and issues against progress and changes external to the endeavor.

Functional Disciplines – Concerning the products that the foresight unit provides the rest of the enterprise.

Scanning: Collection of appropriate and relevant information in a format and timeframe that supports useful retrieval.

- Map the domain of the system into a framework of areas to explore.
- Continue to collect pertinent information from a range of diffuse and credible sources.
- Identify outliers or **outside the system** signals of change that provide insight to possible changes which can impact the system.
- Integrate external and internal information into a common

framework and language.
- Create a useful and accessible information repository.

Forecasting: Description of long-term outcomes that contrast with the present to enable better decision-making.

- Acquire insight into emerging ideas or themes with the aggregation of information into categorized clusters.
- Consider the widest possible set of plausible alternatives in evaluating choices or decisions affecting the system.
- Distill and detail plausible alternative futures into the operating set for consideration.
- Validate foresight with an integrative view of prioritized alternatives.

Visioning: Creation of a preferred future that imaginatively captures values and ideals.

- Elicit and incorporate goals, values, and aspirations of stakeholders.
- Surface the underlying assumptions, espoused beliefs and values, and operational artifacts which establish the culture.
- Articulate the unique contribution that frames the organization's view moving forward.
- Craft the vision in a manner that is both inspirational and motivational, resonating with the hearts and minds of those who will follow it.

Appendix II
Corporate Foresight, Rene
Rohrbeck (2011)

Tables 1 and 2 contain 20 characteristics within five dimensions of an organization's foresight capability that Rohrbeck[3] identified. Some of these characteristics are purely descriptive, such as Mode (top-down versus bottom up and continuous versus project-based). Some are evaluative, such as Reach, Scope, and Time Horizon, where more is better although those can be taken to an extreme so a level appropriate to the organization and its problems is best. (See Match with Context and Match with Problem.)

TABLE 1 – Core Dimensions of Foresight Capability – Information, Methods, People and Networks

Information Usage	
Reach	Describes how deeply a company scans; current business, adjacent business, and white spaces.
Scope	Describes how broadly a company scans (technology, sociocultural, customer, competitors, and political environment).
Time horizon	Describes the time horizons of foresight activities (ranging from the near future to 30 years into the future).
Method Sophistication	
Sources	Describes the sources of information; differentiated into internal vs. external, formal vs. informal.
Match with Context	Describes how deliberately the method is chosen, given a certain context.
Match with Problem	Describes how deliberately the method is chosen, given a certain problem.
Integration Capacity	Describes the usefulness of a method portfolio for integrating various types of information.
Communicative Capacity	Describes the usefulness of a method portfolio for communicating insights internally and externally.
People and Networks	
Characteristics of Foresighters	Describes the degree to which characteristics of the foresighters meet the ideal characteristics. (Ideal characteristics are listed below.)
External network	Describes the extent and intensity of external ties.
Internal network	Describes the extent and intensity of internal ties.

TABLE 2 – Core Dimensions of Foresight Capability – Organization and Culture

Organization	
Mode	Describes the ways in which companies engage in foresight activities: top-down vs bottom-up and continuous vs project-based.
Integration with other processes	Describes the number of processes that are linked to the foresight activity.
Formal diffusion of Insights	Describes the role and effectiveness of formal communication to transfer future insights.
Accountability	Describes the extent to which employees are responsible for detecting and acting on weak signals.
Incentives	Describes whether rewards or bonuses are awarded to encourage future orientation and a wider vision.
Culture	
Willingness to share across functions	Describes the degree of openness and inclination to share information across functions.
Readiness to listen to scouts and external sources	Describes the openness and inclination to listen to external sources of information.
Informal diffusion of Insights	Describes the role and effectiveness of informal communication for the diffusion of future insights.
Attitude of the organization toward the periphery	Describes the level of curiosity of the top management toward the periphery.
Willingness to test and challenge basic assumptions	Describes the degree of willingness of executives to challenge underlying assumptions.

Ideal characteristics of foresighters:

- Deep knowledge in one domain, in order to understand how far a topic needs to be understood to come to conclusions.
- Broad knowledge, to quickly access new information domains and relate them to one another.
- Curiosity and receptiveness, to ensure the eagerness to capture external information.
- Open-mindedness and passion, to ensure that issues outside the dominant worldview of the company are considered and disseminated.
- Strong external networks, for ensuring access to high-quality information. Strong internal networks.

Appendix III
Foresight Certificate
Programs

Certificate in Strategic Foresight, University of Houston TX – *http://houstonfutures.org/certificates.html*

Corporate Foresight, European Business School, Frankfurt DE – http://*www.ebs.edu/downloadcenter.html?&no_cache=1&L=1&download_id=94*

Executive Education, Swinburne University, Melbourne AU – *http://www.swinburne.edu.au/executive-education/our-programs/strategic-foresight.html*

Foresight: Exploring the Future, Shaping the Present, University of Manchester UK – *https://research.mbs.ac.uk/innovation/Executive-courses/ForesightExploringtheFutureShapingthePresent.aspx*

International Certified Future Strategist, Kairos, Stockholm SE – *http://www.certifiedfuturestrategist.com/*

International Foresight Academy – *http://ifa.cgee.org.br/index.php?option=com_content&view=article&id=1&Itemid=101*

Scenario Thinking, Strathclyde Business School, Glasgow UK – *http://www.strath.ac.uk/business/cee/scenariothinking/*

Scenarios Programme, University of Oxford UK – *http://www.sbs.ox.ac.uk/programmes/execed/scenarios*

School of International Futures, Wilton Park UK – *http://www.soif.org.uk/summer-school-wiki/*

Singularity University, Ames Research Center,

FUTURESCAPES

Mountain View CA – *http://singularityu.org/*

Technology Futures, Inc., Austin TX – *http://www.tfi.com/conferences-seminars.html*

The Futures School, Orlando FL – *https://plus.google.com/113601518452534541768/posts/ew9Rr8FtH9n*

The mega-list from FERN – *http://www.globalforesight.org/foresight-certificate-programs*

Business Management in a Time of Change: The Importance of Futures Studies

By Francisco Jose Martinez Lopez and Mercedes García Ordaz

How can futures studies methodologies help businesses understand current and future change?

This chapter analyzes the changing socio-economic era, its effects on business, and explores how futures studies can benefit businesses in such times of significant change.

A change of era

We are lucky to be living in an age that is seeing some of the greatest changes in human history. One of its most important features is the emergence of the knowledge society – rendering agricultural, industrial, and food products less economically important. The main product of our age is information.

To understand the information society and its impact on the company, we need to analyze how it has evolved. There have been three major socio-economic eras:

- *Local-Agricultural:* this period dates from the beginning of human economic activity to about five hundred years ago. The main concern of society was to feed itself and most people worked in food production. In the political sphere, people were most affected by what occurred at a local level. Certain factors common to today – such as businesses or workers – did not exist; instead there were servants, slaves, or subjects.[434] Then, when half the workforce was able to feed the rest, the next significant era began.
- *National-Industrial:* this era has occupied the last five hundred years. In the economy, the main products were, and are industrial, and we saw the emergence of concepts that we consider fundamental to our system of social relations today – such as the company and the worker. This type of economic activity led to the establishment of our legal system and forms of coexistence based on the concept of nation. In this age, people are now directly affected by everything that happens in their country. Advances in this era lay the foundations for the new era that we live in today.
- *Worldwide-Informational:* In the coming years we will need to adapt to a new model in which fundamental social concepts will be in crisis due to the impacts of this new era. The main concerns of society now are to produce food and industrial products, and to make them environmentally sustainable.[435] We also now produce and consume information, which is the main economic product. In this new era people are affected by events that happen all over the world.

The main effect of this new era is that the concept of the company and the worker will change radically, since more than two thirds of the global workforce will now use only information as the principal component of their work.

It is noteworthy that the working population in western countries is converging towards a curious pattern of stabilization. Approximately four percent are engaged in agriculture, 28 percent in industry and 68 percent in macro-sector services in which tourism and tele-communications account for the majority of private investment.[436] When agriculture became mechanized, labor surplus transferred from Local-Agricultural to the National-Industrial sector, and now surpluses are moving into the Worldwide-Informational sector.

In addition, new information and communications technologies (ICTs) are generating many of the emerging jobs – which are aimed at producing what we increasingly consume, namely information. Some would argue that the debate over whether ICT creates or destroys jobs is now in the past, as it has to date generated many more jobs than it eliminated. That debate may resurface with the potential impact of automation, robotics, and artificial intelligence (AI). A key problem is that ICT eliminates jobs in many other industry sectors and creates them in the information sector. Some believe that this new era could bring full employment, although one of the characteristics of these new jobs is that they will not always be financially remunerated.

The next two to three decades could see radical shifts as automation eliminates even professional roles and new industries rely increasingly on ICT rather than human labor. These developments will herald a fourth socioeconomic phase where we will have to work out how to manage a largely automated economy and keep the populace happy. Note that the first era lasted more than five thousand years, the second five hundred, and the third era in which we are already living, could last fifty years or less.[437]

In response, nations may have to combine into new larger political structures (the European Union, for example), possibly to the detriment of those that will lose their sense of National-Industrial era purpose. Today, big multinationals operating in global markets sometimes fail to comply with national laws and international regulations. In future there will be new forms of business regulations to ensure consistent corporate behavior across the globe.

Interestingly, companies are also getting smaller, a phenomenon that began in the early 70s and which is increasingly evident. Concepts such as a person, a company, and a worker are more prominent. And it will be micro-companies that will mostly shape the new economic model. Perhaps one of the main challenges that many companies face, be they large or small, is understanding how to deal with a future subject to great change. It is therefore necessary to look to the role futures studies can play in company management.

Futures studies and company management

One of the most important effects of the changes taking place in today's business world is the speed of occurrence of critical events that companies have to deal with. A few decades ago, when markets and technological landscapes were relatively stable, a company could trust their medium to long term forecasts as a basis to plan their future activities.[438] The focus of many companies was solely on achieving the current year's budget. Subsequently, the practice of company strategic management emerged, which endowed organizations with new tools to adapt to the future. In the main, these were strategic plans, with a short and medium term perspective, which could keep the company on track for the potential transformation of its activities.[439]

Today however, flexibility and adaptation to the environment are just two of the qualities that companies need to acquire if they want to survive. Most companies still plan for the short term with their budgets (up to one year ahead), and for the medium term with their strategic plans (from two to five years). However, for many, long-term measures that could point the company in the right future direction are not considered practical or worthwhile in a rapidly changing and uncertain environment. In addition, the acceleration of organizational and technological processes makes what was once the short term now very short term, and the medium term has now become the short term.[440]

An alternative perspective is to argue that in the face of disruptive change and uncertainty – genuine future thinking has never been more important. I would argue that given the pace of change and the scale of potential disruptive developments on the horizon, it is now critical for organizations to consider their long-term (five to ten years) and very long-term (10-25 years) strategy and direction.

To develop this new way of understanding business management, the step after strategic management, we can use company foresight and futures studies.[441] This is an approach that allows managers to deploy well-established tools to define the scenarios companies might need to adapt to in five to ten years, and from 10 to 25 years. The longer-term timeframes (over 25 years) will be of more interest on the social or political level for some, but perhaps not all firms. Through this process, businesses are seeing the emergence of trends and gaining experience with tools that can help to clarify company planning in the future.[442]

So far, managers have relied on their intuition and generic reports to see the path ahead. Now is the time for executives to complement that intuition. The environment is far more changeable and must be tackled with the help of adequate information. Analyses should consider more variables and each company should carry out in-depth analyses to establish trends that enable managers to view the new scenarios with confidence. Companies that have already glimpsed the importance of corporate foresight are those that are best prepared for the changes to come in the near future.

Three practical closing questions for business

- *What are the risks and benefits of adopting relatively short planning business horizons?*
- *What approaches is your organization exploring to help it address the need for long term thinking in a turbulent and uncertain operating environment, where business cycles are getting shorter and faster?*
- *How can organizations balance the requirement for deep investment in the science and technology that will shape the future with the need to be agile, small and fast moving in today's markets?*

Is The Pace of Change Accelerating?

By Stephen Aguilar-Millan

What is the evidence to suggest that the pace of change is changing – what could the impact be of slowing down?

Introduction

Our recent past is one in which we have enjoyed an accelerating pace of change for about 40 years. It has become normal for us to assume that this will continue indefinitely into the future. The purpose of this piece is to question that assumption. Why could the pace of change stop accelerating? What could be the consequences of this? We will consider these questions in turn before drawing some tentative conclusions.

The pace of change and Moore's Law

The impression of an accelerating pace of change is supported both by the increasing deployment of information technologies and the growth in their uses and applications. More and more technology appears to become available each year. As we move into the future, there is no reason why technologies should not be smaller, faster, more compact, more connected, and cost far less than they do today.

This has led many observers to speculate about the shape of our technological future. They would point to the growing integration of machine and body and take the view that humans are becoming more machine-like in their functioning. For example, we take for granted now the use of pacemakers to augment the functioning of hearts. There are those who acknowledge this trend, but who point to some of the more uncertain consequences that it may bring. If we accept the continued operation of Moore's Law, then there will come a point where computing power could have sufficient capacity to become sentient. This is a rather radical and extreme view. The point to note is that it is based on the assumption that the pace of technology, as embodied in Moore's Law, will continue to accelerate.

Limiting the pace of change

In this currently prevalent view of the future, not only will the accumulation of technology grow, it will also happen at a faster rate. This may not be possible. For the pace of change to continue growing exponentially, there has to be no finite limit to the resources that provide the inputs to that process. I believe this assumption is questionable. For example, in current manufacturing processes, rare earth elements are critical to the production of much of the hardware that makes up the information age. By definition, these elements are rare – they are not completely abundant. Unless alternatives or new sources of the elements can be found, they could present a physical limit to the pace of change.

There are also those who call into question whether technological change is growing that fast in any case. From the perspective of absolute levels of technology, it has to be granted that we currently have the largest stock of tools to hand in the history of humanity. There are those who argue however, that this reflects the fact that we have more people on earth than ever before. If we look at the pace of technological change per capita, then some hold that the most productive period in history was the 1870s, and that the pace of technological advance per capita has been falling throughout the 20th century. If these people are right, then the pace of change is actually decelerating rather than accelerating.

Assessing the pace of change - what should we be measuring

This view is not without its critics. In the modern world, technological developments consist less of major breakthroughs and are more about the incremental enhancement of existing technologies. The per capita pace of change may appear to be slowing, but we are measuring the wrong thing. If we examine total technological development (new innovations plus improvements to existing technologies), we may find that the pace of change could be accelerating.

This leaves us in an interesting position. From the perspective of an individual person or business, what really matters is the ready availability of effective and useful technology at an affordable price. Evidence suggests that such availability comes and goes in waves. As a new wave emerges, it becomes integrated into existing business processes, delivering higher productivity and lowering the cost base. There is nothing to suggest that this process is abating. Eventually, it may be that the resource constraint kicks in. If it does, then the cost of technology will rise, thus altering the balance between the cost and usefulness of the technology. Businesses acting with foresight would have a contingency plan in place should that day arrive.

The maturing of technologies

This situation represents the maturing of a set of technologies and the businesses that provide them. With maturing technologies, the business environment will change. The key to competition will shift away from the pursuit of innovation and first mover advantage towards the exploitation of mass markets and the integration of the new technologies into an existing technology set. It is likely, for example, that the path to driverless cars will be through the existing car manufacturers, who have a mass distribution network, but who will need to integrate the innovations from technology companies into a current product range.

This suggests a world in which the path to scale is dominated by mergers and acquisitions (M&A) rather than the organic growth which technology companies have seen to date. This M&A activity is likely to be both horizontal (technology companies blending into each other) and vertical (existing sectoral market leaders acquiring technology companies in their value chain for their intellectual property portfolio, and vice-versa). All of this acts towards lowering the cost of the end product to the consumer.

The focus of all companies in the future is more than ever likely to be global in scope. As the urban middle class of the developing world expands, and as the cost of innovative technologies falls, we can forecast greater sales of a wider range of products to those consumers. This growth is not without challenges – at some point the resource constraint will start to apply, forcing up the cost of goods to the mass market. It is then that the pace of change would slow.

Conclusion

The assumption of an accelerating pace of change is probably justified for a little while yet. However, at some point it would be reasonable to expect the pace of change to slow down as technologies mature and resource constraints start to bite. It is important for business to be alert to this possibility because it could significantly change the operating environment.

Those in business might like to consider three questions to forewarn themselves of this change of trend. All of these could indicate that the pace of change is slowing, and business would do well to be forewarned of them:

- *How should your organization respond in the face of evidence that resource markets are tightening and resource constraints starting to apply?*
- *What strategies can you adopt if the evidence suggests that consumers are buying new technologies less frequently and that markets are heading towards saturation?*
- *If evidence suggests that obsolescence rates are falling, what are the implications for the frequency with which you replace operating equipment?*

The Outside Context Problem, A Concerned Observers Guide

By Benjamin Mottram

In a potentially complex and uncertain future, how can you make sense of unexpected problems when they challenge your business environment?

Introduction

The anticipated pace and scale of economic, social, technological, and environmental change over the next two decades will generate an increasing number of unforeseen and potentially ever-more complex problems for individuals, businesses, and governments. New techniques and ways of thinking will be required to help us understand and respond to the array of challenges we could face. This chapter introduces the concept of **Outside Context Problems** (OCP) as a technique for addressing the type of unexpected and complex problems that will be created by a world experiencing dramatic transitions and disruptive innovations.

For every problem we are faced with there is a toolbox of responses available to help address the challenge. These come in the form of technologies, procedures, and policies that have been finessed through experimentation as well as painful trial and error. For example, fires are extinguished by trained professionals wielding fire hoses, disease outbreaks are quarantined, inoculations are developed through the scientific method, and political change has been largely tamed by the normalization of democratic process.

Despite the range of potential solution approaches, a set of problems still exists that confound our responses. These are the OCPs.

Definition

The term was coined by the late author Iain Banks in his science fiction novel *Excession*. There he describes the OCP as, "an event, which to those affected by it have no previous frame of reference to it, or indeed have even considered such a thing could occur."

Problem type

There are two flavors of OCP, the **alien** and the **excession**.

Alien – The alien OCP is entirely novel. To those affected, they have never come across its like before or were never even aware of its possibility. It is this lack of knowledge that makes it so dangerous, since there is no previous prescient of response to draw upon. Examples include disruptive businesses like Uber, natural phenomena such as climate change, and unanticipated political upheaval.

Excession – The excession OCP is a known problem magnified to a degree where it is no longer manageable. Examples here include the Black Death and hyperinflation in post-World War One Germany.

Problem source

The source of the OCP must also be considered since it has a direct relation to the kind of response that can face it.

Environmental – Environmental OCPs emerge from the natural laws of the universe, be they earth bound or extra-terrestrial.

Examples include excessive natural disasters and pandemics.

Political – Where the OCP occurs due to the machinations of human politics. Such OCPs tend to be violent due to the way humans typically respond to large scale societal change.
Examples are the assassination of Archduke Ferdinand leading to the outbreak of World War One and the Arab Spring.

Systemic – Systemic OCP's come from the complexities of systems created by humans. They may emerge as unintended consequences of the system's design or the variables within it. Alternatively they may arise from the partial or complete collapse of the system.
Examples include the global financial crisis of 2008 and the collapse of the Soviet Union.

Technological – Technology tends to change the facts on the ground by making tried and tested systems obsolete. In the modern world, the development of new technologies creates new OCPs, for example: the combustion engine, nuclear power, Smartphones, social networks, and 3D printing.

Severity

Every OCP is unique and because of this the metrics required to measure its impact will vary according to its problem type. The best way to classify the severity of an OCP is through the permanence of its effects. Mild effects only cause temporary disruption (no matter how serious). Moderate effects inflict permanent change to those involved. Severe effects can occur when the very existence of the victim of the OCP is threatened.

The severity of an OCP is entirely subjective. For example, the finical crisis of 2008 was moderate in severity for most nations involved, forcing permanent change in fiscal policy. Yet the same OCP was severe for many banks which either collapsed or required vast bailouts.

Responses

Humans tend to respond in two manners. The first is to resist the forces of change and the second is to adapt to the new conditions.

Status Quo – The goal of the response is to maintain the existing conditions and implement methods to enforce this. This tends to be a reactionary response that rarely achieves its aims, since the OCP has changed the conditions rendering the status quo position no longer optimal. Examples include the music industry's attempt to maintain a physical media business model in response to Napster's digital music sharing service and political lobbying by taxi firms against Uber's expansion.

Violence – Violence is rarely an optimal response though sometimes it seems hard to avoid. It may resolve existing problems but often creates further unintended consequences in its wake. For example pogroms against Jewish populations who were believed to be responsible for the Black Death and the War on Terror in response to 9/11.

Policy Change – Policy change represents a more adaptive approach to resolving an OCP, and as such it tends to be more effective since it recognizes the facts on the ground have changed. Examples include Roosevelt's New Deal in response to the great depression and the mutually assured destruction philosophy that has governed nuclear weapons policy.

Technological Innovation – New technology implemented well can turn the tables on the severity of an OCP quickly. Examples include the UK's code breaking computer at Bletchley Park during World War 2 and the USA's Star Wars missile defense initiative that helped bankrupt the Soviet Union.

Summary

Change is coming, thanks to the development of a whole slew of technologies and no organization or nation is safe from the resulting disruptions. Where the policy is to resist change through an attempt to maintain the status quo or even through violence, the result is often counterproductive. The better option is to adapt to the change, to embrace different policy ideas or to seek out new technologies to augment your abilities.

Most important however is to prepare and plan. Organizations need to undertake regular assessments of their industries, or sphere of influence to identify and categorize any potential OCPs that could threaten their position. It is in our best interest to create a set of contingencies that seek to adapt to – rather than resist – the forces of change.

Here are three questions you might pose in your business:

- *On reflection, what Outside Context Problems do you see facing your business now or over the next 5-10 years?*
- *How does your business differentiate between the different types of problems it encounters and then design appropriate responses?*
- *How is your business gearing up to adapt to a constantly changing reality?*

Be There Now

By Paul Brooks

How can we prepare more confidently for the future in rapidly evolving times?

This chapter emphasizes the importance of openness, dynamism, and scalability in helping a business prepare for the future.

Emergence of the "Spaceman Economy"

Through the identification of new trends and emerging tools we can strategize more effectively for changing times. The environment is experiencing rapid change. We now see the explosion of business models and approaches such as Peer-to-Peer, Freemium, and Open-source. **Pull** marketing has been given a boost through developments such as big data, and new channels like social media, and blogging. In economics we are seeing the emergence of new concepts such as the circular economy and new forms of currency known as **crypto-currencies**. All of these things can be considered emerging resources that are and will be instrumental in the formation of a new information economy that Kenneth Boulding called the "Spaceman Economy", where "throughput is by no means a desideratum".[443]

Viewing the present from the future

To visualize the future of business without getting too out of touch with reality, it is helpful to have some sort of lens through which we can view the present from the future. The future of our economic systems will have three basic qualities that are inherent in all living systems, such as humans, societies, and the Internet. These systems are open, dynamic, and scalable. If we stand in the future look back to view the present state of affairs, we will be able to peer through this three-fold lens and use it as a checklist of questions to help ensure that we are on track toward a sustainable future. In a sort of holographic way, each of these three qualities, individually or as a system, can be applied to a person's workload, a team or committee, a department, the whole business, or even an industry.

Understanding and envisioning the future requires Systems Thinking, which happens in three steps. We start by seeking to understand the system we are working with and its objectives, carbonated beverages for example. Perhaps our objective is to find a niche soft drink that is considered healthy. Then we view the broader system that our system is a part of the bottled drinks industry. Lastly, rather than designing a product similar to those currently generating the most profit, we observe the relationship between these two systems in order to design for society's needs. We note that **healthy** is trending, and see that the market is flooded with soft drinks that are loaded with sugar. At the same time, carbonated juices are generally expensive to produce and other sweeteners are difficult to produce at scale or have an unfavorable market response. And then kombucha! We have a highly successful product that no soft drink manufacturer would have dreamed of – a fermented, carbonated, semi-sweet vinegar water! Who knew?

A guide to the qualities of the three-fold lens

Let's examine each element separately (figure 1):

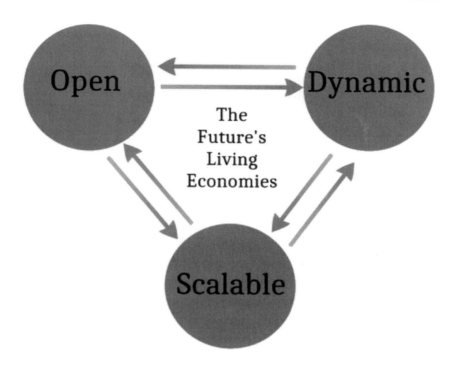

FIGURE 1 – Open, Dynamic and Scalable Systems

Openness means collaboration. That is to say that we are not shutting out any potential for growth or progress. Business-to-Business and Peer-to-Peer collaborations are becoming important parts of strategy, and **collaborative consumption** has given rise to the Sharing Economy. Airbnb, Amazon, and Ebay for example, would not exist if it were not for open participation. The Open-source Android platform is another example. Google gave it away for free and by doing so generated a greater profit.

This means that within our businesses we should allow our different teams and/or departments to share information freely and as much as possible. After all, this is an information economy were talking about, even if it is standing on the shoulders of the outdated industrial one. Also, if we crunch numbers every day and make immediate adjustments, we will never know if perhaps a revenue decrease was only a natural ebb toward a much greater flow; be patient. It's not a recession, it's a transition.

Dynamic means adapting to change. This aspect of business gives us the ability to evolve as markets and economies evolve. A failure to adapt will not only decrease the likelihood of success, it will also leave little if any room for progress. This is not to say that we should abandon old strategies or business models either, but rather make them secondary to a new default. This means meeting the demands of new industry paradigms; feed forward, envisioning, thinking ahead. The real task at hand is then to identify what aspects of business and economics are changing most rapidly and then prepare for major shifts on the horizon. Have you embraced the post-Friedman business ethic of **conscious capitalism**, the **Triple-Bottom-Line**? Is your company prepared for future competition in augmented reality advertising, 3D printing, driverless delivery, and drones?

Applied to a business internally dynamic management might mean allowing workers more autonomy with less micro-management. At 3M there is the legendary **15 percent rule** in which employees are encouraged to spend 15 percent of their time working on their own project. Creativity drives innovation and creativity needs freedom.

Scaleable in an industrial economy means the ability to meet demand without creating a wasteful surplus. Digitization is perhaps the most practical tool for achieving this. Digital resources can be multiplied or eliminated without creating waste and most of the production costs are eliminated after the prototype stage. Scalability also means sharing. If we can create a cost free resource that is valuable or helpful to our clients, customers, and/or competitors, this will serve us as a valuable publicity tool. It may be a blog, an app, a Software as a Service (SaaS) opportunity, a crypto-currency, or even a well written white paper.

For meeting the demands of the future, radical change may be the best solution. If your business is vibrant and participatory, if it is animated and flexible, and if it is alive and growing to meet evolutionary needs, you've created a healthy living economy and the future welcomes you.

So which three questions could businesses pose to help them

prepare for the future in rapidly evolving times?

- *Do we encourage open participation from our customers, the community at large, and even other businesses in the design, manufacture, management, sales, and marketing of our products and services?*
- *Are we willing to make radical shifts to drive innovation, even if it means a significant temporary decrease in profits?*
- *What obstacles would our business face if we had a 10x increase in sales over night?*

Section 10

Conclusions - Navigating Uncertainty and a Rapidly Changing Reality

By Rohit Talwar

How can we make sense of the waves of change coming towards us and map a future path for our organization?

The Future of Business - a Response Framework

This chapter sets out a framework to help leaders respond to the ideas and questions presented in the book and then use the resulting insights to shape future strategy.

Trying to respond to every force, trend, development, and idea individually would be next to impossible. Instead, it may be more appropriate to use a framework through which to filter and interpret the myriad "future factors" of change and map out the preferred direction and operational strategy for the organization. There are ten key elements of this framework that help us analyze these future factors that will shape our business choices. Each of these elements is summarized below along with key questions we need to ask ourselves and our organizations.

Five of the elements focus on **market facing decisions and behaviors** – mission, markets, magic, models, and message. The second five elements address **internal choices** we need to make – myths, mastery, muscle, mindset, and management.

Market facing decisions and behaviors

Mission. We are entering a world where everything we know and understand about the purposes of business and the mission of our own organization will be challenged. In the face of relentless change we need real clarity about what role we believe business should play in society and the mission of our own organization.

- What are the needs or opportunities we should be addressing in tomorrow's emerging economic, societal, and business landscape?
- Who are the core stakeholders we should be serving?
- What are our ambitions and what would success look like?

Markets. Developing a viable business proposition will require a clear understanding of the potential evolution of current and potential markets (products, services, geographies) and how customers might respond to these changes. It also requires a sense of how the evolution of adjacent and emerging sectors might impact our core offerings. We also need scenarios of how the market for talent could play out in the locations where we most need the brightest minds and most capable leaders, managers, and operational staff.

- How might the key future factors shape the behavior of current markets and customers?
- What new market opportunities could open up – how would customer needs differ in these emerging sectors?
- How might the needs, expectations and availability of talent change over the short, medium, and longer term?

Magic. As we automate our products and services, the risk of commoditization increases. The challenge is to ensure our offerings and service experience stand out from the crowd and create a "wow factor" for customers.

- What stands out about the brands that deliver us the biggest "wow factor" today – what makes their offerings and experiences noteworthy?

- How can we differentiate customers' experience of our brand in tomorrow's increasingly commoditized markets?
- Where might the biggest potential opportunities be to inject magic into our future product and service offerings?

Models. Profit-making can no longer be assumed as the prime objective for every enterprise. Even the very need for profits and money are being challenged in emerging economic paradigms. Business models are changing – for example, greater emphasis is being placed on usership over ownership. Firms are looking to market-based solutions such as crowdfunding to validate and finance new product ideas. Greater experimentation is taking place in how we charge for goods and services with freemium pricing models, aggregated buying, auctions, pay with a tweet, and a range of other options becoming more common.

- What are the trade-offs between usership (rental) and ownership (purchase) in the design of tomorrow's company?
- How might the adoption of crowdsourcing to test new ideas impact our approach to the development and marketing of future offerings?
- What experimentation are we doing around alternative approaches to charging for products and services?

Message. The internet and social media provide instant rewards for brands that back marketing promises with operational action. Customers are keen to see us deliver on our commitments in terms of product and service quality, customer experience, business ethics, innovation, employee welfare, operational processes, contribution to society, and the management of environmental impacts. An ever-more transparent future with increasing levels of scrutiny will reinforce the importance of alignment between promise and delivery.

- What are the critical values and beliefs we want our brand to be synonymous with?
- How can we ensure constant alignment between our innovation agenda and marketing messages?
- What role could our broader social commitment play in determining our "license to trade" in the eyes of tomorrow's customer?

Internal choices

Myths. Every organization has a set of myths that are essential to its effective functioning. They enable us to make sense of the world and provide the stories that help simplify complex systems and influence the core operational decisions that guide our every action. These stories, worldviews, assumptions, metaphors, and mental models shape the way we do things internally. They also define how we view the operating environment and determine our marketplace behaviors.

- What are the core stories, worldviews, assumptions, metaphors, and mental models that underpin our current strategies and operating models?
- What new models and metaphors could help us make sense of the emerging environment?
- How should we evolve our current organizational mythology to help us reframe strategy, drive the resulting organizational changes, and navigate the emerging landscape?

Mastery. For the last 20 to 30 years, business schools and strategy consultants have emphasized the importance of developing the firm's critical capabilities. A fast changing environment places even greater emphasis on ensuring excellence in the core activities that help the firm stand out against its competition. However, with ever-shorter and faster business cycles and unruly new competitors, the lifespan of our capabilities is declining. We have to reassess what it takes to win and act to ensure mastery on a more frequent basis. This implies that change management becomes a capability where being average could be mission-threatening. Given the central role of information and communications technology (ICT), effective management of ICT and the associated data assets also rise to the fore as areas where firms have to pursue excellence or risk being left behind.

- Which existing capabilities will we require mastery of to deliver our strategy in the markets we plan to serve in the future?
- What actions can we take to close any gaps between our current and desired strength in these capabilities?
- How will we decide on the capabilities to retain and develop in-house and those we should procure from external providers?

Muscle. Alongside refining internal capabilities, the most agile firms will act to identify and acquire new capabilities quickly. As the shape of next economy starts to reveal itself, many firms are already focusing on identifying and developing key new muscles. In a fast-changing world, such capabilities will include accelerated decision making, rapid execution, and ever-faster resourcing approaches to match talent to short-lived opportunities at speed.

- Where is the organization beginning to experience pain due to a lack of capability?
- What are the capabilities you most admire in the firms that seem to be navigating change most effectively?
- What steps can be taken to accelerate the acquisition and embedding of critical new capabilities?

Mindset. Throughout this book, the authors have emphasized the need for mindset change to embrace digital and exponential ways of viewing the world in traditionally linear thinking organizations. Leaders and managers in particular are being encouraged to develop the capacity to look ahead, see round corners, embrace uncertainty and complexity, and abandon long-cherished assumptions in the face of change. Seeing ourselves as players not victims, and learners rather than knowers, are becoming essential traits of organizations that are willing to embrace the future.

- How is the organization planning to facilitate the shift to more digital and exponential ways of viewing future possibilities?
- What frameworks are in place to explore, interpret, and act on the future factors that could impact the organization over key timeframes? (Twelve months, one to three years, four to ten years)
- How is the need for foresight, future sensing, and scenario planning being embedded in training and development programs?

Management. Leading the organization into an unknown and potentially unknowable future will require fundamental shifts in how we lead and manage. An entirely new set of skills will be required to help deliver on our goals. These will include scenario planning, complexity management, cross-cultural awareness, collaboration, systems understanding, design thinking and extreme creativity. Understanding and responding to change will also require us to free up time and space for people across the enterprise to engage in serious research, analysis and choice-making about our preferred futures. These in turn require us to prune our currently overloaded "To-Do" lists. In their place we need "To-Stop" lists – encouraging "orgies of elimination" to tackle unnecessary complexity and kill off the reports, meetings, and processes that no longer add value.

- How is the corporate learning agenda being updated to reflect the skills required of tomorrow's workforce, management and leadership?
- What is being done to drive the simplification of current activities to reduce workloads and enable the business to respond faster to external stimuli?
- What new management and leadership models are being evaluated to help steer the enterprise on the next stage of its journey?

A point of departure

This book provides a range of potentially conflicting views, forecasts, visions and ideas of how the future could unfold for society and the businesses that serve it. We have deliberately avoided trying to package up a neat set of recipes and seven-step plans for creating your future. They simply can't and won't work in the complex and fast-changing environment that will unfold over the next twenty years.

The authors have deliberately sought to provoke, inspire, enthuse, and challenge our readers. We believe the most valuable role of these provocations is to stimulate the reader to explore the issues raised and resolve them in the context of their own organizations. The questions posed at the end of each chapter and here in this conclusion will hopefully encourage and stretch you to think broadly about the emerging future and how your organization can survive and thrive in a rapidly changing reality.

The Editorial Team

Rohit Talwar - Series Curator and Lead Editor

Rohit is a global futurist, strategic advisor and award winning keynote speaker on emerging change. He is the founder and CEO of both Fast Future Research and Fast Future Publishing. In his consulting work, Rohit advises global corporations, governments, NGOs and professional bodies on how to anticipate and respond to the forces, trends, developments and ideas shaping the future. He helps clients understand how new business models and disruptive developments in science and technology could impact individuals, society, business, industries and government. He specialises in designing and delivering future-focused exponential development programmes that drive step-change improvements in business ambition, innovation, performance and growth.

Rohit's interests include the evolving role of technology in business and society, emerging markets, the future of education, sustainability and embedding foresight in organisations. He has consulted and spoken to leadership audiences in over 60 countries on six continents. His clients include 3M, Airbus, American Express, Barclays, Bayer, Boeing, BT, Citibank, Deloitte, DeutscheBank, Dubai Airports, EY, Etisalat, Gartner, GE, IBM, Intel, Jardines, Juniper Networks, KPMG, Linklaters, Microsoft, Morgan Stanley, Norton Rose Fulbright, Panasonic, Pepsi, Pfizer, PwC, SAP, Sara Lee, Shell, Siemens, Snecma, Standard Life, Tata, and Vodafone.

Rohit is the editor of Achieving Transformation and Renewal in Financial Services and the lead author of Designing your Future.

rohit@fastfuture.com
www.fastfuture.com

Steve Wells – Co-Editor

Steve is an experienced Strategist, Futures Analyst and Partnership Working Practitioner. Before working as Co-Editor and in the role of Author Liaison on this project, Steve's recent client project work has included research and analysis of emerging technologies, scenario development and futures analysis for the UK affiliates of a number of global pharmaceutical companies. He has researched and reported on the pharmaceutical industry / NHS partnership working landscape; conducted a competitive analysis of partnership working practice of major pharmaceutical companies in the UK for a major pharma company; led a collaborative futures project on the aging population in Northern Ireland, Scotland, and Wales for the Future Analysts' Network, a network of public and private sector futures practitioners formerly facilitated by the Department for Business, Innovation and Skills. In his previous staff roles, Steve led the strategic planning process for Pfizer Ltd in the UK; developed a collaborative approach to trend and driver analysis; and led the development of UK health-care system scenarios to support strategy development.
steve@fastfuturepublising.com

April Koury – Co-Editor, Designer and Production Management

April is a recent graduate in Foresight from the University of Houston, a futurist, and a foresight researcher at Fast Future Research. Her research has covered a wide range of topics from the futures of food, water, and distribution, to human enhancement and AI. April joined the Fast Future Publishing team in April 2015. Her role on the project covers a wide spectrum of tasks including editing, design work, and website and social media management. April was a co-author of the Drivers of Change that appear at the start of sections one to seven of the book. She was also responsible for researching and negotiating US printing and fulfillment options and investigating a range of marketing approaches. April also provides first line customer support for enquiries about the book and is responsible for the FutureScapes newsletter.
april@fastfuturepublishing.com

Alberto Rizzoli – Co-Editor and Designer

Alberto is a young Italian futurist, educational innovation entrepreneur and Singularity University student exploring how schools and learning could evolve as a result of the rapid adoption of new technologies and educational models. By bringing 3D printers into schools and studying the way technology impacts how we learn, Alberto is aiming to revolutionise education both within and outside of schools. He descends from a lineage of entrepreneurs who pioneered the printing, cinema, and television industries in Europe for the past century. At a very young age he began working on the next generational step, by exploring the potential of 3D printing and digital distribution of educational media. Today he is part of a futurist think-tank and directs a startup in the education-technology market. On this project he led the completion of the web design, typesetting of the epub version of the book and contributed to the interior design. Alberto was also responsible for researching and negotiating UK printing and fulfillment options.

alberto@fastfuturepublising.com

Fast Future Publishing and FutureScapes

The company was established in February 2015 to become a specialist publisher focusing on making leading edge future insights accessible to a broad audience. The aim is to bring exponential thinking to publishing - delivering depth of insight and high quality writing from leading and emerging thinkers in a fraction of the time that publishers would normally take to deliver a similar outcome. Fast Future Publishing is pursuing an innovative business model that shares profits equitably with contributing authors and sets aside a proportion of the profits from each book to fund relevant causes.

FutureScapes is designed to be a series of multi-contributor books that will address a range of futures topics of interest to a wide audience. The Future of Business is the first book in the series and further titles are in planning.

Fast Future Publishing will also publish the work of individual futures authors and is open to receiving proposals from potential authors and those interested in compiling a multi-contributor book as part of the FutureScapes series.

info@fastfuturepublishing.com
www.fastfuturepublishing.com